ISBN: 9781313112505

Published by:
HardPress Publishing
8345 NW 66TH ST #2561
MIAMI FL 33166-2626

Email: info@hardpress.net
Web: http://www.hardpress.net

PHILIP STUBBES'S ANATOMY

OF THE

ABUSES IN ENGLAND

IN

SHAKSPERE'S YOUTH,

A.D. 1583.

PART I.

[*Collations for the title-page of May 1, 1583, opposite.*]

[1] description F (1595).

[2] corruptions E (1585) ; enormities F (1595).   [3] now *om.* F.

[4] Christian *not in* B (1 Aug. 1583), *or* F.

[5] the countrie of E ; this Realme of F.   [6] verie *not in* B.

[7] England F.   [8] Gods heauie F.   [9] inflicted F.

[10] euerie where *not in* B.   [11] chiefly E.

[12] Gent., *added in* F.

[13] And now newly reuised recognized and augmented the third time by the same Author. E (1585) ; Now, the fourth time, newly corrected and inlarged by the same Author F (1595).   [14] *omitted* F.

[15] saith Christ *not in* E.

[16] Imprinted at London by Richard Iohnes, at the sign of the Rose and Crowne, next aboue S. Andrewes Church in Holborne. 1595. F.

[17] 16. August *in* B, *not in* E.   [18] 1585 *in* E.

Series VI. No. 4.

JOHN CHILDS AND SON, PRINTERS.

The Anatomie

of Abuſes:

Contaŋning[1]

A [1]DISCOVERIE, OR BRIEFE
Summarie,[1] of ſuch Notable Vices and Imperfections,[2] as now[3] raigne in many Chriſtian[4] Countreyes of the Worlde: but (eſ-
peciallie) in [5]a verie[6] famous ILANDE
called[5] AILGNA[7]· Together, with
moſt fearefull Examples of Gods[8] Iudgementes, executed[9] vpon the wicked for the
ſame, aſwell in AILGNA[7] of late, as in
other places elſewhere.

Verie Godly, to be read of all true Christians,

euerie where[10]; but moſt needefull,[11] to
be regarded in ENGLANDE.

Made dialogue-wiſe by Phillip Stubbes.[12]
[13]Seene and allowed, according to order.[13]

[14]MATH. 3. ver. 2. Repent, for the kingdome of God
is at hande.
LVC. 13. ver. 5. I ſay vnto you (ſaith Chriſt)[15] except
you repent, you ſhall all periſh.[14]

[16] ¶ Printed at London, by Richard
Iones. 1. Maij.[17] 1583.[18]

[[1] The collations are on the opposite page.]

To the [1]Right Hono-

rable,[2] Phillip Earle of Arundell: Phillip
Stubbes wifheth helth of body & foule,[1] fauour
of God, increafe of Godly honour, reward of laudable vertue, and eternall felicitie, [3]in the Heauens,[3]
by[4] IESVS Chrift.

[5]NOBILITAS Patriæ DECVS.[5]

[6]HE Lord our God (right honorable)[6] hauing by the power of his word, created Heauen and Earth, with all [7]thinges what foeuer, for the comfort[7] and vfe of Man, the laft of all other (euen the fixt daye) [8]made Man, after his owne fimilitude and likeneffe,[9] that[10] in [God made man in His own likeness, him he might be glorified aboue all other Creatures. And therfore, wheras in making of other thinges he vfed onely this Woord, FIANT, be they made or let them be made, when he came to make Man, [11]as it weare aduyfing[12] himfelfe and[11] afking councell at his wifdome, he faid FACIAMVS HOMINEM, let vs make Man; that is, a wonderful Creature: and therfore is called in greek MICRO-COSMOS, a litle world in himfelf. And truely he is no leffe, whether a little world in himself.] we confider his fpirituall foule, or his humaine body. For what Creature is theare vppon the face of the Earth comparable to man,

---

[1]—[1] Christian Magistrates and godly Gouernors of England, whose authority & offices are to reforme vice and maintain virtue, P. S. wisheth the F.

[2] and his singuler good Lorde *added in* E (1585).

[3]—[3] in the Heauenly hierarchie E; *om.* F.   [4] through E.   [5]—[5] *om.* F.

[6]—[6] Right Honourable, worshipfull and welbeloued, the Lord our God F.

[7]—[7] other thinges, for the benefit, F (benifite E).

[8] he made A, F.   [9] to what end? namely *inserted in* B (1 Aug., 1583).

[10] to this end, that F.   [11]—[11] consulting with himself, & as it were E, F.

[12] consulting with *in* B.

either in body or [1]in mind? what creature hath a ſoule immortall inherent in his body,[1] but onely Man? what Creature can forſee things
[2]to come, remember things paſt, or iudg of things preſent, but onely
[3]man? what Creature beareth the ymage of God [4]about with him,[5] but
Man? what Creature is made ſo erect to behould the Heauens as man?
What Creature may be likened to man, [6]either in proportion of body,
or gifts of the ſoule[6]? And (finally) what Creature hath the promiſe
of the reſurrection & glorification of their bodies, & of eternall life,
but onely Man? Than, ſeeing the Lorde hath made Man thus glorious, and preferred him in[7] [8]euery degree[8] before[9] al other Creatures (the
Angelicall Creatures ſet a part) it is manifeſt he hath done it to ſome
end[10] & purpoſe, [11]namely, that he might be glorified in him, and by
him aboue all other his works, according to the meaſure of his integritie, excellency and perfection.[11]   And hereby we may learn that it is
the will of GOD, that we[12] bend all our force to the aduauncing of his
[13]glorious Name,[13] the edification of his People, and the building vp of
his Church, which he hath redemed with the bloud of his deare
Sonne.

Which thing (mee think) is notably figured foorth vnto vs in the
25 of EXODVS, wher the Lord commaunded Moyſes to build him a
Tabernacle, or howſe of prayer, to this end and purpoſe (doubtles) that
therin his lawe might be read[14], his Ceremonies [15]practiſed, Sacrifices,
Victimates & Holocauſtes offred, [15]and his glorious Name called vppon
and obeyed.   To the erection wherof euery one conferred ſome what,
ſome brought gold, ſome ſiluer & ſome braſſe, lead and tinne; other
brought ſilk, purple, ſkarlet, and other ornaments, and the meaneſt
brought ſome what; namely, ſkins, heare, ſand, lyme, morter, wood,
ſtone, and ſuch like. Euen ſo [16](right honorable)[16] would the Lord haue

Marginal notes:

[² Sig. ¶ 2, k. A.]
[³ Sig. A 2, back. E.]
[⁴ Sig. ¶ 2, back. B.]

[God made man, to be glorified in him,

that he might advance God's name.]

[This was typified by Moses's Tabernacle,

to which all men gave something.]

---

[1]—[1] ſoule? For what creature hath an immortall ſoule, F.

[5] abont with him *om.* F.

[6]—[6] whether we respect the lineaments the demensions and proportion of
the body, or the gifts and graces of the mind E, F.

[7] by E, F.   [8]—[8] many degrees F.   [9] above E, F.   [10] ſpeciall end B.

[11]—[11] that, as in perfection and all kinde of integritie, he excelleth all other
Creatures, so he might be glorified in, thorow, and by him aboue al other
Creatures. B.

[12] we should E, F.   [13]—[13] glorie E, F.   [14] read and preached F.

[15]—[15] duly practized, his Sacrifices and offerings faithfully performed F.

[16]—[16] *om.* F.

euery one to conferre fome what, euen fuch as he hath, to the building[1] of his fpiritnall howfe, the Church, purchafed with the bloud of
Chrift.[2] Wherfore feeing it is fo, that euery one is to further this
fpirituall building to his poffible power, I haue rather chofen, with the
fimpleft and meaneft fort, to bring, though but heyre, fand, fkins,
lyme, morter,[3] wood, or[4] ftones, than altogether to[5] contribute nothing.

[So I, to help God's Church, bring now my mite.]

[3 Sig. ¶ 3. A.]

   Not doubting, but that the chief Maifter and Builder of this
howfe, Chrift Iefus, will not diflike, but accept[6] of[7] [8]my poore con-
tribution, no leffe than he did of the [9]poore wydowes Mite, to whom
was[10] imputed that fhe had caft more [11]in Gazophilatium Templi,[11]
into the treafury of the Temple, than all the reft; for what fhe
wanted in effect that fhe fupplyed in affect. And for that, alfo, the
Lord our GOD committing his talents to euery one, whether more or
leffe, not onely requireth of vs the fame againe fimply, but alfo, as a
ftraight computift, demaundeth intereft and gaine of euery one of vs :
& for that not only he is a murtherer & a Homicide before God
who flayeth or killeth a Man with materiall fword, but he alfo who[12]
may[13] preuent the fame,[14] and will not. And[15] not onely he is guiltie
of haynous tranfgreffion that committeth any euill really,[16] but alfo he
who confenteth to it, as he doth, who holdeth his peace, or he who
by any means might auoid it, and either for[17] negligence wil not, or,
for feare of the world dare not. Therfore, albe it, that I haue receiued but one poore talent, or rather the[18] fhadow of one, yet leaft I
might be reproued (with that vnprofitable Seruaunt) for hyding my
fmall talent in the Earth, not profiting therwith at all, either myfelf
or others, I haue aduentured the making[19] of this litle treatife, intituled
(The Anatomy of Abufes) hoping that the fame (by diuyne affiftance)
fhall fomewhat conduce to the building[20] of this fpirituall howfe of the
Lord.

[6 Sig. ¶ 3. B.]

[9 Sig. A 3. E.]

[God bids us use our talents, not hide them,

and so I've written my *Anatomy of Abuses*, to help God's House,]

   And although I be one [21](moft honorable Lord)[21] that can do leaft in
this Godly courfe of life (palpable barbarifme forbidding mee fo much
as once to enter into Wyfdomes fchool), yet for that fome wil not,

[1] building vp F.	[2] the Messyas B.	[4] and F.
[5] to sit idle and F.	[6] rather accept F.	[7] of this E, F.
[10] it was F. [11—11] *om.* F. [12] vho A.		[13] might hinder B.
[14] same murther F.	[15] And for that E, F.	[16] actually F.
[17] through F.	[18] but the E, F.	[19] contriuing F.
[20] building vp & erection E, F.		[21—21] *om.* F.

for feare of loſing worldly promotion (though in the meane tyme they
loſe the Kingdome of Heauen), Other ſome dare not for diſpleaſing
[and from love
to God and my
country.]
the world : I ſay for theſe, & ſemblable cauſes, together with the
zeale and goodwill I beare vnto my Countrey, and feruent deſire of
[¹ Sig. ¶ 3,
back. A.]
their conuerſion and amende¹ment, I haue taken vpon me the contryu-
ing² of this book ; which Goᴅ graunt may be with like plauſible alacritie receiued, as with paines and good will I haue publiſhed³ it for the
[⁴ Sig. ¶ 3,
back. B.]
benefit of my Cuntrey, the pleaſure of the God⁴ly and amendement of
the wicked.   And I doubt not that as none but the wicked and per-
uerſe, whoſe gawld backes are tutched, will repyne againſt mee, ſo
the Godly and vertuous will accept of this my labour and trauaile here-
[⁶ Sig. A 3,
back. E.]
in,⁵ whoſe gentle fauour and good⁶will ſhall counterpoyſe (⁷and farre
ſurmount with mee⁷) the maligne ſtomacks and ſtearn⁸ countenances
of the other.   After that I had ⁹(right honorable)⁹ fully perfected this
[Tho' I was at
first minded to
suppress my
book, my friends
made me publish
it.]
booke, I was minded, notwithſtanding, both in regard of the
ſtraungenes of the matter it intreateth of, and alſo in reſpect of the
rudeneſſe of my penne, to haue ſuppreſſed it for euer, for diuerſe and
ſundrie cauſes, and neuer to haue offred it to the viewe of the world,
But, notwithſtanding, being ouercome by the importunat requeſt, and
infatigable¹⁰ deſire of my freinds, I graunted to publiſh the ſame, as
¹¹now you ſee¹¹ is¹² extant.

¹³But when I had once graunted to imprinte the ſame, I was¹⁴ in
greatter doubt than¹⁵ before, fearinge to whome I might dedicate the
ſame ſo rude and impoliſhed a worke.   And withall I was not ignor-
[I didn't know
whom to
dedicate it to,
till I thought of
you, Lord
Arundel, whose
fame is world-
wide.]
ant, how hard a thing it is in theſe daies to finde a Patrone of ſuch
books as this, which ſheweth to euery one his ſin, and diſcouereth
euery Mans wicked waies, which indeed the vngodly can not at any
hand abyde, but, as it were, mad-men diſgorging their ſtomacks.¹⁶ (*Cum
in Authorem tum in codicem plenis buccis et dentibus pluſquam caninis
rabidè feruntur :*) they rage, they fume, and rayle both againſt the
ᴀᴠᴛʜᴏʀ and his booke. Thus (*vacillante animo*) my minde wandring

² publishing F.   ³ collected F.
⁵ sustained *added in* E, F.   ⁷—⁷ yea farre surmount B ; *om.* F.
⁸ austere F.   ⁹—⁹ *om.* F.   ¹⁰ *orig.* infagitable
¹¹—¹¹ now (God haue the praise therof) B.   ¹² it F.
¹³ *From here to* faile neuer, *last line, p.* vii, *is omitted in* F.
¹⁴ was then B.   ¹⁵ than then E.
¹⁶ and spewing out the poyson of their malicous harts *inserted in* B.

too and fro, and refting, as it weare, in extafie of defpaire, at laft I called to mind your honorable Lordfhip, whofe praifes haue[1] pearced the Skyes, and whofe laudable vertues[2] are blowen not ouer the realme of England [3]onely, but euen to the furtheft cofts and parts of the world. [3 Sig. ¶ 4. A.]

All whofe vertues and condigne prayfes, if I fhould take vppon mee to recounte, I might as well number the ftarres in the Sky, or graffe of[4] the Earth.

For, for Godly Wyfdome, and zeale to [5]the truth, is not your good Lordfhip (without offence be it fpoken) comparable with[6] the beft? For fobrietie, affabilite, and gentle curtefie to euerie one, farre excelling many. [5 Sig. ¶ 4. B.]

For your great[7] deuotion and compaffion to the poore oppreffed, in all places famous : For Godly fidelitie to your Soueraigne, loue to the CVNTREY, and vertues in generall, euerie where moft re-nowmed.

But leaft I might obfcure your Worthie commenda[8]tions with my vnlearned penne (lytle or no thing at all emphaticall) I will rather furceafe than further to proceed,[9] contenting my felfe rather to haue giuen a fhadowe of them, than to haue ciphered them foorth, which indeed are both infinit and inexplicable. [8 Sig. A 3, bk. E.]

In confideration (whereof,) not withftanding that my Booke be fimpler, bafer, and meaner than that it may (without blufhing) pre-fent it felf to your good Lordfhip (being farre vnworthie of fuch an honorable Perfonage) yet, accordinge to your accuftomed[10] clemency, I moft humbly befeache your good Lordfhip to receiue the fame into your honors Patrociny and protection, accepting it as an infallible token of my faithfull heart, feruice, and good will towardes your honorable Lordfhip : For proofe whereof, would GOD it might once come to paffe, that if not otherwyfe, yet with my humble feruice, I might fhewe foorth the faithfull and euer willing heart I beare in breft to your good Lordefhip, protefting before Heauen and Earth, that though power want, yet fhall fidelitie [11]and faithfulnes[11] faile neuer. [Tho' my book is unworthy of you, yet take it under your protection !]

---

[1] have long fince B.   [2] (by the golden trumpe of fame) *inserted in* B.
[4] vpon E.   [6] to E.   [7] your great *not in* E.
[9] hearein *added in* E.   [10] mansuetude, and pristine *inserted in* B.
[11——11] faithfulnes and goodwill B.

[It exposes sins,

[5 leaf ¶ 4, back. A.]

And becauſe this my Booke is ſubiect [1](my verie good Lord)[1] to as many reproches, tauntes and reproofes as euer was any litle book[2] (for that few *can* abyde to [3]haue[4] their ſins [5]detected) therfore I haue had the greatter care to commit the ſame to the guardance and defence of your honour, rather than to manie others, not onely for that GOD hath made your honour [6]a Lamp of light vnto the world of[6]

and you are God's vicegerent to correct sins.]

true nobilitie and of al[7] integritie and perfection, but alſo hath made you his ſubſtitute, or vicegerent, to reforme vices, puniſh abuſes, and correcte ſinne.

[12 Sig. ¶ 4, back. B.]

And as[3] in mercie he[8] hath giuen you this[9] power and autoritie, [10]ſo hath he [11]giuen[10] you a hungrie [11]deſire to ac[12]compliſh the ſame [13]according to his will : Which zeal in your ſacred breſt the LORD increaſe for euer.

[Reform is needed.

Pride is rife.

Commoners wear gentlefolks' dress.

[17 Sig. A 3, back. E.]

Plays, whoredom, and usury go on.]

And[14] as your Lordſhip knoweth,[13] reformation of maners and amendement of lyfe was neuer more needfull, for was pride (the chiefeſt argument of this Booke) euer ſo rype ? Do not both Men and Women (for the moſt part) euery one in generall go attyred in ſilks, veluers[15], damaſks, ſatans, and what not[16] ? which are attyre onely for the nobilitie and gentrie, and not for the other at [17]anie hand ? Are not vnlawfull games, Playes, and Enterluds, and the like, euery where vſed[18] ? Is not whordome, couetouſnes, vſurie, & the like, daylie practiſed without all puniſhment or lawe[19] ?

But hereof I[20] ſay no more, [21]referring the[21] conſideration, both[22] of theſe and[23] the reſt, to your[24] Godly wyſdome.[25] Beſeaching[26] your

[1]—[1] *om.* F.   [2] book subiect vnto E, F.

[3]—[3] heare their faults discouered) I thought it most meetest to be dedicated to all good Magistrates and men in authoritie, to reforme vice, & maintaine vertue : Vnto whom, in al humble dutie I doe willinglie present the same. And therefore, as the Lorde God F.

[4] heare E.   [6]—[6] a mirror of E.

[7] a rare Phœnix of *for* of al E.   [8] *om.* F.   [9] his E, F.

[10]—[10] to reforme vices and abuses, so I beseech him to giue euery one of F.

[11]—[11] by the operation of his Holy Spirite infused into your heart an earnest B.

[13]—[13] for as you know F.

[14] the rather for that *inserted in* B ; For, E.

[15] Velvets F.   [16] not els ? F.   [18] frequented E, F.

[19] or execution of iustice *added in* E ; F *adds*, Was there euer seene lesse obedience in Youth of all sortes both men-kinde and women-kind towards their superiors, Parents, Masters and gouernors ?

[20] I nead to E.   [21]—[21] reseruyng the good E, F.   [22] as well E, F.

[23] as of E, F.   [24] your Lordships E.   [25] Wisedomes F.   [26]—[26] you F.

good Lordship[20] to perdon my prefumption in fpeaking thus much, for (*Zelus domini huc adegit me*) the zeal of my God hath dryuen me heather.

[1]Knowinge that the LORD hath ordeined you to himfelfe, a chofen veffell of honour, to purge his Church of thefe Abufes and corruptions, which, as in a table, are depainted and fet foorth in this litle [2] booke.[1]

[You, Lord Arundel, are God's Minister to purge his Church.]

Thus I ceafe to moleft your facred[3] eares any further with my rude fpeaches, moft humbly befeaching [4]your good Lordship,[4] not onely to admit this my Book into your [5]honours patronage and defence[5,6] but alfo to perfift the iuft Defender[7] therof againft the fwynish crew of rayling [8]ZOILVS and flowting MOMVS, with their complices[9]; to whome [10]it is eafier to depraue all things, than to amend any thing them felues : Which[11] if I shall perceiue to[12] be accepted of your honour, befides that I shal not care for a thoufand others difliking the fame, I shall not only think my felf to haue receiued a fufficient guerdon for my paines, *and* shalbe therby greatly incoraged (if GOD permit) hereafter to take in hand fome memorable thing to your immortall prayfe, honour and renowne ; but alfo shall daylie pray to GOD for your good Lordship long to continue, to his good pleafure, and your harts defire, with increafe of Godly honour, reward of laudable vertue, and eternall felicitie in the HEAVENS by Iefus Chrift.

[Protect me against the swinish crew of railers and mockers !] [10 leaf ¶ 5. A.]

Columna gloriæ virtus.

Your Honors to commaund,[13]

PHILLIP[14] Stubbes.[8]

[1—1] *Not in* E.   [2] treatise B.   [3] *om.* F.
[4—4] you F.   [5—5] protection F.   [6] protection E.   [7] defenders F.
[8—8] F *has the following*, and slaunderous tongues, so shall I ackowledge my felfe most bounden to pray vnto god for the prosperous & good estates of you all, whom I beseech for Christ his sonnes sake, to blesse and prosper you in all your godly proceedings now and for euer.
Your Honours and Wisdomes most bounden,
P. S.
[9] complies of braging Thrasoes and barking Phormions E.
[11] but E.   [12] the same to E.
[13] in the Lorde *added in* E.   [14] P. *in* B.

[leaf ¶ 5, bk]

A PREFACE[1]

to the Reader.

Thought it conuenient (good Reader, who foeuer thou art *that* fhalt read thefe my poore laboures) to admonifh thee (leaft haply *tho*u mighteft take my woords otherwife than I meant them) of this one thing: That wheras in the proceffe of this

[Tho' I blame Plays, Dances, &c.,

my booke, I haue intreated of certen exercyfes vfually practifed amongeft vs, as namely of Playes and Enterludes, of dauncing, gaming and fuch other like, I would not haue thee fo to take mee, as though

I don't want to abolish all amusements, but only the abuses in them.]

my fpeaches tended to the overthrowe and vtter difliking of all kynd of exercyfes in generall: that is nothing my fimple meaning. But the particulare Abufes which are crept into euery one of thefe feuerall exercyfes is the onely thing which I think worthie of reprehenfion.

For otherwife (all Abufes cut away) who feeth not *that* fome kind of plays, tragedies and enterluds, in their own nature are not onely

[² leaf ¶ 6]

[Some plays are useful for good example

of great ancientie, but alfo very honeft and very commend²able exercyfes, being vfed and practifed in moft Chriftian common weales, as which containe matter (fuch they may be) both of doctrine, erudition, good example, and wholfome inftruction; And may he vfed, in tyme and place conuenient, as conducible to example of life and reformation of maners. For fuch is our groffe & dull nature, that what thing we fee oppofite before our eyes, do pearce further and printe deeper in our harts and minds, than that thing which is hard onely with the eares, as Horace, the hethen Poet, can witneffe: *Segnius irritant animum dimiffa per aures, quam quæ funt hominum occulis obiecta.* So that when honeft & chaft playes,

and Godly recreation.

tragedies & enterluds are vfed to thefe ends, for the Godly recreation of the mind, for the good example of life, for the auoyding of that which is euill, and learning of that which is good, than are they

[1] This Preface is omitted in the editions of 16 August 1583, of 1585, and of 1595.

very tollerable exercyfes. But being vfed (as now commonly they be) to the prophanation of the Lord his fabaoth, to the alluring and inuegling of the People from the bleffed word of God preached, to Theaters and vnclean affemblies, to ydlenes, vnthriftynes, whordome, wantonnes, drunkennes, and what not; and which is more, when they are vfed to this end, to maintaine a great fort of ydle Perfons, doing nothing but playing and loytring, hauing their lyuings of the fweat of other Mens browes, much like vnto dronets denouring *the* fweet honie of *the* poore labouring bees, [1] than are they exercyfes (at no hand) fufferable.

But being vfed to the ends that I haue faid, they are not to be difliked of any fober and wife Chriftian.

And as concerning dauncing, I wold not haue thee (good Reader) to think that I condemne the exercyfe it felf altogether; for I know the wifeft Sages, and the Godlyeft Fathers and Patriarches that euer liued, haue now and than vfed the fame, as Dauid, Salomon, and many others: but my woords doo touch & concerne the Abufes thereof onely. As being vfed vppon the Sabaoth day, from morning vntill night, in publique affemblies and frequencies of People, Men & women together, with pyping, fluting, dromming, and fuch like inticements to wantonneffe & fin, together with their leapinges, fkippings, & other vnchaft geftures, not a few: Being vfed, or rather abufed, in this fort, I vtterly difcommend it.

But vppon the other fide, being vfed in a mans priuat-chamber, or howfe, for his Godly folace and recreation in the feare of GOD; or otherwife abroade, with refpeĉt had to the time, place and perfons, it is in no refpeĉt to be difalowed.

And wheras I fpeake of gaming, my meaning is not that it is an exercife altogether vnlawful. For I know that one Chriftian may play with another at any kind of Godly, honeft, ciuile game, or exercife, for the mutuall recreation one of the other, fo that they be not inflamed with co[2]neytoufnes, or defire of vnlawfull gaine; for the commaundement faith, thou fhalt not couet: wherfore, if any be voide of thefe affeĉtions, playing rather for his Godly recreation, than for defire of filthie lucre, he may vfe the fame in the feare of God: yet fo as the vfe therof be not a let or hinderance vnto him to any other Godly exploit.

But if a man make (as it weare) an occupation of it, fpending

[Haunting gaming-houses to win money, is wrong. both his tyme and goods therein, frequenting gaming howfes, bowling allyes, and fuch other places, for greedineffe of lucre, to him it is an exercife altogether difcommendable and vnlawfull.   Wherfore, as thefe be exercyfes lawfull to them that know how to vfe them in the feare of God, fo are they pradtifes at no hand fufferable to them that

I want the abuses of amusements removd.] abufe the*m*, as I haue fhewed.   But take away the abufes, the thinges in themfelues are not euill, being vfed as inftruments to Godlynes, not made as fpurres vnto vice.   There is nothing fo good but it may be abufed; yet becaufe of *th*e abufes, I am not fo ftridt that I wold haue the things themfelues remooued, no more than I wold meat and drinke, becaufe[1] it is abufed, vtterly to be takén away.

[So in Dress. Noble folk may wear sumptuous apparel.] And wheras alfo I haue fpoken of the exceffe in Apparell, and of the Abufe of the fame, as wel in men as in women generally, I wold not be fo vnderftood, as though my fpeaches exte*n*ded to any, either noble, honorable, or worfhipful; for I am farre from once

[² leaf ¶ 7, bk] thinking that any kind of fump²tuous or gorgeous attire is not to be worn of any of them, as I fuppofe them rather Ornaments in them, than otherwife.

And that they both may, and, for fome refpedts ought, to were fuch attire (their birthes, callings, fundtions, and eftats requiring the fame) for caufes in this my Booke laid downe, as maye appeare ; and for the diftindtion of them from the inferiour forte it is prouable, both by the Woord of God, Ancient Writers, and common practife of all ages, People and Nations from the beginning of the World to this day.

And therfore, when I fpeake generally of the exceffe of Apparell,

[But lower folk must not flaunt in velvets, gilt daggers, &c.] my meaning is of the inferiour forte onely, who for the moft parte do farre furpaffe either noble, honorable, or worfhipfull, ruffling in Silks, Veluets, Satens, Damafks, Taffeties, Gold, Siluer, and what not, with their fwoords, daggers, and rapiers guilte and reguilte, burnifhed, and coftly ingrauen, with all things els that any noble, honorable, or worfhipfull Man doth, or may weare, fo as the one cannot eafily be difcerned from the other.

[I am against abuse, not use.] Thefe be the Abufes that I fpeake of, thefe be the euills that I lament, and thefe be the perfons that my words doo concerne, as the

¹ be- it is

tenure of my Booke, confideratly wayed, to any indifferent READER doth purport.

This much I thought good (Gentle Reader) to informe thee of, for thy better inftruction, as [1] well in thefe few points, as in all other the like, wherfoeuer they fhall chaunce to occurre in my Booke; Befeaching thee to conftrue al things to the beft, to beare with the rudenes therof, and to giue the fame thy good-woord and gentle acceptaunce.   And thus in the LORD I bid thee farewell.

[1 leaf ¶ 8]

Thyne to vfe in the Lord,

PHILLIP Stubbes.

[Sig. B i. E,
B.]

Phillippus Stubeus

CANDIDO LECTORI.[1]

[I don't wonder,
reader, if my
book offends you
with its worse
than Vandalic
words and dull
themes; so read
something more
useful.]

Offendit nimia te garrulitate libellus
    fortè meus, Lector; miror id ipfe nihil.
Obfitus eft etenim verborum colluuione
    plusquam vandalica, rebus *et* infipidis.
Quare fi fapias, operam ne perdito pofthac
    noftra legendo; legas vtiliora, vale.

¶ *Idem in Zoilu.*

[Since, Zoilus,
you rage like a
mad dog,

Zoile, cum tanta rabie exardefcis in omnes,
    non aliter rabidus, quam folet ipfe canis:
Dente Theonino rodens alios, calamoque,[2]
    inceffens hos, qui nil nocuere tibi:

and dart out
your viper's
tongue against
everybody, and
can never be
quiet,
and are always
swelling like the
frog, I wonder
you too don't
burst.]

Viperam in cunctos vibrans, O Zoile, linguam,
    linguam quam inficiunt toxica dira tuam:
Cum debacchandi finis fit, Zoile, nullus,
    hora quieta tibi nullaque prætereat:
Cum tumeas veluti ventrofus, Zoile, bufo,
    demiror medius quod minus ipfe crepes.

¶ *Aliud in eundem.*

[To the devil
with Zoilus!
But why so with
one who carries
about the devil
in his own
bosom?

Dæmonis ad tetrum defcendat Zoilus antrum,
    hunc[3] lacerent furiæ, Cerborus ore voret.
Imprecor at mifero quid pænas, cui fatis intus?
    dæmona circumfert pectore namque fuo.

¶ *Eiufdem aliud.*

If the book
before you
seems too long,
make it short by
reading but
little of it.]

Si tibi prolixus nimium liber ifte videtur,
    pauca legas; poterit fic liber effe breuis.

[1] *This page is omitted in* F.
[2] calomoque *in* B, E.   [3] hunce *in* B.

[¹C. B. In commendation of the Auctors lucubrations.

[¹ Sig. B 1, back. B, E ; not in A.]

You Sages graue with heares so hoare
    attend what you doe heare :
And eke you youthfull gallants all,
    marke well and giue good eare.
You princely peeres, and Senatours,
    in facred breafts imprint :
These faiynges wife, and prudent eke,
    to practize doe not ftint.
You Bifhoppes, and you Prelates all,
    learn here your flock to keepe :
You Minifters, and Preachers eke,
    to feade your feely fheepe,
You Commons all, whiche doe enioye,
    bothe high and lowe degree :
Step boldly in amongeft the route,
    and view with fingle eye,
This perfect glaffe, and mirror pure,
    which doeth your finnes defcrie :
And facred precepts doeth prefcribe,
    by name Anatomie.
Approche therefore both high and lowe,
    this Booke fee that thou buye :
And learne thy felf by facred lore,
    in vertue for to dye.
To God, to Queene, to all men eke,
    how thou thy felf fhouldft frame :
To liue, to dye in vertues lawes,
    to win immortall fame.
²Loe here (you readers all) the gaine,
    which you herein maie haue :
Delay not then, giue *Stubbes* the praife,
    fince freely he it gaue.

Side notes:
[Sages,
Gallants,
Peers,
Bishops,
Preachers,
Commons,
see here your sins describ'd !
Buy this book,
learn your duty by it,
[² Sig. B ij. B, E.]
and praife Stubbes.]

xvi

Loe, here my freende, his freendly harte,
    which he to Countrey beares,
His taken paines, to all his[1] fendes,
    with fighes and tricklyng teares:
In his behalfe, I, as his freende,
    doe humbly of you craue:
His willyng minde accept, and giue
    hym praife he ought to haue.

Finis.

[I, Stubbes's
friend, ask you to
take his work in
good part, and
praise him.]

.

τῆς ἀρετῆς διεγοῦ· η τευχ' ἡ αλδιαιακαί. B, E.]

[1] ? he

[leaf A.]

¹A. D. In commendation of the Author and his Booke.

[Sig. B ij. B, E.]

IF Mortall-man may challenge prayfe
 For any thing done in this lyfe,²
Than may our *Stubbes*, at all affayes,
 Inioy the fame withouten ftryfe :
Not onely for his Godly zeale,
 And Chriftian life accordinglie,
But alfo for this³ booke in fale,
 Heare prefent, now before thine eye.
Herein the Abufes of thefe dayes,
 As in a glaffe thou mayeft behold :
Oh! buy it than ; hear what he fayes,
 And giue him thankes an hundred fold.

[Stubbes should
be praisd for his
Christian life,
and this book
which mirrors
the abuses of our
days.]

¹ This page is omitted in F.   ² like B.   ³ his B, E.

I. F. In Commendation of the Avthor and his Booke.

S Hall men prophane, who toyes haue writ,
    And wanton pamphlets ftore,
Which onely tend to noorifh vice,
    And wickednes the more,
Deferue their praife, and for the fame
    Accepted be of all,

And fhall not this our AVTHOR than
    Receiue the Lawrell pall ?
Who for goodwill in facred breft
    He beares to natiue foyle,
Hath publifhed this Godly Booke
    With mickle paine and toyle.
Wherein, as in a Mirrour pure,
    Thou mayeft behold and fee

The vices of the World difplayed
    Apparent to thy[1] eye.
He flattereth none, as moft men do,
    In Hope to gaine[2] a price ;
But fhewes to all their wickedneffe,
    And Gods diuyne Iuftice.
A Godlyer booke [3]was neuer[3] made,
    Nor meeter for thefe dayes :
Oh ! read it than, thank GOD for it ;
    Let TH' AVTOR[4] haue his praife.

[1] the E, F.   [2] get F.   [3—3] hath not beene E, F.
T' HAVTOR A ; Th' Author B, E, F.

[1]The Avthor and his Booke.

N ow hauing made thee, feelie booke,
　　and brought thee to this frame,
Full loth I am to publifh thee,
　　left thou impaire my name.

The Booke.

Why fo, good Maifter? what's the caufe
　　why you fo loth fhould be
To fend mee foorth into the World,
　　my fortune for to trye?

The Author.

This is the caufe; for that I know
　　The wicked thou wilt moue;
And eke becaufe thy ignoraunce
　　is fuch as none[2] can loue.

The Booke.

I doubt not but all Godly Men
　　will loue and like mee well;
And for the other I care not,
　　in pride although they fwell.

The Author.

Thou art alfo no leffe in thrall,
　　And fubiect euery way
To Momvs and to Zoilvs crew,
　　who'le dayly at thee bay.

---

[1] This and page xx are omitted in F.　　　[2] fewe B, E.

The Booke.

Though MoMvs rage and ZoiLvs carpe,
    I feare them not at all;
The Lord my GoD, in whom I truſt,
    ſhall ſoone cauſe them to fall.

The Author.

Well, ſith thou wouldeſt ſo faine be gone,
    I can thee not withhold;
Adieu, therfore; GoD be thy ſpeade,
    And bleſſe thee a hundred fold.

The Booke.

And you alſo, good Maiſter mine,
    GoD bleſſe you with his grace;
Preſerue you ſtill, and graunt to you
    In Heauen a dwelling place.

¹*The Anatomie of*
²*the Abuſes in AILGNA.*

[¹ Sig. B i. A. Sig. B. iij, back. B, E.]

¶ The Interlocutors, or Speakers.
Spudeus, Philoponus.

God geue you good morow, Maiſter *Philoponus.*
    Philo. And you alſo, good brother *Spudeus.*
    Spud. I am glad to ſee you in good health, for it was ³bruted abroad euery where³ in our countrey (by reaſon of your diſcontinuance,⁴ I thinke) that you were dead long agoe.⁵

Flying fame oftentimes lyeth.

    Philo. In deede, I haue ſpent ſome tyme abroad, els where then in my native countrey (I muſt needs confeſſe), but how falſe that Report is (by whom ſoeuer it was firſt rumored,⁶ or how farre ſo euer it be diſperſed) your preſent eyes can witneſſe.

    ⁷*Spud.* I pray you, what courſe of lyfe haue you lead in this your longe abſence foorth of your owne countrey?

[⁷ Sig. B j, back. A.]

    Philo. Truely (brother) I haue lead the life of a poore Trauayler in a certaine famous Ilande, once named ⁸*Ainabla,* after *Ainatirb,*⁸ but nowe preſently called *Ailgna,*⁹ wherein I haue liued theſe ſeuen winters and more, trauailing from place to place, euen all the Land ouer indifferently.

The place wher the Authour hath trauayled. [*Albania, Britania, Anglia.*]

    ¹⁰*Spud.* That was to your no litle¹¹ charges, I am ſure.¹²

[¹⁰ leaf ɪ. B.†]

    ¹³*Philo.* It was ſo, but what than? I thank God I haue atchieued it, and by his dyuine aſſiſtance proſperouſly accompliſhed it, his glori-

[¹³ leaf ɪ. E.] Trauailing chargeable.

---

² the *not in* B, E, F.   ³—³ reported F ; euery where *not in* B, E.
 ⁴ from thence *inserted in* B, E, F.   ⁵ agone F.
    ⁶ broched B, E, F.   ⁸—⁸ Albania, after Britania F.
    ⁹ Anglia F.   † leaf ɪ. The Author a Trauailer. B.
¹¹ small E ; no litle *omitted in* F.   ¹² F *adds* was it not I pray you?

ous name (worthie of all magnificence) bee eternally prayſed there fore.

Spud. And[1] to what ende did you take in hand this great trauayle? if I may be ſo bould as to aſke.[2]

Philo. Truely, to ſee faſhions, to acquainte my-ſelfe with the natures, qualities, properties, and conditions of all men, to breake my ſelfe to the worlde, to learne nurture, good demeanour, & cyuill be-hauiour; to ſee the goodly ſituation of Citties, Townes, and Countryes, with their proſpeɕts and commodities; and finally to learne the ſtate of all thinges in generall : all which I could neuer haue learned in[3] one place.[3] For[4] [5]who ſo[5] ſitteth at home, euer [6]commorante or[7] abid-ing[8] in one place, knoweth nothinge in reſpeɕte of him that trauayl-eth abroade : and hee that knoweth nothing, is lyke[9] a brute Beaſte; but hee that knoweth all thinges (whiche thing none doeth but God alone) hee is[10] a God amongeſt men. And ſeeing there is a perfeɕtion in knowledge as in euery thing els, euery man ought to deſire that per-fection[11]; for in my iudgement there is as muche difference (almoſt)[12] betwixt a man that hath trauayled much, and him that hath dwelt euer in one place, (in reſpect of knowledge and ſcience of things,) as is be[13]twen a man lyuinge, & one dead in graue; And therfore I haue had a great felicytie in trauayling abroade.[14]

[15]*Spud.* Seing that by diuyne prouidence we are heare[16] met toge-ther, let vs (vntill we come to *the* end of our purpoſed[17] iorney) vſe ſome conference of the ſtate of the World now at this daie, as well to recreate our minds, as to cut of the tedyouſnes of oure iorneye.

Philo. I am very well contente ſo to doe, beinge[18] not a litle glad[19] of your good companie; for *Comes facundus in via, pro vehiculo eſt.* 1. A good Companion too trauayle withall, is in-ſteade of a Wagon [20]or Chariot. For as the one doth eaſe the painfulneſs of the way, ſo doth the other alleuiat *the* yrkſomnes of the iourney intended.

The causes that moued the author to take this tra-uaile in hand.

[⁶ Sig. B ij. A.]

The difference betwixt a man that * hath tra-uayled, and a man that hath not.
[* the A; that B.]
[¹³ leaf ɪ, back. B.†]
[¹S leaf ɪ, back. E.]

The benefite of a good Com-panion to tra-uayle withall.
[²⁰ Sig. B ij, back. A.]

¹ And *not in* B, E, F. ² aske you F.
³—³ my owne countrey E ; my owne countrey at home F.
⁴ For (in my poor iudgement) E, F. ⁵—⁵ hee that F.
⁷ commorante or *not in* F. ⁸ or abiding *not in* B, E.
⁹ like *not in* E, F. ¹⁰ is (as it were) E, F.
¹¹ F *adds* aboue al other things. ¹² *om.* F. ¹⁴ F *adds* all my life long.
† leaf ɪ, back. The benefite of trauailyng. B. ¹⁶ *om.* F.
¹⁷ *om.* F. ¹⁸ reioysing E, F. ¹⁹ glad *not in* E, F.

Spud. But before I enter combat[1] with you (becaufe I am a countrey man, rude and vnlearned, & you, a Cyuilian indued with great wifdome, knowledge, and experience,) I moft humbly befeech you that you wyl not be offended with me, though I talke *with* you fomwhat grofly,[2] without eyther polifhed wordes, or fyled fpeeches, which your wifdom[3] doth require, and[4] my infufficiencie and inabylitie[5] is not [6] of power to affoorde.[6]

A request to auoid [fcandal or E.] offence.

Phil. Your fpeeches (I put you out of doubt) fhall not[7] be offenfiue to mee, if they be not offenfiue to God firft.

Spud. I pray you[8] what maner of Countrey[9] is that *Ailgna*,[10] where you fay you haue trauailed fo much ?

[9 leaf 2. B.†]

Philo. A pleafant & famous Iland, immured aboute with the Sea, as it were with a wall, [11]wherein the aire is verie[12] temperate, the ground fertile, and[13] abounding with all things, either [14]neceffary to[14] man or needefull[15] for beaft.

Ailgna a goodly cuntry. [Anglia, England.] [11 leaf 2 E.]

Spud. What kinde of people are they that inhabite there[16] ?

Philo. A ftrong kinde of people, audacious,[17] bold, puiffant, and heroycal ; of[18] great magnanimitie, valiauncie, and prowes, of an incomparable feature,[19] of an excellente complexion, and [20]in all humanitie inferiour to none vnder the Sunne.

The people of Ailgna.

[20 Sig. B iij. A.]

Spud. This people, whome God hath thus bleffed, muft needes bee a verie godly people, eyther els they be meere ingrate[21] to God, the authour of all grace, & of thefe their bleffinges efpecially.

Philo. It greeueth me to remember their liues, or to make mention of their wayes[22] ; for, notwithftanding that the Lorde hath bleffed [23]that Lande[23] with the knowledge of his truth aboue all other Landes in the world, yet is there not a people more abrupte,[24] wicked, or peruerfe, liuing vpon the face of the earth.

The liues of the people of Ailgna.

Spud. From whence fpring all thefe euills in man ? for we fee

---

[1] into difpute F.   [2] rudely B, E, F.
[3] F *adds* peraduenture   [4] and whiche B.   [5] being such *added in* E, F.
[6]—[6] able to perform B, E ; able for to yeelde F.   [7] uot A.
[8] you then E, F.   † leaf 2. Ailgna described. B.
[10] is England F.   [12] verie *not in* B, E, F.   [13] the earth B, E, F.
[14]—[14] needfull for F.   [15] necessarie F.   [16] that Countrey E, F.
[17] most audacious F.   [18] and of F.   [19] of body *added in* F.
[21] meerlie vngratefull F.   [22] workes F.   [23]—[23] them F.
[24] corrupt E, F.

euerie one is inclined to fin naturally, and there is no flefhe which liueth and finneth not.

From whence
all euilles
spring in man.
[² leaf 2, back.
B.*]

[⁶ leaf 2, back.
E.]
We ought to
haue no deal-
ing with the
workes of the
flesh.
[¹⁰ Sig. B iij, bk]

Philo. All wickednes, mifchiefe, and finne (doubte you not, brother *Spud.*) fpringeth of[1] our [2]auncient ennemie the Deuill, the inueterate corruption of our nature, and the inteftine malice of our owne hearts, as from the[3] [4]originals of all vncleannes & impuritie[4] whatfoeuer. But we are now newe creatures, and [5]adoptiue children,[5] [6]created in Chrift Iefus to doe[7] good woorkes, which God hath pre- pared for vs to walke in. [8]Wherefore wee[8] ought to haue no fellow- fhip with the workes of darkneffe, but to put on the armour of light, [9]Chrift [10]Iefus,[9] to walke in newneffe of life, and to worke our falua- tion in[11] feare and trembling, as the Apoftle faith[12]; and our fauiour Chrift biddeth vs fo[13] work as our workes may glorifie our heauenlye Father. But (alas!)[14] the contrarie is moft true; for there is no finne that[15] was euer broached in any age, which[16]florifheth not nowe. And therfore the fearfull daie of the Lord cannot be farre of; at which day all the World fhall ftand in flafhing fier, and than fhall Chrift our Sauiour come marching in *the* clowdes of heauen, with his[17] *Taratan- tara* founding in each mans eare, 'arife you Dead, and come to iudge- ment!' and than fhall the Lord reward euery Man after[18] his owne workes. But how little this [19]is efteemed of, & how fmally re- garded,[19] to confider, it [20]greeueth me to the very harte, and there is almoft no life in mee.[20]

The day of
Dome not re-
garded.

Spud. It is but a follie to greeue at[21] them who forowe not for them felues. Let them finck in their owne finne: lyue well your felfe, & you fhall [22]not anfweare for them, nor they for you. Is it not writen, *vnufquifque portabit fuum onus*[23]? Euery one fhall beare his own bur-

Euery Man
must answer
for him selfe.
[²² leaf 3. B.†]

---

[1] from E, F.   * leaf 2, back. The originall of sinne. B.
[3] the causes and E.
[4]—[4] efficient causes and stinking puddles of all vncleannes and filthinesse F.
[5]—[5] adoapted (*sic*) children of God F.   [7] *om.* F.
[8]—[8] and therefore B, E; and therefore we F.
[9]—[9] *not in* E, F.   [11] with F.   [12] speaketh F.   [13] so to F.
[14] F *omits* alas.   [15] which F.   [16] that F.
[17] this dreadfull *instead of* his B, E, F.   [18] according to F.
[19]—[19] daie is feared, ‡how smally perpended,‡ and how slenderly regarded in Ailgna§ B, E, F. ‡—‡ *om.* F; § England F.
[20]—[20] would grieue any Christian hart to consider F.   [21] for F.
† leaf 3. Of Christian charitie. B.   [23] onus suum F.

den. *Anima quæ peccauerit, ipſa morietur :* the foule that ſinneth
ſhall dy. wherfore ſurceaſe[1] to ſorow or greeue any more for them,
for[2] they are ſuch as the Lord hath caſt of[3] into a [4]reprobat ſence,
&[4] [5]preiudicat opinion, & preordinat[5] to [6]deſtruction, that his power,   [6 Sig. B iiij. A.
his glorie, and[7] iuſtice may appeare to all the World.

     Philo. Oh, brother ! ther is no[8] chriſten man in whoſe hart ſhineth   [The Christian's
ſcintillula aliqua[9] *pietatis,* any ſparke of [10]God his grace, which[11] will   grief at English-
not greeue to ſee[10] his brethren & ſiſters in the Lord, members of the   men's sins.]
ſame body, coheyres of the ſame kingdom, & purchaſed with one
& the ſame ineſtimable price of Chriſt his bloud, to runne thus[12] deſ-
peratlie into[13] the gulphe of deſtruction and laberinth of[14] perdition.[15]
If the leaſt and[16] meaneſt member of thy whole body be hurt, wounded,
cicatriced, or bruſed, doth not the hart and euerie member of thy[17]
body feele the anguiſh and paine of the grieued parte, ſeking & en-
deuouring [18]them ſelues,[18] euery one in his office & calling,[19] to repaire   The mutuall
the ſame, and neuer ioying vntill that[20] be reſtored again to his former   harmonie of
integritie & perfection? Which thinge, in the balance of Chriſtian   with an other.
charity, conſideratly weighed, may[21] mooue any good Man[22] to mourn
for their defection, and to aſſay [23]by all poſſible means[23] to reduce[24]
them home [25]again, that their ſoules maie be ſaued in the daye of the   [25 leaf 3, back.
Lord. And the Apoſtle commandeth vs,[26] [27]that we be[27] (*alter*[28]   B.†]
alterius emolumento) an[29] ayde and helpe one to an other. And that
we do good to all men, *dum tempus habemus,* whyleſt we haue tyme.
To weepe with them that weepe, to mourne with them that mourne,
and [30]to be of like affection one towardes an other. And common   [30 Sig. B iiij,
   back]

---

[1] cease F.

[2] by all probable conjectures *added in* B, E ; F *adds* by all likelihood

[3] *not in* F ; of=off.   [4—4] *not in* B, E, F.   [5—5] destinate F.

[7] and his F.   [8] not any F.   [9] vlla F.

[10—10] Gods grace, but will grieue, seeing F.   [11] who B, E.

[12] thus *not in* B, E, F.   [13] headlong into B, E, F.

[14] laberinth of *not in* F.   [15] F *adds* both of body and soule for euer.

[16] or B, E, F.   [17] the E, F.

[18—18] by al meanes possible B, E, F.   [19] nature F.   [20] it F.

[21] ought to B ; mooveth me and ought to E, F.   [22] Christian man B, E, F.

[23—23] *not in* B ; assaying by al meanes possible E, F.

[24] and to bring *added in* E ; reclaime them, and to bring F.

† leaf 3, back. The Authors intent. B.

[26] to the vttermost of our power *added in* B, E, F.   [27] *om.* F.

[28] vt simus alter B, E, F. (alteri *in* F.)   [29] That we should be an F.

reaſon aduertiſeth[1] vs, that wee are not borne for our ſelues onelie ; for *Ortus noſtri partem patria, partem amici, partem parentes vendicant :* Our Countrey challengeth a part of our byrth, our brethren and frendes require an other parte, and our parentes (and that *optimo iure*) doe vendicate a third parte : Wherefore I will aſſay to doe them good (if I can) in[2] diſcouering their abuſes, and laying open their inormities, that they, ſeeing the greeuouſnes of their maladies, & daunger of theyr diſeaſes, may in time ſeeke to[3] the true Phiſition [4]& expert Chirurgion[4] of their ſoules, Chriſt Ieſus, of whome onelie commeth all health & grace, and ſo eternally be ſaued.

Spud. Seeing that ſo many and ſo haynous ſinnes[5] do raigne and rage in *Ailgna,*[6] as your wordes[7] import, and which mooue you to ſuch inteſtine ſorrowe and griefe of minde, I pray you deſcribe vnto me more perticularly ſome of thoſe Capitall [8]crimes, and chiefe Abuſes[8] which are there frequented, and which diſhonour the maieſtie of God the[9] moſt, [10]as you ſuppoſe.[10]

A particuler deſcription of P<small>RIDE</small>, the principall
Abuſe[11] ; and how manifold it is
in A<small>ILGNA</small>.[11]

P<small>HILOPONVS</small>.

Y<small>Ou</small> do well to requeſt me to cipher[12] foorth vnto you[13] parte[14] of thoſe great Abuſes (and Cardinall Vices) vſed[15] in A<small>ILGNA</small>,[16] for no man in anie [17]Catalogue, how prolixe ſoeuer,[17] is able to comprehend the ſumme of all [18]abuſes there in praſtiſe.[18] And whereas you woulde haue mee to ſpeake of thoſe Capitall or[19] chiefe Abuſes, which both are deadly in their owne nature, and which offende the maieſtie of

**No man born
for himſelfe.**

**[leaf 4 : Sig.
B. v.]**

**The number of
Abuſes [in
Ailgna E.]
infinite.**

---

¹ teacheth F.   ² by E, F.   ³ to *om.* F.   ⁴—⁴ *om.* F.
⁵ inormities B, E, F.   ⁶ England F.   ⁷ words doe B, E, F.
⁸—⁸ abuses and horrible crimes E, F. (vices *for* crimes F.)
⁹ the *not in* B, E, F.   ¹⁰—¹⁰ in your iudgment F.
¹¹ in Ailgna (in England *in* F.) *comes after* Abuse *in* B, E, F.
¹² discipher B, E ; describe F.   ¹³ unto you *not in* B, E.   ¹⁴ some F.
¹⁵ which are vsed F.   ¹⁶ England F.   ¹⁷—¹⁷ competent volume F.
¹⁸—¹⁸ the abuses there practised F.   ¹⁹ and B, E.

God moſte.[1] Mee thinke you[2] ſhake hands with the ſworne enemies of God, the Papiſtes, who ſay there are two kindes of ſinne, the one veniall, the other lethall or deadly.   But you muſt vnderſtand that there is not the leaſt ſinne, that is committed, eyther in thought, woorde or deede (yea, *Væ vniuerſæ iuſtitiæ noſtræ, ſi remota miſeri-cordia iudicetur:* Wo be to all our righteouſnes, if, mercy put away, they[3] ſhould bee iudged) but it is damnable, *dempta miſericordia Dei,* if the mercie of God be [4]not extended.[4]   And againe; there is no ſinne ſo[5] greeuous, which[6] the grace and mercy of God is not[7] able [8]to [9]coun[10]teruaile withal, & if it bee his[11] pleaſure to blot it out for euer.[9] So *that* you ſee now, there is no ſinn ſo venial, but if the mercie of God be not [12]ſtretched out,[12] it is damnable; nor yet anie ſinne ſo mortall, which by the grace and mercie of God may not bee done away.   And therfore as we are not to preſume of the one, ſo wee are not to deſpaire of the other.   But to returne againe to *the* ſatisfying of your requeſt.   The greateſt abuſe, which[13] both offendeth god moſte, & is there not a little aduaunced, is the execrable ſinne of Pride, and exceſſe in apparell, which is there ſo ripe,[14] as the filthie fruits[15] thereof haue long ſince preſented themſelues before the throne of the maieſtie of God, calling and crying for vengeance day and nighte inceſſantly.

Spud. Wherfore haue you intended to ſpeak of Pride the firſt of all, geuing vnto[16] it the firſt place in your traƈtation[17]? Becauſe it is euill in it-ſelfe, and the efficiente cauſe of euill, or for ſome other purpoſe?

Philo. For no other cauſe but for that I thinke it to bee[18] not onely euill and damnable in it owne nature, but alſo the verie efficient cauſe of all euills.   And therfore the wiſe man was bolde to call it *Initium omnium malorum,* the beginning and welſpring of al euils. For as from the roote all natural thinges doe grow, & take their

Side notes:
All ſinne in it owne nature is mortall.

[8 Sig. B. v, back]
[10 leaf 4, back. B.†]

The greateſt abuſe which offendeth god moſt is pride.

Pride the be-gyning of all euill.

ECCLES. 10.

---

[1] as I suppose *added in* B, E.
[2] you herein B, E.   [3] the B; it E, F.   [4]—[4] taken away E.
[5] lethall nor yet any offence so *added in* B, E ; so lethall or deadly, nor yet any offence so F.   [6] but F.   [7] *om.* F.
[9]—[9] pardon and remit, if it be his good pleasure so to do F.
† leaf 4, back. Pride, the roote of all vices. B.   [11] his good E.
[12]—[12] stretched forth E ; extended F.
[13] in my judgemente *added in* B, E, F.   [14] so stinckyng B, E ; so rotten F.
[15] and lothsome dregges *added in* B E ; dregges F.
[16] *om.* F.   [17] discourse F.   [19] to bee *not in* F.

[¹ Sig. B vj.]
[² leaf 5. B.*]

beginning, fo from *the* curfed ¹roote of ²peftiferous Pride do all other³ euilles fproute, and thereof are ingenerate.   Therfore may Pride be called not improperly, *Matercula* et *origo omnium vitiorum*, the mother and nurfe of al mifchief : for what thyng⁴ fo haynous,

What is it but pride dares attempt it.

what cryme fo flagitious, what deed fo perillous, what attempt fo venterous, what enterprife fo pernicious, or what thing fo offenfiue to God, or hurtful to man, in⁵ all *the* world, which man ⁶(of himfelfe a very Sathanas,)⁶ ⁷to maintain his pride withall,⁷ wil not willingly atchieue⁸ ? hereof ⁹wee haue too muche experience euerye day, more is the pittie.⁹

Spud. How manyfold is this fin of Pryde, whereby the glorie of God is defaced, and his maieftie fo greeuoufly offended !

Philo. Pride is tripartite¹⁰ ; namely, *the* pryde of the hart, the pride

Pride is three-fold : pride of the hart, pride of the mouth, and pride of apparell.

of the mouth, & the pryde of apparell, which¹¹ (vnles I bee deceiued) offendeth God more then the other two.   For as *the* pride of the heart &¹² mouth is¹³ not oppofite to *the* eye, nor vifible to the fight, and therefor ¹⁴intice not¹⁴ others to vanitie & fin (notwithftanding they be greeuous finnes in the fight of God) fo the pride of apparel, ¹⁵remaining in¹⁵ fight, as an exemplarie of euill, induceth the whole man to wickednes and finne.

Spud. How is the pride of *the* hart committed ?

[¹⁶ leaf 5, back. B.†]
[¹⁸ Sig. B vj. back]

¹⁶*Philo.* Pride of the hart is perpetrate¹⁷ when as a man lifting him felfe on highe, thinketh ¹⁸of himfelf aboue that which he is ¹⁹of him-felfe,¹⁹ dreamyng a²⁰ perfection of²¹ himfelfe, when he²² is nothyng leffe ; And in refpect of himfelfe contempneth, ²³vilefieth, and re-proacheth²³ all men,²⁴ thinking none comparable to him felfe, whofe

[Isaias 50. E.]

righteoufnes, notwithftanding, is lyke to the polluted cloth of a men-ftruous woman.   Therfore the Pryde of the Heart maye bee faide too

What pride of the hart is.

bee a Rebellious elation, or lyftynge vppe of the mynde agaynfte the

* leaf 5.   Three fortes of Pride. B.   ³ other *not in* B, E.
⁴ facte B, E, F.   ⁵ is there in B, E, F.   ⁶—⁶ *not in* F.
⁷—⁷ *come after* atchieue *in* B, E, F.   ⁸ attempt E ; commit F.
⁹—⁸ euery daies successe ministreth proof sufficient B, E, F.
¹⁰ threefold F.   ¹¹ the laste whereof B, E, F.   ¹² and of the B, E, F.
¹³ are F.   ¹⁴—¹⁴ cannot intice B, E, F.
¹⁵—¹⁵ obiecte to B, E ; which is obiect to the F.
† leaf 5, back.   Pride deuided. B.   ¹⁷ committed F.
¹⁹—¹⁹ *not in* E, F.   ²⁰ of a F.   ²¹ in F.
²² there F.   ²³—²³ and despiseth   ²⁴ others E, F.

Lawe of God, attrybutynge and aſcrybynge that vnto himſelfe whiche is proper to God onely. And although it bee the Lorde, *Qui operatur in nobis velle*[1] et *poſſe*, who worketh in vs both the wil and power to do good, *Ne gloriaretur omnis caro*, leaſte anie fleſhe ſhould boſte of his owne power and ſtrength, yet Pride, with his Coſin germayn *Philautia*, which is *Selfeloue*, perſwadeth him *that* he hath neede of no mans helpe but his owne ; that he ſtandeth by his own proper ſtrength & power, and by no mans els, & that he is al in all ; yea, ſo perfect and good as no more can be[2] [3]exacted of hym.[3]

Philavtia.

Spud. How is[4] Pride of wordes, or pride of[5] mouthe, committed ?

Philo. Pride of the mouth, or of[6] wordes, is when we boaſt, bragge, or glorie, eyther of our ſelues, our kinred,[7] conſanguynitie, byrth, parentage, and ſuche like : or when we extol our [8]ſelues [9]for any[9] vertue, ſanctimonie of lyfe,[10] ſincerytie of [11]Godlynes[11] which eyther is in vs, or which we pretend to be in vs. In this kinde of Pride (as in the other) almoſt euery one offendeth ; for ſhal you not haue all (in a maner) boaſt & [12]vaunt themſelues[12] of their Auncetors and progenitors ? ſaying & crying[13] with open mouth, I ˙ am a Gentleman, I am worſhipful, I am Honourable, I am Noble, and I can not tell what : my father was this, my father was that : I am come of this houſe, and I am come of that.[14] ' Wheras, Dame *Nature* bryngeth vs all into the worlde after one ſorte, and receiueth all againe into the wombe of our mother, I meane[15] the bowelles of the earth, al in one and the ſame order and manner, without any difference or diuerſitie at all ; wherof more hereafter ſhalbe ſpoken.

How pride of wordes or of the mouth is committed.

[8 leaf 7 ; † *there is no leaf* 6. B 7.]

[Vain glorious oſtentation of birthes, & parentage, &c. B, E.]

Spud. How is Pride of Apparell *committed* ?

Philo. By wearyng of Apparell more gorgeous, ſumptuous, & precious than our ſtate, callyng, or condition of lyfe requireth ;

How pride of

---

[1] et *velle* F.   [2] be required or B, E.
[3]—[3] required of him in this life F.   [4] is the E, F.
[5] of the E ; the pride of the F.   [6] *om.* F.   [7] affinitie *added in* F.
† leaf 7. Pride vainglorious. B.
[9]—[9] in respect of E ; in respect of some F.   [10] of lyfe *om.* F.
[11]—[11] integrity or perfection F ; and the like *added in* E.
[12]—[12] bragge F.   [13] *aperto ore* added in F.
[14] I was borne of this race, and I was borne of that, I am ‡come of this stocke, and I am come of that,‡ *added in* B, E, F ; *but* E & F *have* sprong of [descended *in* F.] this stock, and I of that *for* ‡—‡   [15] I meane *not in* E, F.

apparel is per-
petrate &
co*m*mitted.

wherby we are puffed vp into Pride, and inforced[1] to thinke of our ſelues more than we ought, beyng but vile earth, and miſerable ſinners. And this ſinne of Apparell (as I haue ſayde before) hurteth more then the other two; For the ſinne of the heart hurteth none but the Author in whom it breedeth, ſo long as it burſteth not foorth into [2]exteriour action[2]; [3]and the [4]Pride of the mouth [5](whiche conſiſteth, as I haue ſayd, in oſtenting and braggyng of ſome ſingular vertue, eyther in himſelfe or ſome other of his kinred, and which he arrogateth to himſelfe (by[6] Hereditarie poſſeſſion or lineall diſſent)[5] though it be meere vngodly in it own nature; yet it is not[7] permanent (for [8]wordes fly[8] into the aire, not leauing any print or character behinde them to offend the eyes[9]) But this ſinne of[10] exceſſe of Apparell remayneth as an Example of euyll before our eyes, and as[11] a prouocatiue[12] to ſinne, as Experience daylye ſheweth.[13]

[3 leaf 7, back.
B.†]
[4 B 7, back]

A decorum to
be obſerued.

Spud. Would you not haue men to obſerue a decencie, a comlineſſe, & a *decorum* in their vſuall[14] Attyre? Doeth not the worde of God commaund [15]vs to do all things[15] *decenter* et *ſecundum ordinem ciuilem,* decently and after a cyuile maner[16]?

Philo. I[17] would wiſh that a decencie, a comly order, and, as you ſay, a *decorum* were obſerued, as well in Attyre as in all things els: but would God the contrarie were not true; for [18]moſt of our nouell[19] Inuentions and new fangled faſhions [20]rather deforme vs[21] then adorne vs, diſguiſe vs then become vs, makyng vs rather to reſemble ſauadge Beaſtes and ſtearne[22] Monſters, then continent, ſober, and chaſte Chriſtians.

Our apparell
rather deform-
eth than
adorneth vs.

[23 B viij]

Spud. Hathe this contagious infection of [23]Pride in[24] Apparell infected and poyſoned any other countrey beſide *Ailgna,*[25] ſuppoſe you?

---

[1] induced F.   [2—2] outward shew and appearance F.

    † leaf 7, back.   Men become Monsters.   B.

    [5—5] *not in* F ; from his progenitors *added in* E.

    [6] as it were by B, E.   [7] is it not so F.

    [8—8] Verba cito avolant, et euanescunt in aerem, words soone fly away and vanish E, F.   [9] eies withal F.   [10] of the F.   [11] is E, F.

    [12] prouocation F.   [13] prooueth F.   [14] vsuall *not in* F.

    [15—15] vs al thinges to be done E, F.   [16] order F.

    [17] yes truly I B, E ; Yea trulie I F.   [18] do not *the* E.   [19] fond F.

    [20] dooe thei not *added in* B.   [21] vs *omitted in* F.

    [22] bruitish F.   [24] of F.   [25] countries besides Engla*n*d F.

[1] *Philo.* No doubt but this poyſon hath ſhed foorth his influence, [¹ leaf 8. B.*]
and powred foorth his ſtinking dregges ouer all the face of the earth; [Circes cuppes and Medeas pottes haue made England dronken with Pride. E.]
but yet I am ſure there is not .any people vnder the Zodiacke[2] of
heauen, how [3]clowniſh, rurall,[3] or brutiſh ſoeuer, that is[4] ſo poiſoned
with this Arſnecke of Pride, or[5] hath drunke ſo deepe of [6]the dregges
of this[6] Cup as *Ailgna*[7] hath; with griefe of conſcience I ſpeake it,
with ſorow I ſee it, and with teares I lament it.

Spud. But I haue heard them ſaye that other Nations paſſe them
for exquiſite[8] brauery in Apparell: as the *Italians,* the *Athenians,* the No Cuntrey ſo drunken with pride as Ailgna.
Spaniards, the *Caldeans, Heluetians, Zuitzers, Venetians, Muſcouians,*
and ſuch lyke: now, whither this be true or not I greatly deſire to
knowe.

Philo. This is but a viſour, or cloke, to hide[9] their Sodometrie[10]
withall; onelye ſpoken, not prooued; forged in the deceiptfull Mint
of their owne[11] braynes: For (if credit may be giuen to ancient writers)
the *Egyptians* are ſaid neuer [12]to haue changed[12] their faſhion, or altered
the forme [13]of their firſt[13] Attire from the beginning[14] to this day: as
Iacobus Stuperius, *lib. de diuerſis noſtræ ætatis habitibus, Pag.* 16, [Stuperius. B, E.]
affirmeth. The *Grecians* are ſaide to vſe but one kynde of Apparell
without any chaunge: that is, to [15]wit, a longe Gowne reaching [¹⁵ B 8, back]
downe to the grounde.

The *Germaynes* are thought to be ſo preciſe in obſeruing one
vniforme faſhion in Apparell, as they haue neuer receeded from their
firſt Original; as the ſaid *Stuperius* ſayth in theſe [16]wordes: *Non* [¹⁶ leaf 8, back. B.†]
enim mores leuiter mutare vetuſtos, Germanus vnquam conſueuit incola:
Whiche in Englyſh Verſe is thus muche in effect:

¶ *The Germayne people neuer vſe*
lightly[17] *to chop and chaunge* [Cp. my *Andrew Boorde,* p. 159, 152, 149.]
Their cuſtomes olde, or els Attyre,
wherin abroade they range.

¶ The *Muſcouians, Athenians, Italians, Braſilians, Affricanes,*

* leaf 8. Newfangledneſſe in Ailg. B.
[2] face F.　　　[3—3] ſauage F.　　　[4] that is *not in* B, E, F.
　[5] or that B, E, F.　　　[6—6] this impotionate B, E, F.
[7] England F.　　[8] fineneſſe and *added in* F.　　[9] couer B, E, F.
[10] owne ſhame E, F.　　[11] own lying F.　　[12—12] to chaunge F.
[13—13] or faſhion of their F.　　　[14] of the world *added in* F.
† leaf 8, back. Foreigne guiſe of Apparell. B.　　　[17] at all F.

Aſianes, Cantabrians, Hungarians, Ethiopians,[1] or els what Nation[2]
foeuer vnder the Sunne, are ſo farre behinde the people of *Ailgna*[3] in
exquiſitneſſe of Apparell, as in effect they eſteeme it litle or nothyng
at all, ſo it repell the colde and couer their ſhame ; yea, ſome of them
are ſo ſmally addicted therto, that, fettyng apart all honeſtie and
ſhame, they go cleane naked.   Other ſome, meanly apparelled ; ſome
in Beaſts ſkinnes, ſome in haire, & what euer they can get[4] : ſome in
one thing, ſome in another, nothing regarding eyther hoſen, ſhoes,
bands, ruffes, ſhirts, or any thing els.   And the ciuileſt nations that
are, bee ſo farre eſtraunged from the pride of [5]Apparell, that they
eſteme him as brauelye attyred that is clothed in our carzies, frizes,
ruggs, and other kinds of cloth, as we do him that is clad all ouer in
ſilkes, veluets, ſatens, damaſks, grograins, taffeties, and ſuch like.   So
that herby you ſee that they ſpeak vntruly, that ſay that other nations
exceede them in brauerie of apparell.   For it is manifeſt that all other
Nati[6]ons vnder the ſun, how ſtrange, how new, how fine, or how
comly ſoeuer they think their faſhions to be, when they be compared
with the dyuerſe faſhions & ſundrie formes of apparell in *Ailgna*,[7]
are moſt vnhandſome, brutiſh, and monſtrouſe.   And herby it appeareth that no People in the World is[8] ſo curiouſe in new fangles as they
of *Ailgna*[7] be.   But graunte it were ſo, and admit that others excelled
them (which is falſe), ſhall we do euill becauſe they do ſo ? ſhall their
wickedneſſe excuſe vs of ſinne, if we commit the like & worſe ?
ſhall not the ſoule that ſinneth dye ? wherfore let vs not ſinne of[9]
preſumption with the multitude, becauſe they do ſo, leaſt we be
plagued with them becauſe we doe the like.   Moreouer, thoſe Cuntreyes are rich and welthie of them ſelues, abounding with all kinde
of preciouſe ornaments and riche attyre, as ſilks, veluets, Satens,
damaſks, ſarcenet, taffetie,[10] chamlet, and ſuch[11] like (for al theſe are
made in thoſe foraine cuntreyes), and therfore [12]if they weare them
they are not muche[13] to bee blamed, as not hauing anie other kind of
cloathing to couer themſelues withall.   So if wee would contente
ourſelues with ſuch kinde of attire as our owne Countrey doeth

[All nations
inferiour to
Ailgna for
pride of apparell
B, E.]

[5 C 1]

[No people so
curious in newe
fangles as thei of
Ailgna. B, E.]
[6 leaf 9. B.†]

Other coun-
treyes not to
be blamed·
though they
go in silks,
veluets, and
why.
[12 C 1, back]

---

[1] Dutch, French *added in* F.   [2] nations F.   [3] England F.
    [4] get *not in* F.   † leaf 9.   Brutishe fashions in Ailgna. B.
[7] England F.   [6] are B, E, F.   [9] in B, E.   [10] Taffeta F.
            [11] the B, E, F.   [13] *not in* F.

[1]miniſter vnto[1] vs, it were much[2] tollerable. But wee are ſo ſurpriſed[3] in Pride, that if it come not from beyond the ſeas, it is not worth a ſtraw. And thus we impoueriſh our ſelues in buying their trifling merchandizes, more pleſant tha*n* neceſſarie, and [4]inrich them, who rather[5] laugh at vs in their ſleeues than otherwiſe,[6] to ſee our gret follie in affecting of trifles, & departing[7] *with* good merchandizes[8] for it.[9] And howe litle they eſteeme of ſilkes, veluets, ſatens, damaſks, [10]and ſuch like,[10] wee maye eaſely ſee, in that they ſell them to vs for[11] wolles, frizes, rugges, carzies, and the lyke, whiche they coulde[12] neuer doe[13] if they eſteemed of them as much as we doe. So that you ſee they are forced of neceſſytye to weare ſuch riche attyre, wanting other things (whereof we haue ſtore) to inueſt themſelues withall. But who ſeeth not (excepte wilfullie blynde) that no neceſſitie compelleth vs to weare them, hauing abunda*n*ce of other things to attire our ſelues with,[14] both hanſomer, warmer, [15]and as comlie as[15] they in euerie reſpecte? But 'farre fetched and deare boughte' is good for Ladyes,[16] they ſay.

Spud. Doe you thinke it not permitted to any, hauinge ſtore of other neceſſary clothing, [17]to weare ſilks, veluets, taffeties, & other ſuche riche attyre, of what calling ſoeuer they be of[18]?

Ph. I doubt not but it is lawfull for *the* poteſtates,[19] the nobilitie, the gentrie, [20]yeomanrie, and for euerye priuate ſubiecte els[20] to weare [21]attyre euery one in [22]his degree, accordinge as his calling and condition of life requireth; yet a meane is to be keept, for *omne extremum vertitur in vitium,* euery extreme is turned into vice.[22] The nobilitye [23](though they haue ſtore of other attyre) and the gentrie (no doubte) may vſe a rich and precioſſe kynd of apparell (in the feare of God)[23] to innoble, garniſhe, & ſet forthe their byrthes, dignities,[24] functions, and callings; but for no other reſpecte they may not in any maner of

Margin notes:

Other Countryes eſteme not ſo muche ſilkes, veluets, as we do.

[4 leaf 9, back. B.†]

[Foreigners change their velvets, &c.· for our wools. Cp. *Stafford,* p. 54, 87, &c.]

[17 C 2]

Euery man may apparell according to his callinge.

The nobility may weare gorgiouſe attire, and why

1—1 afford B, E; yeeld F.　　[2] ſomewhat B, E, F.　　[9] captiuate F.
† leaf 9, back. Pride and Pleaſure in Ailg. B.　　[5] rather *not in* B, E, F.
　[6] than otherwiſe *not in* B, E, F.　　[7] parting F.　　[8] wares F.
　[9] them B, E, F.　　10—10 Taffetaes, and ſuch, F.　　[11] for our B, E, F.
　[12] would F.　　[13] *not in* F.　　[14] with-all F.
　15—15 and comlier then B, E, F. (comelier F.)　　[16] ladies as B.
　[18] of *not in* B, F.　　[19] the potestates *not in* B, E, F.　　[21] weare riche B, E, F.
22—22 their calling B, E, F.　　23—23 *omitted in* B; and gentrie E, F.
　　24—24 & ẽſtates. The magiſtery B, E, F.

wyſe. The maieſtrats alſo & Officers in the weale publique, by what tytle ſoeuer they be called (accordinge to their abylities), may were (if the Prince or Superintendent do Godly commaund) coſtlie ornaments and riche attyre,[24] to dignifie their callings, and to demonſtrat [1]and ſhewe forth[1] the excelency[2] and worthines of their offices and functions, therby to ſtrike a terroure & feare into the harts of the people to offend againſt [3][4]the maieſty of their callings[4] : but yet would I wiſh that what ſo is ſuperfluous or ouermuche, either in the one or in *the* other, ſhold be diſtributed to[5] the helpe of[6] the pore members of Chriſt Ieſus, of whom an infynite number [7]daylie do[8] periſh thorowe wante of neceſſarie refection and due ſuſtentation to their bodies. And as for the priuat ſubiects, it is not at any hand lawful that they ſhould weare ſilks, veluets, ſatens, damaſks, gould, ſiluer, and what they liſt (though they be neuer ſo able to maintain it), except they, being in ſome kinde of office in the common wealth, do vſe it for the dignifying and innobling of the ſame.[9] But now there is ſuch a confuſe mingle mangle of apparell in *Ailgna*,[10] and ſuch prepoſterous[11] exceſſe therof, as euery one is permitted to flaunt it out in what apparell he luſt[12] himſelfe, or can get by anie kind of[13] meanes So that it is verie hard to knowe [14]who is noble,[14] who is worſhipfull, who is a gentleman, who is not : for you ſhall haue thoſe which are neither of the nobylitie, gentilitie, nor yeomanry ; no, nor yet anie Magiſtrat, or Officer in the common welth, go daylie in ſilkes, veluets, ſatens, damaſks, taffeties, and ſuch like, notwithſtanding that they be both baſe by byrthe, meane by eſtate, & ſeruyle by calling. [15]This is[15] a great confuſion, & [16]a general diſorder : [17]God be mercyfull vnto vs[17] !

Spud. If it be not lawfull for euery one to weare ſilks, veluets,

[1]—[1] *not in* B.   [2] the maieſtie *added in* B, E, F.
 * leaf 10. Sumptuous Attyre. B.   [4]—[4] their office and authoritie B, E, F.
[5] and erogate to B, E, F.   [6] and subvention of B, E, F.   [8] do *not in* F.
   [9] Or at the commaundement of ‡ their superintendent, or Archprimate,‡ for some speciall consideration or purpose, *added in* B, E, F. (‡—‡ the chiefe Magiſtrate F.)
          [10] England (*and so in every other place where* Ailgna *occurs*) F.
 .   [11] horrible F.   [12] listeth F ; lusteth B, E.   [13] kind of *not in* F.
[14]—[14] *not in* F.   [15]—[15] And this I compt [accompt F.] B, E, F.
          † leaf 10, back.   Riche ornaments. B.
          [17]—[17] in a christian common wealth E, F.

Maieſtrats may were sumptuouse attyre, & why.
[3 leaf 10. B.*]

[7 C 2, back]
[Men die for want of food.]

Not lawfull for priuate ſubiectes to weare ſumpteous attyre.

Hard to know a Gentleman from another by apparell.

[16 leaf 10, back. B.†]

ſatens, damaſks, taffeties, gold, ſiluer, precioufe ſtones, & what not, wherfore did the Lord make & ordein them ?

Philo. I denie not but they may be worne ¹ of them who want other things to cloth them withal, or of *the* nobylity, gentilytie,² or magiſtery, for the caufes abouefaid, but not of euery proud fixnet³ indifferentlie, that haue⁴ ſtore of other attyre inough.   And yet did not the Lord ordeane thefe riche ornaments and gorgioufe veſtments to be worne of all men, or of anie, fo muche as to garnish,⁵ bewtifie, and fet forth, the maieſty & glorie of this his earthly kingdome : For as cloth of gold, Arafe, tapeſtrie, & fuch other riche orname*n*ts, pendices, and hangings in a houfe of eſtate, ſerue not onely to manuall vfes and feruyle occupatio*n*s, but alfo to decorate,⁶ to bewtifie, & become⁷ the houfe, and to shewe the riche eſtate and glorie of the owner ; fo thefe riche ornaments, and fumpteoufe veſtments of the earthly territory of this World, do not onelie ſerue to be worn of them, to whome it doth appertaine (as before) but alfo to shew forth *the* power, welth, dignity, riches, and glorie of the Lord, the Author of all goodneffe.⁸   And here in the prouidence and mercy of God appeareth moſt plainelye ; for wher there is ſtore of other clothing, there hath he geuen leffe ſtore of filks, veluets, fatens, damaſks, ⁹ and fuch like : and wher there is plenty of them, there is no clothing els almoſt ; & thus the Lord ¹⁰did deale¹⁰, for that euery cuntrey ¹¹ought to contente themfelues¹¹ with there owne kind of attyre ; except neceffytie inforce ¹²the contrarie ; for than we are to vfe our libertie, in the feare of God.

Spud. I praye you, let mee intreate you to ſhewe me wherefore our apparell was giuen vs, and by whome ?

Philo. Your requeſte is both diffufe and intricate, and more than my weake and infirme knowledge is able to comprehend¹³ ; yet leaſt I might bee adiudged vnwilling to doe good, I will affay to doe the beſt¹⁴ I can.

When the Lord our God, a fpiritual, intelle&ible vnderſtanding fubſtance, incomprehenfible, immenfurable, & inacceffible, had, by

Marginal notes:

[¹ C 3]

Wherfore the lord made riche orna-mentes.

Wherto riche ornamentes do ſerue.

[⁹ leaf 11. B.†]

[¹² C 3, back]

When, where, and for what caufe our apparell was geuen vs.

---

² Gentry F.   ³ Thraso B, E, F.   ⁴ hath B, E, F.
⁵ splendishe B, E, F.   ⁶ decore B, E, F.   ⁷ adorne F.
⁸ thynges B, E, F.   † leaf 11. By whom App[arell] was giuen. B.
¹⁰—¹⁰ hath dealt B, E, F.   ¹¹—¹¹ should be content B, E, F.
¹³ performe B, E, F.   ¹⁴ best that B, E, F.

his woord and heauenly wifedome, Chrift Iefus, created and made *the* world & all things therin contayned, *the* fixte day he created man after his own fimilitude and likenes, in innocencie, holines, righteoufnes, & all kind of perfection, [1]he placed[1] him in Paradife tereftrial, commaunding[2] him to tyl & manure *the* fame.   Than *the* deuil, an old maligner of mankind, who before was an Angel in heauen, & through fin[3] of pride in arrogating to himfelfe *the* feate & throne of Gods maiefty, caft down into *the* lake of hell, enuying mans glorious eftate, which he than had loft, came vnto man in Para-

[4 leaf 11, back. B.*]

dife, & [4]inticed him (oh,[5] torteoufe ferpent !) to eat of *the* forbidden fruite, wherof the Lorde God had forbidden him to taft on pain of

The fall of man by the malice of the deuill. [7 C 4]

his life : notwithftanding *Adam*, condefcending to [6]his wife her per- fwafions,[6] or [7]rather to[8] the Serpent,[9] hauing buzzed his venemous fuggeftions into their[10] eares, tooke of the apple & did eat, contrary to *the* expreffe commandement of his God.   This done, their eyes were opened, thei faw their nakednes, & were not a litle afhamed ; (& yet before fin was committed, they, being both naked, were not afhamed ; but fin once committed[11] they became vncleane, filthie, loth- fome, & deformed,) & fewed them garments of fig leaues together, to couer their fhame withall.   Than the Lord, pittying their miferie & loathing their deformity, gaue them pelts & [12]felles[13] of beafts[12] to make them garments withall, to the end that their fhamefull parts

Impudent beasts, [that shewe their priuities. E.]

might leffe appeare ; yet fome are fo brafen faced & fo impudent that, to make *the* deuill & his members fport, will not fticke to make open fhew of thofe parts which God commaundeth to be couered, nature willeth to be hid, & honefty is afhamd once to be- hold or looke vpon.

Spud. I gather by your words three fpeciall poynts.   Firft, *that* fin was the caufe why our apparell was giuen vs ; Secondly, *that* God is the author & giuer therof ; Thirdly, *that* it was giuen vs to couer

[14 leaf 12. B.†]

our fhame withall, & not [14]to feed *the* infatiable defires of mens wanton & luxurious eies.

---

[1]—[1] and placing B, E, F.   [2] commanded B, E, F.   [3] the sinne B, E, F.
    * leaf 11, back.   The fall of Adam. B.   [5] like a F.
    [6]—[6] the perswasions of his wife B, E, F.   [8] of B, E, F.
    [9] in his wife *added in* F.   [10] her F.   [11] contracted F.
        [12]—[12] beasts felles and skinnes F.   [13] and skins E.
            † leaf 12.   Proude Ap[parell] the Deuils nets. B.

Philo. Your collection is very true. Than, ſeeing *that* our apparel
was giue*n* vs of god to couer our ſhame, to keep our bodies from cold,
& to bee as pricks in our eies to put vs in mind of our miſeries,
[1] frailties, imperfections, and ſin, of our backſlyding from the com-
maundements of god and obedience of the higheſt, and to excite [2] vs
the rather to contrition and compunction of the [3] ſpirit, to bewayle our
miſery, & to craue mercy at *the* mercifull hands of God, let vs be
thankfull to God for them, be ſorie for our ſinnes (which weare the
cauſe [4] therof,) and vſe them to the glory of our God, & the benefyte
of our bodies and ſoules, [5] againſt the great day of the Lord appeare.[5]
But (alas) theſe good creatures which the Lord our God gaue vs for
the reſpects before rehearſed, we haue ſo peruerted as now they ſerue,
in ſtead of the deuills nettes, to catche [6] poore ſoules in; for euery
one now adaies (almoſt) couet to [7] deck and painte their liuing [8]
ſepulchres, [9] or erthly graues [9] (their bodies I meane) with all kind of
brauerie, what ſoeuer can be deuiſed, to delight *the* eyes of the vnchaſt
behoulders, wherby God is diſhonored, offence [10] is encreaſed,[10] and
much ſinne daylie committed, as in further diſcourſe ſhall plainly
appeare.

Spud. Did the Lord cloth our firſt parents in leather, as not
hauing any thing more precioufe to attyre them withall, or for that it
might be [11] a permanent [12] rule, or patern, vnto vs (his poſterity) for
euer, wherafter we are of force to make all our garments, ſo as it
is not now lawfull to [13] go in [14] richer arraye,[14] without [15] offendinge
his maieſtie?

Philo. Although *the* Lord did not cloth the*m* ſo meanly, for that
he had nothing els more precioufe to attyre them withall, (for *Domini*
eſt terra, et *plenitudo eius,* the earth is the Lords and the fulneſſe
therof, ſaith the Lord by his Pſalmiſt; And by his Prophet, Gold is
myne, ſiluer is myne, and all the riches of the world is my[16] own,) yet,
no doubt, but he would *that* this their meane & baſe attyre ſhould
be as a rule, or pedagogie, vnto vs, to teach vs *that* we ought rather

Wherfor our
apparell was
geuen vs.
[¹ C 4, back]

Mens bodies
lyuing ſepul-
chres.

[¹¹ leaf 12, back
B.†]

[¹⁵ C 5]

---

[2] exercise F.   [3] the *not in* F.   [4] causes F.
[5]——[5] at the last F.   [6] intangle B, E, F.   [7] couet to *not in* B, E, F.
[8] liuing *not in* B, E, F.   [9]——[9] *not in* B, E, F.   [10]——[10] miniſtred B, E, F.
† leaf 12, back. The right vſe of App[arell]. B.   [12] perpetual F.
[13] for vs to F.   [14]——[14] riche attire B, E, F.   [16] mine F.

to walke meanelye and fimplye, than gorgioufly or pompoufly ; rather
feruing prefente neceffitye, than regarding the wanton appetits of our
lafcinioufe mindes. Not-withftandinge, I fuppofe not that his heauenlye maiefty would that thofe garments of lether fhould ftand as a rule
or pattern of neceffytie vnto vs, wherafter we fhold be bound to fhape
all our apparell for euer, or els greeuouflye to offende ; but yet by
this we may fee his bleffed will is,² that we fhould rather go an ace
beneth our degree, than a iote aboue. And *that* any fimple couering
pleafeth the Godly, fo that it repell the colde and couer the fhame, it
is more than manifeft, as well by the legends both³ of prophane
Hiftoryographers, Cronologers, and other writers, as alfo by the cen-

fures, examples, ⁴and lyues of all Godly fince the beginning of the
world. And if the Lord would not ⁵ that the attyre of Adam fhould
haue beene a figne or patterne of mediocritie vnto vs, he both in
mercy would &, in his almighty⁶ power, could, haue inuefted them in
filks, veluets, fatens, grograins, gold, filuer, & what not.⁷ But the
Lord our God forefawe that if he had clothed man in rich and
gorgioufe attyre (fuche is our proclynitye to finne), he wold haue bene
proude therof, ⁸as we fee it is come to paffe at this day (God amend
it !), and therby⁸ purchafe to himfelfe, his body and foule, eternall
damnation.

Spud. Than, it feemeth a thinge materiall, and of great importance,⁹ that we refemble our firft Parents in aufterity ¹⁰and fimplicity of
apparell,¹⁰ fo muche as maye be poffible, doth it not ?

Philo. I put no religion in goinge, or not goinge, in the like
fimple attyre of our parents Adam & Eua (as ¹¹our Papiftes, Papifts ?
no, Sorbonifts, Sorbonifts? no, Atheifts, atheifts? no, plaine Sathanifts¹¹
do, placing all thier religion in hethen garments & Romifh raggs)
fo that we obferue a meane, and exceade not in pride. But notwithftanding, if we approched a litle nearer them in Godly fimplicitie
and Chriftian fobrietie, both of apparell and maner of lyuinge, we
fhould not onely pleafe God a great deale the more, and enritche our

Cuntrey, but alfo auoyd many fcandals & of¹²fences which grow

¹ oby A. ² was then, & is now F. ³ both *not in* B, E, F.
† leaf 13. No conscience reposed in App[arell]. B. ⁶ mighty E.
⁷ not els F. ⁸—⁸ and so F. ⁹ moment F.
¹⁰—¹⁰ of apparell and simplicity of attire B, E, F.
¹¹—¹¹ Sorbonicall Papists B, E, F (F *prefixes* the).

daily by our exceſſiue ryot, and ryotouſe exceſſe in apparell. For doth not *the* [1] apparell ſtyrre vppe the heart to pride? doth it not intice others to ſinne? and doth not ſin purchaſe hell, the guerdon of pride?

Spud. But they ſay they pleaſe God, rather than offend him, in wearing this gorgiouſe attyre, for therby the glory of his workmanſhip in them doth more[2] appeare. Beſides that, it maketh a man to be accepted and eſteemed of in euery place; wheras otherwiſe they ſhould be nothing leſſe.

Philo. To think that the Lorde our God is delighted in the ſplendente ſhewe of outward apparell, or that it ſetteth forth *the* glory of his Creatures, and the maieſty of his kingdom, I ſuppoſe ther is no ma*n* (at leaſt no perfeᄃ chriſtian man) ſo bewitched or aſſotted: For that weare as much as to ſay, that ſtinking pride & filthie ſinne tended to the glory of God; ſo that the more we ſyn, the more we increaſe his prayſe and glorye. But the Lord oure God is ſo farre from delightinge in ſinne, that he adiudgeth them to eternall Death and damnation that committe the ſame. Than, who is he that will take pleaſure in vayne apparell, which, if it be worne but a whyle, will fall to ragges, and if it be not worne, will ſoone rotte, or els be eaten with mothes. His wayes are not oure [3] wayes, his ·iudgements not[4] our iudgements, as he ſayth by his Prophet: and wheras they holde that Apparell ſetteth foorth the glory of his Maieſtie in his creatures, makynge them to appeare fairer, than other wyſe they would of them-ſelues, [5] it is blaſphemouſly ſpoken, and muche derogateth from *the* exellency and glory of his name. For, ſaith not God by his prophet Moyſes, that after he had made all creatures, he beheld them all, & behould they weare (and eſpecially ma*n*, the excellenteſt of all other his creatures, whom he made after his own ſimilitude & likneſſe) excedinge good? And were all creatures good & perfeᄃ, & only ma*n* not perfeᄃ, nor faire inough? If theſe their ſpeeches were true (which in the[6] fulneſſe of their blaſphemie they ſhame not to ſpeake) than might we eaſily conuince the Lord of [7] vntrue ſpeak-

[[1] leaf 13, back. B.*]

The fruite of Pride.

The Lord ac-cepteth no man after his apparell.

[3 C 6, back]

No attyre can make the crea-ture of God ſeeme fayrer.
[5 leaf 14. B.†]

---

² more *not in* E ; more brauely F.

⁴ are not F.   † leaf 14.   Man comely of hymſelf. B.
    ⁶ the *not in* F.   ⁷—⁷ untruthe B, E, F.

ing,[7] who in his facred word informeth[1] vs, that man is the perfecteft Creature, & the fayreft of al others, *that* euer he made (excepting the heuenly fpirits, & Angelical creatures) [2]after his own likneffe,[2] as before.   O[3] man! who arte thou, that reafoneft with thy Creator?

Euery one is to contente him felfe with his creation, and to prayfe God for it.

fhall the clay fay vnto the potter, why haft thou made me thus?   Or can *the* clay make himfelfe better fauored than the potter, who gaue him his firft ftamp & proportion?   Shall we think that ftinking pride can make the workmanfhippe of the Lord to[4] feeme fayrer?

[5 C 7]

Than, why did not the Lord cloth vs [5]fo at *the* firft? or at leaft, why gaue he not commaundement in his will & teftament, which he fealed with the [6]price of the[6] bloud of his fonne, to cloth our felfes in riche & gorgioufe apparel to fet forth his glory *the* more?   But away with thefe[7] dogs & hellifh haggs, who retaine[8] this opinion,[9]

[10 leaf 14, back. B.†]

that cur[10]fed pride glorifieth God, & fetteth forth or bewtifieth his workmanfhippe in his creatures!   In vain is it for me to expoftulat with them, for doubtles non hould this, but fuch as be[11] mifecreants (or

The Lord our God is a con-suming fire to destroy all impenitent sinners.

deuills incarnate) [12]& men[12] caft of[f] into a reprobate fence,[13] whom I befeech the Lord, in the bowels of his mercy, either fpeedely to con-uert, that they perifh not, or els confounde, *that* they hurte not, that peace may be vppon[14] Ifrael.   Thus, hauing fufficiently (I truft) refelled their falfe pofitions, I leaue them to the Lord, befeechinge them (as they tender their own faluation, *linguas compefcere digitis*, to ftoppe their facrilegioufe mouthes with ther fingers, & not to fpit againft heauen, or kicke againft the pricke, as they do, anie longer: For the Lord our God is a confuming fier, & vpon obftinate finners fhal raine down fire & brimfton, & confume them in his wrath. This is our[15] portion acquired by finne.

   Spud. But what fay you to the other branch of their conclufion, namely, that Apparell maketh them to be accepted, and well taken in euery place?

[16 C 7, back]

   [16]*Philo.* Amongeft the wicked and ignorante Pezants, I muft needes

---

[1] teacheth B, E, F.   [2—2] *not in* B, E, F.   [3] But O F.
[4] to *not in* F.   [6—6] *not in* F.   [7] sauage *added in* E, F.
[8] are of B, E, F.   [9] mind F.
          † leaf 14, back.   Proude Appa[rell] deformeth man. B.
     [11] as be *not in* B, E, F.   [12—12] as the Lord hath B, E, F.
[13] and preiudicate opinion *added in* F.   [14] vnto F.   [15] their B, E, F.

confeſſe, they are the more eſtemed in reſpeᶜt of their apparell; but nothing at all the more, but rather the leſſe, amongeſt the godly wyſe. So farre of[f] will all wyſe men be from accepting of any for his gay apparell onely, that (be he neuer ſo gallantly pain[1]ted or curiouſly plumed in the deceiptfull fethers of pride) they wil rather contemne him a great deale the more, taking him to be a man puffed vp with pride and vaine glorie, a thing both odiouſe, [2]& deteſtable to God & good men.[2]   And ſeeing it cannot ſtand with the rule of god his iuſtice, to accept, or not to accept,[3] any man for[4] his apparell, or any other externe ſhew of deceiptfull vanytie, it is manifeſt, that man, doinge the contrarie, is a *Iudas* to the truth, a Traytor to iuſtice, & an enemy to the Lord: wherfore farre be that from al good chriſtians; and if thoſe that go richly clothed ſhould be eſteemed the rather for their rich apparel than *à contrario*, muſt thoſe that go in meane and baſe attire, be the more contemned, and deſpiſed for their pouertie. And than ſhould Chriſt Ieſus, our great Ambaſſador from[5] the king of heauen, [6]& only Sauiour,[6] be comtemned, for he came in poore & mean array: but Chriſt Ieſus is bleſſed in his pore raggs, and all others are contemned in their rich & precious attyre.   Vnder a ſimple cote many tymes lyeth hid great wiſdom & knowledg; & contrarely, vnder braue [7]attyre ſomtime is couered great ydiotacy[8] and folly.   [9]Hereof euery daies ſucceſſe offreth proofe ſufficient: more is the pytie[9]!

Spud. Wherfore would you haue men accepted, if not for Apparell?

Philo. If any be ſo fooliſh to ymagin that he ſhalbe worſhipped, reuerenced, or accepted the rather for his apparell, he is not ſo wyſe as I pray [11]God make me.   For ſurely, for my part, I will rather wor-ſhippe & accept of a pore man (in his [12]clowtes & pore raggs[12]) hauing the gifts and ornaments of the mind, than I will do him that roiſteth & flaunteth[13] daylie & howrely in his ſilks, veluets, ſatens,

[1 leaf 15. B.*]

The wise will not accept of any after 1 apparell.

[Wisdom not tyed to exteriour pompe of apparell. B, E.]
[7 C 8]

10 Reuerence due to vertue, not to attyre.10
[11 leaf 15, back B.†]

* leaf 15.   No estimation due to App[arell]. B.
[2]—[2] before men and detestable before God B, E, F.   [3] accept of E, F.
      [4] after E.   [5] sent from B.
  [6]—[6] *not in* B, E, F.   [8] adiocie F.   [9]—[9] *not in* B, E, F.
  † leaf 15.   Reuerence due to Vertue. B.   [10]—[10] *not in* E.
      [12]—[12] torne cloutes and ragges E ; ragged cloutes F.
                [13] flaunteth it out F.

damaſks, gold or ſiluer, what ſoeuer, without *the* induments of vertue, wherto only al reuerence is due.   And therfor as any man is indued, or not indued, with vertue, & true godlyneſſe, ſo will I reuerence, or not reuerence, accept or not accept of him : wherfore if any gape after reuerence, worſhip or acceptation, let them thirſt after vertue, as namely,[1] wiſdome, knowledge, diſcretion, modeſtie, ſobrietie, affability, gentleneſſe & ſuche like ; than can they be without reuerence or acceptation, no more than *the* ſonne can be without light, the fire without heat,[2] or the water without his naturall moyſture.

Sp. Than I gather, you would haue men accepted for vertue & true Godlines,[3] wold you not?

Ph. I would not only haue men to be accepted & reuerenced for their virtue (though the [4]chiefeſt reuerence is only to be attributed to him, whoſe ſacred breſt[5] is fraught with vertue, as it may well be called the *Promptuarie* or *Receptorie*[6] of true wiſdome and Godlines, but alſo (in parte) for their byrthes ſake, parentage and conſanguinitie[7]; and not only that,[8] but [9]alſo in reſpect of their callings, offices and functions, whether it be in the Temporal Magiſtery, or[10] Ecclefiaſtical presbitery (ſo long as they gouerne godly and well): For the Apoſtle ſayth, that thoſe Elders which[11] gouerne wel amongſt vs are worthie of double honor.   But yet the man whom God hath bleſſed with vertue and true godlynes, thoughe he be neyther of great byrth nor callynge, nor yet any Magiſtrate whatſoeuer, is worthie of more reuerence and eſtimation then any of the other without the ornaments of *th*e minde, & gifts of vertue aboue ſaid.   For what preuayleth it to be borne of worſhipfull progenie, and to be deſtitute of all vertue, which deſerueth[12] true worſhip? what is it els then to carie a golden Swoorde in a Leaden Scabbarde ?   Is it any thyng els then a golden Coffyn or painted Sepulchre, makyng a fayre ſhowe outwardly, but inwardly is full of all ſtinche & lothſomnes ?   I remember once I red a certaine ſtorie of one, a Gentleman by byrth and parentage, who greatly reproched, and withall diſdayned an other, for that he was come to great autho[13]rytie onely by vertue,

[All reuerence due to vertue and not to riche attire. B, E.]

[4 C 8, back]

Wherfore man is to be worshiped and had in reuerence.

[9 leaf 16. B.†]

Gentilitie without vertue is no gentilitie.

[An exelent apothegme. E, F.]

[13 D 1]

---

[1] F *adds* feare of God, zeale to religion
[2] the heat. E.   [3] onely *added in* F.   [5] brest is so B, E.
[6] storehouse F.   [7] discent F.   [8] for that E.
† leaf 16. How to know a Gentleman. B.
[10] a or (*sic*) A.   [11] that F.   [12] maketh B, E, F.

being but a poore mans child by byrthe : "What! faith[1] the Gentle-man by birth,[2] arte thou fo luftie ? Thou arte but a coblers fonne, and wilt thou compare with me, being a Gentleman by[3] byrth and call-ing ?" To whome the other anfweared,[4] "thou arte no Gentleman, for thy gentilitie endeth in thee, and I am a Gentleman, in [5]that my gentilitie beginneth in me :" Meaning (vnleft[6] I be deceiued) that the wante of virtue in him was the decay of his gentility, and his vertue was the beginning of true gentilitie in him felfe : for virtue therfore, not for apparell, is euerye one to be accepted ; For if we fhould accept of men after apparell onely, refpecting nothinge els, than fhold it come to paffe, that we might more efteme[7] of one, both meane by birth, bafe without[8] virtue, feruyle by calling, & poore in eftate, more than of fome, by birthe noble, by virtue honorable, and by callinge laud-able.[9] And the reafon is becaufe euery one, tagge and ragge, go brauer, or at leaft as braue as thofe that be both noble, honorable and worfhipfull.

Spud. But I haue hard fay, there is more holyneffe in fome kynd of apparell than in otherfome ; which makes them fo much to affecte vary[e]tie of fafhions, I thinke.

Philo. Indeed, I fuppofe that the fumme[10] of their religion doth confifte in apparell. And, to fpeake my confcience, I thinke there is more, [11]or as muche holyneffe in the apparell, as in them ; that is, iuft none at all. But admit that there be holyneffe in apparell (as who is fo infatuat to beleue it) than[12] it followeth that the holynes pretended is not in them ; & fo be they plaine Hipocrits to make fhew of that which they haue not. And if the holines by there attire prefaged be in them felues, than is it not in the [13]garments ; & why do they than attribute that to the garments whiche is neither adherente to the one, nor yet inherent in the other ? Or if it wer fo, why do they glory of it to the world ? but I leaue them to their follie, haftinge to other matters more profitable to intreate of.

Spud. But I haue hard them reafon thus : That which is good in it own nature cannot hurt ; apparell is good, and the good Creature of

[5 leaf 16, back. B.*]

The exordium of virtue is the exordium of gentilitie & worfhip, and want of the one is the decay of the other.

[11 D 1, back]

No holynes in apparell

[13 leaf 17. B.†]

1 quoth B, E, F.	2 by birth *not in* F.
3 both by B, E, F.	4 repliyng, faide B, E, F.
* leaf 16, back. Vertue maketh Gentilitie. B.	6 vnleffe F.
7 accept B, E, F.	8 in B, E, F.	9 venerable B, E, F.
10 and enargie *added in* B, E ; and substance *added in* F.	12 then B.
† leaf 17. An obiection to maintain Pride. B.

An argument trimly contryued.

God: *ergo* no kynde of apparell can hurte. And if there be anie abufe in it, the apparell knowethe it not; Therfore take awaye the abufe, and let the apparell remaine ftill, for fo it maye (fay they) without anie hurte at all.

Philo.   Thefe be well feafoned reafons, and fubftantiall affeuerations in deed; but if they haue no better arguments to leane vnto

[But shortly to fall, without hope of recovery.]

than thefe, their kingdome of Pride will fhortlie fall [1]without all[1] hope of recouerie againe.   The apparell in it owne nature is good,

[[2] D 2]

and the good Creature of God (I will not de[2]nie) and cannot hurte, except it be thorowe ouer[3] owne wickedneffe abufed.   And therfore wo be to[4] them that make the good Creatures of God inftruments of dampnation to them felues, by not vfing them, but abufing them. And yet, not withftanding, it maye be faid to hurte, or not to hurte, as it is abufed or not abufed; And wheras they would haue the abufe of apparell (if any be) taken away, and the apparell to remain ftill, it

[[5] leaf 17. back. B.†]

is impoffible to fupplant the one, without [5]the extirpation of the other alfo.   For it is trulye faid, *fublata caufa, tollitur effeĉtus;* But not *fubrepto*[6] *effeĉtu tollitur caufa;* Take away the caufe and the effeĉte falleth,[7] but not contrarylye, take away the effeĉt and the caufe

Vnpossible to take away pride, except sumptuouse apparell be taken away also.

falleth.[7] The[8] efficiente caufe of Pride is gorgioufe attire; [9]the effeĉt is pride it felfe ingenerate by attire[9]: But to begin to plucke awaie the effeĉte (to wit, pride) and not to take awaye the caufe firft (namelie fumptuoufe attyre) is as if a man, intendinge to fupplante a Tree by the rootes, fhould begin to pull the fruite and braunches onelye; or, to pull downe heauen, fhould dig in the earthe, workinge altogether prepofterouflie and indyreclye.[10]   And the reafon is,[11] thefe two col-

Apparell and pride combined together as mother & daughter.
[[12] D 2, back]

laterall Cofins, apparell and Pride (the Mother and Daughter of mifchiefe) are fo combinate together, and incorporate the one in [12]the other, as the one can hardlie be dyuorced[13] from the other, without the diftruĉtion of them both.   To[14] the accomplifhmente wherof, God graunte that thofe holfome lawes, fanĉtions, and ftatuts, which, by our moft gracious and ferene princeffe (whome Iefus preferue for euer)

---

[1]—[1] withall B.   [3] through our F.   [4] to *not in* F.
† leaf 17, back. Appa[rell] the Mother of Pride. B.
[6] sublato B, E, F.   [7] fayleth F.
[9] The externe B, E, F.   [9]—[9] *not in* F.   [10] and contrarily *added in* F.
[11] is for that B, E, F.   [13] plucked F.   [14] For F.

and her noble and renoumed Progenitors, haue beene promulgate and
enaɕted hertofore, may be put in execution.   For, in my opinion, it is
as impoſſible for a man to were precious apparell and gorgiouſe
attyre, and not to be proude therof (for if he be not proud therof, [¹ leaf ɪ8. B.*]
why doth he weare ſuche riche attire, wheras mea¹ner is both better
cheape, eaſier to be had, as warme to the bodie, and as decent and
comly to any chaſt chriſtians eye) as it is for a man to cary fire in   Vnpoſſible not
his boſome and not to burne. Therfore, would God euery man might   to be proud of
                                                                        rich attyre.
be compelled to weare apparell according to his degree, eſtat, and
condition of life ; which, if it were brought to paſſe, I feare leaſt ſome
who ruffle now in ſilks, veluets, ſatens, damaſks, gold, ſiluer, and what
not,² ſhold be glad to weare frize cotes, & glad if they might get
them.³

   Spud. What is your opinion ? did the people of the former world
ſo much eſteeme of apparell as we doe at this preſent day, without
reſpect had either to ſex, kind, order, degree, eſtat, or callinge ?

   ⁴ *Philo.* No doubt but in all ages they had their imperfections⁵ and   [⁴ D 3]
faults, for *Hominis eſt errare, labi* et *decipi ;* it is incident to man to
erre, to fall, and to be deceiued.   But, notwithſtandinge, as the wicked
haue alwayes affected, not onelie pride in apparell, but alſo all other
vices whatſoeuer, ſo the chaſte, Godly, and ſober Chriſtians haue euer   The Godly
eſchewed this exceſſe of apparell, hauing a ſpeciall regard to weare   haue euer de-
                                                                        tested pride of
ſuche attyre as might neyther offend the maieſtie of God, prouoke   apparell.
them ſelues to pride, nor yet offend ⁶any of⁶ their Brethren in any
reſpecte.   But (as I haue ſaid) not onely the Godlie haue deteſted and   The verie
hated this vaine ſuperfluitye of apparell in all tymes ſince the be⁷gin-   hethen haue
                                                                        contemned
ning of the Worlde, but alſo the verie panims, the heathen *Philoſo-*   sumptuouse
phers, who knew not God (though otherwiſe wyſe Sages and great   apparell.
                                                                        [⁷ leaf ɪ8, back.
Clarks), haue contemned it as a peſtiferouſe euill ; in ſo muche as   B.†]
they haue writ (almoſt) whole volumes againſt the ſame, as is to be
ſeene in moſt of their Books yet extant.

   Spud. Are you able to proue that ?

   Philo. That I am, verie eaſilye ; but of an infinyte number,
take a taſte of theſe few.   *Democrates* beeing demaunded, wherin the   Testimonies of

---

* leaf ɪ8. The godly abhorre Pride. B.   ² not els F.
   ³ them too F.   ⁵ blemishes *added in* F.
⁶—⁶ *not in* B, E, F.   † leaf ɪ8, back. Vertue the comeliest ornament. B.

hethen people
who derided
riche attire.

[¹ D 3, back]

Vertue is the
comlyest orna-
ment of all.

[³ leaf 19. B.†]

Diogines his
ansuerity.⁴

[⁵ D 4]

[The example of
a Philosopher,
deriding
pride. E, F.]

bewtie and comlie feature of man, or woman, confifted? aunfwered, iu fewnes of fpeaches well tempered together, iu virtue, in integrity ¹of life, and fuche like. *Sophocles*, feinge one weare gorgeoufe apparell, faid to him, 'thou foole! thy apparell is no ornamente to the, but a manifeft fhewe of thy follie.' *Socrates*, being afked what was the greatteft ornamente in a woman, anfwered, '*that* which moft fheweth her chaftitie, and good demeanoure of body and mind, & not fumptuoufe attyre, which rather fheweth her adulterate life.' *Ariftotle* is fo diftrict² in this point, that he would haue men to vfe meaner apparell than are permitted them by the lawe. The Wife of *Philo*, the *Philofopher*, being vppon a tyme demaunded why fhe ware not gold, filuer and precioufe garments, faid, fhe thought the vertues of her hufbande fufficiente ornaments for her. *Dionifius*, the king, fente the richeft garments in all his wardrobes to the no³ble Wome*n* of the *Lacedemonians*, who returned them from whence they came, fayinge, they would be a greatter fhame to them than honore. Kinge *Pirrus* fente riche attyre to the Matrones of Rome, who abhorred them as menftruous clowtes. The conceiued opinion among*e*ft the Grecians to this day is, that it is neither gold nor gorgioufe attyre that adorneth either Man or Woman, but vertuous conditions, and fuch like. *Diogines* fo much contemned fumptuous attyre, that he chofe rather to dwell in wilderneffe amon⁵geft brute beafts all his lyfe longe, than in the pompoufe courts of mightie kings one daye to be commorante.⁶ For he thought, if he had the ornaments of the minde, that he was than faire ynoughe, and fine inough alfo, not needing any more. A certen other *Philofopher* addreffed himfelfe towards a kings courte in his Philofophers attyre, that is, in meane, bafe and poore aray; But foe fone as the Officers efpied him, they cried, 'awaie with that rogue! what dothe he foe nie the kinges maiefties courte?' The poore Philofopher, feing it lighten fo faft, retyred back for feare of their thunderclappes,⁷ and repayringe home, appaireled himfelfe in riche Attyre, and came againe marchinge towards the court: he was no fooner in fight, but euery one receiued him plaufiblie, and with great fubmiffion and reuerence. When he came in prefence of the kinge, and other

ˀ strict F.   † leaf 19. Philosophers examples. B.
⁴ austerie [austerity] *in* B, E.   ⁶ resiant F.
⁷ thunderboltes F.

mightie potentats, he kneled[1] down, and[2] ceafed not to kiffe [3]his
garments. The king and nobles marueylinge not a litle therat, afked
him, wherfore he did fo? Who aunfwered, ' O noble kinge ! it is no
marueyle ; for that whiche my vertue and knowledge could not doe,
my Apparell hath brought to paffe : For I, comminge to thy gates
in my PHILOSOPHERS [4]weede, was repelled ; but hauing put vpon me
this riche attyre, I was brought to thy prefence with as great venera-
tion and worfhip as could be.' Wherby is[5] to be feene in what de-
teftation he had the ftinkinge Pride of apparell, takeing this occafion
to giue the King to vnderftand the inormious abufe thereof, and fo
to remoue the fame as a peftilent euill out of his whole dominion &
kingdome. I read of a certen other *Philofopher* that came before a
king, who, at the fame tyme, had inuited his nobles to a feast or banquet : the Philofopher comming in and feinge no place to fpit in (for
euery place was hanged with cloth of gold, cloth of filuer, tinfell,
arrace, tapeftrie, and [6]what not[6]) came to the kinge and fpat in his
face, faying, 'it is meet (o king !) that I fpit in the fowleft place.'
This good *Philofopher* (as we may gather) went about to withdraw
the king from taking pleafure or delight in the vaine gliftering fhewe,
either of apparell or any thing els, but rather to haue confideration of
his owne filthynes, miferie & finne, not ryfing vp into pride, and
fpitting againft heauen, as he did, by dilighting in prowde attyre and
gor[7]geoufe ornaments. Thus we fee the verie painims and heathen
people haue from the beginning difpyfed this exceffe of apparell, both
in them felues and[8] others, whofe examples heerin god graunt we may
folowe.

[9]*Spud.* But you are not able to proue that any good Chriftians
euer fet light[10] by precious attire, but alwayes efteemed it as a fpeciall
ornament to the whole man. As for thefe Heathen, they were fooles,
neyther is it materiall what they vfed, or vfed not.

Philo. I am able to prooue that euen from the beginning of the
world, the chofen and peculiar people of God haue contemned proude[11]
Apparel, as things (not onely) not neceffarie, but alfo as very euilles

[3 leaf 19, back B.*]

The example of a Philoso- pher deriding the pompe of the World.

[4 D 4, back]

The example of a Philoso- pher who spat in the kings face.

[7 leaf 20. B.†]

[9 D 5]

Probation that the former world hath

---

[1] kneelyng, B, E, F.   [2] *not in* B, E, F,
* leaf 19, back. The Heathen dispise Pride. B.   [5] it is E, F.
[6]—[6] the like F.   † leaf 20. The base attire of the former age. B.
  [8] and in F.   [10] lightlie F.   [11] gorgious F.

themſelues, and haue gone both meanely and poorely in their vſuall attyre. What ſay you to our Grandfather *Adam,* and *Eua* our Mother ? Were they not clothed in peltes, and ſkins of beaſts ? Was not this a meane kinde of Apparell, thinke you ? Was it not vnfitting[1] to ſee a woman inueſted[2] all ouer in leather ? But yet the Lord thought it precious and ſeemelie ynough for them. What ſaye you to the noble Prophet of the world, *Elias* ? did hee not walke in the ſolitude[3] of this worlde in a ſimple playne mantell, or gowne, girded to him with a girdle of leather ? *Elizeus, th*e Prophet, did not he in a manner the verie ſame ? And what ſay you to *Samuell,* the golden mouthed Prophet, notwithſtanding *that* [4]hee was an Archprophet, and a chiefe ſeer of that time ? did hee not walke ſo meanely, as *Saul,* ſeking his fathers Aſſes, could not know him from the reſte, but aſked him, where was [5]the ſeers houſe ? This muſt needs argue that he went not richer then the common ſorte of people in· his time ? The Children of *Iſraell,* beeing the choſen people of God, did they not weare their Fathers attire fortie yeeres togither in the wildernes ? was not *Iohn* the *Baptiſt* clothed with a garment of Camels heare, girded with a thong of the ſkin of the ſame, in ſted of a girdle or ſuccinctorie about his loines ? *Peter,* the deere Apoſtle of our Sauiour, was not diſtinct from the reſt of his Felowes,[6] Apoſtles, by any kinde of rich apparel, for then the maid would not haue ſaid, ' I know thee by thy tung,' but rather, ' by thy apparel.' The Apoſtle *Paul,* writing to the *Hebrues,* ſaith that the perſecuted Church, bothe in his time and before his dayes, were clothed, ſome in Sheep ſkinnes, and ſome in Gote ſkinnes, ſome in Camels heare, ſome in this, and ſome in that, and ſome in whatſoeuer they coulde get ; for if it would hide their ſhameful parts, and kept[7] them from the colde, they thought it ſufficient, they required no more. but, to ſpeak in one woord for all : did not our Sauiour *Ieſus Chriſt* weare the very ſame fashion of apparell that his Cuntrey-men vſed, that is, a cote without a ſeame, either knit or weaued[8] ? which fashions the [9]*Paleſtynians* vſe there yet to this day, without any alteration, or chaunge, as it is

Marginalia:
contemned pompouse attyre.

Elias.

Elizeus.

Samuell.

[4 leaf 21, back. B.*]

[5 D 5, back]

The children of Israell.

Iohn Baptist.

Peter.

[The early Church.]

The humility and pouertie of Christe vppon earth.
[9 leaf 21. B.†]

---

[1] ſtraunge F　　　[2] couered F.　　　or wildernesse *added in* F.
* leaf 21, back. Christ his example for Appa[rell]. B.　　　[6] fellow F.
[7] keepe F.　　　[8] wouen F.
† leaf 21. Greate ſuperfluitie of Ap[parell]. B.

thought.   This his attyre was not [1] very hanfome (one would think) :   [¹ D 6]
at the [2] leaft it was not curious, or new fangled, as ours is ;   [3] but, as the
Poet wel faid,[3] *nitimur in vetitum, femper cupimufque negata,* we defire
things forbid, and couet thinges denied vs.   We lothe the [4] fimplicitie
of Chrifte, and abhorring the chriftian pouertie, and godly mediocritie
of our Forefathers in apparel, are [5] neuer content except wee haue   [Modern
fundry futes of apparel, one diuers from an other, fo as our Preffes   extravagance.]
crack withall, our Cofers bruft, and our backs fweat with the cariage
therof : we muft haue one fute for the forenoone, another for *the*   [* Side-note here
afternoone, one for the day, another for the night ; one for the   in B, E, F.]
workeday, another for the holieday, one for fommer, another for
winter ; one of the newe fafhion, an other of the olde, one of this
colour, another of that, one cutte, an other whole, one laced, another
without, one of golde, and other of filuer, one of filkes and veluets,   * Superfluitie of
and [6] another of clothe, with more difference and varietie than I can   apparell With
expreffe.   god be merciful vnto vs, and haften his kingdome, [7] that all   dyuersitie of
imperfections may be doon away [7] !   fashions.

A perticuler Difcription of apparell in Ailgna
by degrees.

[9][*Spud.*] YOu haue borne me in hand of many and greeuous   [9 leaf 21, back.
abufes reigning in *Ailgna*,[8] but now fetting aparte thefe [10] ambages   B.†]
and [11] fuperfluous vagaries, I pray you defcribe vnto me more [12] par-   [¹¹ D 6, back]
ticularly the fundrie abufes in [13] Apparell there vfed ; running ouer by
degrees the whole ftate thereof, that I maye fee, as it were, the perfect
Anatomie of that Nation in Apparell, whiche thinge I greatlye defire
to knowe.

Philo. Your requeft feemeth both [14] intricate and harde,[14] confider-

[2] the *not in* F.
[3]—[3] For of us that Poeticall Apothegme maie very well be verified B, E, F.
[4] this F.   [5] wee are F.   [6] and *not in* B, E, F.
[7]—[7] for his electes sake B, E, F.   [8] England F.
† leaf 21, back. Hattes of sundry fashions. B.
[10] these impertenent B, E, F (ambagies *not in* F.
[12] more *not in* B, E.   [13] of B, E, F.
[14]—[14] harde and intricate B, E, F.

ing [1]there bee *Tot tantæ mæryadæs inuentionum,* So manie and fo
fonde fafhions, and inuentions of Apparell euerie day.[1] But yet, left
I might be iudged vnwilling to fhewe you what pleafure I can, I will
affay (*pro virili mea,* [2]*omnibus neruulis vndique extenfis*)[2], with all the
might and force I can, to fatisfie your defire. Wherefore, to begin
firft with their Hattes.

[3]Sometimes they were[4] them fharp on the crowne, pearking vp
like a[5] fphere,[6] or fhafte of a fteeple, ftanding a quarter of a yard

The diuersity
of hattes in
Ailgna.

aboue *the* crowne of their heades; fome more, fome leffe, as pleafe
the phantafies of their[7] mindes. Otherfome be flat and broad on the
crowne, like the battlements[8] of a houfe. An other fort haue round
crownes, fometimes with one kinde of bande, fometime with an
other; nowe blacke, now white, now ruffet, now red, now greene,
now yellowe, now this, nowe that, neuer content with one colour or
fafhion two dayes[9] to an ende. And thus in vanitie they fpende the

[[10] D 7]
[[11] leaf 22. B.†]

[10]Lorde his treafure, [11]confuming their golden yeares and filuer dayes
in wickednes & fin. And as the fafhions bee rare and ftraunge, fo

The sundrye
things wherof
hattes be
made.

[12]are the thinges[12] wherof their Hattes be made, diuerfe alfo; for fome
are of filke, fome of veluet, fome of taffetie, fome of farcenet, fome of
wooll : & which is more curious, fome of a certaine kind of fine
haire, [13]far fetched and deare bought, you maye bee fure[13] ; And fo
common a thinge it is, that euerie Seruingman, Countreyman, and
other, euen all indifferently, do weare of thefe hattes. For he is of
no account or eftimation amongft men,[14] if hee haue not a veluet or
a[15] taffatie Hatte, and that mufte bee pincked and cunningly carued
of the befte fafhion; And good profitable Hattes bee they,[16] for the
longer you weare them the fewer holes they haue.[17] Befides this, of

---

[1]—[1] the innumerable *meriades* of fondrie fashions daiely inuented amongest
them B, E, F.

[2]—[2] *not in* F.   [3] A description of the Hattes of England *added in* F.

[4] vse B, E, F.   [5] the B, E, F.   [6] speare F.

[7] their inconstant B, E ; their waueringe F.   [8] battlement F.

[9] moneths F.   † leaf 22. Varietie of Hattes. B.

[12]—[12] is the stuffe B, E, F.

[13]—[13] These thei call Beuer hattes of xx, xxx, or xl shillinges price fetched
from beyond the seas, from whence a greate sorte of other varieties* doe come
besides B, E, F. (* vanities F.)

[14] them F.   [15] a *not in* F.   [16] these B, E, F.

[17] F *adds :*—They haue also Taffeta hattes of all collours quilted, and im-

late there is a new fafhion of wearing their Hattes fprung vp amongft them, which they father vpon *the* Frenchmen, namely to weare them without bandes; but how vnfeemelie (I will not fay how Affy) a fafhion that is, let the wife iudge.   Notwithftanding, howe euer it bee, if it pleafe them, it shall not difpleafe me.   An other[1] fort (as phantafticall as the reft) are content with no kind of Hatt without a great bunche[2] of feathers of .diuerfe and fundrie colours, peaking on toppe of their heades, not vnlyke (I dare not fay) Cockfcombes, but [3] as fternes of pride and en[4]figns of [5]vanitie; and[3] thefe fluttering fayles and fethered flags of defiance to vertue (for fo they are[6]) are fo aduaunced in *Ailgna,* that euery Childe hath them in his hat or cap: many get good liuing by dying and felling of the*m*, and not a fewe prooue them felues more then fooles[7] in wearing of them.

Wering of hattes without bandes.

[Wearyng of Feathers in hattes. B, E, F.]

[4 D 7, back]

[5 leaf 22, back. B.†]

Spud. Thefe Fethers argue the lightnes of their fond imaginations, and plainly co*n*uince them of inftabilitie and folly; for fure I am, hanfome they cannot be, therefore Badges[8] of pride they muft needs be, which I think none wil weare, but fuch as be like them felues.   But to your intended difcourfe.

[9]*Philo.* They haue great and monfterous ruffes, made either of Cambrick, holland, lawn, or els of fome other the fineft cloth that can be got for money, whereof fome be a quarter of a yard deep, yea, fome more, very few leffe; So that they ftand a full quarter of a yarde (and more) from their necks, hanging ouer their shoulder poynts, infted of a vaile.[10]   [11]But if *Aeolus* with his blafts, or *Neptune* with his ftormes chaunce to hit vppon the crafie bark of their brufed ruffes, then they goe flip flap in the winde, like rags flying[12] abroad, [13]and lye[13] vpon their shoulders like the difhcloute of a flut.[11]   But wot

Great ruffes deformed & ill fauored.

broydered with golde, filuer, and silke of sundrie sortes, with monsters, antiques, beastes, foules, and all maner of pictures and images vpon them, wonderfull to behold.

> [1] And another B, E, F.   [2] plume F.
> [3—3] fooles bables if you list: And yet notwithstanding F.
> † leaf 22, back. Feathers, Flagges of vanitie. B.   [6] be E, F.
>   [7] Asses F.   [8] Ensignes. F.
>   [9] *heading :*—Of great Ruffes in England. F.   [10] Pentise F.
> [11—11] F *has :* But if it happen that a shoure of raine catch them before they can get harbour, then their great ruffes strike sayle, and downe they fall, as dishcloutes fluttering in the winde, like Windmill sayles.
>   [12] that flew B, E.   [13—13] liyng B, E.

you what? the deuil, as he in the fulnes of his malice, firſt inuented

[¹ D 8]

thefe ¹great ruffes, ſo hath hee now found out alſo two great ſtayes²

Two arches or
pillers to vn-
der proppe the
kingdom of
great ruffes
withall, *vide-
licet* support-
asses and
starche.
[⁵ leaf 23. B.*]

to beare vp and ³maintaine that³ his kingdome of ⁴great ruffes⁴ (for the
deuil is ⁵king and prince ouer all the children of pride): the one arch
or piller wherby⁶ his kingdome of great ruffes is vnderpropped, is a
certaine kinde of liquide matter which they call Starch, wherin the
deuill hath willed⁷ them to wash and diue his⁸ ruffes wel, which,
⁹when they be⁹ dry, wil then ſtand ſtiffe and inflexible about their
necks.¹⁰ The other piller is a certain deuice made of wyers, creſted for
the purpoſe, whipped ouer either with gold, thred, ſiluer or ſilk, &
this hee calleth a ſupportaſſe, or vnderpropper. This is to be applyed
round about their necks vnder the ruffe, vpon the out ſide of the band,
to beare vp the whole frame & body of the ruffe from falling and
hanging down.

Spud. This is a deuice paſſing all the deuices that euer I ſawe or
heard of. Then I perceiue the deuill not onely inuenteth miſcheif,
but alſo ordaineth inſtrumentall¹¹ meanes to continue the ſame. Theſe
bands are ſo chargeable (as I ſuppoſe) that¹² but fewe haue of them:
¹³if they haue, they are better monyed then I am.¹³

Philo. So few haue¹⁴ them, as almoſt none is without them; for

[¹⁵ D 8, back]

Euery pesant
hath his stately
bands &
monsterouse
ruffes, how
costly soeuer
they be.

[¹⁷ leaf 23, back.
B.†]

euery one, how meane or ¹⁵ſimple ſoeuer they bee otherwiſe, will
haue of them three or foure apeece for fayling. And as though
Camericke,¹⁶ Holland, Lawne, and the fineſt cloth that maye bee got
anie where for money, were not good inough, they haue them
wrought all ouer with ſilke woorke, and peraduenture laced with
¹⁷golde and ſiluer, or other coſtly lace of no ſmall price. And whether
they haue Argente¹⁸ to mayntaine this geare withall, or not, it ¹⁹forceth
not muche,¹⁹ for they will haue it by one meane or other, or els they

---

² pillers B, E, F.   ³—³ vphold this F.   ⁴—⁴ Pride withall F.
* leaf 23. Great Ruffes and Supportasses. B.   ⁶ wherewith F.
⁷ learned F.   ⁸ their B, E, F.   ⁹—⁹ beyng B, E, F.
¹⁰ F *adds*:—And this startch they make of diuers substances, sometimes of
Wheate flower, of branne, and other graines : sometimes of rootes, and somtimes
of other thinges: of all coloùrs and hewes, as White, Redde, Blewe, Purple, and
the like.
¹¹ instrumentes and F.   ¹² that *comes before* as F
¹³—¹³ such as are of the richer sort F.   ¹⁴ haue of F.   ¹⁶ Cambricke F.
† leaf 23, back. Costly shirtes and bandes in Ailg. B.   ¹⁸ Unde F.
¹⁹—¹⁹ is not greatly material B, E, F.

will eyther[1] ſell or[2] morgage their Landes [8](as they haue good ſtore)[8] on Suters hill & Stangate hole,[4] with loſſe of their lyues at Tiburne in a rope.[5]

Spud. The ſtate and condition of that Land muſt needes be miſerable, and in tyme growe to greate ſcarcitie and dearth, where is ſuch vayne[6] Prodigalitie, and[6] exceſſe of [7]all thynges[7] vſed.

[8]*Philo.* Their Shirtes, which all in a manner doe weare (for if the Nobilitie or Gentrie onely did weare them, it were ſomedeal[9] more tollerable) are eyther of Camericke, Holland, Lawne, or els of the fineſt cloth that maye bee got.   And of theſe kindes of Shirts euerie one now doth weare alike: ſo as it may be thoght our Forefathers haue made their Bandes & Ruffes (if they had any at all) of groſſer cloth and baſer ſtuffe than the worſt of our ſhirtes [10]are made of now a dayes.   And theſe ſhurts (ſomtimes it happeneth) are wrought through out with nedle work of ſilke, and ſuche like, and curiouſlie ſtitched with open ſeame, and many other knackes beſydes, mo than I can deſcribe.[11]   [In ſo much as I haue heard of Shirtes that haue coſt ſome ten ſhillynges, ſome twentie, ſome fortie, ſome fiue pound, ſome twentie Nobles and (which is horrible to [12]heare) ſome ten pounde a peece, yea, the meaneſt ſhirt that commonly is worne of any, doeſt coſt a crowne, or a noble at the leaſt: and yet this is ſcarſly thought fine enough for the ſimpleſt perſon that is.   B, E, F.]

Spud. Theſe be goodly ſhurts indeed, & ſuch yet[13] as will not[14] chafe their tender ſkinnes, [15]nor[16] vlcerat their[17] lyllie white[15] bodyes; or if they[18] do, it wil not be much to their greeuances, I dare be bound. Is it anie maruell, *ſi Criſtas erigant & cornua attollant,* if they ſtand vppon their pantoffles, and hoyſe vp their ſayles on highe, hauinge

[New kind of Ruffes, called Three ſtepps and a halfe to the Gallowes. F:]

The ſhirts vſed in Ailgna.

[10 E 1]

[The cost of these Shirts.]

[12 leaf 24. B.†]

---

[1] eyther *not in* B, E, F.   [2] or at the least F.   [3—3] *not in* F.
          [4] F *adds,* and Salisburie plaine.
   [5] F *adds :—*& in sure token therof, they haue now newly found out a more monstrous kind of ruffe of xii. yea, xvi. lengthes a peece, set 3 or 4 times double, & is of some, fitlie called: *Three steppes and a halfe to the Gallowes.*
   [6] vaine *comes after* and *in* B, E, F.   [7—7] thinges is F.
   [8] *heading in* F :—Of costly Shirtes in England.   [9] *not in* F.
   [11] recount F.   † leaf 24. Nice Appa[rell] make tender bodies. B, F.
        [13] yet *not in* B, E, F.   [14] neither B, E, F.
      [15—15] nor yet fret their delicate F.   [16] nor *not in* B, E.
      [17] tender fleshe, nor yet make perforation into their *added in* B, E.
                 [18] it F.

thefe dyamond fhurts on their [1]delicate bodies[1]: but how foeuer it is, I gather by your words that this muft needs be a nice and curious[2] People, who [3]are thus nuffeled vp[3] in fuch daintie attyre.

Philo. It is very true, for this their curiofity, and nicenes in apparell (as it were) tranfnatureth them,[4] makinge[5] them weake, tender and infirme, not able to abide fuch [6]fharp conflicts and bluftering ftormes[6] as many other people, both abroade farre from them, and in their confines nie to them, do daylie[7] fuftaine. I haue hard my Father, with other wyfe Sages affirme, that in his tyme, within the compaffe of foure or fyue fcore yeres, when men went clothed in black or white frize coates, in hofen of Hufwyues carzie of the fame colore, [8]that the fheep bore[9] them ([10]the want of making and wering of which clothe, together with the exceffiue wering of filks, veluets, fatens, damafks, taffeties, and fuch like, hath and doth make many a thoufand in *Ailgna* [11]as poore mendicants[11] to begge their bread) wherof fome weare ftrait to the thigh, otherfome litle bigger: and when they ware fhurts of hempe or flax (but now thefe are to groffe, our tender ftomacks cannot eafilye difgeft fuch roughe and crude[12] meats) men weare ftronger than we,[13] helthfuller, fayrer complectioned, longer lyuinge,[14] and finallye, ten tymes harder than we,[15] and able[16] to [17]beare out[17] any forowe[18] or paynes whatfoeuer. For be fure, this pampering of our[19] bodies makes them weker, tenderer and nefher, than otherwyfe they would be, if they were vfed to hardneffe, and more fubiect to receiue anye kind of infection or maladie; And[20] rather abbreuiat[21] oure dayes by manye yeres, than extenuate our liues one minut of an houre.

Spud. I thinke no leffe; for how ftronge men were in tymes paft, how long they lyued, and how helthfull they weare before fuche Nicenes, and vayne pamperinge curiofitie was inuented, we may reade, and many that lyue at this daye can teftifie. But now,

[1]—[1] backes F.   [2] womanish kind of F.
[3]—[3] thus pamper their bodies B, E, F.   [4] them, and B.   [5] and maketh F.
[6]—[6] blustering stormes and sharpe showers F.   [7] dayly beare and F.
[9] bare F.   † leaf 14, back. Men strong in tymes past. B.
[11]—[11] *not in* B, E, F.   [12] a hard F.
[13] than we *not in* B, E, F.   [14] liued F.   [15] we be now B, E, F.
[16] abler F.   [17]—[17] undure F.   [18] any discrasie B, E.   [19] their B, E, F.
[20] and doeth B, E, F.   [21] shorten F.

through our fond toyes and nice inuentions, we haue brought our felues into fuche pufil[1]lanimitie and effeminat condition, as we may feeme rather[2] nice dames and yonge[3] gyrles than puiffante[4] agents or manlie[4] men, as our[5] Forefathers haue bene.

[1 E 2]

[5 leaf 25. B.*]

[6] *Philo.* Their dublettes are noe leffe monftrous than the refte ; For now the fafhion is to haue them hang downe to the middeft[7] of their theighes, or at leaft to their priuie members, beeing fo harde-quilted, and[8] ftuffed, bombafted and fewed, as they can[9] verie hardly eyther ftoupe downe,[10] or decline[11] them felues[12] to the grounde, foe ftyffe and fturdy they ftand about them.

The monstrous dublets in Ailgna.

Now, what handfomnes can be in thefe dubblettes whiche ftand on their bellies like, or[13] muche bigger than, a mans codpeece (fo as[14] their bellies are thicker than all their bodyes befyde) let wyfe men iudge ; For for[15] my parte, handfomnes in them I fee none, and muche leffe profyte. And[16] to be plaine, I neuer fawe any weare them, but I fuppofed him to be a man inclined to gourmandice, gluttonie, and fuche like.[16]

For what may thefe great bellies fignifie els than that either they are fuche, or els[17] are affected that way ?[17] This is the trueft fignification that I could euer[18] prefage or diuyne[18] of them. And this maye euerye one[19] iudge of them that feeth them ; for certaine I am there was neuer any kinde of apparell euer inuented that could more difproportion the body of man then thefe Dublets *with* great bellies, ha*n*ging down beneath their *Pudenda* (as I[20] haue faid), & ftuffed with foure, fiue or fix pound of Bombaft at the leaft. I fay nothing of what their Dub-

Great bellied dublets betoken gourma*n*dice, gluttony, and such like.

[19 E 2, back]

[20 leaf 25, back. B.||]

[2] rather seeme F.   [3] wanton B, E ; wayrish F.
[4—4] valorous and hardy F.   * leaf 25. Monsterous Dublets in Ailgna. B.
          [6] *heading to chapter :—*English Doublets. F.
          [7] middle B, E, F.   [8] and *not in* B, E, F.
[9] neither woorke, nor yet well plaie in them, through the excessiue heate †
thereof : & therefore are forced to weare them lose about them for the most part
otherwise they could *added in* B, E, F. († F *adds* and stifnesse)
          [10] downe *not in* B, E, F.   [11] bowe F.   [12] themselues *not in* B, E.
          [13] as big or F.   [14] that F.   [15] 2nd for *not in* F.
[16—16] besides that I see no good end wherto thei serue, except it be to shewe
the disposition of ye wearer, how he is inclined, namely ‡, to gluttonie gourmandice, riotte §, and excesse. B, E, F. (‡ as namely F ; § drunkennesse *added in* F.)
          [17—17] would be thought to be such F.   [18—18] gather F.
          || leaf 25, back. Pride in Dublets, and Hose. B.

Dublettes of
dyuerse [1] fash-
ions.

lets be made, fome of Saten, Taffatie, filk, Grogram,[2] Chamlet, gold,
filuer, & what not; flafhed, iagged, cut, carued, pincked and laced
with all kinde of coftly lace of diuers and fundry colours, for if I
fhoulde[3] ftand vpon [4] thefe particularities,[4] rather time then matter
would be wanting.

Spud. Thefe be the ftrangeft doublets that euer I heard of; and
the furdeft from hanfomnes in euery refpe&, vnleffe I be deceiued.

Hosen of
diuerse &
sundry fash-
ions.
[French hosen
of two sortes. E,
F.]

[5] *Philo.* Then haue they Hofen, which as they be of diuers fafhions,
fo are they of fundry names.   Some be called french-hofe, fome
gally-hofe,[6] and fome Venitians.   The french-hofe are of two diuers
makings, for the common french-hofe (as they lift to call them) contayneth length, breadth, and fidenes fufficient, and is made very round.
The other contayneth neither length, breadth nor fidenes (beeing not
paft a quarter of a yarde fide) wherof fome be paned, cut and drawne
out with coftly ornaments, with Canions annexed[7] reaching down
beneath their knees.

[Gally hosen. E,
F.]
[8 E 3]

[8] The Gally-hofen are made very large and wide, reaching downe
to their knees onely, with three or foure guardes a peece laid down
along either hofe.   And the Venetian-hofen, they reach beneath the
knee to the gartering place to[9] the Leg,[10] where they are tyed finely

[11 leaf 26. B.†]

with [11] filk points, or fome fuch like, and laied on alfo with rewes of
lace,[12] or gardes as the other before.   And yet notwithftanding all this

[* Side-note here
in D.]

is not fufficient, except they be made of filk, veluet, faten, damafk, and
other fuch precious things[13] befide: yea, euery one, Seruing man and
other inferiour to them, in euery condition, wil not fticke to flaunte it
out in thefe kinde of hofen, with all other their apparel futable
therunto.

* The great ex-
cesse vsed in
hosen.

In times paft, Kings (as olde Hiftoriographers in their Bookes yet
extant doo recorde) would not difdaine to weare a paire of hofen of a
Noble, tenne Shillinges, or a Marke price, with all the reft of their
apparel after the fame rate; but now it is a fmall matter to beftowe
twentie nobles, ten pound, twentie pound, fortie pound, yea, a

[1] diuers B, E, F.   [2] grograine B, E, F.   [3] could F.
[4—4] particularlie F.   [5] *heading in* F : Costly Hosen in Englande.
[6] Gallie *in* B, E ; Gallie hosen F.   [7] adioyned F.   [9] of F.
[10] beneathe the knee *added in* B.   † leaf 26. Great excesse in hose. B.
[12] of lace *not in* F.   [13] stuffe F.

hundred pound of one paire of Breeches. (*God be mercifull vnto vs !*) [1]

Spud. This is a wunderful exceſſe as euer I hearde of, woorthy with the Swoorde [2] of *Iuſtice* rather to be puniſhed, then with paper and pen to be [3] ſo gentlie [3] confuteed. [4]

[5] *Philo.* Then haue they nether-ſtocks to theſe gay hoſen, not of cloth (though neuer ſo fine) for that is thought to baſe, but of *Iarnſey* worſted, [6] ſilk, thred, and ſuch like, or els at the leaſt of the fineſt yarn *that* can be, [7] and ſo curiouſlye knit with open ſeam down the leg, with quirks and clocks about the ancles, [8] and ſometime (haply) interlaced with gold or ſiluer threds, as is wunderful to behold.   And to ſuch [9] inſolency & [10] outrage it is now growen, that euery one (almoſt) though otherwiſe verie poor, hauing ſcarce fortie ſhillings of wages by the yeer, wil [11] be ſure [11] to haue two or three paire of theſe ſilk neither-ſtocks, or els of the fineſt yarne that may be got, though *the* price of them be a Ryall [12] or twentie ſhillinges or more, as commonly it is ; for how can they be leſſe, when as the very knitting of them is worth a noble or a royall, and ſome much more ? The time hath beene when one might haue clothed all his body well [13] for leſſe then a pair of theſe neither-ſtocks wil coſt.

Spud. I haue ſeldome hearde the like : I think verely that *Sathan*, prince of darknes & Father of pride, is let looſe in *the* [14] land, els it could neuer ſo rage [15] as it dooth ; for *the* like pride (I am fully per-ſwaded) is not vſed vnder the ſonne of any nation or people how bar-berous ſo euer : wherfore wo be to this age, and thriſe accurſed be theſe dayes, which bring [16] foorth [17] ſuch ſowre [18] frutes ; & vnhappie are that people whom *Sathan* hath ſo bewitched & [19] captiued in ſin. *The Lord holde his hand of mercy ouer vs !* [19]

Philo. To theſe their nether-ſtocks, they haue corked ſhooes, pinſnets, and fine pantofles, which beare them vp [20] a finger or two [20]

The diuersity of neither-stocks worne in Ailgna.

[5 E 3, back *]

[8 leaf 26, back. B.†]

The miserie of these daies.

[17 E 4]

---

[1] and yet is this thought no abuse neither *added in* B, E, F.

[2] Rodde F.   [3]—[3] *not in* F.   [4] confuted F.   [6] crewell *added in* B, E, F.

* *heading to chapter :*—Costly Nether Stockins in England. F.   [7] be got F.

† leaf 26, back. Costly netherstockes in Ailgna. B.   [9] such impudent B, E, F.

[10] and shamefull B, E, F.   [11]—[11] not sticke B, E, F.   [12] royal F.

[13] from top to toe *added in* F.   [14] that F.   [15] so far exceed F.

[16] bringeth F.   [18] vnsauorie B, E, F.

[19]—[19] captiuate in Pride. (*heading*) Corked shooes in England. F.

•   [20]—[20] two inches or more F.

Corked shoes,
Pantoffles and
pinsnets.
[¹ leaf 27. B.*]

from the ground; wherof ſome be of white leather, ſome ¹of black, and ſome of red, ſome of black veluet, ſome of white, ſome of red, ſome of green, raced, carued, cut, and ſtitched all ouer with ſilk, and laid on with golde, ſiluer, and ſuch like: yet, notwithſtanding,² to what good vſes ſerue theſe pantofles,³ except it be to wear in a priuate houſe, or in a mans Chamber to keepe him warme? (for this is the onely vſe wherto they beſt ſerue in my iudgement) but to go abroad

Pantoffles &
slippers are a let
to those that
go abrode in
them.

in them, as they are now vſed al together, is rather a let or hinderance to a man then otherwiſe; for ſhall he not be faine to knock and ſpurn at euery ⁴ſtone, wall,⁴ or poſte to keep them on his feet? ⁵ wherfore, to diſcloſe euen the bowels of my iudgement vnto you,⁵ I think they be rather worne abrode for nicenes, then either for any eaſe which they

Pantoffles vn-
easie to go in.

bring (for the contrary is moſte true), or any hanſomnes which is in them.   For how ſhould they be eaſie, when ⁶ as the heelé hangeth an inch or two ouer the ſlipper on⁷ the ground? Inſomuch as I haue

[⁸ E 4, back]

knowen diuers mens legs ſwel with the ſame.   ⁸And handſome how ſhould they be, when ⁹ as with their flipping & flapping⁹ vp and down in *the* dirte ¹⁰ they exaggerate a mountain of mire, & gather a heape of clay & baggage together, loding the wearer with importable burthen. ¹⁰

[¹¹ leaf 27, back.
B.†]

Spud. Thoſe kinde of pantoffles can neither ¹¹ be ſo handſome, nor yet ſo warme as other vſuall ¹² common ſhoes be, I think.   Therfore the weringe of them abrode rather importeth a Nicenes (as you ſay) in them that weare them, than bringeth any other commodytie, els vnleſſe I be deceiued.

The varytie
of coates and
ierkins.

¹³*Philo.* Their coates and Ierkins, as they be diuerſe in colors, ſo be they diuerſe in faſhions; for ſome be made with colors, ſome without, ſome cloſe to the bodie, ſome looſe,¹⁴ couering the whole

---

* leaf 27. Greate excesse in shooes. B.   ˣ I see not *added in* F.
   ³ doe serue *added in* F.   ⁴—⁴ wall, stone F.
       ⁵—⁵ And therefore to tell you what I iudge of them F.

   ⁶ a man can not goe steadfastly in them, without slipping and sliding at euery pace ready to fall doune: Againe how should thei be easie where *added in* B, E, F.
       ⁷ from B, E, F.   ⁹—⁹ they go flip flap F.
           ¹⁰—¹⁰ casting vp mire to the knees of the wearer F.
     † leaf 27, back. Coates and Ierkins. B.   ¹² *not in* F.
           ¹³ *heading in* F:—Coates and Ierkins in England.
               ¹⁴ which they cal Mandilians E, F.

body downe to the theighe, like baggs or ſacks that weare drawen
ouer them, hidinge the dimenſions and proportions[1] of the body: [The ſhapes * of
coats and jer-
ſome are buttened downe the breſt, ſome vnder the arme, & ſome kins.]
(* varitie (*sic*)
downe the back; ſome with flappes ouer the breſt, ſome without, F.)
ſome with great ſleeues, ſome with ſmall, and [2]ſome with non at all[2];
ſome pleated and creſted behind, & curiouſlye gathered; ſome not
ſo[3]; & how many dayes [4](I might ſay houres, or minuts of houres,[4]
in the yeare) ſo many ſortes of apparell ſome[5] one man will haue, and
thinketh it good prouiſion in faire weather to lay vp againſt [6]a ſtorme![6]
But if [7]they would conſider that their clothes (except thoſe that they [7 E 5]
weare vppon their backs) be non of theirs, but the poores, they would
not heap vp their preſſes and wardrobes as they do.   Do they think
that it is lawfull for them to haue millions[8] of ſundry ſortes[8] of apparell
lying rotting by them, when as the poore members of Ieſus [9]Chriſte The poore
ought to be
die at their doores for wante of clothing?   God commaundeth in his prouided for.
[9 leaf 28. B.†]
law, that there be no miſerable poore man, nor begger amongeſt vs,
but that euery one be prouided for and maintained of that abund- Our ſmal regard to the
ance[10] which God hath bleſſed vs withal.   But we thinke it a great poore.
matter if we geue them an old ragged coate, dublet, or a paire of
hoſen, or els a penny or two, wheras not withſtanding we flow in
abundance of all things.   Than we thinke we are halfe way to
heauen, and we need to do no more.   If we geue them a peace of
brown bread, a meſſe of porredge (nay, the ſtocks & priſon, with
whippinge cheare now and than, is the beſt portion of almes which
many Gentlemen geue) at our dores, it is counted meritorious, and a
worke of ſupererogation, when we fare full delicatelye oure ſelues,
feeding on many a dainty[11] diſh.   There is a certen Citye in *Ailgna*
called *Munidnol*,[12] where as the poore lye in *the*[13] ſtreats vppon pallets [Londinum in
Anglia.]
of ſtraw, and well if they haue that to, or els in the mire and dirt, as
commonlie it is ſeene, [14]hauing neither houſe to put in their heads, Cold charitie
to the poore.
couering to keep them from the cold, nor yet to hide their ſhame [14 E 5, back]
withall, penny to buy them ſuſtenance, nor any thing els, but are
permitted[15] to dye in the ſtreats like dogges, or beaſts, without anie

---

[1] lineaments B, E, F.   [2—2] *not in* F.   [3] ſo *not in* B, E, F.   [4—4] *not in* F.
    [5] ſome ſome (*sic*) F.   [6—6] foule F.   [8—8] of ſutes F.
    † leaf 28. Cold Charitie in Ailgna. B.   [10] ſtore F.   [11] danity A.
    [12] Londou F.   [13] the *not in* F.   [15] ſuffered B, E, F.

mercie or compaſſion ſhewed to them at all. And if anye be ſicke of the plague (as they call it) or any other[1] diſeaſe, their Maiſters and Maiſtres[2] are ſo impudent[3] (being,[4] it ſhould ſeeme, at[5] a league with Sathan, a couenante with Hell, and [6]as it were obliged them-ſelues by[6] obligation to[7] the deuil neuer to haue to do with *the* works of mercy) as ſtraight way thei throw them out of their dores. And ſo being caried foorth, either in carts or otherwyſe, [8]and thrown[8] in the ſtreats, [9]there[9] they end their dayes moſt miſerably. Truely, Brother, if I had not ſeen it, I would ſcarſly haue thought that the like Turkiſh cruelty had bene vſed in all[10] the World. But they ſay *vnus teſtis occulatus plus valet quam mille auriti,* one eye witneſſe is better to be belyued than a thouſand eare witneſſes beſydes. But to leaue theſe excurſions, and to returne from whence I haue digreſſed, I think it the beſt; for I am perſwaded, they will [11]as much reſpect[11] my words (or amend their maners) as the wicked[12] World did at[13] the preaching[14] of our Sauiour Chriſte Ieſus ; that is, iuſt nothing at all.

[15]*Spud.* Well then, ſeeing they are ſuche a ſtifneckned People, leaue them to the Lord ; and proceed to your former tractation.[16]

[17]*Philo.* They haue clokes there alſo in nothing diſcrepante[18] from the reſt, of dyuerſe and ſundry colors, white, red, tawnie, black, greene, yellowe, ruſſet, purple, violet, and infynite other colors : ſome of cloth, ſilk, veluet, taffetie, [19]and ſuch like, wherof ſome be of the Spaniſh, French, & Dutch faſhion[20] : Some ſhort, ſcarſely reach-inge to the gyrdleſtead, or waſt, ſome to the knee, and otherſome traylinge vppon the ground (almoſt) liker gownes than clokes. [21]Theſe clokes muſt be garded, laced, & thorowly faced ; and ſom-times[21] ſo lyned as the inner ſide ſtandeth almoſt in as much as the

---

[1] other mortall B, E, F.   [2] Mistresses F.
* leaf 28, back. Turkishe impietie in Ailgna. B.
[4] hauing made B, E, F (as *added in* F.)   [5] at *not in* B, E, F.
[6]—[6] an B, E ; sealed an an F.   [7] with B, E, F.
[8]—[8] are laied doune either B, E, F ; *but* E F *have* or laide
[9]—[9] or els conueied to some olde house in the fieldes, or gardens, where for want of due sustentation B, E, F. (and good tending *added in* F.)
[10] any place of F.   [11]—[11] regard as much F.   [12] former B.   [13] at *not in* F.
[14] of Noah, or the latter worlde at the preachyng *added in* B, E, F.
[16] discourse F. | [17] *heading in* F : Cloakes in Englande.
[18] different F.   † leaf 29. Costly Clokes in Ailgna. B.   [20] fashions F.
[21]—[21] Then are thei garded with Veluette gardes, or els laced with costly lace,

outſide : ſome haue ſleeues, otherſome haue none ; ſome haue hoodes
to pull ouer the head, ſome haue none ; ſome are hanged with points
& taſſels of gold, ſiluer, or ſilk, ſome without al this.　But how
ſoeuer[1] it be, the day hath bene when one might haue bought him
two clokes for leſſe than now he can haue one of theſe clokes made
for,[2] they haue ſuch ſtore of workmanſhip beſtowed vppon them.

Spud.　I am ſure they neuer learned this [3] at the hands of our *Pro-
conſul,* and chief Prouoſt,[3] Chriſt Ieſus, nor of any other *that* euer lyued
godly in the Lord ; but rather out of the deceiptfull forge of their own
braines haue they [4]drawen[5] this [6]curſed Anatomy[6] to their owne
deſtruction[7] in the end, except the[8] repente.

[9]*Philo.*　They haue alſo bootehoſe which are to be wondered at ;
for they be of the fyneſt cloth that may be got, yea, ſine inough to
make any band, ruffe, or ſhurt[11] needful to be worn : yet this is bad
inough to were next their greſie boots.　And would[12] God this weare
all[13] : but (oh,[14] phy for ſhame !) they muſt be wrought all ouer, from
the gartering place vpward, with nedle worke, clogged with ſilk of all
colors, with birds, foules, beaſts, and antiques purtrayed all ouer in
comlie[15] ſorte.[16]　So that I haue knowen the very nedle work of ſome
one payre of theſe bootehoſe to ſtand, ſome in iiij pound, vi. pound,
and ſome in x. pound a peece.　Beſides this, they are made ſo wyde
to draw ouer all, and ſo longe to reach vp to the waſte, that as litle, or
leſſe, clothe would make one a reaſonable large ſhurte.　But tuſh !
this is nothing in compariſon of the reſte.

Spud.　I would thinke that boote-hoſen of groſſer lynnen, or els
of[17] wollen clothe, weare both warmer to ride in, as comly as the
other, though not ſo fine, and a great deal more durable.　And as for

either of golde, ſiluer, or at the leaſt of ſilke three or fower fingers broade doune
the back, about the ſkirtes, and euery where els. And now of late thei vſe to garde
their clokes rounde about the ſkirtes with (bables) I ſhould ſaie Bugles, and
other kinde of glaſſe, and all to ſhine to the eye. Beſides al this, thei are ſo
faced, and withal B, E, F.

The counting
house of all
euill is mans
braine.
[4 E 6, back]

[9 leaf 29, back.
B.†]
10 The vain ex-
cesse of bote
hosen.10

The varitie of
fashions con-
uince vs of
follie.

Bugled clokes.

1 howeuer E, F.　　2 for *not in* F.　　3—3 of our sauiour F.
5 sucked E, F.　　6—6 filthy poyson F.　　7 confusion B, E, F.　　8 they F.
† leaf 29, back. Great excesse, in Boote hose. B. *Heading in* F : Boothose
in England.　　10—10 *not in* E.　　11 shirt of F.
12 would to E, F.　　13 all too F.　　14 oh *not in* F.　　15 sumptuous B, E, F.
16 yea and of late, imbroydered with Golde and Siluer very costly *added in* F.
17 of *not in* E.

thofe gengawes wherwith you fay they be blaunched and trimmed, they ferue to no end but to feade *the* wanton eyes of gazing fools, & planly argue *the* vertiginie, and inftability of their more than fantaftical brains.

[1]*Phil.* To thefe haue they their Rapiers, Swoords and Daggers, gilt twife or thrife [2]ouer the hilts, with [3][good Angell golde, or els argented ouer with filuer both within and without, and if it be true as I heare fay it is, there be fome hiltes made all of pure filuer itfelf, and couered with golde. Otherfome at the leaft are Damafked, Vernifhed, and ingrauen marueilous goodly: and leaft any thyng fhould be wantyng to fet forthe their pride, their][3] fcaberds and fheathes of[4] Veluet or the like; for leather, though it be more proffitable and as feemely, yet wil it not carie fuch a [5]porte or countenance like[6] the[5] other.   And wil not thefe golden fwoords & daggers almofte apale a man[7] (though otherwife neuer fo ftout a *Martialift*) to haue any deling with them? for either to *that* end they be worne, or els other fwoords, daggers and rapiers of bare yron and fteele were as hanfom as they, & much more conducible[8] to that end whereto fwoords and rapiers fhould ferue, namely,[9] for a mans lawful and godly defence againft his aduerfarie in time of neceffitie.   But wherfore they be fo clogged with gold and filuer I know not, nor yet wherto this exceffe ferueth I fee not; but certain I am, a great fhewe of pride it is, an infallible token of vain glorie, and a greeuous offence to God, fo prodigallie and licentiouflie[10] to lauifh foorth his treafure, for which we muft render accounts at the day of Iudgement, when it fhall be faide to euerie one, *Redde rationem Vilicationis tuæ.* Come, giue accounts of thy Stewardfhip.

[1] *Heading in* F :—Rapiers, Daggers, Swords, gilte in Englande.
† leaf 30. Swordes, Rapiers, and Daggers. B.   [3]—[3] *in* B, E, F.
[4] are of B, E, F.   [5]—[5] Maiesty or glorious shewe as the F.   [6] as B, E.
[7] thinke you *added in* F.   [8] auaileable F.   [9] that is F.   [10] wastfully F.

Marginal notes:

[1 E 7]
Swords and
daggers guilt
& damasked.
[2 leaf 30. B.†]

[Scabbards and
sheaths of
velvet.]

[Why gilt
swordes, and
daggers be
worne. E, F]

Lucc. 16.

[1]*A particulare Diſcription of the Abuſes of Womens* [2] [[1] E 7, back; leaf 30, back. B.]
apparell in *Ailgna*.

THus hauinge geuen thee a[3] ſuperficiall[4] viewe, [5]or ſmall taſt[5] (but not diſcouered the hundreth part) of the guyſes of *Ailgna* in mens apparel, *and* of the abuſes contained in the ſame, now wil I, with like [6]celeritie of matter,[6] impart vnto thee the guyſe and ſeuerall Abuſes of the apparell of wemen there vſed alſo : wherfore, geue attentiue eare. [The abuses in women's apparel.].

Sp. My eares be preſt to heare : begin when you wil, and truely herin you ſhal pleaſur me much, for I haue greatly defired to know thorowly the ſtate of *that* Land, euen *a crepundiis* (as they ſay) from my tender yeres, for the great prayſe I haue hard therof. Wherfore I pray you proceed to the ſame, & though I be vnable *with* any benefit to counteruail your great pains,[7] yet *the* Lord, I doubt not, wil ſupplie my want.

Ph. The Lord our God is a mercifull God, & a bountiful Rewarder of euery one that truſteth in him ; but yet (ſuch is *the* magnificency[8] & liberalitie of that gentle ſex) that I truſt I ſhall not be vnrewarded at their hands, if[9] to be called a thouſand knaues be a ſufficient guerdon for my pains. But though it wilbe[10] a corroſiue[11] to their hautie[12] ſtomacks, & a *nippitatum* to their [13]tender breſts[13] to heare their dirtie dregs ript vp and caſt in[14] their dia[15]mond faces, yet hope[16]ing that they, ſeeing the horrour of their impieties, and tragicall abuſes laide open to the world (for now they ſleep in the[17] graue of obliuion) wil at the laſt, like good Conuertes and[18] Penitentiaries of *Chriſte Ieſus*, leaue of their wickednes, call for mercie at the hands of God, repent and amend. I will proceed to my intended purpoſe. [The rewarde of the female sex. B, E.]   ['5 leaf 31. B.†]   ['6 E 8]

[2] Womans F.   [3] a taste or B, E, F.   [4] *not in* F.
[5]—[5] *not in* B, E, F.   [6]—[6] expedition F.   [7] curtesie F.
[8] munificencie B, E, F.   [9] if at the least B, E, F.
[10] maie bee perhappes B, E, F.   [11] corrasiue F.
[12] tender F.   [13]—[13] haughty minds F.   [14] into F.
† leaf 31. Colouryng of faces in Ailgna ? B.   E *has a new head-line here,*
Abuse of the female sex.   [17] dust of silence and *added in* E, F.
[18] become faithfull B, E ; become the faithfull F.

¹The Women of *Ailgna*² vfe to colour their faces with certain oyles, liquors, vnguents and waters made to that end, whereby they think their beautie is greatly decored : but who feethe not that their foules are thereby deformed, and they brought deeper into the difpleafure and indignation of the Almighty, at whofe voice the earth dooth tremble, and at whofe prefence the heauens fhall liquifie and melt away. Doo they think thus to adulterate the Lord his woorkmanfhip, and to be without offence? Doo they not know that he is *Zelotipus*,³ a ielous God, and cannot abide any alteration of his woorkes, other wife then he hath commaunded⁴?

Yf an Artificer or Craftsman fhoulde make any-thing belonging to his art or fcience, & a cobler fhould prefume to correct the fame, would not *the* other think him felf abufed, and iudge him⁵ woorthy of reprehenfion ?

And ⁶thinkeft thou (oh Woman!)⁶ to efcape the Iudgement of God, who hath fafhioned thee⁷ ⁸to his glory, when thy⁹ great, and more then prefumptuous, audacitie¹⁰ dareth to alter, & ¹¹chaunge his woorkmanfhip in thee¹² ?

¹³Thinkeft thou that thou canft make thy felf¹³ fairer then God, who¹⁴ made vs all? Thefe muft needes be their inuentions,¹⁵ or els they would neuer go about to coulour their faces with fuch fibberfawces. And thefe beeing their inuentions,¹⁵ what can derogate more from the maieftie of God in his creation ? For in this dooing, they plainly conuince the Lord of vntrueth in his word, who faith he made man glorious, after his owne likenes, and the fayreft of all other terreftiall¹⁶ Creatures. If he be thus faire, then what need they to make them fayrer? Therfore this their colouring of their faces importeth (as by probable coniecture may be prefuppofed) that they think them felues not faire enough,¹⁷ and then muft GOD needs be vntrue in his woord.

Coloring of faces with oyntments and waters.

Adulteration of the Lord his workmanfhip in his Creatures.

[⁸ E 8, back]

[¹¹ leaf 31, back. B.[*]]

They that colour their faces, deny the Lord of glory to bee true God, and so no God at all.

¹ *Heading in* F :—Collouring of womens faces in England.
² (many of them) use B, E, F.   ³ deus *added in* B, E, F.
⁴ made them B, E, F.   ⁵ the reproouer F.
⁶—⁶ doe these women thinke B, E, F.   ⁷ them B, E, F.   ⁹ their B, E, F.
¹⁰ audacicitie A.   * leaf 31, back. Coloured faces abhord of God. B.
¹² them B, E, F.
¹³—¹³ Doe they suppose that they can make themselues B, E, F.
¹⁴ that B, E, F.
¹⁵ intentions B, E, F : (suppositions *for the* 1st *word* F.)   ¹⁶ terrestriall F.
¹⁷ els why doe thei goe about to make themselues fairer *added in* B, E, F.

And alſo they deny the Lord to be either merciful or almightie,
or bothe, and ſo conſequently no God at all; for if hee could not
haue made them faire, then is hee not almightie; and if hee could and
would not, then is hee not a merciful God; and ſo euery way they
[1] fall in to the ſinck[1] of offence, [2] beeing[2] aſhamed of the good creation
of the Lord in them; but[3] it is to be feared leaſt at the day of Iudgement the Lord wil be aſhamed of them, & in his wrath [4] denounce
this heauie and ineuitable ſentence con[5]demnatorie againſt them:
" *Departe from mee, you curſed, into euerlaſting fire, prepared for the*
deuil and his Angels : I knowe you not : (I ſay) departe, for you were
aſhamed of mee, and of my creation in you.[6] "

[4 F 1]
Sentence con-
demnatory
against those
that coulour
their faces.
[5 leaf 32. B.†]

Spud. Wherof doo they make theſe waters, and other[7] vnctions
wherwith they beſmeare their faces, can you tel ?

Philo. I[8] am not ſo ſkilful in their [9] matters of pride,[9] but I holde
this for a *Maxime*, that[10] they are made of many mixtures, and ſundry
compounded[11] ſimples, bothe farre fetched and deer bought, cunningly
couched[12] together, and[13] tempered with many goodly condiments and
holſome confections, I warrant you; els you may be ſure they woulde
not applye them to their amorous[14] faces, for feare of harming or
blemiſhing the ſame.

[Materials of
waters, &c. for
women's faces.]

[*Spud.* I praie you ſhewe me the [15] iudgements, and[15] opinions of
the Fathers, concernyng theſe colourynges[16] of faces [17] with ointmentes
and waters, that I maie the better know, what to iudge of it[18] my ſelf.[17]
B, E, F; *part inſerted with the pen in* A.]

Philo. S. *Ciprian*, amongſt all[19] the reſt, ſaith, a Woman, thorow
painting and dying of her face, ſheweth her ſelf to be more then
whoriſh. For (ſaith hee) ſhee hath corrupted and defaced (like a
filthie ſtrumpet or brothel) the woorkmanſhip of Goᴅ in her: what
is this els but to turne trueth into falſhood with painting and ſibber-

Inuectiues of
the Fathers
against paynt-
ing and cou-
louring of
faces.

---

[1]—[1] stumble at the stone of B, E, F.

[2]—[2] whiche one day will cruſhe them all to peeces, excepte they repent. And
as they be B, E, F.   [3] so B, E, F.

† leaf 32. Harlottes vſe painted faces. B.   [6] in you *nòt in* F.

[7] other *not in* B, E, F.   [8] Truly I, F.   [9]—[9] dealings.

[10] that *not in* E.   [11] compounde B, E; *not in* F.   [12] mingled B, E, F.

[13] and artificially B, E, F.   [14] amiable F.   [15]—[15] *not in* A, pen.

[16] this colouringe A, pen.   [17]—[17] *not in* A, pen.   [18] them E, F.

[19] all *not in* B, E, F.

fawces, wheras the Lord ſaith, " *Thou canſt not make one haire white or black.*"   In an other place hee ſaith, *Qui* [1]*ſe pinguunt*[2] *in hoc ſeculo, aliter quam creauit* [3]*Deus, metuant ne, cum dies reſurrectionis venerit, artifex creaturam ſuam non recognoſcat.*   Thoſe which[4] paint or collour them ſelues in this world otherwiſe then God hath made them, let them feare, leaſt when the day of iudgement commeth, the Lorde wil not know them for his Creatures.   Againe, *Feminæ crines ſuos inficiunt malo præſagio, capillos enim flammeos auſpicari*[5] *non metuunt.*   Whoſoeuer doo color their faces, or their haire, with any vnnaturall collour, they begin to prognoſticate of what colour they ſhalbe in hel.

[1 leaf 32, back. B.*]
[3 F 1, back]
[St Cyprian against face-painting.]

S. Ambroſe ſaith that from the coullouring of faces ſpring the inticements to vices, and that they which[6] color their faces doo purchaſe to them ſelues the blot and ſtain of chaſtitie.

For what a dotage is it (ſaith hee) to chaunge thy naturall face which God hath made thee for a painted face, which thou haſt made thy ſelf? If thou beeſt faire, why painteſt thou thy ſelf to ſeeme fairer? and if thou be not faire, why dooſt thou hippocrittically deſire to ſeeme faire, and art nothing leſſe? Can thoſe things which, beſides that they be filthie, doo cary the brand of God his curſſe vpon their backs for euer, make thee to ſeeme fayrer? I could ſhow you the ſharp Inuections, and grounded reaſons of many moe, as of *Aug[u]ſtine, Hierome, Chriſoſtome, Gregorie, Caluin, Peter Martyr, Gualter,* and of an infinite number moe; [7]yea, of all generally ſince the beginning of [8]the world, againſt this[9] whoriſh and brothellous painting and coulouring of faces; but to auoid *prolixitie* I will omit them, deferring them to further oportunitie, for *pauca ſapienti,*[10] To a wiſeman few woords are ſufficient.

No painting can make any to ſeem fairer, but fowler.

[7 F 2]
[8 leaf 33 B.†]

Spud. It muſt needs be graunted, that the dying and coulouring of faces with artificiall colours, and vnnaturall Oyntments, is moſte offenſiue to God, and derogatorie to his Maieſtie : [And when thei haue doen all that thei can, and the cunningeſt artiſt that euer liued beſides, yet ſhal thei neuer be able to make ſo ſplendent, ſo orient, and

‡ Colouring of faces, the deuils net.

---

[2] pingunt E.   * leaf 32, back. Colouryng of faces detestable. B.
[4] that F.   [5] auspicare F.   [6] which *comes before* that *in* F.
† leaf 33. Painted faces, the Deuilles nets. B.   [9] those E.
[10] sapientia B, E, F.

ſo naturall a colour, as dame Nature hath giuen to the herbes in the feeld. Then if God hath imprinted ſuche an excellent colour in the graſſe of the feeld, which to-day [1]is ſtanding,[1] and to-morrow is cut doune; how muche more hath he ingrauen a beautifull colour in man, the excellenteſt creature of all others[2]? Therefore ought euery one to content himſelf with the ſhape that God hath giuen hym, without ſekyng of alteration or change. B, E, F.] for doo they think that the God of all glorie, and who only decketh and adorneth the Sun, the Moon, the Starres, and all the hoaſt of heauen with vnſpeakable glorie, and incomparable beautie, cannot make them beautiful and faire enough (if it pleaſe him) without their ſibberſawces? And what are they[3] els then the Deuils inuentions, to intangle poore ſoules in the nets of perdition?

    [4] *Philo.* Then followeth the trimming and tric[5]king of their heds in laying out their hair to the ſhewe, which of force muſt be curled, friſled and criſped, laid out (a World to ſee!) on wreathes & borders from one eare to an other. And leaſt it ſhould fall down, it is vnder propped with forks, wyers, & I can not tel what, rather[6] like grime[7] ſterne monſters, then chaſte chriſtian matrones. Then, on the edges of their bolſtred heir (for it ſtandeth creſted round about their frontiers, & hanging ouer their faces like [8]pendices[9] with glaſſe windowes an[10] euery ſide) there is layd great wreathes of gold and ſiluer, curiouslie wrought & cunninglie[11] applied to the temples of their heads. And for feare of lacking any thing to ſet foorth their pride withal, at their heyre, thus wreathed and creſted, are hanged bugles (I dare not ſay bables) ouches, rings, gold, ſiluer, glaſſes, & ſuch other[12] gewgawes and[13] trinckets beſides, which, for that they be innumerable, and I vnſkilfull in wemens termes, I can not eaſily recount.[14] But God giue them grace to giue ouer theſe vanities, and ſtudie to adorn their heads with the incorruptible ornaments of vertue & true Godlyneſſe.

    Spud. The Apoſtle *Paul* (as I remember) commaundeth wemen to cheriſh their heyre, ſaying that it is an ornament to them; &

---

[1]—[1] standeth E.   [2] other F.   [3] but F.
    [4] *heading in* F :—Attiring of womens heades in England.   •
     † leaf 33, back. Laying out of coloured haire. B.
   [6] rather *comes before* than *in* F.   [7] and *added in* F.
[9] or vailes *added in* B, E, F.   [10] on F.   [11] cunning = (*sic*) F.
  [12] other childishe B, E, F.   [13] and foolish B, E, F.
     [14] expreſſe B, E ; recompt F.

therfor me think this abufe of curling and laying it out[1] (if eyther were lawfull) is muche more tollerable than dying their faces.

[2 leaf 34. B.*]

Curling and crisping and laying out of heyre.

Bought heyre and colored vsed to be worn.

[Children's hair cut off by women in London.]

[10 F 3]

[Women dye their hair.]

[16 leaf 34, back. B.†]

[2]*Philo.* If curling, & laying out of[3] their own naturall heyre weare all (which is impious, and at no hand lawfull, [4]notwithftanding for[4] it is the[5] enfigne of Pride, and the ftern[6] of wantonnes to all that behould it) it were the leffe matter; but they are not fimply contente with their owne haire, but buy other heyre,[7] dying it of what color they lift themfelues: [And if there be any poore women (as now and then, we fee God doeth bleffe them with beautie, as well as the riche) that hath faire haire, thefe nice dames will not reft, till thei haue bought it. Or if any children haue faire haire, thei will intice them into a fecrete place, and for a penie or two, thei will cut of their haire: as I heard *that* one did in the citie of Munidnol[8] of late, who metyng a little child with verie faire haire, inuegled her into a houfe, promifed her a penie, and fo cutte off her haire. B, E, F.] & this they were[9] in the fame order as you haue [10]heard, as though it weare their owne[11] natural heir: and vppon *the* other fide, if any haue heyre[12] which is not faire inough, than will they dye it into[13] dyuerfe colors, almoft chaunginge the fubftance into accidentes by their dyuelifh, & more than thrife curfed deuyfes.   So, wheras their heire was geuen them as a figne of fubiection, and therfore they were commaunded to cherifh the fame, now haue they made [14](as it were) a *Metamorphofis* of it, making[14] it an ornament of Pride, and deftruction to them felues [15]for euer,[15] except they repent.

[16]*Spud.* This is a ftyfnecked People, & a rebellious, I fee well, that thus dareth, in euerie refpecte, to peruert the ftraight wayes of the Lord, digginge vp to them-felues cefterns of iniquity, [17]& pittes of aduerfity,[17] which in th'end, without the great mercy of God, will be their vtter confufion.

---

[1] forth F.   * leaf 34. Bought haire & coloured, worne. B.
[3] of *not in* B, E, F.   [4]—[4] beyng as B, E, F.   [5] an B, E; and F.
[6] standerd F.
[7] either of Horses, Mares, or any other straunge beastes *added in* E, F.
[8] London F.   [9] weare F.   [11] owne owne F.
[12] haire of her owne naturall growyng B, E, F.   [13] in E, F.
[14]—[14] *not in* B, E, F.   [15]—[15] *not in* F.
† leaf 34, back. Capitall ornamentes for heads. B.
[17]—[17] *not in* F.

[1] *Philo.* Than, on toppes of theſe ſtately turrets (I meane their goodly heads wherin is more vanitie than true Philoſophie now and than) ſtand their other capitall ornaments, as french hood, hat, cappe, kercher, and ſuche like; wherof ſome be of veluet, [2] ſome of taffatie, ſome (but few) of woll,[2] ſome of this faſhion, ſome of that, [3] and ſome of this color, ſome of that,[3] according to the variable fantaſies of their ſerpentine minds. And to ſuch exceſſe [4] is it growen, as [4] euery artificers wyfe [5] (almoſt) wil [6] not ſtick to goe in her hat of Veluet euerye day, euery marchants wyfe and meane Gentlewomen in her french-hood, and euerye poore Cottagers Daughter in her taffatie hat, or els of woll at leaſt, wel lined with ſilk, veluet or taffatie. But how they come by this (ſo they haue it) they care not; who payeth for it they regard not, nor yet what hurt booth to them ſelues and others it [7] dooth bring,[7] they feare not, But runne daylie *a malo ad peius* (as they ſay) from one miſchiefe to an other, vntill they haue [8] filled vp the meſure of their euill [9] to their owne [10] perdition at that day.[10]

[11] They haue alſo other ornaments beſydes theſe to furniſh foorth their ingenious heads, which they cal (as I remember) cawles, made Net-wyſe, to th' ende, as I thinke, that the clothe of gold, cloth of ſiluer, or els tinſell, (for that is the worſt) wherwith their heads are couered and attyred withall [12] vnderneath their cawles maye [13] appeare, and ſhewe it ſelfe in the braueſt maner. Soe that a man that ſeethe them (there heads gliſter and ſhine in ſuche forte) wold [14] thinke them to haue golden heads. [And ſome weare Lattice cappes with three hornes, three corners I ſhould ſaie, like the forked cappes of Popiſhe Prieſtes, with their perriwincles, chitterlynges, and the like apiſhe toyes of infinite varietie. B, E, F.]

Thus lauiſhe they foorth the goods of the Lorde, which are none of their owne (but lent them for a tyme) vppon Pride and naughti-neſſe, delighting (as it ſeemeth) in nothing ſo [15] muche as in the ſtinck-ing puddle of vanitie and ſinne, which will be their owne decay [16] at the

Marginal notes:

Capitall ornaments for the head.

[6 F 3, back]

Hattes of veluets: taffaty worn in common

Trahit sua quenque voluptas.

[11 leaf 35. B.†]

Cawles made Netwyse.

Golden heads fraught with leaden wit.

[15 F 4]

---

[1] *heading in* F :—French Hoodes in England.   [2]—[2] *not in* F.

[3]—[3] *not in* F.   [4]—[4] it is grown that F.   [5] wyse A.

[7]—[7] bringeth F.   [8] haue *not in* F.   [9] iniquitie B, E, F.

[10]—[10] confusion at the last F.   † leaf 35. Golden heads with leaden wit. B.

[12] *not in* F.   [13] may the better B, E, F.   [14] he would F.

[16] in the end F.

laſt.[16] Another forte of diſſolute minions & wanton *Sempronians* (for I can term the*m* no better) are fo far bewitched, as they are not

aſhamed to make holes in their eares, wherat they hang rings, and other Iewels of gold and precious ſtones. But what this ſignifieth in them I will hould my peace, for the thing it felfe ſpeaketh fufficiently. There is a certen kinde of People in the [1]Orientall parte of

the World[1] (as Writers affirme), that are fuche *Philautoi,* [2]louers of them felues, and fo prowde with all, that, hauing plentie of precious

Stones and Margarits amongeſt them, they cut and launce their ſkinnes and fleſhe, fetting therin theſe precious Stones, to the end they maye gliſter and ſhine to the eye.

So, except theſe Women weare minded to tread their pathes, and[3] folowe their direfull wayes in this curfed kind of [4]vnhard of[4] Pride, I wonder what they meane.

But becaufe this is not fo muche frequented amongeſt Women as Men, I will fay noe more thereof, vntill further occaſion be offred.

Spud. Except it weare a People wedded to [5]the deuills eldeſt

Daughter[5] Pride (for I thinke chaſtitie[6] amongeſt them maye dwell [7]a Virgin for any that wil marry her), and giuen ouer of God, I neuer heard the like. I am perſwaded [8]neither the *Libertines,* the *Epicures,* nor yet the vile *Atheiſts,* euer[9] exceeded this people in pride, [10]nor[11] the wickednes of them might euer counterpeafe with the wickednes of theſe people[10]: *God be merciful vnto them!*

Philo. You heare not the tenth parte, for no pen is able fo wel to difcribe it, as the eye is to difcry[12] it. The Women there vfe great

ruffes, & neckerchers of holland, lawne, camerick, and fuch cloth, as the greateſt thred ſhall not be fo bigge as the leaſt haire that is : then,[13] leaſt they ſhould fall down, they are fmeared and ſtarched in the

deuils liquore, I meane *Starch;* after that, dryed with great diligence, ſtreaked, patted, and rubbed [14]very nicely, and fo applyed to their goodly necks, and, withall, vnderpropped with fupportaſſes (as I tolde you before) the ſtatelie arches of pride : beyond all this they

haue a further fetch, nothing inferiour to the reſt; as, namely, three
or foure degrees of *minor* ruffes, placed *gradatim*, ¹ſtep by ſtep,¹ one   Minor ruffs.
beneath another, and all vnder *the* Maiſter deuil ruffe. the ſkyrts,
then, of theſe great ruffes are long and ſide euery way, pleted and
creſted ful curiouſly, God wot. Then, laſt of all, they are either
clogged w*ith* golde, ſiluer, or ſilk lace of ſtately price, wrought all
²ouer with needle woork, ſpeckled and ſparkled heer & there with   [² F 5]
the ſonne, the moone, the ſtarres, and many other antiquities³ ſtraunge
to beholde. Some are wrought with open woork down to the midſt   The great
of the ruffe and further,⁴ ſome with purled lace ſo cloyd, and other   curioſity of 5
gewgawes ſo peſtred, as the ruffe is the leaſt parte of it ſelf. Some-   neckcerchers.
times they are pinned vp to their eares, ſometimes they are ſuffered to
hang ouer their ſhoulders, like ⁶ windmil ſayles fluttering in the winde;
and thus euery one pleaſeth her ſelf with⁷ her fooliſh deuices, ſor *ſuus cu-*
*iuſq*ue *crepitus ſibi bene olet*, as *the* prouerb ſaith : euery one thinketh his
own ⁸wayes beſt⁸, ⁹though they leade to diſtruction of body and ſoule,
which I wiſh them to take heed of.⁹ [¹⁰ And¹¹ amongeſt many other
fearfull examples of Gods wrathe againſt Pride,¹² to ſett before their
eyes, the fearfull Iudgement of ¹³ God, ſhewed upon a gentlewoman of   [¹³ leaf 36, back.
Eprautna ¹⁴ of late, euen the 27 of Maie 1582, the fearfull ſound where-   B.†]
of is blowen through all the worlde, and is yet freſh in euery mannes   [Antwarpe. E.]
memorie. This gentlewoman beeyng a very riche Merchaunte
mannes daughter : vpon a tyme was inuited ¹⁵ to a Bridall, or Weddyng,
whiche was ſolemnized in that Toune, againſte whiche daie ſhe made   [A fearfull
greate preparation, for the plumyng of her ſelf in gorgious arraie, that   example against
as her body was moſte beautifull, faire, and proper, ſo her attire in   vpon a gentle-
euery reſpecte might bee coreſpondent ¹⁶ to the ſame. For the accom-   woman in
pliſhment whereof, ſhe curled her haire, ſhe died her lockes, and laied   Antwarpe. E, F]
them out after the beſt maner, ſhe coloured her face with waters and
Ointmentes : But in no caſe could ſhe gette any (ſo curious and   [Womens
daintie ſhe was) that could ſtarche, and ſette her Ruffes, and Necker-   lubricious
chers to her mynde : wherefore ſhe ſent for a couple of Laundreſſes,   mindes neuer
                                                                          content with
                                                                          anythinge when
                                                                          it is well. E.]

¹—¹ *not in* B, E, F.   ³ antiques B, E, F.
    ⁴ some with close woorke, *added in* B, E, F.   ⁵ in E.
⁶ flagges or *added in* F.   ⁷ in B, E, F.   ⁸—⁸ foist the sweetest F.
⁹—⁹ *not in* F.   ¹⁰ *added in* B, E, F.   ¹¹ But F.
¹² I would wish them *added in* F.   † leaf 36, back. *No head-line.* B.
    ¹⁴ Antwerpe F.   ¹⁵ inuiled A ; inuited F.   ¹⁶ answerable F.

[The fearful end of the proud Antwerp lady.]

who did the beſt thei could to pleaſe her humors, but in anywiſe thei could not. Then fell ſhe to ſweare and teare, to curſſe and banne, caſtyng the Ruffes vnder feete, and wiſhyng that the Deuill might take her, when ſhe[1] weare any of thoſe Neckerchers againe. In the meane tyme (through the ſufferaunce of God) the Deuill, tranſform-yng himſelf into the forme[2] of a young man, as braue, and proper as ſhe in euery poinƈte in outward appearaunce, came in, fainyng

[3 leaf 37. B.ª]

himſelf to bee a woer or ſuter vnto her. [3]And ſeyng her thus agonized, and in ſuche a peltyng chafe, he demaunded of her the cauſe thereof, who ſtraight waie tolde hym (as women can conceale no thyng that lieth vppon their ſtomackes) how ſhe was abuſed in the ſettyng of her Ruffes, which thyng beeyng heard of hym, he promiſed to pleaſe her minde, and thereto[4] tooke in hande the ſetting of her Ruffes, whiche he performed to her greate contentation, and likyng,

[The deuil pleaseth women better then any bodie els. E, F.]

in ſo muche as ſhe lokyng her ſelf in a glaſſe (as the Deuill bad her) became greatly inamoured with hym. This dooen, the yong man killed her, in the doyng whereof, he writhe her necke in ſonder, ſo ſhe died miſerably, her bodie beyng [5]Metamorphoſed, into blacke and blewe[5] colours, moſt vggleſome to behold, and her face (whiche be-fore was ſo amorous) became moſte deformed, and fearfull to looke vpon. This being knowen, [6]preparaunce[6] was made for her buriall, a riche coffin was prouided, and her fearfull bodie was laied therein, and it[7] conered verie ſumpteouſly. Foure men immediatly aſſaied to lifte vp the corps, but could not moue it, then ſixe attempted the like, but could not once ſtirre it from the place, where it ſtoode. Whereat the ſtanders by marueilyng, cauſed the Coffin to bee opened, to ſee the cauſe thereof. Where thei founde the bodie to be taken awaie, and

[The deuil found setting of great Ruffes. E.]

[8 leaf 37, back. B.†]

a blacke Catte verie leane and deformed sittyng in the Coffin, ſetting of great Ruffes, and frizlyng of haire, to the great feare, and [8]wonder of all the beholders. This wofull ſpeƈtacle haue I offered to their viewe, that by looking into it, in ſtead of their other looking Glaſſes

---

[1] shee did F.   [2] shape F.

* leaf 37. *No head-line* B. E *has head-line*, A fearfull example agaynst Pride.

[4] so F.   [5]—[5] straight waies changed into blew and black F.

[6]—[6] in the cittie, great preparation F.   [7] it *not in* F.

† leaf 37, back. Women wearyng Dublets. B. E *has* The deuil found setting of ruffes.

thei might ſee their own filthineſſe, & auoyde the like offence, for
feare of the ſame, or worſer iudgement: whiche God graunt thei
maie doe[1].]

Spud. As in a *Camelion* are ſaid to be all coulours, ſaue white, ſo
I think in theſe people are all things els[2], ſaue Vertue and chriſtian
ſobrietie. *Proteus*, that Monſter, could neuer chaunge him ſelf into   Proteus.
ſo many fourmes & ſhapes as theſe women doo: belike they haue
made an obligation with hel, and are at agreement[3] with the deuil,
els they would neuer outrage thus, without either feare of God or reſpeĉt to their weak Bretheren, whom heerin they offend.

[4] *Philo.* The Women alſo there haue dublets & Ierkins, as men   Women wer-
haue heer, buttoned vp the [5]breſt, and made with wings, welts, and   ing dublets
                                                                        and Ierkins.
pinions on the ſhoulder points, as mans apparel is [6]for all the world[6];   [5 F 5, back]
& though[7] this be a kinde of attire appropriate[8] onely to man, yet they
blush not to wear it; and if they could as wel chaunge their ſex, &
put on the kinde of man, as they can weare apparel aſſigned onely to
man, I think they would as verely become men indeed, as now they
degenerat from godly, ſober women, in wearing this wanton lewd
kinde of attire, proper onely to man.

It is written in the 22 of *Deuteronomie*, that what man ſo euer   A curse to
weareth [9]womans apparel is accurſed, and what woman weareth   them that
                                                                        weare co*n*trary
mans apparel is accurſed alſo. Now, whether they be within the [10]bands   apparell to
                                                                        their sex.
and lymits[10] of that curſſe, let [11]them [12]ſee to it them ſelues[12].[11] Our   [9 leaf 38. B.†]
Apparell was giuen vs[13] as a ſigne diſtinctiue to diſcern betwixt ſex
and ſex, & therfor one to weare the Apparel of another ſex is to
participate with the ſame, and to adulterate the veritie of his owne
kinde. Wherefore theſe Women may not improperly be called
Hermaphroditi, that is, Monſters of bothe kindes, half women, half   Hermaphro-
men.[14]   diti.

Spud. I neuer read nor heard of any people, except drunke*n* with

----

[1] *added in* B, E, F.   [2] els *not in* E.   [3] a league F.
[4] *heading in* F :—Doublets for Women in England.   [6]—[6] in all respectes F.
[7] although F.   [8] proper F.   † leaf 38. A curse for Apparell. B.
    [10]—[10] compasse F.   [11]—[11] they themſelues iudge F.
        [12]—[12] take heede B, E.   [13] us *not in* E, F.
[14] Who if thei were naturall women, and honest matrones, would blushe to go
in suche wanton and leude attire, as is proper* onely to man *added in*
B, E, F. (* incident F.)

Cyrces cups, or poyfoned with the *exorcifms* of *Medea,* that famous and renoumed Sorcereffe, that euer woulde weare fuche kinde of attire as is not onely [1]ftinking before the face of God,[2] offenfiue to man, but alfo[3] painteth out to the whole world the [4]venereous inclination[4] of their corrupt conuerfation.

[5]*Philo.* There Gownes be no leffe famous alfo[6]; for fome are of filk, fome of veluet, fome of grogram, fome of taffetie, fome of fcarlet, and fome of fine cloth, of ten, twentie, or fortie fhillings a yard. But if the whole gowne be not filke or veluet, then the fame fhall[7] be layed with lace, two or three fingers broade, all ouer the gowne, or els the mofte parte.

Or, if not fo (as lace [8]is not fine enough fometimes[9]), then it muft be garded with great gardes of veluet,[10] foure or fix fingers broad at the leaft, and edged with coftly lace; and as thefe gownes be of diuers and fundrie colors, fo are they of diuers fafhions, changing with the Moon, for fome be of the new fafhion, fome of the olde, fome of this fafhion, and fome of that, fome with fleeues hanging down to their fkirts, trayling on the ground, and caft ouer their fhoulders, like Cow-tayles.

Some haue fleeues much fhorter, cut vp the arme,[11] and pointed with filk-ribons very gallantly, tyed with true-looues knottes (for fo they call them).

Some haue Capes reaching downe to the middeft of their backs, faced with Veluet, or els with fome fine wrought filk [12] Taffatie [13]at the leaft, and fringed about very brauely; & (to fhut vp all in a word) fome are pleated & ryueled[14] down the back wonderfully, with more knacks than I can declare.[15] Than haue they Petticots of the beft cloth that can be bought, and of the faireft dye that can be made. And fometimes they are not of cloth neither, for that is thought to bafe, but of fcarlet, grograin, taffatie, filk, and fuche like, fringed about the

---

[2] and *added in* B, E, F.   [3] such as *added in* F.   [4]—[4] dissolutenesse F.
[5] *heading in* F :—Womens Gownes in England.
[6] then the rest *for* also B, E, F.   [7] muft F.
† leaf 38, back. The great excesse in Gownes. B.   [9] now and then F.
[10] euery gard *added in* B, E, F.
[11] drawne out with diuers and sundry collours *added in* F.
[12] silk *not in* F.   [14] creasted F.
[15] expresse F.

fkirts with filk fringe of chaungable coloure. But which is more
vayn, of whatfoeuer their petticots be, yet muft they haue kyrtles
(for fo they call them), eyther of filk, veluet, grograin, taffatie, faten,
or fcarlet, borde¹red with gards, lace, fringe, and I cannot tell what [¹ leaf 39. B.⁵]
befydes. So that when they haue all thefe goodly robes vppon them,
women feeme to be the fmalleft part of themfelues, not naturall
women, but artificiall Women; not Women of flefh & blod, but Women the
least part of
rather puppits or mawmets of² rags & clowtes compact together. themfelues.
So³ farre hath this cancker of pride eaten into the body of the common welth, that euery poore Yeoman his Daughter, euery Husband
man his daughter, & euery Cottager his Daughter, will not fpare⁴ Poore Mens
Daughters
to flaunt it out in fuche gownes, petticots, & kirtles as thefe. And excesse.
not withftanding that their Parents owe a brafe of hunndred
pounds more than they are worth, yet will they haue it, *quo iure*
quaue iniuria, eyther ⁵by hooke or⁶ crooke, by right or wrong, as they [⁵ F 7]
fay, wherby it commeth to paffe that one can fcarfly know who is a
noble woman, who is an honorable or worfhipfull Woman, from them
of the meaner forte.

Spud. Their parents & Freinds are muche to be blamed for fuf- Parents to
blame.
fering them to go in fuche wanton attyre. They fhould not allowe
them fuch large pittance, nor fuffer them to meafure their apparell
after their own licentious yardes of felfe will, and wicked defires.⁷

Philo. Than shall they ⁸ be fure neuer to haue good day with them,
For they are fo impudent ⁹ that, all be it their poore Parents haue but The impud-
ency of proud
one cow, horfe, or sheep, they wil neuer let them reft til they be harlots.
fould to maintain them in their braueries, ¹⁰paft all tongue can tell.¹⁰ [⁹ leaf 39, back.
B.‡]
And, to fay the truth, fome Parents (worthie to be inaugured¹¹ with
the lawrell Crowne of triple follie,) are fo buxome to their shame-
leffe defires, and fo exorable to their proftitute requefts, *tha*t they
graunt to their too too nice daughters more than they can¹² defire

---

* leaf 39. The impudencie of Harlottes. B.   ² consistyng of B, F.
  ³ Yea, so F.   ⁴ stick E, F.   ⁶ or by F.
  ⁷ then should thei not rage† so farre as thei doe *added in* B, E, F ; *but* E F
have could ; †F *has* exceede, *which comes after* far.
                        ⁸ theyr Parents F.
              ‡ leaf 39, back. What makes youth wicked. B.
  ¹⁰—¹⁰ beyond all measure B, E, F.   ¹¹ for fooles *added in* E, F.
                    ¹² do E, F.

Our remiſſe
leuitie of Pa-
rents to their
Children.

themſelues, taking a ſingular felicity &[1] ſurmounting pleaſure in
ſ[ee]ing them [2]to go plumed and decked[2] in the Feathers of
deceiptfull vanity.

Sp. This ouer great lenitie & remiſſe libertie in[3] the education
of youthe, in reſpect of the euent and ſucceſſe[4] in the end, maye rather

[5 F 7, back]

be counted an extrem cruelty, than a Fatherly [5]pitie[6] of them towards their children ; For what maketh them ſo ſoone whores, ſtrum-
pets,[7] and bawdes, as that cockering of them doth ?

8 what maketh
whores and
strumpets.8

What maketh them apt & prone to all kind of naughtyneſſe but
this ? Nothing in the World ſoe muche ; For, giue a wild horſe the
libertie of the head neuer ſo litle, and he will runne headlonge to
thyne and his owne deſtruction alſo.

So long as a ſprigge, twiſt,[9] or braunche, is yong, it is flexible
and bowable [10]to any thing[10] a man can deſire ; but if we tarie till it be
a great tree, it is inflexible and vnbowable. If wax be taken whyleſt
it is hote, anye character maye be eaſilye imprinted[11] ; but tarying till it

[12 leaf 40. B.*]

be hard, it re[12]ceiueth no printe at all.

So, correct Children in their tender yeres, and you may bow them
to what good lore you will your ſelfe ; but tarie till they be old, than
[13]is it[13] to late, as experience teacheth daylie.

Netherstocks
of gernsey or
silk.

[14] *Philo.* Their neitherſtockes, in like maner, are either of ſilke
gearnſey,[15] worſted, crewell, or, at leaſt, of as fyne yarn, thread, or
cloth, as is poſſible to be had, [yea thei are not aſhamed to weare
hoſe of all kinde of chaungable colours, as greene, red, white, ruſſet,
tawny, and els what,[16] whiche wanton light colours, any [17] ſober chaſte
Chriſtian [18](except for neceſſitie ſake)[18] can hardly, without any [19] ſuſpi-
tion of lightneſſe, at any tyme weare ; but whatſoeuer is a deformitie
or ſhame in [20] others is an ornament to them that be paſt all ſhame.
Then theſe delicate hoſen muſt bee, B, E, F] cunningly knit and curi-

---

[1] and farre B, E, F.　　　　[2]—[2] decked and plumed B, E, F.
[3] of theirs in B, E, F.　　　　[4] that it bringeth *added in* F.
[6] loue or pittie B, E, F.　　　　　[7] Harlots *added in* F.
[8]—[8] *not in* E, F.
[9] a twist F.　　[10]—[10] which way F.　　[11] in it *added in* F.
[*] leaf 40. New fashions euery daie. B.　　　[13]—[13] it is F.
[14] *heading in* F :—Netherstockes of women in England.
[15] Iarnsey F.　　[16] what not F.　　[17] no F.　　[18]—[18] *not in* F.
[19] any *not in* E, F.　　　　　　[20] to F.

ouſly indented in euery point[1] : wherto they haue korked ſhooes, pinſnets, pantoffles, and [2]ſlippers, ſome of black veluet, ſome of white, ſome of greene, and ſome of yellowe; ſome of ſpaniſh leather, and ſome of Engliſh lether,[3] ſtitched with ſilk,[4] and imbrodered with Gold and ſiluer all ouer the foote, with other gewgawes innumerable. All which, if I ſhould [5]endeuoure my ſelfe[5] to expreſſe, I might [6]with more[7] facilitye[6] number the ſands of the Sea, the Starres in the ſkye, or the graſſe vppon the Earth, ſo infinit and innumerable be their abuſes. For weare I neuer ſoe experte an Arithmeti[8]cian [9], [10]or[11] Mathematician[10], I weare neuer [12]capable of[12] the[13] halfe of them, the deuill brocheth ſoe many new faſhions euery day.

Corked shoes, pinsnets, pantoffles, & such like, for women.
[2 F 8]

The innumerable fashions of womens attire.
[8 leaf 40, back B.†]

Wherfore to their *Author* I leaue them, not omittinge to tell you by the way ([14]as an *interim*[14]) of a certen kynde of ſweete Pride vſed amongeſt[15] Gentlemen and Gentlewomen in *Ailgna*.

Spud. I haue learned out of the Booke of God, that all Pride is ſtincking before the face of GOD; wherfore I greatlye deſyre to knowe what abortyue Miſcreant this is,[16] for it is ſome portenteous miſhapen monſter, I am[17] perſwaded.

Pride stinking before the face of God.

[18]*Philo.* Is not this a certen[19] ſweete Pride to haue cyuet, muſke, ſweete powders, [20]fragrant Pomaunders, odorous perfumes, & ſuch like, wherof the ſmel may be felt and perceiued, not only all ouer the houſe, or place, where they be preſent, but alſo a ſtones caſt of almoſt, yea, the bed wherin they haue layed their delicate bodies, the places where they haue ſate, the clothes, and thinges which they haue touched, ſhall ſmell a weeke, a moneth, and more, after they be gon. But the Prophet *Eſaias* telleth them, inſtead of their Pomaunders, muſks, ciuets, balmes, ſweet odoures and perfumes, they ſhall haue ſtench and horrour in the nethermoſt hel. Let them take heed to it, and amend their wicked liues.[21]

[20 F 8, back]
The hauing of ciuet, musk, and other perfumes, a sweet kind of Pride.

Esai, Cap. 3.

---

[1] with quirkes, clockes, open seame, and euery thing els accordingly *added in* B, E, F.   [3] lether *not in* B, E, F.
[4] with silke *repeated in* F.   [5]—[5] take vpon me F.   [6]—[6] as easily F.
[7] like B, E.   † leaf 40, back. Costly Perfumes and Muskes. B.
[9] Arithmetrician A.   [10]—[10] *not in* F.   [11] never so skilfull a *added in* B, E.
[12]—[12] able to recompt F.   [13] the one B, E, F.
[14]—[14] *comes after* you *in* B, E, F.   [15] amongest the B, E, F.
[16] may be B, E, F.   [17] am fully B, E, F.
[16] *heading in* F :—Muske, Ciuet, and sweet powder in England.
[19] certen *not in* E, F.   [21] in tyme *added in* B, E, F.

[¹ leaf 41. B.•]

Nofegayes &
posies of flow-
ers worn and
caried abrod.

And in the Sommer-time, whilft floures be greene and fragrant, yee shall not haue any ¹Gentlewoman almoft, no nor yet any droye or puffle in the Cuntrey, but they will carye in their hands nofegayes and pofies of floures to fmell at; and which is more, two or three Nofegayes² fticked in their brefts before, for what caufe I cannot tel, except it be to allure their³ Paramours to catch at them,⁴ wherby, I doubt not, but they get many a flabbering kiffe, and, paradeuenture, more freendfhip befides : they know beft⁵ what I mean.

Beware the
Spanish pip.

Spud. You wil be thought very ftraight laced to fpeak againft thefe thinges, for I haue heard it faid, that thefe⁶ fweet fmels ⁷are bothe corroboratiue to the fences, and confortatiue ⁸ to the fpirits, and which doo viuifie and recreate afwel the body as the minde.⁷

[⁸ G ɪ]

These ¹¹ curious
smelles obnu-
hilat the
spirits &
darken the
sences.

Philo. They are fo far from comforting the braines⁹, or lightning¹⁰ the fpirits of men ¹², that as myftes and exhalations which euaporate from thefe earthly bodyes, and are drawen vp by the attractiue power of the Sun, Moon, and ftarres, doo rather¹³ obnubilate ¹⁴ and darken the beames of the Sun, ¹⁵not fuffering his radiations to difparcle abrode¹⁵ ; So thefe (in a maner) palpable odors, fumes, vapours ¹⁶, fmells of thefe ¹⁷ mufks, cyuets, pomanders, perfumes, balmes, & fuche like, afcend-ing to the braine, do rather denigrate¹⁸, darken, and obfcure *the* fpirit ¹⁹

Sweet smells
of musks,
cyuet, and such
like, do ²¹ anoy
the spirits.

and fences, then either lighten them, or comfort them ²⁰any manner of way. But howfoeuer it falleth out, fure I am they are enfignes of pride, allurements to ²²finne, and prouocations to vice. After all

[²² leaf 41. back.
B.†]

this, when they haue attired them felues²³ in the midft of their pride, it is a world to confider their coyneffe in geftures, their minfednes in woords and fpeaches, their gingerlynes²⁴ in trippinge on toes like yong goats, their demure nicitie and babifhnes, and withall their

The vain
gestures &
coynes of
women in the
middest of

---

² nosegayes *not in* B, E, F.   ³ their amorous B, E, F.
⁴ and to smell at their breastes *added in* F.   ⁵ hest *not in* E, F.
⁶ these *not in* B, F ; the *for* that these *in* E.
⁷—⁷ doe corroborate the sences, comfort the spirits, and recreate both the body & mynd of man greatly, doe they not so ? B, E, F.   ⁹ braine F.
¹⁰ illuminating E ; reuiuing F.   ¹¹ The F.   ¹² man F.
¹³ doo rather *not in* B ; rather *not in* E, F.   ¹⁴ obnubilate *not in* F.
¹⁵—¹⁵ *not in* F.   ¹⁶ vapours and B, E, F.
¹⁷ these *not in* B, E, F.   ¹⁸ denigrate *not in* F.   ¹⁹ spirites F.
²⁰ by any B.   ²¹ do *not in* F.
† leaf 41, back. Looking glasses, the deuils spectacles. B.
²³ thus *added in* B, E, F.   ²⁴ gingernesse B, E, F.

hawtie ſtomackes and more than Cyclopicall countenances. their
fingers are[1] decked with gold, ſiluer and precious ſtones, their
wriſtes with bracelets and armlets of gold, and other precioufe[2]
Iewels: their hands are[3] couered with their ſweet wa[4]ſhed gloues,
imbrodered with gold, ſiluer, and what not; & to ſuch abhomination is it[5] grown, as they muſt haue their looking glaſſes caryed
with them wherfoeuer they go. And good reaſon, for els how cold
they ſee the deuil in them? for no doubt they are the deuils
ſpectacles to allure vs to pride, & conſequently to diſtruction for
euer. [6]and aboue al things they muſt[6] haue their ſilk ſcarffes caſt
about their faces, & fluttering in the winde, with great taſſels at
euery end, either of gold, ſiluer, or ſilk. But I know wherfor they
wil ſay they weare theſe ſcarfes; namely, to keep them from Sun-
burning; But I wold aſke theſe Nicelings one queſtion, wherin if
they can reſolue mee, then I will ſay, as they ſay, *that* ſcarffes are
neceſſary, and not flags of pride. Can that thing which is moſte
glorious & fair of it ſelf, make any thing foule or ilfauored? the
ſun is a moſt glorious & fair creature, & therfor cannot make them
fowler then they are of their own nature. From whence then is it[8]
that the Sun burneth them, & altereth their orient colour into
woorſer hue? The cauſe therof proceedeth from their own genuine
corruption and natural imperfection[9]; for no more is their fowlenes to
be aſcribed to the ſtelliferous[10] beames of *the* gliſtering[11] Sun, then *the*
ſtench of a dead carcaſſe may be ſaid to [12]come of[12] *the* ſun, & not
rather of it own corruption & filthines. They buſie themſelues in

their pecok
fethers.
Fingers clog-
ged with
rings.
Womens
trinckets.
Sweeted
gloues.
Loking
glaſſes, the
deuills specta-
cles.
[4 G 1, back]

Silk skarfes.

A question to
skarfe werers.

---

[1] must be B, E, F.   [2] costly B, E, F.   [3] are *not in* B, E, F.   [5] it is F.

[6]—[6] *Spud.* The deuill could neuer haue found out a more pestilent euill then
this, for hereby man beholding his face, and being naturally giuen to flatter hymself too muche, is easely drawen to thinke well of hymself: and yet no man seeth
the true proportion of his face, but a counterfaite effigie, and false image therof
in the glaſse, whiche the Deuill suffereth hym to see, that thereby he maie rise
into Pride, and so [so *not in* E, F] offende the Diuine Maiestie. Therefore maie
these lookyng glasses [7] be called the deuils bellowes, wherewith he bloweth the
blast of Pride into our hartes: and those that looke in them may be said to looke
in the Deuilles arse, whilest he infuseth the venemous winde of Pride into their
soules. *Philo.* * Then must thei B, E, F. * *Heading in* F :—Scarffes and
Maskes in England.

[Looking-glasses
the deuils
bellowes. E, F.]
[7 leaf 42. B.†]

† leaf 42. Silke Scarffes in Ailgna. B.

[8] it is F.   [9] prauitie F.   [10] splendent F.   [11] glistering *not in* F.

[12]—[12] proceed of B, E, F.

[¹ G 2]
[³ leaf 42, back.
B.*]

preſeruing the beautie of their bodyes, which laſteth but for a time, & in time ¹is cauſe of his² own corruption, & which, ³in effeʓ, is nothing els then⁴ putrifaction it ſelf, & a dunghil couered with white & red; but for the beautie of the ſoule they care nothing at

Visors or
inuiſories of
veluet to ride
abrode in.

all. When they vſe to ride abrod, they haue ⁵inuiſories,⁶ or⁵ ⁷viſors made of veluet,⁸ wherwith they couer all their faces, hauing holes made in them againſt their eyes, whereout they look. So that if a man, that knew not their guiſe before, ſhould chaunce to meet one of them, hee would think hee met a monſter or a deuil; for face hee can

Sues voluta-
bris versantur.

ſee⁹ none, but two brode holes againſt her¹⁰ eyes with glaſſes in them. Thus they prophane the name of God, & liue in al¹¹ kinde of voluptuouſnes & pleaſure, wurſſe then euer did the hethen.

Sp. What think you, are not the inuentors & firſt finders out of theſe new toyes & dyuelish deuices, in great daunger, and partakers with them of the euill committed ?

[† side-note here
in B.]

Philo. It cannot be but the Inuentors of theſe new toyes are in great daunger before God, as they who ſhall render accounts to god, not only for the inuention of them, but alſo for the euil committed by

† The first
finders and
inuentors of
new fashions
are culpable of
all the euil
that commeth
by them.
[¹⁹ leaf 43. B.‡]

[²⁰ G 2, back]

them. For whoſoeuer is author of any euil muſt needs anſwer for the euil. And ſurely the authors¹² of theſe newfangles are ¹³not vnworthy¹³ to be canonized ſaints when the yeere of *Iubilie* commeth (I meane ſaincts of ſathan); for ¹⁴there is no¹⁴ deed ſo flagicious, no¹⁵ faʓ¹⁶ ſo dangerous, ¹⁷nor any¹⁷ thing¹⁸ ſo hainous, which ¹⁹with alacritie is not plauſibly committed for the ²⁰maintenance of theſe Diueliſh toyes and deuices: And albeit that the Perſons themſelues who offend this way ſhal dye in their ſinnes, their owne bloud being powred vppon their owne heads, yet the *Authors* of theſe new toyes, wherthorow they offended, ſhalbe giltie of their deathes, and ſurely anſwear for their deſtruʓion in the day of the Lord.

A vaine
excuse.

Spud. But ſay they, 'if I make them not, an other wil, & it is as good for me to make them as an other; & it is my lyuing; wherfore

² it B, E, F.   * leaf 42, back. Veluet Viſours to ride with. B.
⁴ but E, F.   ⁵—⁵ *not in* B, E.   ⁶ masks F.   ⁷ and F.
⁸ (or in my judgement thei maie rather be called invisories) *added in* B, E, F.
⁹ shew F.   ¹⁰ their E, F.   ¹¹ all in B, E.   ¹² author F.
¹³—¹³ worthy F.   ¹⁴—¹⁴ what B, E, F.   ¹⁵ what B, E, F.   ¹⁵ attempt F.
    ¹⁷—¹⁷ or what B, E, F.   ¹⁸ fact F.
         ‡ leaf 43. A Caueat for Artificers. B.

I am diſcharged of blame, if I make them (being commaunded) with ſweat of my face, and with trauaile and paine to get my lyuing.'

Philo. We are commaunned (*sic*), indeed, to get our lyuing with the ſweate of our face; but how? Not in doing thoſe things which are euill of themſelues, and alſo drawe and intice others to euill, but in things lawful and good,[1] & which induce to goodneſſe.[2] And to ſay ' others will make them, if I[3] do not,' no more excuſeth them of offence,[4] than for a Murtherer or[5] Thief to ſay, if I had not robbed, or killed this man, another wold, diſchargeth him from the penaltie of the iudiciall[6] lawe [7]to be infliĉted againſt[8] him.[7] Is it lawfull for vs to do euill becauſe others do it? Or dooth the wickednes of an other delyuer me[9] from blame, if I[10] commit the ſame offence? no, nothing leſſe. Wherfore let Taylers and Artificers be[11]ware how [12]they eyther inuente or make theſe new deuyces and Dyueliſh faſhions euery day: And being requeſted to make them, if they perceiue them[13] tende to vice, and[14] allure to ſinne, let them refuſe them in the name of God, more tendering the ſaluation of many, than the priuat commodytie of themſelues alone: which thing, if euery one wold do, he ſhould delyuer his own ſoule, & ſupport an infinit number from falling into the gulphe of ſinne; and ſo in ſhort tyme theſe new toyes, fond deuyces, and childiſh babelries (new faſhions I ſhould ſay) wold ſoone vaniſh away and come to naught[15]: which God graunt may [16]once be ſeene[16]!

[17]*Spud.* Did the women of the former world attire themſelues in ſuche ſorte as theſe women do?

Philo. The Women of the former age, you may be ſure, neuer appareled themſelues like one of theſe. But leaſt you ſhould thinke that the Godly onelie lyued thus auſterly, you ſhal heare how litle the very hethen and barbarian Women haue, and do at this preſent, eſteeme of apparell; as *Stuperius* witneſſeth, whoſe words are theſe,

Side notes:
We are bouηd to get our lyuing in well doing, not in euill doing.

A caueat to Artificers that inuent new faſhions.

[[11] leaſ.43, back. B.†]
[[12] G 3]

[A caueat for Tailours and Artificers. F.]

[Heathen women despise dress.]

---

[1] honest F.   [2] godlinesse E, F.   [3] they B, E, F.
[4] before God *added in* F.   [5] or a F.   [6] *not in* F.
[7]—[7] or guilt of the fact F.   [8] upon B, E.   [9] vs E, F.   [10] we E, F.
          † leaf 43, back. Mans saluation to be regarded. B.
[13] to *added in* E, F.   [14] and to F.   [15] naughe (*sic*) F.
          [16]—[16] come to passe E, F.
[17] *heading in* F: The meane attire of both Heathen and other Women in olde time.

[Egyptian and other heathen women are modest in dress.]

fpeking of the Egiptian women : " *Veſtimenta ſciunt̄ nec noua priſtinis mutare, verum ſemper his in cultibus gaudent perpetuo tempore congredi, quaſcunque gentes hunc per orbem viſitent ;* Which may be thus turned into Englifh verfe :

[¹ G 3, back]

¹ *The Egiptian Matrones neuer vſe*
Their faſhion ² of attyre to change,

[³ leaf 44. B.*]

⁸ *But euer keep one forme to chuſe,*
Although they viſite Nations ſtrange.

AND as all Writers doo affirme, all the Women there indifferently go with their haire hanging downe, with a broade hat vppon their heads, and other attyre as playne as the reſt, foo farre are thefe People from Pride, and hunting after ſtrange faſhions as our Women doo.

[The meannes of other Nations in attire. B, E, F ; *with* maners *for* meannes.]

The Women of *Affrica* are witneffed, by the fame *Stuperius,* and others, to be ſo farre from affecting⁴ ſtrange faſhions, or curiofity in aparel, that they cloth themfelues, in a manner, all ouer *ferinis pellibus,* with beafts ſkinnes, furres, and fuch like. And this they think fo riche attire, as they vfe it altogether when they celebrat their feſtiual folemne daies, or when they go abrode to be feene.

The *Braſilian* Women efteeme ſo litle of apparell alfo, as they rather chofe to go naked (their fecret partes only being couered) then they wold be thought to be proud, or defirouſe of ſuch vanities.⁵

The *Cantabrian* Women likewyfe, with many others,⁶ do the fame.

[German women dress plainly.]

In High *Germany,* the Women vfe in effect one kind of apparel or habite, without any difference at all, nothing like other Nations delighting in new fangles, ⁷yea, the wiues there are ſo far from pride

[⁷ G 4]

that they will not difdaine to carie all their houfehould ſtuffe, and other trinckets,⁸ about with them vppon their backs in tyme of extremitie.⁹ Thefe ¹⁰ Mayds & Virgins go very plain, with kerchers

[¹¹ leaf 44, back. B.†]

only on their heads, their ¹¹haire hanging down behinde, in token of Virginitie.

Thus, you fee, euery Nation, how barbarous foeuer, are much inferiour to *the* people of *Ailgna* in pride & exceffe of apparell ; and

---

² fashions F.   * leaf 44. Women*s* habit, in other Countries. B.
    ⁴ affecting of E, F.   ⁵ vanity F.   ⁶ other F.
    ⁸ supellectiles E, F.   ⁹ necessity F.   ¹⁰ Their B, E, F.
        † leaf 44, back. Brutish Attire not commendable. B.

yet theſe examples I alledge not to th' end I wold wiſh all others to vſe *the* ſame, or *the* very like brutiſh[1] kind of auſter[2] habite, but to ſhew how farre they be from Pride, & how much the other be wedded to *the* ſame.　And as for the vertuous, & godly chriſtian women : from the beginning of the world they haue ſo litle cared for the vain glory of apparell, & ſo litle (or rather nothing at al) were they acquainted therwith, as they hunted for nothing els ſo much as for the ornaments of the mind, as wiſdom, continency, chaſtitie, & true godlyneſſe, thinking the ſame bewtie ſufficient.　They counted it great ſhame to cloth their bodies with ſumpteous apparel, & their minds to be naked, & voide of true vertue.　So, if theſe women wold ſeek after *the* bewtie of *the* mind, they wold not affect apparell ſo much ; for if they be faire in body alredy, than need they not gorgeous apparel to make them fairer : & if they be deforme[3] in body, it is not *the* apparell[4] that can make them fairer.　And either their bewtie confiſteth in them, or in their apparel : If in them, than not in the Apparell, & ſo it is meere foolery to were them ; And if in apparel, than not in them, and ſo cannot the garments make them fayre whome God & na[5]ture hath made otherwiſe : wherfor look in what ſhape, forme, or condition, euerye one is created by God, let him content himſelfe with the ſame, without any alteration or chaunge, with praiſe to his Creator.

[The contempt of apparell of the former age. B, F.]

[4 G 4, back]

[5 leaf 45. B.†]

Spud. They hold (notwithſtanding) that it is the pride of the heart, which God ſo muche hateth and deteſteth.

Philo. It is verye true that GOD puniſheth the pride of the heart with eternal damnation (if they repent not), for he will be ſerued and obyed either with the whole man, or els with none.　Than, if he puniſh the pride of the heart with euerlaſting damnation, he muſt needs (in iuſtice) puniſh the pride of Apparell with the like, being booth ioyned in one predicament of ſinne, and the pride of apparell much more hurting before the world than the other.

Pride of the heart.

Pride of apparel equiualent with Pride of the heart.

Alſo it is manifeſt that the pride of apparel riſeth firſt from the corruption of the heart, as the effects from the cauſe, the fruite from the roote of the tree : than, if the pride of *the* heart which, notwith-ſtanding it hurteth not outwardly, but is ſecret betwixt God and him-

---

[1] ſauage F.　　　[2] *not in* F.　　　[3] deformed F.
† leaf 45. Pride of the harte, and of Ap[parell]. B.

[¹ G 5]

[Pride of apparel more damnable than pride of heart.]

[² leaf 45, back, B.*]

¹felfe, be damnable in it owne nature before God, than muft it needs be that the Pride of apparell (which fheweth its felfe to the world, both offenfiue to God, and hurtfull to man, and which alfo is the fruite of the pride of the heart, and throweth almoft as many as behold it, at leaft as many as followe it, into the deep dungion of hell,) is ²much more pernicious and damnable than the other.

Spud. Hath the Lord plagued this finne of pride with any notable torture³ or punifhment euer from the beginning of the World vnto this day, or hath he ⁴omitted the reuenge therof⁴ as a thing of fmall force, or⁵ importance?

⁶*Philo.* Moft fearfull plagues and dreadfull iudgements of God haue in all ages beene powred vppon them that offended herein, as all Hiftories, both holy and prophane, do beare record. For proofe wherof I will geue you a tafte but of a few, wherby may appeare how

Examples of God his punifhments executed vppon them that offended in Pride in all ages.

wonderfully the Lord, in all ages, tymes, kinreds, & peoples, hath punifhed thofe that thorow pride (like wicked recufants⁷ and backflyders from God) haue rebelled againft his maieftie. The deuill, who before was an Angell in Heauen, arrogating to himfelfe the imperial throane of the maiefty of God, was caft downe into the deepth⁸ of Hell, burning with fire⁹ and fulphur for euer.

[¹⁰ G 5, back]

Adam, defiring to be a God (for the ferpent ¹⁰tould him, he fhould be as God, knowing both good & euill), was for the fin of Pride throwne downe to the bottome of Hell, & not onely he but all his pofteritie to the end of the World. The hoaft of *Core, Dathan,* and *Abiram,* for their exceding pride in ftirring vp mutenie,¹¹ ¹²rebelling againft their lawfull Magiftrate, were fwallowed vp¹³ quick into hell,

[¹⁴ leaf 46. B.†]

the earth opening her mouth & deuouring them, ¹⁴with all their complices whatfoeuer. The People of *Babylon,* intending to builde a

[The Tower of Babel.]

tower, whofe top fhould ¹⁵tutche the Skye,¹⁵ thinking that if God fhould drown the world againe with water, they would be fure inough on the toppe of their high turrets; yea, they intending¹⁶ to

---

* leaf 45, back. Gods punishments for Pride. B.
³ plague F.   ⁴—⁴ passed it ouer F.   ⁵ force or *not in* F.
⁶ *heading in* F:—Pun[i]shments of pride in all ages.
⁷ runnagats F.   ⁸ lake E, F.   ⁹ brimstone B.   ¹¹ mutinies F.
¹² and rebelling B ; and rebellion E ; and rebellions F.   ¹³ up *not in* E.
† leaf 46. Punishments for Pride. B.   ¹⁵—¹⁵ reach the heauens F.
¹⁶ intended F.

ſit with God himſelfe (if need weare) weare all confounded, and a
diuerſe language put into euery mans mouth, that none knew what
an[1] other ſpake. And thus were they forced to leaue there building,
and diſperſed themſelues abroad vppon the face of the earth, wherof[2]
ſprang the firſt diuerſitie of languages in the world. Wherfore when
we heare any language ſpoken we[3] know not, it may be a *memo-* A memoran-
randum to[4] vs to put vs in minde of our Pride, which was the cauſe dum.
therof.

    Goliah, the great Gyant, the huge Cyclops, and ſworne enemy to
the Children of *Iſraell,* for his pride againſt the Lord was ſlaine by
Dauid, the fait[h]full Seruaunt of the Lord.

    [5]*Antiochus,* intending to ouerthrowe and ſacke *Ieruſalem,* to ſpoile Antiochus.
the Sanctuarie and Temple of the Lord, and to kill the people of [5 G 6]
God, was for his pride ouerturned in his chariet, ryding thetherward,
his belly bruſt,[6] and filthy wormes crawled[7] out moſte lothſomly; and,
in fine, beganne ſo to ſtinke and ſwell,[8] as neither his Seruants, nor he
himſelfe, cold abide his owne fauoure; and thus ended his lyfe in
great miſerie and wretchedneſſe.

    Nabuchodonoſor[9] was for his pride caſt out of [10]his Kingdom, and[11] Nabuchodo-
forced to eat graſſe with wild beaſts in the wilderneſſe. nosor. Daniel 4.
                                                         [10 leaf 46, back
    King *Saule,* for his pride and diſobedience, was depoſed of his B.†]
principallitie and Kingly regimente, and in the end ſlewe him ſelf on K. [Saul.]
mounte *Gelboe* moſt deſperately.

    Sodoma and *Gomorra* were both deſtroyed with fire & brimſtone
from heauen for their ſin of pride & contempt of the Lord. All the
world in the daies of *Noah* was drowned with [12]vniuerſall deluge for
pride & contumacy of heart.

    King *Hezekiahs*[13] for his pride in ſhewing to the Ambaſſadors of 2 Reg. Cap. 20.
the king of *Babylon* all his treaſure (for he ſent Meſſengers vnto him
with gifte[14] & lettres, congratulatorie[15] for the recouerie of his helth)
loſt al his iewels, treſures, & riches, with his owne[16] ſonnes alſo,
being tranſported captiues into *Babilon.* K. *Dauid,* for his pride in
numbring the people contrary the wil of god, [17]was grenouſlie pun- [17 G 6, back]

    [1] an *not in* E, F.   [2] and hereof F.   [3] that we B, E ; that me (*sic*) F.
    [4] vnto F.   [6] burſting B, E, F.   [7] crawling B, E, F.   [8] smell E, F.
    [9] Nabuchadnezar F.   † leaf 46, back. Proude Kynges puniſhed. B.
    [11] and and (*sic*) F.   [12] with an B, E, F.   [13] Ezekiah F.
    [14] giftes F.   [15] reioycing *added in* F.   [16] owne *not in* B, E, F.

2 Samuel 1, c.
24, Ver. 15.

ifhed, and threefcore and ten thoufand of his People flaine with a greeuous peftilence for the fame.

King *Pharao*, for his pride againft the Lord (for he thought him felfe a GOD vppon the Earth, and therfore afked he *Moyfes*, in derifion, who is the Lord?), was drowned in the read Sea with all his hoaft.

The proude
Pharisey.

The proude *Pharifey*, iuftifying himfelfe, for his pride was reproued of the Lord, and reie&ed.

K. Herode.

[¹ leaf 47. B.*]

King *Herode*, for attiring himfelfe in fumpteous aray & not afcribing glory to the ¹Lord, was ftrucken² dead by an Angel, and wormes confumed his flefh immediatly.   Al thefe, with infinit mil-lions moe in al ages, haue perifhed thorow pride; and therfore let not this people think that they fhall efcape vnpunifhed, who drinke vp pride as it weare fweet wyne, feede vppon it as vppon delicious meats, and wallowe in it as a³ filthie fwyne doth in the dirtie⁴ myre. will the Lord punifh his peculiare people and ele& veffels, and let them goo free?

Wherfore I wold wyfhe them to be warned, for it is a terrible thing to fall into *th*e hands of GOD, who is a confuming fire & a

God his Plagues
are prepared, if
we repent not.

fearfull God.   His bowe is bente, his arrowes of iudgements⁵ are drawen to the head, his fire is kyndled, his wrath is gone out, & ready to be powred vppon the contemners of his lawes.   Tempt not

[⁶ G 7]

the Lord any longer; prouoke not ⁶his wrath, exafperate not his iudgements towards thee; for as mercy proceedeth *fro*m him, fo doth iuftice alfo; And, be fure of it, he payeth home at the laft.   For as in mercie he fuffreth no good deed to be vnrewarded, fo, in his iuft iudgmente, there is no wickednes⁷ which he leaueth vnpunifhed.   And yet, notwithftanding, their wickedneffe and pride is fuch as ftincketh before the face of God, and maketh the Enemies to blafpheme and fpeake euill of the wayes of the Lord: for, fay they, the men of *Ailgna* are wicked & licentious⁸ in all their wayes, which eafily

[⁹ leaf 47, back.
B.†]

appeareth by their apparell & ⁹new fangled fafhions euery day in-uented.   The beaftly Epicures, the Drunkards & fwilbowles, vppon their ale benches, when their heads are intoxicat with new wine,¹⁰ wil

---

* leaf 47. Gods iudgementes for Pride. B.   ² striken F.   ³ a *not in* E, F.
⁴ dirtie *not in* F.   ⁵ iudgement F.   ⁷ without repentance *added in* F.
⁸ dissolute F.   † leaf 47, back. Our liues, a slaunder to the Gospell. B.
¹⁰ and strong drinke *added in* F.

not ſtick to belch foorth and ſay, that the inhabitantes of *Ailgna* go brauelye in Apparell, chaunging faſhions euerie daye, for no cauſe ſo much as to delight the eyes of their harlots[1] withall, and to inamoure the mindes of their fleſhly paramours.   Thus be this People a laughing ſtock to all the world for their pride, a ſlaunder to the word of God & to their profeſſion, ſcandalles to their brethren, a dishonor and reproch to the Lord, and very caterpillers to themſelues in waſting and confuming their goods and treaſures vppon vanyties & trifles.

Our new fangles and toies are occaſions why all nations mocke and floute vs.

Our lyuing a ſlaunder to the truth.

[[2] *Spud.* I perceiue theſe are nice dames, I pray you what exerciſes followe thei, for the moſte parte beyng thus clothed in their robes, and how doe thei ſpende the tyme? For I ſtand in doubte thereof?[3]

Philo. You neede not to doubt.   For thei ſpend their time very well, I warrant you, and to their owne contentation.[4]   For ſome of them lye in bed (I will not ſaie with whom) till nine or tenne of the clocke every mornyng; then, beyng rouzed forthe of their dennes, thei are twoo or three howers in puttyng on their Robes, which beeyng[5] doen, thei go to dinner, where no delicates either of wines or meates are wanting.   Then their bo[6]dies beeyng ſatiſſied, and their heades pretely mizzeled with wine, thei walke abrode for a time, or els confer with their familiars (as women you know are talkative enough, & can chat like Pies) all the world knoweth it.   Thus ſome ſpende the daie till ſupper tyme, and then the night, as before.   Other ſome ſpende the greateſt parte of the daie, in ſittyng at the doore, to ſhewe their braueries, to make knowen their beauties, to beholde the paſſengers by, to viewe the coaſt, to ſee faſhions, and to acquainte themſelues with the braueſt fellowes: for if not for theſe cauſes, I ſee no other cauſes why thei ſhould ſitt at their doores, from Mornyng till Noone (as many doe) from Noone to Night; thus vainly ſpendyng their golden daies in filthie idleneſſe and ſinne.   Againe, otherſome being weary of that exerciſe, wil[7] take occaſion (aboute vrgent affaires you muſt ſuppoſe) to walke into the Towne; & leaſt any thing

[The great paynes that theſe gentlewomen take. E.]

[⁰ leaf 48. B.†]

[Exercises and practiſes of the gentlewomen of Munidnol. B, E.]

---

[1] whorish mates F.

[2] *From here to p.* 89, *l.* 24, *is from* B: *it's not in* A.   *Heading in* F :—The dayly exercises of the Women of England.

[3] they scarse spend it wel *instead of* thereof F.   [4] contentments F.

[5] beeyng *not in* F.

† leaf 48 ; *no head-line* B.   E *has* Hand baskets clokes to sinne.

[7] wil *not in* E, F.

[*This page is not in* A.]
[Hand baskets clokes to siune. E.]

[might bee gathered, but that thei goe about fereous matters indeede, thei will [1] take their baſkets in their hands, or vnder their armes; vnder which pretence, pretie conceites are practized, and yet maie no man ſaie blacke is their eye.   But if al other waies faile them, yet haue thei one which be ſure will ſpeede.

Spud. What waie is that, I praie you declare vnto me.

[[3] leaf 48, back. B.*]
[Garden in the fieldes no better then the Stewes. E.]

[2] *Philo.* Seyng you are ſo deſirous to knowe I will tell you. In the Feeldes and Suburbes [3] of the Cities thei haue Gardens, either palled, or walled round about very high, with their Harbers and Bowers fit for the purpoſe. And leaſt thei might bee eſpied in theſe open places, they haue their Banquetting houſes with Galleries, Turrettes, and what not els therin ſumpteouſly erected : wherein thei maie (and doubtleſſe doe) many of them plaie the filthie perſons. And for that their Gardens are locked, ſome of them haue three or fower keyes a peece, whereof one they keepe for themſelues, the other their Paramours haue to goe in before them, leaſt happely they ſhould [4] be perceiued, for then were all their [5] ſporte daſht. Then to theſe Gardens thei repaire when thei liſt, with a baſket and a boy, where thei, meeting their ſweete hartes, receiue their wiſhed deſires. Theſe Gardens are exelent places, and for the purpoſe ; for if thei can ſpeak with their dearlynges no where els, yet there thei maie be ſure to

[Gardens, places of baudry. B, E.]

meete the*m*, and to receiue the guerdon of their paines : thei know beſt [6] what I meane. But I wiſhe them to amende, for feare of Gods heauie wrathe in the daie of vengeaunce.

Spud. Why ? doe you condemne the vſe of Gardens [7] and houſes [7] then altogether ?

Philo. No nothyng leſſe. For I knowe they bee very healthful, comfortable, and holſome for mans bodie, and ſuche thynges, as the vſe whereof we can [8] not lacke. But I condemne theſe abuſes, theſe

[[9] leaf 49. B.†]
[Euery thing abused, is not to be remoued, but the abuse to be taken away onely. E.]

corruptions, and enormities there vſed, [9] and I pray God thei maie be reformed.   There is no thyng ſo good but it maie be abuſed : yet I am not ſo preciſe that I would haue the thyng remoued for the abuſe, but the abuſe to be taken awaie, whereby the thyng it ſelf is made

---

[1] will *not in* E, F.   [2] *heading in* F :—Gardens in Englande.
* leaf 48, back ; *no head-line* B. E *has* Gardens places of baudrie.
[4] might F.   [5] the F.   [6] best *not in* E, F.   [7]—[7] and garden houses F.
[8] can we F.   † leaf 49 ; *no head-line* B. E *has* Women good and badd.

[worſe. Nor I ſpeake not againſt the good and Godly women, for I [*This page to l. 24, is not in* A.]
knowe there bee a greate number,—and the Lorde increaſe the num-
ber of them that are chaſt, wiſe, ſober, continent, and verteous Ma
trones, and voyde of all theſe corruptions!—But againſt thoſe light, [I denounce the lewd Harlots, not the virtuous Ma-trons.]
leaude,[1] and incontinent Harlottes (as it is well knowne there bee too
many) that runne to thoſe places, as faſt as euer did the brothelles to
the Stewes. And truely I thinke ſome of theſe[2] places are little better
then the Stewes and Brothell houſes were in tymes paſt: I beſeeche
the Lorde to make[3] them cleane, either with the Oliue braunch of
his mercie, or with the broome[4] of his iudgement, that this wickedneſſe maie be doen[5] awaie.

Spud. Are theſe[6] nice Dames, gentle, ſober and diſcrite, or otherwiſe, giuen to chiding, braulyng, and vnquietneſſe : For thei ſhewe
themſelues abroade (by reporte) as though butter would not melt in
their mouthes.

Philo. There are ſome, ſober, wiſe, gentle, diſcrite, and verteous
Matrones, as any be in al the worlde. And there be other ſome (yea
maior numerus) that are neuer well, but when thei be, either brawl- [Women good and bad, but the greater number naught. E, F.]
yng, ſcoldyng, or fightyng with[7] ſome [8]of their houſholde[9] : and ſuche [8 leaf 49, back. B.*]
deuilles, as a man were better to be hanged then to dwel with them.
But becauſe I haue ſmall experience hereof[10] my ſelf; [11]but onely by[11]
reporte of them that haue made triall thereof themſelues, I will ſaie
no more, committyng them ouer to the Lorde, to whom thei either
ſtand if thei doe well, or fall if thei doe euill. B, E, F.]

Spud. Seeing that by diuyne aſſiſtance you [12]haue now finiſhed [12 G 7, back]
your traſtation[13] of the Apparell of *Ailgna*,[14] ſhew me (I pray you)
what other abuſes be there vſed; for I am perſwaded that pride,
the Mother of all[15] ſinne, is not without her Daughters of ſinne[16]
ſemblable to her ſelfe.

---

1 lewd F.   2 those F.   3 sweepe E ; purge F.   4 sharpe rod F.
5 put F.   b those F.   7 eyther with F.
* leaf 49, back. Horrible whordome in Ailgna. B.
9 or some others *added in* F.   10 therof E, F.
11—11 saue onely by the E, F.   13 discourse F.
14 *This is always printed* England *in* F.   15 all *not in* B, E, F.
16 of sinne *not in* B, E, F.

The horryble vice of Whordome in *Ailgna.*

Philo. THE horryble vice of Whordome alfo[1] is ther too too much
frequented, to the great difhonor of God, the prouoking of his iudgements againft them, the ftaine and blemifh of their profeffion, the
euill example of all the world, and finally to their owne damnation
for euer, except they repente.

Spud. I haue heard them reafon,[2] that mutuall coition betwixt
man and woman is not fo[3] offenfiue before God; For do not all
Creatures (fay they) as wel *reptilia terræ* as *volatilia Cæli*, the[4] creeping
things vpon the earth, as the[4] flying [5]Creatures[6] in the aire, and all
other Creatures in generall, both fmall & great, ingender together?
hath not nature and kynd ordained them fo.? & geuen them members incident[7] to that vfe? & doth not the Lord (fay they) (as it were
with a ftimule or prick, by his mandat, faing *crefcite & multiplicamini
& replete terram*: increafe, multiplie & fill the earth,) ftirre them

[8]vp to the fame? Otherwyfe the World wold become barren, and
foone fall to decay: wherfore they conclude that whordome is a
badge of loue, a cognizance of amitie, a tutch of luftie youth, a
frendlie daliance, a redintegration of loue, and an enfigne of vertue,[9]
rather meritorious than damnable: thefe, with the like, be [10]the[11]
exceptions[10] [12]which I haue hard them many times to obiect[13] in
defence of their carnal pollutions.

Philo. Curfed be thofe mouths that thus[14] blafpheme the mightie
God of *Israell* and his facred word, making the fame, clokes to couer
their finne withall: [15]worfe are they[15] than Lybertines who thinke all
things lawfull, or Atheiftes who denie there is any God. The diuells
themfelues neuer finned fo horribly nor erred fo groffely as thefe (not
Chriftians, but dogges) do, that make whordom a vertue and meritorious: but becaufe you fhal fee their deceptions difplayed & their
damnable abufes more plainly difcouered, I will reduce you to the

---

[1] also *not in* F.   [2] reason thus B, E, F.   [3] so much F.
[4] the *not in* F.   † leaf 50. Libertines defend whordome. B.
[6] Creatures *not in* F.   [7] proper F.   [9] good will B, E, F.
[10]—[10] their ridiculous reasons F.   [11] their childishe B, E.
[12] and friuolous obiections *added in* B, E.   [13] pretende B, E; alleadge F.
[14] dare to *added in* B; care *in* E; do *in* F.   [15]—[15] Thei are much worser B, E, F.

firſt inſtitution [1] of this Godly ordenance of matrimony. The Lord our God, hauing created all things in Heauen, earth or Hell whatſoeuer, created of euery ſex two, male & female [2] of both kindes [2]; and laſt of al other creatures he made man after his own likeneſſe & ſimilitude, geuing him a woman, made of a ribbe of his own body, to be his [3] companion, & comforter [4]; & lincking them together in the honorable ſtate of [5] venerable wedlocke, he bleſſed them both, ſaying ' creſcite, multiplicamini & *replete terra*m '; Increaſe, multiplie, & repleniſh *the* earth : wherby it is more than apparent that the Lorde, whoſe name is *Iehouah*, the mightie GOD of *Iſraell*, is the Author of Godly matrimony, inſtituting it in the tyme of mans innocency [6] in *Paradice* ; and that, as mee ſeemeth, for foure cauſes. Firſt, for the auoydaunce of whordom; Secondly, for the mutuall comforte & conſolation that the one might haue of the other in all aduerſities & calamities whatſoeuer : Thirdly, for the [7] procreation and Godly [7] propagation of Children in the feare of the Lord, that both the world might be increaſed therby, and the Lord alſo [8] in them glorified.[8] And, fourthlie, to be a figure or type of our ſpirituall wedlocke betwixt Chriſt and his church, both militant and triumphante. This congreſſion, and mutuall copulation, of thoſe that be thus ioyned together in the Godlye ſtate of bleſſed matrimony is pure virginitie, and allowable before God and man, [9] as an action wherto the Lorde hath promiſed his bleſſing thorow his mercy, not by our merite, *ex opere operato,* as ſome ſhame not to ſay. All other goinges together and coitions are damnable, peſtiferous, and execrable. So, now you ſee that wheras the Lord ſaith ' increaſe, multiplie, & fill the earth,' he alludeth to thoſe that are cheyned [10] together [11] in the [12] Godly ſtate of [12] matrimonie and wedlock, and not otherwyſe : For to thoſe that go together after any other ſorte, he hath denounced his curſe and wrath for euermore, as his alſauing word beareth record. And wheras they ſay that all creatures vppon the Earth do ingender together, I graunte it is true ; But how ? *in ſuo genere*, in their owne kinde. There is no

Marginal notes:

The firſt inſtitution of matrimonie.
[[1] leaf 50, back. B.*]

Gene. 2.
Mat. 19.
Marc.
Luc. 16.
1 Cor. 6.
Ephe. 5.
[[5] G 8, back]

Mariage inſtituded for 4 cauſes.

[Procreation.]

[As type of Chriſt and his Church.]

[[9] leaf 51. B.†]

All mutuall copulation except mariage is vnlawfull.
[[11] H 1]

How all creatures do goe togither in their kinde.

---

* leaf 50, back. Gods curse for Whordome. B.
[2]—[2] *not in* E, F.   [3] a *for* his E, F.
[4] vnto him *added in* E, F.   [6] inconcency A ; innocencie B, E, F.
[7]—[7] *not in* B, E, F.   [8]—[8] be glorified in him E, F. (be *not in* F.)
† leaf 51. Fidelitie in maried couples. B.
[10] linked F.   [12]—[12] state of godly F.

creature creeping on the earth, or flying in the aire, how irrationable foeuer, that dooth[1] degenerate as man dooth, but keepethe the fame ftate and order wherein they were made at the firft; [2]and fo[2] if man did, he fhould not commit[3] abhominable whordom and filthie finne as hee dooth.   It is faid of thofe that write *de natura animalium*, that (almoft) all vnreafonable beafts and flying fowles, after they haue once linked and vnited them felues togither to any one of the fame kinde, and after they haue once efpoufed them felues the one to the other, wil[4] neuer after[5] ioyne them felues with any other, til the one be diffolued from the other by death.   And thus they keepe the knot of matrimonie inuio[6]lable to the end.   And if any one[7] chaunce to reuolte, and go togither with any other, during *the* life of his firft mate, al the reft of the fame kind affemble togither, as it were in a councel or parliament, and either kil or greeuoufly punifh the adulterer or adulterefle, whether [so]euer[8] it be; which lawe I [9]would God were amongft Chriftians eftablifhed.   By all which it may appeer how horrible a finne whordome is in nature, that the very vnreafonable creatures doo abhorre it.   The Heathen people, who know not God, fo much lothe this ftinking finne of whordome, that fome burne them quick, fome hang them on gibbets, fome cut off their heds, fome their armes, legs and hands; fome put out their eyes, fome burne them in the face, fome cut of their nofes, fome one parte of their bodye, fome another, and fome with one kind of torture, and fome with another; but none leaueth them vnpunifhed : fo that we are fet to fchoole to learn our [10]firft rudiments[10] (like yung Nonices or Children fcarce crept out of the fhel[11]) how to punifh whordome, euen by the vnreafonable creatures, and by the heathen people[12] who are ignorant of the deuine goodnes.   [13]*God be merciful vnto vs !*[13]

Spud. I pray you rehearfe fome places out of the woord of God, wherin this curfed vice of whordome is forbidden, for my better inftruction.

Philo. Our Sauiour Chrifte, in the eight of *Iohn*, fpeaking to the

The fidelitie of vnreasonable creatures in mariage one towards an other.

[6 leaf 51, back. B.†]

[9 H 1, back]

How much the Heathen haue detested whordome.

Sundery punishments of whordome amongst the Heathen.

---

[1] doeth so B, E, F.   [2]—[2] whiche thing B, E, F.   [3] commit such E, F.
[4] thei wil B, E, F.   [5] after *not in* B ; *follows* themselves *in* E, F.
† leaf 51, back. The Heathen detest whoredome. B.   [7] one *not in* B, E, F.
[8] soeuer B, E, F.   [10]—[10] A. B. C. *in* F.
[11] swadling cloathes F.   [12] people themselues B, E, F.
[13]—[13] *not in* B, E, F.

woman whom the mali[1]cious *Iewes* had apprehended in adulterie, bad her go her way, and fin no more. If it had not been a mofte greeuous fin, he would neuer haue bid her [2]to fin therin[2] no more.

[3]In the fift of *Mathew* he faith, 'Who fo lufteth after a woman in his hart, hath committed the fact alredy, and therfore is guiltie of death for the fame.' To the *Pharifes*, afking him whether a man might not put away his wife for any occafion? *Chrifte* anfwered, 'for no caufe, faue for whordome onely'; inferring that whordome is fo hainous a finne, as for the perpetration therof it fhalbe lawful for a man to fequefter[4] him felf from his owne wife, and the wife from her owne hufband. The Apoftle *Paul* fayth, 'know you not that your bodyes are the members of *Chrifte?* fhall I then take the members of *Chrifte* (faith he), and make them the members of an whore? *God forbid!* knowe yee[5] not that he who coupleth him felf with a[6] harlot is become one body with her?' 'flee[7] fornication (faith he), therfore, for euery finne that a man committeth is without the body, but who committeth fornication, finneth againft his owne body.' And in an-other place : 'knowe you not that your Bodyes are the temples of the holy ghoft, which dwelleth within you? And who fo deftroyeth the Temple of God, him fhall God deftroy.'

In an other place he faith : 'be not deceiued, for neither Whoremonger, Adulterer, Fornica[8]tor, inceftuous perfon, nor fuch like, fhall euer enter into the kingdome of heauen.' Again, '*Coniugium honorabile eft inter omnes:* [9]Mariage is honorable amongft all men, and the bed vndefiled; but whooremongers and adulterers, God fhall iudge.' In the Reuelation of Saint *Iohn* it is faid, that they who were not defiled with women doo waite vpon the Lamb, whetherfoeuer he goeth. The Apoftle *Paul* willeth vs to be fo far from fornication, that it[10] be[11] not once named amongft vs, as becommeth Saints; with infinit fuch places, which for breefnes[12] I omit, referring you in the olde Teftament to thefe and fuch like[13] places, namely, the 20 of *Exodus*, 20 of *Leuiticus*, [14]*Deutronomie* 22, *Deutro.* 27, 2 *Reg.*[14] 11,

Testimonies out of the woord of god wherin whordome is forbid.
[1 leaf 52. B.*]
[3 H 2]
Mat. 5.

Mat. 19; Mat. 10 ; Luc. 16.

1 Cor. 6.

[The Bible against whoredom.]

[8 leaf 52, back. B.†]

[9 H 2, back}

---

　* leaf 52. Examples against whoredome. B.　　　　[2—2] sin F.
　　　[4] deuide F.　　　　[5] you F.　　　　[6] an F.　　　　[7] Flie F.
　　　　　† leaf 52, back. The rewarde of chast liuers. B.
[10] it maie B, E, F.　　　[11] be *comes after* once *in* F.　　　[12] breuitie F.
[13] like *not in* E, F.　　　[14—14] 22. Deuteronomy.‡ 27. 2. Kinges F.　(‡ 22 Deuteronomie *for* Deutronomie 22, Deutro. *in* B, E.)

[Bible bits against whoredom.]

Leuit. 18,[1] *Exodus* 22. *Num.* 5, *Eccle.* 9, *Pro.* 23, *Pro.* 7 [2] *verfe,* 24.

Spud. As you haue now prooued by inuincible teftimonies of holy Scripture, that whordome is forbidden by the Lord, fo, I pray you, fhew mee the greeuoufnes thereof by fome feuere & rare examples

Genesis 7, 8.
of Gods iuft iudgement, executed[3] vppon the fame from the begining.

Punishments of whordom in all Ages.
[4] *Philo.* The whole world was deftroyed with water, not any liuing thing left vpon the erth (faue in the Ark of *Noath*[5]) for the fin of whordom, inceft, & brothelry, vfed in thofe daies. *Sodoma* and *Go-morra,* two famous Cities, were confumed with fire and brimftone

[6 leaf 53. B.†]
Genesis 19 ; Genesis 24.
Genesis 20.
[7 H 3]
from heauen for the like fin of whordom, adul[6]terie, and fornication. The citie of the *Sichemits,* man, woman, and childe, weare put to the edge of the [7]fwoord for the rauifhing of *Dina,* the daughter of *Iacob.* The Lord alfo tolde *Abimelech* that if he did not let go vntouched *Sara, Abraham* his[8] wife, bothe he and all his houfholde fhould[9] dye the

C. 26.
Ge. 18.
death, notwithftanding he did it ignorauntly. The very fame hapned to *Ifaac* alfo. *Iudah,*[10] vnderftanding that his daughter in law was impregnate and great with childe, and not knowing by whom, com-

2 Reg. 16.
[Absalon,
Ge. 29.
Reuben,]
manded that she fhould be burned without any further delay.[11] Was not *Abfalon,* king *Dauid* his fonne, plagued all his life for going into his Fathers Concubines? And did not *Achitophel,* who gaue councel fo to do, hang himfelf? Was not *Ruben,* the firft borne fonne of *Iacob,* accurfed for going vp to his Fathers bed ; and loft he not his birth-right, his dignitie, his[12] primacie, ouer his Bretheren 'for the

Iudi. 20.
2 Reg. 13, 12.
[David,
fame? Were there not aboooue threefcore and fiue thoufand men flain for the adulterie doon with one *Leuits* wife? Was not king *Dauid* punifhed all the daies of his life for his adultery doon with *Berfabe, Vrias* his wife? Was not his fonne *Amon,* for lying with[13]

Solomon,]
[1 Reg. 11. B, E, F.]
Thamar, flain? Was not *Salomon,* beeing peruerted with[14] hethen women, caft out of the fauour of GOD, notwithftanding being otherwife the wifeft Prince in all the world? [15]Did not[15] *Achab,* at the perfwa-

---

[1] Leuiticus 11 B, E, F.

[2] 2 Prouer. 7 B, E.   [3] poured forth E, F.

[4] *heading in* F :—Examples of whoredom punished in all ages.

[5] Noah F.   † leaf 53. Punishmentes for Whordom. B.

[6] Abrahams F.   [9] shall F.   [10] Iudas A.   [11] de-delay (*sic*) F.

[12] and B, E, F.   [13] his Sister *added in* F.   [14] with many F.

[15]—[15] *not in* F.

fions of *Iefabel*, his curfed wife, falling [1] to Idolatrie and woorfhiping of Idolles [2] and deuils, fuffer [3] mofte cruel punifhment in this life all his dayes; befides, what he fuffereth now, God onely knoweth. Were not the *Ifraelite* and *Madianitifh* woman both flain [4] by that woorthy man *Phinees*, who ran them both thorow the [5] priuy members with his Iauelin or fwoord? Was not *Sampfon* brought to a miferable end, his eyes beeing bothe put out, and he made to be a laughing ftock to all men, thorow his too much fauouring of wanton women? Was not king *Pharao* wunderfully plagued, but for intending euil in his hart towards *Sara, Abraham* his wife? Did not the Lord flay (with a mofte greeuous mortalitie) foure & twentie thoufand of *the Ifraelites* in one day, for whordome and adulterie with the women of the *Moabites* and *Madianits*?

By thefe, and fuch like fearful Examples of the iuftice of God powred vpon thefe whoremongers & adultrers, we may learn to know the greeuoufnes of the fame, and the punifhment due to all whoremongers and fornicatours, either in this life, or in the World [6] to come, or els in both: for if the Lord deferre the punifhment of whordome in this life, hee referueth it for the world to come, fuffering the wicked to wallow in their finne, and to fil vp the meafure of iniquitie, that their damnation may be iuft. And if the Lord left not fin vnpunifhed, no, not in [7] his moft deer Saints, [8] what he wil [9] doo in them who dayly crucifie him anew, let the world [10] iudge.

Spud. Now am I fully perfwaded, by your inuincible reafons, that there is no fin greater before the face of God then whordome; wherfore, *God graunt that all his may auoid it.*

Philo. You haue faid true, for there is no finne (almoft [11]) comparable vnto it; for befides that it bringeth euerlafting damnation to all that liue therin to the end without repentance, it alfo bringeth thefe inconueniences, with many mo: *vidilicet*, it dimmeth the fight, it impaireth the hearing, it infirmeth *the* finewes, it weakneth the ioynts, it exhaufteth the marrow, confumeth the [12] moifture and fupplement of the body, it riueleth the face, appalleth the countenance, it dulleth

Margin notes:

3 Reg. 21.
[1 leaf 53, back. B.*]
[2 H 3, back]
Num. 25.
Iud. 16.
[Sampfon,

Pharaoh,]
Gene. 12.

[24,000 Israelites

were all punifht for whoremongering.]

[7 leaf 54. B.†]
[8 H 4]

What euils whordome bringeth to mans body in this life.

---

        * leaf 53, back. Examples for Whoremongers. B.
  3 *should be* suffer'd *in* F.   4 for Whoredome *added in* F.
      5 their B, E, F.   6 life E, F.
† leaf 54. Many euils come by whordome. B   9 wil B; shall E, F.
  10 godly E, F.   11 almost *not in* F.   12 the radicall F.

the fpirits, it hurteth the memorie, it weakneth *the* whole body, it bringeth [1]it into a[1] confu*m*ption, it bringeth[2] vlcerations,[3] fcab, fcurf, blain, botch, pocks, & biles; it maketh hoare haires &[4] bald pates; it induceth olde age, &, in fine, bringeth death before nature vrge it, malady enforce it, or age require[5] it.

Sp. Seeing *that* whordome bringeth fuch foure fauce with it, namely,[6] death euerlafting after this life, and fo many difcom*m*odities befides in this life, I wunder that men dare com*m*it the fame fo fecurely as they doo now a dayes.

Philo. It is fo little feared in *Ailgna,* that, vn[7]till [8]euery one hath[8] two or three Baftardes a peece, they efteeme him no man[9] (for that they call a mans deede); infomuch as[10] euery fcuruie boy of twelue, fixteen, or twenty yeeres of age, wil make no confcience of it to haue two or three, peraduenture half a dofen feuerall women with childe at once; and this exploite beeing doon, he fhowes them[11] a faire pair of heeles, and away goeth he, *Euro*[12] *velocius,* as [13]quick as a Bee[13] (as they fay) into fome ftrange place where he is not knowen, where, how he

liueth, let the wife[14] iudge, for, *cœlum non animum mutant qui trans mare currunt;* though they chaunge their place of abode, yet their naughtie difpofitions they retaine ftil.   Then, hauing eftraunged them felues thus for a fmall fpace, they returne againe, not to their priftine curfed life, I dare fay, but vnto[15] their cuntrey, and then no man may fay black is their eye; but all is wel, & they as good chriftians as thofe that fuffer them vnpunifhed.

Spud. The ftate and condition of that Cuntrey is moft miferable, if it be true you report : it weare much better that euerye one had his lawful wife, and euery woman her lawfull husband, as the Apoftle commaundeth, then thus to be[16] drowned[17] in the filthie fin of whordome.

Philo. That is the only falue and foueraine remedy which the lord ordained againft whordome, that thofe who haue not the gift of

---

1—1 *not in* B, E, F.   2 causeth B, E, F.   3 vlceration F.
4 and *not in* B, E, F.   5 constraine F.   6 as namely B, E, F.
          † leaf 54, back. Causes of bastardie in Ailgna. B.
8—8 one hath had F.   10 that E, F.
11 all *added in* E, F.   12 pilo F.
13—13 round as a hall F.   14 world F.   15 to E.
16 lye B, E.   17 and immerged *added in* E ; plunged F.

continencie might mary, and ſo keep their veſſels [1]vndefiled to the

Lord. But, notwithſtanding, in *Ailgna* there is ouer great libertye permitted therin; for litle infants in ſwadling clowts, are often maried by their ambicious Parents and frends, when they know neither good nor euill; and this is the origene of much wickedneſſe, & directlie againſt the word of God, and examples of the primityue age. And beſydes this, you ſhall haue euery ſawcy boy of x, xiiij, xvi, or xx yeres of age, to catch vp a woman & marie her, without any feare of God at all, or reſpect had, either to her religion, wiſdom, integritie of lyfe, or any other vertue; or, which is more, without any reſpecte how they maye lyue together with ſufficient maintenance for their callings and eſtat. No, no; it maketh no matter for theſe things : ſo he haue his pretie puſſie to huggle withall, [2]it forceth not,[2] for that is the only thing he deſireth. Than build they vp a cotage, though but of elder poals, in euery lane end, almoſt, wher they lyue as beggers al their life.[3] This filleth the land with ſuch ſtore of poore people,[4] that in ſhort tyme (except ſome caution[5] be prouided to preuent the ſame), it is like to growe to great pouertie and ſcarſnes,[6] which, God forbid !

Sp. I canot ſee how this geare ſhold be holpen.

Philo. What if a reſtraint were made *that* [7]none (except vppon ſpeciall and vrgente cauſes) should marie before they come to xx or xxiiij [8]yeeres, or, at *the*[9] leaſt, before they be xiiij or xviii yeeres old, would not this make fewer beggers than now there are ?

Sp. But if this were eſtabliſhed, than ſhould we haue moe Baſtards; and of the two, I had rather we had many [10]legittimats than many illegittimates.[10]

Philo. The occaſion of begetting of manye Baſtards were ſoone cut of, if the puniſhment which either [11] God his lawe doth allowe, or

---

* leaf 55. Causes of many beggers in Ailgna. B.
[2]—[2] *not in* B, E, F.   [3] life after B, E, F.
[4] Mendicantes, or to speak plainely §, of Beggers as wee call them B, E.   § E *has* plainlyer. *For* 'of poore people,' F *has* of Beggers as we call them F.
[5] remedy F.   [6] extream misery F.
† leaf 55, back. Remedies to suppresse whordome. B.   [9] the *not in* E, F.
[10]—[10] children lawfully begot than many Bastards F.
[11] either *not in* F.

els which good pollicy [1]doth conftitute,[1] were [2]aggrauated and executed[2] vppon the Offenders.

For the punifhment appointed for whordom now is fo light that
they efteeme not of it; thei feare it not, they make but a ieft of it.
For what great thing is it to go ij or three dayes in a white fheete[3]
before the congregation, and that fomtymes not paft an howre or two
in a day, hauing their vfuall garments vnderneth, as commonly they
haue?[4] This impunitie (in refpecte of condigne punifhement,
which that [5]vice requireth) doth rather animate and imbolden them
to the acte, than feare them from it. In fo much as I haue heard
fome mifcreants impudently fay, that he is but a beaft that for fuch
white lyuered punifhment would abftaine from fuche gallant paftyme :
but certen it is that they who thinke it fuche fweet meate here, fhall
find the fawce fowre [6]and ftiptick[7] enough in Hell. [[8]And yet as
light and as eafie as this punifhment is, it may be, and is daiely
difpenfed[9] with-all for monie : and this is thought to be the beft
kinde of punifhment, to punifhe them by the purfe. Then the whiche,
what can be a greater diforder in a Chriftian common wealth ? Is this
any thyng els then to buye and fell the bodies and foules of Chriftians
for monie ? Can the Pope himfelf doe any more then this ? Is not
this a maintenance of the Stewes ? Yea, fo long as this is vfed, the
Stewes fhall neuer be out of Ailgna. Let the Magiftrates therefore
of the Ecclefiaftical Hierarchie (for to them I fpeake) take heede
that thei be not maintainers of Stewes and whoredome, whereof thei
would fo faine bee thought to bee fuppreffors. For this kind of
difpenfing with Whoredome, Adulterie, and Fornication for monie,
and fettyng of them free a *culpa, rubore*,[10] *& pœna*, [11]in this worlde,[11]
from the falte [12]it felf, [13]from the fhame,[13] and punifhment due for the
fault ? What is it els then not onely a maintenaunce, but alfo a

The punish-
ment for
whordome
ouer remisse.

[5 leaf 56. B.†]

[6 H 6]

[Whoredome
ought not to be
punished by the
purse. E, F.]

[Let the Arch-
deacons look to
it!]

---

[1]—[1] hath constituted F.   [2]—[2] executed and aggravate B ; inflicted F.
   [3] or els in a Cope (a ridiculous kinde of punishmente) *added in* B, E, F.
   [4] [And truely I can not a little admire, nor yet sufficiently deplore the *
(* that F.) wickednesse of the Ecclesiasticall Magistrates, in not punishing more
greeuously, this horrible sinne of whoredome : for to goe in a sheete with a
white wande in their handes, is but a plain mockyng of God, and of his Lawes.
Added in B, E, F.]   † leaf 56. *No head line.* B.
   [7] bitter F.   [8] *From this, to p.* 99, *l.* 16, *not in* A.
   [9] suspensed *in* E.   [10] *not in* F.   [11]—[11] *not in* E, F.
    [12] falte B, E ; fault F.   [13]—[13] *not in* F.

[ſtirryng of them vp to commit whoredome, when for a little monie thei [1]maie be diſcharged of all gilte?   And this beyng certaine, or at leaſt very likely, *that* whoſoeuer getteth one with child, of what reputation or degree ſoeuer ſhe be of, (if he be ſingle) he ſhall be forced to marie her, and that[2] for a little peece of monie, thei may both haue a Bull of diſpenſation. This beyng ſo, who, I ſaie, will not ſeeke to aſpire as high as he can,[3] and aſſay[4] to deflower (in hope of further gaine) as many as he maie.[5]   This ſiluer puniſhment is it, that defileth honeſt Matrones, polluteth chaſt Virgines, and diſhoneſteth poore Maides, to their vtter ſhame and vndoyng for euer. I ſaie nothyng, how the monie receiued for theſe diſpenſations is beſtowed, how ſpent, nor wherevpon[6] imployed. The Lord for his mercies ſake, giue them grace to puniſhe vice ſeuerely, as the worde of God doeth commaunde, and not after their owne ſenſuall deſires,[7] and licencious luſtes, that God maie be glorified, and their conſciences diſburdened[8] at the greate daie of the Lorde. *Added in* B, E, F.]

Spud. What puniſhment would you haue inflicted vppon ſuch as commit this horrible kinde of ſinne?

Philo. I would wiſh that the Man or Woman, who are certenlye knowen, without all ſcruple or doübte, to haue committed the horryble fact of whordome, adulterie, inceſt, or fornication, eyther ſhould[9] drinke a full[10] draught of *Moyſes* cuppe, that is, taſt of preſent death [as Gods word doth [11] commaunde, and good pollicie allowe B, E]; or els, if *that* be thought too ſeuere (for[12] in euill, men will be more mercifull than the Author of mercie him ſelfe, but in goodneſſe, fare well mercy) than wold Goᴅ they might be cauterized and ſeared with a hote yron on[13] the cheeke, forehead, or ſome other parte of their bodye that might be ſeene, to the [14]end the honeſt and chaſt Chriſtians might be diſcerned from the adulterous Children of Sathan.[14]   But (alas!) this vice (with the reſt) wanteth ſuch due puniſhement as Goᴅ his Word doth commaunde to be executed[15] thervppon.[16]

[*To l.* 16 *is not in* A.]

[To diſpence with whoredome for money, is a playne maintenance of whoredome. E, F.]
[[1] leaf 56, back. B.*]

---

* leaf 56, back. Due punishment for whordome. B.   [2] thus F.
[3] may *in* E, F.   [4] assay *not in* E, F.   [5] can *in* E, F.
[6] whereunto *in* E, F.   [7] appetites F.   [8] discharged F.
[9] eyther *comes after* should *in* F.   [10] full *not in* F.
† leaf 57. A late exa*m*ple for whordom, in Ailg. B.
[12] as *in* E, F.   [13] vppon F.
[14]—[14] end that the adulterous children of Sathan, might be discerned from the honest and chast Christians B, E, F.   [15] inflicted F.   [16] vppon them E, F.

[Magiftrates
wink at whore-
dom.]
The Magiſtrates wincke at it, or els, as looking thorowe their fingers, they fee it, and will not fee it.

[1] And therfore the Lorde is forced too take the ſword into his owne hands, and to execute puniſhment him felfe, becaufe the Magiſtrates will not.[2]

[3 H 6, back]
[3] For better proof wherof, marke this ſtrange & fearful iudgment of god, shewed vpon two adulterous perſons there,[4] euen the laſt day in effect, the remembrance wherof is yet green in their heds.

[A most dread-
full example of
two notorious
whoremongers.
E.]
[5 W. Brustar.]
There was a man whoſe name was *W. Ratſurb*[5], being certenly knowen to be a notorious vſerer (and yet pretending alway a ſingular zeale to religion, fo that he wold feldom tymes go without a byble about him : but fee the iudgements of God vpon them that will take his word in their mouthes, and yet lyue cleane contrarie, making the
[6 leaf 57, back.
B.†]
[Bridewell.]
word of God a cloke to couer their [6]finne and naughtyneffe withall[7]); who, vppon occaſion of buſines, viſiting *Lewedirb*, a place appointed for the correction of ſuch that[8] be wicked lyuers, faw there a famous whore, but a very proper Woman, whom (as is faid) he knew not; but whether he did or not, certen it is that he procured her delyuery from thence, bayled her, &, hauing put away his owne wife before, kept her in his chamber, vfing her at his pleafure. Whyleft thefe two
[Whoremongers
members of the
Deuill. E.]
members of the deuil were playing the vile *Sodomits* together in his chamber, & hauing a litle pan of coles before them, wherin was a very litle fire, it pleafed GOD, euen in his wrath, to ſtrike thefe two perfons dead in a moment. The Woman, falling ouer the pan of coles, was burned, that all her bowels gushed out : the man was
[9 H 7]
[The punish-
ment of whor-
dome by the
Lord himself
from heauen. E.]
founde lying by, his [9]cloths in fome partes being fcorched and burned, & fome partes of his body alfo. But, which is moft wonderfull, his arme was burned to the very boone, his shirt fleeue and dublet not once perished, nor tutched with the fire. Wherby may be thought, & not without great probabilitie of truth, that it was euen the fire of God his wrath from Heauen, and not any natural fire from the earth. And in this wonderfull & fearfull maner weare thefe cupple founde : which God graunt may be a document[10] to all that

[1] *From here to p.* 101, *end of line* 3, *not in* F.
[2] not do it *added in* E.   [4] in Munidnol, *for* there E.
† leaf 57, back. Two Adulterers burned in Ailgna. B.
[7] as many do in these daies *added in* E.   [8] as B, E.
[10] or lesson admonitorie *added in* B, E.

heare or read the ſame, to avoyde the like offence, and to all Magiſ-
[1]trates an Example to ſee the ſame puniſhed with more ſeueritie, to　[¹ leaf 58. B.*]
the glorie of God and their owne diſcharge.

But ſo farre[2] are ſome from ſuffering condigne puniſhment for this
horrible ſinne, that they get good maintenance with practiſing the
ſame.　For ſhall you not[3] haue ſome, yea many thouſands, that liue
vppon nothing els, and yet go clothed Gentlewomenlike, both in their
ſilks,[4] and otherwyſe, with[5] their fingers clogged with rings, their wriſts
with bracelets & Iewels, and their purſes full of gold and ſiluer.　And
hereof they make no conſcience, ſo their Husbands know it not.　Or　[Many gette
great liuinges
with practiſing of
whordome. E,F.]
if they doo, ſome are ſuch peaſants, and ſuch maycocks, that either
they will not, or (which is truer) they dare not, reproue them for it.
But & if the Husband once reproue them for their miſde[6]meanour,　[⁶ H 7, back]
than they conſpire his death by ſome meane or other.　And all this
commeth to paſſe becauſe the puniſhment therof is [7]no extremer, as it
ought to be[7]; And ſome, both Gentlemen and others (wherof ſome I
know) are ſo nuſled herein, that hauing put awaye their owne wyues,
do[8] keepe whores openly, without any great puniſhment for it; and　[Putting away
honest wiues,and
retaining of ¹⁰
whores. E, F.]
hauing beene conuented before the [9]magiſtery, and there beene[9]
depoſed vppon a booke to put away their whores, haue put them
foorth at one doore, and taken them in at the other.

And thus they dally in their othes with the Lord, and ſtoppe the
courſe of the lawe [11]with *rubrum argentum*,[12] wherof they haue ſtore　[¹¹ leaf 58, back.
B.†]
to beſtowe vppon ſuch wickedneſſe, but [13]haue not a mite[13] to giue
towards any good purpoſe.

Wherfore, in the name of God, let all men that haue put away　[Lawe ought to
be executed
without par-
tialitie. E, F.]
their honeſt wyues be forced to take them again, and abandon all
whores, or els to taſte of the law.　And let all whores be cut of with
the ſword of [14]right iudgement[14]; For as long as this immunitie and
impunitie is permitted amongeſt vs, let vs neuer looke to pleaſe God,
but rather prouoke his heuie iudgements againſt vs.　And the reaſon

---

* leaf 58. Knowne whores kept openly. B.　² Yea ſo farre of F.
³ not *omitted in* F.　⁴ and Veluets *added in* F.　⁵ *not in* F.
⁷—⁷ ſo eaſie and gentle as it is F.　⁸ they E, F.
⁹—⁹ magiſtrates and there F.　¹⁰ of *not in* F.
† leaf 58, back. Great exceſſe and belly cheere. B.　E *has* Whoredome:
Honeſt wiues put away.　¹² vnguentum F.
¹³—¹³ not a peny F.　¹⁴—¹⁴ juſtice F.

is, for that there is no ſinne in all the World, but theſe whores and
whoremaiſters will [1] willingly attempt and atcheiue for the[1] inioying of
their whordome. [2] And Hell, deſtruction, and death euerlaſting, is the
guerdon therof, and yet men cannot [3] be aware[3] of it. The Lord
[4] remooue it from all his Children,[4] and preſent them blameles before
his tribunall ſeate, without ſpotte or wrincle at that[5] great day of the
Lord !

Spud. What [6] memorable thing[6] els haue you ſeen there frequented ? for ſeeing you haue begun in parte, I pray you deſcribe the
whole.

Gluttonie[7] and drunkenneſſe[8] in Ailg[na].

Philo. I Haue ſeene that which greeueth mee to report. The
People there are marueilouſly giuen to daintie fare, gluttonye, belli-
cheer, & many alſo to drunkenneſſe & gourmandice.

[9] *Sp.* That is a manifeſt argument of good hoſpitality, which
both is commended in the word of God, & which I know you wil not
reprehende.

Ph. Godly hoſpitalitie is a thing in no wiſe worthy of reprehenſion, but rather of great commendation ; for many haue receiued
Angels into their houſes, at vnawares, by vſing the ſame, as *Abraham,
Lot, Tobias,* & many others.   Yet if hoſpitality flow ouer into ſuperfluitie & riotous exceſſe, it is not tolerable : for[10] now adaies, if the
table be not couered[11] from the one end to the other, as thick as one
diſh can ſtand by another, [12] with delicat meats[13] of ſundry ſorts, one
cleane different from an other, and to euery diſh a ſeuerall ſawce
appropriat to[14] his kinde, it is thought there vnworthye the name of a
dinner.   Yea, ſo many diſhes ſhal you haue peſteruing the table[15] at
once, as the infaciableſt *Helluo,* the denouringeſt glutton, or the greed-
ieſt cormorant that is[16], can ſcarfe eat of euery one a litle. And theſe
many ſhall you haue at the firſt courſe ; as many at the ſecond ; and,
peraduenture, moe at the third ; beſydes other ſweet condyments,[17] and
delicat confections of ſpiceries, and I cannot tell what. And to theſe

[²H 8]

Daintie fare,
gluttony and
gourmandice
vsed in Ailg.
[⁹ leaf 59. B.*]

Godly hospi-
talitie to be
commended.

[¹² H 8, back]

Varitie of
dishes and]
meats, with
their curious
sawces.

Excesse of
meats.

[1]—[1] gredily commit for F.   [3]—[3] beware B, E, F.
   [4]—[4] keep all his children from it F.   [5] the F.   [5]—[6] notable abuses F.
         [7] The Gluttonie B, E, F.   [8] excesse B, E, F.
   * leaf 59. Great excesse in delicate fare. B.   [10] and B, E.   [11] pestered F.
   [13] meat F.   [14] in F.   [15] thereon F.   [16] ever was B, E, F.   [17] iunkets F.

dainties, all kind of wynes are not wanting, you may be fure. Oh, what nifitie[1] is this! what vanitie, exceffe,[2] ryot and fuperfluitie is heare! Oh, farewell former world! For I haue heard my Father fay *that* in his dayes, one difh or two of good wholfome [3] meate was thought fufficient for a man of great worfhip to dyne withall; and if they had three or four kinds, it was reputed a fumptuous feaft. A good peece of beef was thought tha*n* good meat, and able for the beft; but now it is thought too groffe, for their tender ftomacks [4]are not able[4] to difgeft [5]fuch crude and harfh meats[5] : For if they fhold, (their ftomacks being fo queafie as they be, and not able[6] to concoct it) they fhould but[7] euacuat the fame againe, as other filthie excrements,[8] their bodies receiuing no noorifh[9]ment therby, or els [10]they fhould[10] lye ftincking in their ftomacks, as dirte in a filthie finck or pryuie. If this be fo, I marueile how oure fore-Fathers lyued, who eat litle els but cold meats, groffe and hard of difgefture. Yea, the[11] moft of them fead vppon graine, corne, roots, pulfe, herbes, weeds, and fuch other bag-gage, and yet liued longer then wee, [12]helthfuller then we, were[12] of better complection then we, and much ftronger then we in euerie refpect : wherfore I cannot perfwade my felf otherwife, but that our nicenes and curioufnes in dyet ·hath altered our nature, diftempered our bodies, and made vs more[13] fubiect to millions of[14] difcrafies and[14] difeafes then euer weare our Forefathers fubiect vnto, and confequently of fhorter life then they.

Spud. They wil afke you again, wherfore god made fuch varietie of meats, but to be eaten of men? what anfwere giue you to that?

[15] *Philo.* The Lord our God ordained, indeede, the vfe of meat[16] and drinks for man to fuftain the fraile, caduke,[17] and brittle eftate[18] of his mortall body withall[19] for a time; But he gaue [20]it him not[20] to[21] delight and [22]wallow therin coutinually[22]; for as the olde Adage faith, *Non*

Marginal notes:

The austerity and Godly simplicity of the former World in meats and drinkes. [3 leaf 59, back. B.*]

Nice, tender stomacks. [*not in* F.]

[9 I 1]

The faraginie or rough fare of our Fore-fathers.

Our nice fare hath altered our bodies and chaunged our nature.

[15 leaf 60. B.†]

---

[1] what prodigality *added in* F.　　　[2] what excesse F.
* leaf 59, back. Hard fare holsomest. B. F. *From* such *to* pryuie, *line* 13, *not in* F.　　[4—4 *and* 5—5 *not in*, B, E, F.　　[6] so vnable *for* not able B, E.
[7] but *not in* B ; might happely E.　　[8] crude and indigest B, E.
[10—10] it would B ; might E.　　· [11] the *not in* F.
[12] were *before* helthfuller B, E, F.　　[13] more *not in* B, E, F.　　[14—14] *not in* F.
† leaf 60. How meates bryng destruction. B.　　[16] meates B, E, F.　　[17] *not in* F.
[18] state F.　　[19] withall *not in* F.　　[20—20] the*m* not unto him B, E, F.　　[21] for F.
[22—22] pleasure onely, but for necessitie and neede F ; as the swine do in ye mire *added after* continually *in* B, E.

Medietie to be
obserued in
meats.

[7 I 1, back]

viuendum[1] vt edamus, fed edendum[2] vt viuamus: Wee [3]muft not liue[3] to
eat, but wee muft[4] eat to liue; wee muft not fwill and ingurgitate our[5]
ftomacks fo ful,[6] as no more can be crammed[7] in.   The Lord willed[8]
that they fhould be ordinarie[9] meanes to preferue[10] the ftate of[10] our
bodyes[11] a time, whilfte we liue and foiourne in this vafte wildernes
of the worlde, but not that they fhould be inftruments of deftruction
to vs bothe of body and foule.   And truely they are no leffe when

When meats
and drinks are
Instruments of
destruction
vnto vs.

they are taken immoderatly without the feare of God.   And[12] dooth
not the impletion and facietie of meates and drinks prouoke luft? as
Hiero faith, Venter Mero eftuans fpumat in libidinem, the belly enflamed
with wine burfteth foorth into luft.   Doth not luft bring foorth finne,

Ge. 24.

and fin bring[13] foorth death?   The Children of Ifrael, giuing themfelues to delicat fare & gluttony, fel to Idolatrie, facriledg & apoftafie,
worfhipping ftocks, ftones, and deuils, in-fted of the liuing God.   The
fonnes of Hely the Prieft, giuing themfelues to daintie fare & belly-

1 Reg. 2.[14]
[[15] leaf 60, back.
B.*]
[Bible instances
of the evils of
Gluttony.]

cheere, fell into fuch fin as the Lord flew them all, & their fa[15]ther
alfo, for that he chaftifed them not for the fame.   The Children of
bleffed Iob, in midft of all their banquetings & ryot, were flain by
the lord, the whole houfe falling vpon them, and deftroying them
moft pitifully.   Balthafar, king of the Chaldeans, in midft of all his

Daniel 5,
verse 5.[16]

good cheer, faw a hand writing vpon the wall thefe woords, mene[17]
techel upharfin, fignifiing that his kingdome fhould be taken from him;

[[18] sign. I 2]
Luc. 16.

and fo it was, and he flain the fame night by the[18] hand of the lord.
The rich glutton in the Gofpel, for his riotous feaftings & propofter-
ous[19] liuing, was condemned to the fire of hel.   Our Father Adam,
with all his of-fpring (to the end of the world) was condemned to
hel-fire for taking one apple to fatisfie his glotonus defire withall.

Mat. 4.
[The Devil
tempted Christ
through Glut-
tony.]

Gluttony was one of the chiefeft canons wherwith the deuil affailed
Chrifte, thinking therby to batter his kingdome & to win the feeld
for euer; yet not withftanding the greeuoufnes heerof, the fame is
thought to be a coutenance & a great credit to a man in Ailg[na].   But
true hofpitality confifteth not in many difhes, nor in fundry forts of meats

---

[1] viuimus F.   [2] edimus F.   [3]—[3] liue not F.   [4] must not in F.
[5] so much into our B, E, F.   [6] so ful not in B, E, F.   [8] prouided them E, F.
[9] as F.   [10]—[10] not in F.   [11] for a B, E, F.   [12] Besides that B, E, F.
[13] bringes F.   [14] 3 Reg. 2. in B, E, F.
[*] leaf 60, back. Small reliefe for the poore. B.   E has Gluttony punished.
[16] verse 5. 25. in B, E, F.   [17] mene added in B, E, F.   [19] inordinate F.

(the ſubſtance wherof is chaunged[1] almoſte into accidents thorow
their curious cookries, &[2] which doo help to[2] rot the[3] bodies & ſhorten
their daies) but rather in giuing liberally to the poor and indigent[4]
members of Ieſus Chriſte, helping them to meat, drink, lodging,
clothing, [5]& ſuch other neceſſaries wherof they ſtand in need.

But ſuch is their hoſpitality, *that* the poor haue *the* leaſt part of it :
you ſhal haue 20, 40, 60, yea a C *li.* ſpent in ſome one houſe in ban-
queting & feſting, yet *the* poor ſhall haue litle or nothing : if they
haue any thing, it is but *the* refuſe[6] meat, ſcraps & parings,[7] ſuch as
a dog would ſcarſe eat ſomtimes ; & wel if they can get *that* too : inſted
wherof, [8]not a few haue whipping cheer to feed the*m*[9] withall.   [10]it
is cou*n*ted but a ſmal matter for [11]a man that can ſcarſlie diſpend
fortie pound[12] by the yeer, to beſtow againſt one time, ten or twentie
pound[12] therof in ſpices. And truely, ſo long & ſo greeuouſly hath this
exceſſe of gluttonie and daintie fare ſurffeted in *Ailgna*, as I feare mee,
it will ſpue out many of his Maiſters out of dores before it be long.
But as ſome be ouer largeous,[13] ſo other ſome are ſpare enough ; for
when any meat is ſtirring, then lock they vp their gates, that no man
may come in. An-other forte[14] haue ſo many houſes that they viſit
them [15]once in vii yeer[16] ; many Chimnies, but little ſmoke ; faire
houſes, but ſmall hoſpitalitie. And to be plaine, there are three cankers,
which, in proceſſe of time, wil eat vp the whole common Welth,[17] if
ſpeedy reformatio*n* be not had, namely, daintie Fare, gorgious Build-
ings, and ſumptuous Apparel ; which three *Abuſes*[18], [19]eſpecially, yet
not without their cofin germanes, doo floriſh there. *God remooue them
thence, for his Chriſtes ſake.*

Spud. I had thought that dainty fare & good cheer had both nooriſhed
the body perfe&ctly, and alſo prolo*n*ged life[20] ; & dooth it not ſo think you ?

Philo. Experience, as [by][21] my former intimations you may

Wherin hos-
pitalitie
conſiſteth.

[5 leaf 61. B.*]

The ſmall
releef of the
poore.

[11 I 2, back]

Locking vp of
Gates when
meat is ſtir-
ring.

Three deuour-
ing Cankers.

[19 leaf 61, back.]
B.†]

---

[1] changed E.
[2]—[2] impotionate ſlibber ſawces which B, E, F ; (ſibber *in* B.)
[3] their B, E, F.   [4] needy F.   * leaf 61. Small hoſpitalitie in Ailgna. B.
[6] refuge A ; refuſe B, E, F.   [7] patrings A ; parings B, E, F.
[8] now and then not B, E, F.   [9] themſelues B, E, F.   [10] yea it B, F.
[12] poundes F.   [13] and profluous herein *added in* F.
[14] forte A ; ſorte B, E, F.   [15] not once B, E, F.   [16] yeares F.
[17] of Ailgna *added in* B, E, F.   [18] three deuouryng Cankers B, E, F.
    † leaf 61, back. Diuerſitie of meates hurtfull. B.
[20] life greatly B, E, F.   [21] by F ; in B, E ; *both* by *and* in *wanting in* A.

Who more
subiect to
infirmities
then they that
fare best?
[¹ sign. I 3. A.]

gather, teacheth clean contrary; for who is ficklier the*n* they that fare delicioufly euery day? who is corrupter? who belcheth more? who looketh wurffe, who is weaker [1]and feebler then they? who hath more filthie colour,[2] flegme, and putrifaction (repleat[3] with groffe humors) then they? and, to be breef, who dyeth fooner then they? Doo wee not fee the poor man that eateth brown bread (wherof fome is made of Rye, barlie, peafon, beans, oates, and fuch other groffe graines) & drinketh fmall drink, yea, fometimes water, feedeth vpon milk, butter, and cheefe; (I fay) doo wee not fee fuch a one helth-fuller, ftronger,[4] and longer liuing,[5] then the other that fare[6] daintily euery day? And how fhould it be otherwife? for wil not the eating of diuers and fundry kindes of meats, of diuers[7] operations and quali-ties (at one meale) engender diftemperance in the[8] body? And the

Eating of di-
uers meats
at one time
hurtful.
[¹⁰ leaf 62. B.†]

body diftempered, wil it not fall into fundry defeafes? one meat is[9] of hard difgefture, another of light[9]; & whilft the meate of hard dif-gefture is in concocti*n*g, the other meat[10] of light difgefture dooth putrifie and ftink: & this is the very mother of all difeafes. one is of this qualitie, another of *that*; one of this operatio*n*, another of that; one kind of meat is good for this thing, another is naught for that. Then, how can all thefe contrarieties & difcripancies[11] agree togither in one body at one & the fame time? wil not one contrary impugne his contrary[12]? one enemy refift an other? Then, what wifeman is he that wil receiue all thefe enemies into[13] the caftle

The spedy de-
cay of those
that geue
the*m*felues to
daintie fare.
[¹⁴ I 3, back]

of[13] his[14] body at one time? Doo we not fe, by experie*n*ce, that they *tha*t giue the*m*felues to dainty fare and fweet meats are neuer in helth? dooth not their fight wax dim, their eares hard of hering, their teeth rot & fall out? dooth not their breth ftink, their ftomack[15] belch foorth filthy humors, and their memory decay? doo not their fpirits and fences become heuie & dul by reafon of[16] [17]exhalations & impure vapors, which rife vp in[18] [17]their gingered brefts & fpiced ftomacks? &,

---

² choller E, F.   ³ together E, F.   ⁴ fairer complectioned *added in* B, E, F.
⁵ liued F.   ⁵ fared F.   ⁷ contrary B, E, F.   ⁶ the *not in* F.
⁹—⁹ hard of disgestion, another light F.
† leaf 62. The decay of daintie feeders. B.
¹¹ repugnacies F.   ¹² eontrary A.   ¹³—¹³ *not in* F.
¹⁵ stomackes F.   ¹⁶ of the B, E, F.
¹⁷—¹⁷ the filthy vapours and stinking fumes which rise from F.
¹⁸ from B, E.

fumyng vp to *the* hed, they[1] mortifie *the* vitall fpirits & intellectiue powers. [2]dooth not[2] *the* whole body become[3] purfie & corpulent, yea, fomtimes decrepit therwith,[4] & ful of all filthy corruption? *The Lord keep his chofen from the tafting therof.*[5]

[6]*Sp.* You fpake of drunkennes, what fay you of *that*?

[7]*Phi.* I fay *that* it is a horrible vice, & too too much vfed in *Ail*[gna]. Euery cuntrey, citie, towne, village, [8]& other,[8] hath[9] abundance of alehoufes, tauerns, & Innes, [10]which are fo fraughted[10] with mault-wormes, night & day, that you would wunder to fe them. You fhal haue them there fitting at *the* wine and goodale all the day long, yea, all the night too,[11] peraduenture [12]a whole[12] week togither, fo long as any money is left; fwilling, gulling, & carowfing from one to another, til neuer a one can fpeak a redy woord. Then, when with the fpirit of the buttery they are thus poffeffed, a world it is to confider their geftures[13] & demenors,[14] how they ftut and ftammer, ftagger & reele too & fro like madmen: [15]fome vomiting, fpewing, & difgorging their filthie ftomacks; other fome [16](*Honor fit auribus*)[16] piffing vnder the boord as they fit, & which is moft horrible, fome fall to fwering, curfing, & banning, interlacing their fpeeches with curious tearms of blafphemie, to *the* great difhonour of God, and offence of the godly eares[17] prefent.[18]

Sp. But they wil fay, *that* god ordained wines & ftrong drinks to cheer *the* hart & to fuftain the body[19]; therfore it is lawful to vfe them to *that* end.

Philo. Meats (moderatly taken[20]) corroborate[21] *the* body, refrefh *the* arteries, & reuiue the fpirits, making them apter, euery member, to doo his office as god hath appointed[22]; but being immoderatly taken

[7 leaf 62, back. B.*]

The beaftly vice of drunknees frequented in Ailg[na].

[15 sign. I 4. A.]

The fpirite of the buttery is drunknes and exceffe.

The lothsome qualities of those that be drunke.

[21 leaf 63. B.†]

---

[1] they *not in* B, E, F.   [2—2] in so much that F.
[3] becommeth F.   [4] withall F.
[5] *A new chapter-heading in* B *and* E *here* :—Drunkenneffe in Ailgna.
[6] *heading in* F :—Drunkenneffe in England.
* leaf 62, back. The beaftly vice of drunkenneffe. B.
[8—8] and other places B, E, F.   [9] haue F.
[10—10] in them, which are haunted F.   [11] too *not in* F.
[12—12] all the F.   [13] their countenances *added in* F.
[14] one towardes an other, and towardes every one els, *added in* B, E, F.
[16—16] *not in* F.   [17] hearers B, E, F.   [18] present *not in* E, F.
[19] body withall B, E, F.   [20] by the blessing of God F.
† leaf 63. The discommodities of drunkennes. B.
[22] them *added in* E, F.

The transfi-
guration uf
those that be
drunke.

(as commonly they be), they are inftrumeזts of damnation to *the*
abufers ¹of *the* fame,¹ & noorifh not *the* body, but corrupt it rather,
²& cafteth² it into a world³ of defeafes. And⁴ a man once drunk with
wine or ftrong drink, rather refembleth a brute beafte then a chriftian
man ; for doo not his eies begin to ftare & to be red, fiery & blered,
blubbering foorth feas of teares ? dooth he not frothe & fome at the
mouth like a bore ? dooth not his tung faulter and ftammer in his
mouth ? dooth not his hed feeme as heuie as a milftone, he⁵ not being
able⁶ to bear it vp ? Are not his wits & fpirits, as it were, drowned ?
Is not his vnderftanding altog[et]her decayed ? doo not his hands, & all
his body⁷, quiuer⁸ & fhake, as it were, with a quotidiaז feuer ? ⁹Befides

[¹ˣ I 4, back]

The difcom-
modities of
drunkennes

thefe,⁹ it cafteth him¹⁰ into a dropfie or plu¹¹refie, nothing fo foon ; it
infeebleth the finewes, it weakneth *the* natural ftrength, it corrupteth
the blood, it diffolueth *the* whole man at *the* length, and finally
maketh him forgetful of him-felf altogither, fo that what he dooth
being drunk, he remembreth not, being fober. The Drunkard, in his
drunkennes, killeth his freend, reuileth his louer, difclofeth fecrets,

[¹³ leaf 63, back.
B.†]

and regardeth no man : he either¹² expelleth all feare ¹³of god out of
his minde, all looue of his freends &¹⁴ kinffolkes, all remembrance of
honeftie, ciuilitie, & humanitie ; fo that I will not feare to call drunk-

Drunkerds
wurffe then
Beafts.

erds beafts, and no men ; and much wurffe then beafts, for beafts
neuer exceed in¹⁵ fuch kind of exceffe or fuperfluitie, but alway *modum
adhibent appetitui*,¹⁶ they meafure their appetites by the rule of neceffitie ; *which, would God wee would doo*.

Spud. Seeing it is fo great an offence before God, I pray you
fhow me fome teftimonies of the holy Scripture againft it ; for
whatfoeuer is euil, *the* woord of God, I doubt not, reproueth the
fame.

Philo. It feemeth you haue not read *the* holy fcripture very much,
for if you had, you fhould haue found it not only fpoke againft, but
alfo throweז down euen to hel : for proof whereof, of infinit places I

---

¹——ᵗ thereof E, F.   ²——² caftyng B, F.   ³ sea F.
        ⁴ besides E, F.   ⁵ he *not in* E, F.   ⁶ beeing not able F.
        ⁷ euibrate *added in* B, E ; tremble F.   ⁸ quauer F.
        ⁹——⁹ *not in* E, F.   ¹⁰ also *added in* E, F.   ¹² vtterly E, F.
                † leaf 63, back. Drunkardes worfe then Beafts. B.
        ¹⁴ and *not in* B.   ¹⁵ in any B, E, F.
        ¹⁶ appetitui F ; appetitum A, *with* m *altered by the pen to* i.

wil recite a few.   The Prophet *Eſaias* thundereth out againſt it, ſaying, *ve qui conſurgitis mane ad ebrietate*m *ſectanda*m : ' [1]Wo be to
them that ryſe earlie to followe drunkenneſſe, wallowing therein from
morning to night, vntill they be ſet on fire with wyne & ſtrong
drinke.   Therfore gapeth hell, & openeth her mouth wyde, that the
glory, multitude, and welth of them that delight therin, may go
downe into it,' ſaith the Prophet. The prophet *Hoſeas* ſaith, *fornicatio,*
*vinu*m et *muſtum auferunt* [2] *animum.*   Whordome, wyne, [3]& ſtrong
drinke, infatuat *the* heart of man.

The Prophet *Ioel* biddeth all Drunkards awake,[4] ſaying, ' weepe
and howle, you winebibbers, for the wickedneſſe of deſtrućtion that
ſhall fall vppon you.'

The Prophet *Habacuck* ſoundeth a moſt dreadfull alarme not only
to all Drunkards, but alſo to all that make them drunken, ſaying, ' wo
be to him that geueth his Neighbour drinke till he be drunke, that
thou mayſt ſee his priuities.'   *Salomon* ſaith, ' wyne maketh a Man to
be ſcornfull, and ſtrong drinke [6] maketh a Man vnquiet : who ſo taketh
pleaſure in it, ſhall not be wiſe.' In an other place, 'keep not companie
with wynebibbers and riotous Perſons, for ſuch as be Drunkards ſhal
come to beggerie.' In the xxiij [7] of his Prouerbes he ſaith : 'To whome
is woo ? To whome is ſorow ? to whome is ſtrife ? to whome is murmuring ? to whome are wou*n*ds without cauſe ? and to whome are
red eyes ?   Euen to the*m* that [8]tarie longe at the wyne, to them that
go and ſeek mixt wyne.'   And, againe : ' Looke not thou vppon the
wyne when it is red, and when it ſheweth his colour in the[9] cup, or
gooth downe pleaſantlie, for in the end it will bite like a ſerpent, and
hurt like a Cockatriſe, or Baſilicock, which ſlay [10] or kill men with the
poiſon of their ſighte.'   Again, ' it is not for Kings to drinke wyne,
nor for Princes to drinke ſtrong drinke.' Our Sauiour Chriſt, [11]in the
goſpell of *S. Luke*, biddeth vs take heed that we ' be not ouercome
with ſurffeting and drunknes and cares of this lyfe, leaſt the day of the
Lorde come vppon vs vnawares.'

Paule [13] to the *Epheſians*, biddeth beware that we ' be not dru*n*k [14]

Eſais 5.
[[1] ſign. I 5. A.]

Testimonies
against drunkennesse out of
the word of
GOD.

Hoseas c. 4.
[[3] leaf 64. B.*]

Ioel 1.[5]

Habacuck 2.

Prouerb c. 20.
[Solomon against
drunkenness.]

Prouerb 23.

[[8] I 5, back]

[Solomon against
drunkenness.]

Prouerb 31.
[[11] leaf 64, back.
B.†]

Luc. 21.

Ephe. 5.[15]

---

[2] auferent F.   * leaf 64. Testimonies against Drunkards. B.
[4] wayle E, F.   [5] Joel 2 E.   [6] wine F.   [7] twenty and three F.
   [9] any B.   [10] slea F.   † leaf 64, back. Drunkennesse forbidden. B.
      [13] S. Paule B, E, F.   [14] drunken F.   [16] *not in* E, F.

with wine, wherin is exceſſe, but to be filled with *the* ſpirit.' The ſame apoſtle, in an other place, ſaith, *that* 'neither whoremo*n*ger, adulterer, Drunkard, glutton, ryotous perſon, nor ſuch like, ſhal euer enter into *the* kingdome of Heauen.' By theſe few places, out of many, you may ſee the inormitie[1] of this vice, which is ſo much [2]euery where[2] frequented.

Spud. Let me intreate you to ſhew me ſome examples withall, wherby I may ſee [3]what euill it hath done in all ages.[3]

[4]*Philo.* Drunknes[5] cauſed *Lot* to commit [6]moſt ſhamefull[6] inceſt with his owne two Daughters, who got them both with Child, [7]he not perceuing it, neither when they lay downe, nor when they roſe vp. See how drunkenneſſe aſſotteth a man, depriuing him of all ſence, reaſon, and vnderſtanding.

Drunkenneſſe cauſed *Noah* to lye with his priuities bare in his Tabernacle, in ſuche beaſtlie forte as his wicked Sonne *Cham* ieſted and ſcoffed at the ſame.

Thorow drunkenneſſe, *Holophernes,* that [8]great and inuincible Monarche of the *Aſſyrians,* was ouercome by a Woman, hauing his head cut from his ſhoulders with a fauchone. Thorow drunkenneſſe, King *Herode* was brought to ſuche ydiocie and fooliſhe dotage, that he cauſed the head of good *Ihon Baptiſt* to be cut of, to ſatiſfie the requeſt of a dauncing ſtrumpet. That riche *Epulo,* of whom [9]*Luke* maketh mention, was for his drunkenneſſe and ryotous exceſſe, con-demned to the fire of Hel for euer; with many moe examples, which for ſhortnes I omit. Now, ſeeing than that drunkenneſſe is both of-fenſiue to GOD, and bringeth ſuch euills in this lyfe preſent, let vs, in the name of GOD, auoyde it as a moſt wicked thing and prenicious euill. For euery Drunkard is ſo farre eſtranged from himſelfe, that as one in an extaſie of mind,[10] or rather in a playne Phrenſie, he maye not be ſaid to be *ſui animi compos,* or [11] a man of ſounde wit, but rather a [12]very Bedlem, or muche worſe, no Chriſtian, but an Antichriſtian; no

---

---

[1] vnlawfulnes F.   [2—2] *not in* F.

[3—3] the effectes thereof, and what punishment hath been ſhewed vpon the offendors herein in all ages. B, E, F ; (*but* F *has* therein.)

[4] *heading in* F :—Punishment of Drunkardes.

. [5] Drunkenneſſe B, E, F.   [6—6] *not in* F.

† leaf 65. Examples against Drunkenneſſe. B.   [9] Sainct *added in* B, E, F.

[10] of mind *not in* F.   [11] or *not in* B, E, F.

member of Chriſt Ieſus, but an impe of Sathan and a lymme of the
Deuill.   Wherfore, in the name of God, let vs auoyd al exceſſe, imbrace temperancie and ſobrietie, & receiue ſo much [1]meats and drinks[1]
as may ſatiſſie nature, not the inſaciat appetits of our fleſhly[2] deſires ;
Knowing that, except the Lord bleſſe our meats and drinks within our
bo[3]dyes, and giue them power & ſtrength to nouriſh and feede the
ſame, and our bodyes their naturall powers, euery member to doo his
office and dutie, our meates ſhall lye in our ſtomacks, ſtincking, ſmell-
ing, and rotting, like filthie carion in a[4] lothſom ſinck.[5]   So farre of
ought we to be from abuſing the good creaturs of God by ryot, drunk-
neſſe, or exceſſe, that we ought neuer to take[6] morſell of bread, nor
ſope of drinke, without humble thankes[7] to the Lord for the ſame.[8]
For we neuer read that our Sauiour Chriſt euer eat or dranke, but he
gaue thankes (or, as we call it, ſaid grace) both before the receipt
therof and after. This needed[9] he not to haue done in reſpeĉt of himſelfe, but for our erudition[10] & learning, according to this ſaying, omnis
Chriſti aĉtio noſtrà eſt inſtruĉtio : Euery aĉtion of our Sauiour Chriſte
is our example and inſtruĉtion, to follow as neere as[11] we are able.
[12]And thus much of drunkeneſſe, which god graunt may euery wher
be auoided.[12]

[[13]Or if all that hath been ſaied hetherto,[14] bee not ſufficient to
withdrawe vs from this beaſtly vice of dronkenneſſe : yet lette vs ſette
before our eyes this moſte fearfull iudgement of God, executed vpon
a ſorte of dronkardes, the ſtorie whereof is this. The eight day
of February 1578 in the countrey of Swaben, there were dwellyng
eight menne Citezens, and Citezens, ſonnes, very riotouſly and pro-
digally inclined,[15] the names of whom, for the better credite of the
ſtorie, [16]I haue ſett doune, viz. Adam Giebens, George Kepell, John
Keiſell, Peter Herſdorſe, Jhon Waganaer, Simon Henrickes, Herman
Fron, Jacob Hermans,[18] all whiche would needes goe to the Tauerne,
vppon the Sabboth daie in the mornyng verie earely, in contempt of

[*This page not in* A.]
[The propertie of a good Hoste. E, F.]

[the Lorde and his Sabboth. And commyng to the houfe of one Anthonie Hage, an honeft, godlie man, who kepte[1] a Tauerne in the fame Toune, called for burnte Wine, Sacke, Malmetie,[2] Hipocras, and what not. The hofte tolde them, that thei fhould haue none of all thefe, before the diuine feruice and the[3] fermon tyme were pafte, and councelled them to goe heare the facred woorde of God preached. But thei (faue Adam Giebins, who aduifed them to heare the Sermon, for feare of Gods wrathe) denied, faiyng : That thei lothed that kind of exercife. The good hofte, neither giuyng them any Wine hymfelf, nor fufferyng any other, went to the Sermon, as duetie did binde hym, who beyng gone, thei fell to curfyng, bannyng, and fwearyng, wifh-

[A caueat for cursers and banners. E, F.]

yng that he might breake his necke, or euer he came againe from the Sermon; and bruftyng forthe into thefe intemperate fpeeches, " the Deuill breake our neckes, if wee departe hence this daie, either quicke or dedde, till wee haue had fome wine!" Straight waie, the Deuill appered vnto them, in the likeneffe of a yong manne, bryngyng in

[[4] leaf 66, back. B.†]

his hande, a Flagon of wine, and demaundyng of them, why [4]thei caroufed not, he dranke vnto them, faiyng : " Good fellowes, bee merie,

[The desperate securitie of Dronkerdes. E, F.]

for ye fhall haue wine inough, for you feeme luftie laddes, and I hope you will paie me well," who inconfiderately anfwered, that thei would paie hym, or els thei would guage their neckes, yea their bodies and foules, rather then to faile. Thus thei continued fwillyng, gullyng, and caroufyng fo long, as till one could not[5] fee an other. At the laft the deuill their hofte, tolde them, that thei muft needes paie the fhotte, whereat their hartes waxed cold. But the Deuill comfortyng

[The deuilles rewarde to his darlinges the Dronkardes. E, F.]

them, faied : " Bee of good cheare, for now mufte you drinke boilyng Lead, Pitche, and Brimftone with me in the pit of helle for euermore " : Herevpon[6] immediatly he made their eyes like flames of fire, and in bredth as broad as Saucers. Then beganne thei to call for mercie, but it was to late. And ere thei could call againe for mercie and grace, the Deuill preuented them, and[7] brake their neckes a fonder, and threwe mofte horrible flames of fire, flafhing[8] out of their mouthes. And thus ended thefe feuen dronkardes, their miferable daies, whofe Iudgement I leaue to the Lorde. The other Adam Gibiens, who

---

[1] keep F.   [2] Malmsie F.   [3] the *not in* F.
† leaf 66, back. *No head-line.* B.   [5] scarsely *in* E, F.
[6] Heeeupon (*sic*) F.   [7] and *not in* E, F.   [8] flashing *not in* F.

PHILLIP STUBBES'S ANATOMY

OF THE

ABUSES IN ENGLAND

IN

SHAKSPERE'S YOUTH,

A.D. 1583.

PART II.

𝕿𝖍𝖊 𝕯𝖎𝖘𝖕𝖑𝖆𝖞 𝖔𝖋 𝕮𝖔𝖗𝖗𝖚𝖕𝖙𝖎𝖔𝖓𝖘.

PHILLIP STUBBES'S ANATOMY

OF THE

ABUSES IN ENGLAND

IN

SHAKSPERE'S YOUTH,

A.D. 1583.

PART II.
𝕿𝔥𝔢 𝕯𝔦𝔰𝔭𝔩𝔞𝔶 𝔬𝔣 𝕮𝔬𝔯𝔯𝔲𝔭𝔱𝔦𝔬𝔫𝔰 𝕽𝔢𝔮𝔲𝔦𝔯𝔦𝔫𝔤 𝕽𝔢𝔣𝔬𝔯𝔪𝔞𝔱𝔦𝔬𝔫.

EDITED BY

FREDERICK J. FURNIVALL.

PUBLISHT FOR
𝕿𝔥𝔢 𝕹𝔢𝔴 𝖀𝔥𝔞𝔨𝔰𝔭𝔢𝔯𝔢 𝖀𝔬𝔠𝔦𝔢𝔱𝔶
BY N. TRÜBNER & CO., 57, 59, LUDGATE HILL,
LONDON, E.C., 1882.

Series VI. No. 12.

BUNGAY: CLAY AND TAYLOR, THE CHAUCER PRESS.

To the Chriſtian Reader, a preface
premonitorie.

I Nede not (good Christian Reader) to ſtand vpon either the commendation of the Author of this booke, or the worke it ſelfe, for *Vino vendibili hœdera ſuſpenſa nihil eſt opus*, both the one and the other (ſuch is the exellencie of them both) may ſufficiently commend themſelues. Onely this I am to request at thy hands (good Reader) that what faultes or escapes soeuer thou shalt meete withall in this booke, (as there be some) I beseech thee impute them not to the negligence of the Author, who is greatly agreeued at them, but to the ouersight of the printer, through whom they were cōmitted. Wherefore gentle Reader I beseech thee reade this booke (being I assure thee a learned worke) *cum iuditio*, not *prœiuditio*, with the spirite of modestie, not of contumacie, knowing that (as the Apostle saith) charitie couereth the multitude of faultes, enuieth no man, speaketh ill of no man, but receiueth all thinges in good part. And whersoeuer anie fault shall be committed, freendly to amend it with thy pen, and especially for the pointing thereof. And for the marginal notes, and quotations also, the like ouersights as before are cōmitted, wherfore good reader blame not the author without cause, either for the one, or for the other. A greater volume thou maiest haue, but a learneder treatise for the substance therof, I persuade my selfe, is hard to find. Thus putting thee in mind of the old adage μωμησε ταιτισ φασσον ἡμιμησεται it is easier to find fault, and to carpe than to imitate or amend, I commit thee to God who bleſſe thee with the knowledge of his truth.

Thine in the Lord Phillippe Stubbes.

↓

From :—

A | Godlie and fruitfull Treatise of | Faith and workes. | Wherein is confuted a certaine opinion of me- | *rit by workes, which an aduersary to the Goſpell* | of Christ Iesu, held in the conference, had | in the Tower of London. [Quotes Mat. 7 ver. 31, four lines in B.L.—John 6 ver. 40, four lines italics.] LONDON | Printed for *Gregory Seton*, and are to be sold | (sic) *his ſhop vnder Alderſgate* | *1583.* | A (counts 4) to G in eights. Small 8vo.

Dedication " To his very good Lord, Ambrose Earle of Warwicke . . . . . H. D. wisheth all prosperitie &c."

Signed " Your honors most humble to
      Commaund, H. D.

[I find not this article in any bibliographical work ; nor can I assign the initials, H. D., to any writer of the period.—*A. Wallis.*]

TO

MY FRIEND AND HELPER

𝕿𝖊𝖊𝖓𝖆 (𝕸𝖆𝖗𝖞 𝕷𝖎𝖑𝖎𝖆𝖓) 𝕽𝖔𝖈𝖍𝖋𝖔𝖗𝖙-𝕾𝖒𝖎𝖙𝖍.

CONTENTS.

———◇———

PART II. THE SPIRITUALTY.

This Second Part of Stubbes's *Anatomie* is partially described, after the
First Part, in Sir E. S. Brydges's *Restituta*, i. 530-5, and quotations are given
from the opening, the description of Q. Elizabeth (p. 7 below), the Ruff, Starching
House and Poking-Stick bits (p. 35-6), and the scene in the Barber's Shop (p.
50-1). On p. 527 Haslewood says "that a limited impression of the whole
work would materially assist the spirit of modern researches." A note on p.
530 states that "Copies of this edition [Part II] are attached to the third edition
[1585] of the first part."

There is a copy of Stubbes's *Motiue to good Workes*, 1593 (see Forewords to
Anatomie, Part I, p. 67*), in Emmanuel College, Cambridge.—W. C. Hazlitt.
Bibliog. Collections and Notes, 2nd Series, 1882. I hope we may be able to print
it some day in our *Shakspere's England* Series.

Anthony Stapley, of Framfield, Sussex, grandfather of "Anne Stapley, 9 years
olde, aº 1634," had for his 4th wife a "widow of Mr. Stubbes, but no issue."
Harl. MS. 6164 (Visitation of Sussex, 1634), lf. 22, bk.

FORETALK.

§ 1. IN the Forewords to my edition of the First Part of
Stubbes's *Anatomie* for the New Shakspere Society in 1877-9, I
said that I meant to reprint this Second Part, and I gave a list of
the subjects treated in the first Division of it, that describing the
Corruptions of the Temporalty. Of Stubbes's dealing with the
Spiritualty, I gave only a mention at the foot of p. 35. Now pages
viii-ix of the Contents above sufficiently sketch it.

Readers must not, as I warnd them before, expect to find in this
Part II as much amuzement and interest as they found in Part I[1].
The only lively bit in the book is the scene in the Barber's shop, p.
50-1 below, the humour of which I commend to those who look on
Stubbes as "a mere bitter narrow-sould Puritan." But the Men and
Women who are in earnest themselvs now, will find Stubbes in like
earnest in this Second Part, as in his First, dealing with real abuses in
the Life of his time, demanding that Justice be dealt to the Poor as

---

[1] The pages against Ruffs, those Cartwheels of the Devil, is as fierce as anything in Part I. See too the beastly Ruffians who wear long hair, p. 35-6, p. 50.

fairly as to the Rich ; that endowments be kept for the Poor who
dezerve them, and not jobd in favour of the monied folk who abuze
them ; that Tradesmen shall deal honestly with their Customers,—
Drapers and Clothiers not cheating, Butchers not selling diseazd
meat ;—that rich men's Pleasures and Profit shall not, by Parks and
Sheep, eat up poor men's Homes and Lives ; that Landlords shall
not rack their Tenants to their ruin ; that strong and able Beggars
shall be made to work, or be hung, while an Almshouse shall be set
in every Parish for the sick and aged Poor ; that Doctors shall tend
the Poor as well as the Rich, and that a Parish-Doctor shall be
provided for the Poor ; that the evils of Forestalling shall be
checkt, Astrologers punisht,[1] and that in every act of dealing, Right
shall be done through the land.

As to the Spiritualty and Church matters, the view that Stubbes
was a mere narrow Puritan utterly breaks down. He comes out as
a preacher of implicit obedience to the Sovereign even when he
orders what is wrong (p. 17-18) ; he accepts Bishops, ' My Lord
Bishop ' too (p. 104-5), Surplices, Forkt Caps, and other externals
which the Puritans held as signs of the Whore of Rome (p. 109—
112) ; and his advice about all the trifles of garments about which
men then, and since have, made such a needless fuss, is (p. 116) :—

"And seeing we do all agree togither, and iump in one truth
"having al one God our father, one Lord Jesus Christ our Sauiour,
"one holy Spirit of adoption, one price of redemption, one faith,
"one hope, one baptisme, and one and the same inheritance in the
"kingdome of heauen, Let vs therefore agree togither in these ex-
"ternall shadowes, ceremonies and rites. For is it not a shame to
"agree about the marrow, and to striue about the bone? to contend
"about the karnell, and to vary about the shell? to agree in the
"truth, and to brabble for the shadow?"

This is surely as much a proof of his good sense, as are his
demands that every Congregation shall have the Patronage of its
own living (p. 79), and nominate its own Pastor—presenting two

---

[1] The 5 Eliz. ch. 15, A.D. 1562-3. "An Act agaynst fonde and phantastical
Prophecyes" only applies to folk who put them forth "to thintent therby to
make anye Rebellion, Insurrection, Dissention, losse of Lief or other Disturb-
ance within this Realme and other the Quenes Dominions."

or three to the Bishop that he may pick the best (pp. 90-2, 100), that the abuses of private Patronage shall be stopt (p. 80-2), Pluralism (p. 75-6) and Simony abolisht, and that every Church shall have power to alter its form of external government from time to time (p. 101).

On the whole then, I claim that this Part II of the *Anatomie* more than bears out the favourable opinion of Phillip Stubbes that I utterd in my Forewords to Part I.

§ 2. In proof that Stubbes was not inventing the Abuses of which he complaind, I've thought it right to make some extracts from the Statutes and a Proclamation of Queen Elizabeth, and the Statutes of James I, 1. on the corrupt Presentations to Scholarships and Benefices; 2. on the tricks of Clothiers; 3. the bad work of Tanners and Shoemakers; 4. the thefts and evils (which we still know so well) arising from the wrongly-named 'Brokers'—our Pawnbrokers and Marine-Store Dealers;—and 5. from the practice of Regrating. As of old, I quote mainly the words of the Statutes. Any one who finds em too long and tedious, will skip em.

(I.) A.D. 1588-9, 31 Eliz. chap. VI. "An acte against Abuses in Election of Scollers and presentac*i*ons to Benefices."

"Whereas by the intent of the Founders of Colledges, Churches Collegiat, Churches Cathedrall, Scoles, Hospitals, Halles, and other like Societies within this Realme, and by the Statut*es* and good Orders of the same, the Eleccions, presentac*i*ons and Nominac*i*ons of Fellowes, Schollers, Officers and other P*er*sons to have roome or place in the same, are to be had and made of the fittest and most meete p*er*sons beinge capable of the same Eleccions, presentac*i*ons, and Nominac*i*ons, freelye w*i*thout anye Rewarde, Guyfte, or thinge given or taken for the same; And for true p*er*formaunce whereof, some Ellectors, Prescntors and Nomynators in the same, have or should take a Corporall Oathe to make their Eleccions, Presentac*i*ons and Nominac*i*ons accordinglye; Yet notwithstandinge it is sene and found by experience that the saide Eleccions, Presentac*i*ons and Nominac*i*ons *be many tymes wrought and brought to passe with Monye, Guyft*es *and Reward*es, whereby the fyttest p*er*sons to be presented, elected or nom*i*nated, wanting Money or Friend*es, are sildome or not at all preferred, contrarie to the good meaninge of the saide Founders, and the saide good Statut*es and Ordynaunc*es of the saide Colledges, Churches, Scholes, Halles, Hospitalls and Socyeties, and to the great prejudice of

Learning and the Common Wealthe and Estate of the Realme : ·For Remedye whereof, Be it enacted "—that all Elections effected by Bribery of any kind shall be void, and that the Queen or other Presenter shall appoint fresh persons to the void Offices. § 2 enacts that any one bribing to procure the resignation of a Fellowship or Office, shall lose the place, and that the Resigner accepting the bribe shall forfeit double its value.

§ 4 declares Simoniacal Presentations to Benefices, Dignities, &c. void ; and that the Presentations shall devolve to the Crown, both Briber and Bribee paying a fine of double the amount of the Bribe.

§ 5 fines any one corruptly instituting a man to a Benefice, double the yearly value of it ; declares the Institution void, and empowers the Patron to present some one else.

(II.) As to Cloth, the 35 Eliz. c. 10, A.D. 1592-3, recites the Queen's Proclamation of the year before " for the Reformacion of thinsufficiencies growen in the Clothes called Devonshire Kersies or Dozens,"—cloths " of late marvailouslie discredited by the Invencions and newe Devises of the Weavers, Tuckers, and Artificers "— and " forbiddinge all other Deceiptes in Weaving, and all dymynishinge and unreasonable drawinge, stretchinge, and other Deceiptes in Tuckers," and then enacts that the Cloths shall be properly made, of good wool, and " without rackinge, stretching, streyning, or other Devise to increase the Lengh therof."

In 1597-8 " An Acte aginst the deceitfull stretching and taintering of Northerne Cloth," 39 Eliz. c. 20, is passt, because " the said Northern Clothes and Karsies doe yeerely and daylie growe worse and worse, and are made more light and muche more stretched and strayned . . . which great Enormities your faythfull Subjectes doe chieflye impute to the great nomber of Tenters and other Engins daylie used and practized in the said Counties for the stretchinge and strayninge of the said Clothes and Karsies." So the Act forbids this stretching, and puts a penalty of £20 on any one who

" shall have use or occupie any Tenter, of what sorte or kynde soever, or any manner of Wrinche, Rope, or other Engins to stretch or strayne any Clothes, Kersies, Dozens, Penystones, Rugges, Frises, Cottons, Kighley Whites, Plaine Grayes, or any other Clothes" made within the said Counties. (By the next-quoted Statute this Act is extended to all English Cloths.)

The abuse stretching over other Cloth Districts, and adulteration also prevailing, in 1601 "An Acte for the true workinge and making of Wollen Clothe" was past, saying that the former Acts "for the true makinge and workinge of Wollen Clothe" had been

"frustrated and deluded by strayninge, stretchinge, wante of weighte, Flocks, Sollace, Chalke, Flower, deceitfull things, subtill sleightes and untruethes,[1] soe as the same Clothes beinge put in Water are founde to shrincke rewey, pursey, squallie, cocklinge, baudy, lighte, and notablie faultie, to the great dislike of forraine Princes, and to the hynderance and losse of the buyer and wearer."

It is therefore enacted that

"no person or persons shall put any Haire, Flocks, Thrummes or Yarne made of Lambes Wooll, or other deceivable thinge or things into or upon any broade Woollen Clothe, Half Clothe, Kersey, Frize, Dozen, Pennystone, or Cotton, Taunton Clothe, Bridgewater, Dunston Cotton . . . or other Clothe . . . upon paine to forfeit every suche Cloth. . . . And that no person . . . shall . . . have use or occupye . . . any Tenter, Instrumente, Engine, or other Device . . . with any lower Barre, Pynne, Ringe, or other Engine or Device . . . wherebie . . . any rough and unwroughte Woollen Broad Clothe, Halfe Clothe, Kersey, Cotton, Dozen, Pennystone, Frize, Rugge . . . shall or may be stretched or strayned in breadthe," under a penalty of £20.

(III.) The Statute 1 James I. chapter 22 (A.D. 1603-4), not only confirms Stubbes's complaints about Leather-sellers, but also names another fault of theirs :—

§ x. "Much dammage hath redounded to the Common Wealthe by reason that divers Tanners for theire private lucre have used to convert to Sole Leather suche Hides as are altogether insufficient for that use, which Hides they doe raise in the workemanshippe by divers Mixtures, therebie making the same to seeme verie stronge and substantiall Leather, whereas the same doeth in the wearinge proove hollowe, deceitfull, and altogether unprofitable for the Common wealth,"—and enacts that all such raizd and converted Hides shall be forfeited.

---

[1] Compare in A.D. 1592-3, the 35 Eliz. ch. 8. "An Acte againste deceit-full making of Cordage" : the makers of 'Cables, Halsers and other kinde of Cordage' made em of 'oulde, caste, and overworne' stuff, tarrd em, and sold em as new, whereby not only Ships of the Queen and her Subjects "but also the Lyves of diverse of her saide Subjectes have bene loste, perished and caste awaye."

About the not-enuf tand Leather with which Stubbes finds fault on p. 36, the Statute says (1 Jac. 1, c. 22,[1] A.D. 1603-4. Record Statutes, vol. iv. Pt. 2, p. 1041):

§ xii. "... if any person or persons usinge, or which shall use, the Misterie or Facultie of Tanninge, shall at any tyme or tymes hereafter offer or put to sale any kinde of Leather which shalbe insufficientlie or not throughlie tanned, or which shall not then have beene, after the tanninge thereof, well and thorowlie dried, so that the same by the Triers of Leather lawfullie appointed accordinge to this present Acte for the tyme beinge shalbe founde to be insufficientlie or not throughlie tanned, or not throughlie dried, as aforesaide, that then all and everie suche person and persons so offendinge shall forfeite and loose so much of his or theire said Leather as shalbe soe founde insufficientlie and not throughlie tanned, or not throughlie dryed as aforesaide ..."

Then, as to what Stubbes says of the Tanners taking " vp their hides before they bee halfe tanned," the Statute goes on in § xiii:

"And whereas divers Tanners, for greedines of gaine, doe overmuch hasten the tanning of their Leather, and for that purpose doe use divers craftie and subtile Practises, sometimes layinge theire Leather in theire Fattes set in theire old Tanhils, where it may be tanned in the hott Woozes, takinge unkinde heate in the same Hill, and sometimes by putting of hot Woozes into their Tanne Fats where the same Hides or Leather lie, by which and other like Fraudulent Practises they make theire Leather to seeme bothe faire and well, and sufficientlie tanned within a very short space.[2]   For Reformation whereof, be it enacted by the authoritie aforesaide, That after the saide Feaste of St. Bartholomew next cominge, no person or persons shall sett their Fattes in Tanhils or other Places where the Woozes or Leather that shall be put to tanne in the same, shall or may take any unkinde heates, or shall put any Leather into any hotte or warme Woozes, or shall tanne any Hide, Calve Skinne or Sheep Skinne, with any hote or warme Woozes whatsoever, upon paine that everie person so offendinge shall forfeite for everie such Offence, Tenne Poundes ; And shall also, for everie such Offence, stand upon the Pillorie three severall Markett Dayes in the Market Towne next to the Place where the saide Offence shall be committed."

---

[1] Compare its clauses with those of 5 Eliz. ch. 8, from which some are, more or less, taken.

[2] The right time is enacted by § ix : "Nor shall suffer the Hides for utter Sole Leather to lye in the Woozes any lesse tyme then Twelve Moneths at the leaste, nor the Hides for upper Leathers in the like Woozes any lesse time than Nyne Monethes at the leaste. . ."

The Shoemakers, and their selling Horse hide for Ox-hide, &c. (p. 37, Stubbes), are dealt with in § XXIII. (p. 1043).

And forasmuch as Leather well tanned and curried, may, by the Negligence, Deceite, or evill Workmanshippe of the Cordwainer or Shoemaker, be used deceitfullie, to the hurte of the Occupier or Wearer thereof : Be it further enacted by the authoritie aforesaide, That no person or persons which, after the saide Feast of St. Bartholomew next comminge, shall occupie the Misterie or Occupation of a Cordwainer or Shoemaker, shall make or cause to be made any Bootes, Shoes, Buskins, Startups, Slippers, or Pantofles, or any parte of them, of Englishe Leather, wet curried (other then Deere Skinnes, Calve Skinnes, or Goate Skinnes, made or dressed, or to be made or dressed like unto Spanish Leather) but of Leather well and truelie tanned and curried, in manner and forme aforesaid, or of Leather well and truelie tanned onelie, and well and substantiallie sewed with good Threed well twisted and made, and sufficientlie waxed with waxe well rosoned, and the stitches harde drawen with Hand Leathers, as hathe bene accustomed, without mixinge or minglinge Overleathers, that is to say, parte of the Overleathers beinge of Neates Leather, and parte of Calves Leather, nor shall put into anie parte of anie Shooes, Bootes, Buskins, Startups, Slippers, or Pantofles, any Leather made of a Sheepe Skinne, Bull Hide or Horse Hide, nor into the upper Leather of any Shooes, Startups, Slippers, or Pantofles, or into the neither [nether] parte of any Bootes (the inner parte of the Shooe onlie excepted) any parte of any Hide from which the Sole Leather is cutte, called the Wombes, Neckes, Shancke, Flancke, Powle, or Cheeke, nor shall put into the utter Sole any other Leather then the beste of the Oxe or Steere Hide, nor into the inner Sole any other Leather than the Wombes, Necke, Poll, or Cheeke, nor in the Treswels of the double soled Shooes, other then the Flancks of any the Hides aforesaide : nor shall make or put to sale in any yeere, betwene the laste of September and the twentieth of Aprill, any Shooes, Bootes, Buskins, Startups, Slippers or Pantofles, meete for any person to weare exceedinge the age of foure yeeres, wherein shall be any drie English Leather (other than Calve Skinnes or Goate Skinnes made or dressed, or to be made or dressed like unto Spanishe Leather, or any parte thereof) ; nor shall shew, to the intent to put to sale, any Shooes, Bootes, Buskins, Startups, Slippers or Pantofles upon the Sunday ; upon paine of forfeiture for everie paire of Shooes, Bootes, Buskins, Startups, Slippers and Pantofles made, solde, shewed or put to sale contrary to the true meaninge of this Acte, three shillinges and fourepence, and the juste and full value of the same."

(IV.) Against the evil of miscald 'Brokers'—really our Pawn-brokers and Marine-Store Dealers—buying stolen goods, and thus

inciting folk to pilfer, which Stubbes condemns on p. 38-40, an
Act was past twenty years later :—

1 James I, chap. 21 (A.D. 1603-4; p. 1038). "An Acte
againste Brokers." This Act recites that "of large and ancient
tyme by divers hundred yeeres . . certaine Freemen of the Citie" of
London had been appointed "to be Brokers within the saide Citie
and Liberties of the same, and have taken theire Corporall Oaths
before the saide Mayor and Aldermen from tyme to tyme . . to use
and demeane themselves uprightlie and faithfullie betweene Merchant Englishe and Merchant Strangers and Tradesmen, in the
contrivinge, makinge, and concluding, Bargaines and Contractes to
be made betweene them concerning their Wares and Merchandizes
to be bought and solde and contracted for within the Citie of
London, and Moneys to be taken up by Exchange betweene such
Merchant and Merchantes and Tradesmen, and these kinde of
persons so presented, allowed, and sworne to be Brokers as aforesaide, have had and borne the name of Brokers, and bene knowen,
called, and taken for Brokers, and dealinge in Brokerage or Brokerie,
who never of any ancient tyme used to buy and sell Garmentes,
Houshold stuffe, or to take Pawnes and Billes of Sale of Garmentes
and Apparell, and all thinges that come to hand for Money, laide
out and lent upon Usurie, or to keepe open Shoppes, and to make
open Shewes, and open Trade, as now of late yeeres hathe [bene]
and is used by a number of Citizens assuminge unto themselves the
name of Brokers and Brokerage, as though the same were an honeste
and a lawfull Trade, Misterie, or Occupation, tearminge and naminge
themselves Brokers, whereas in trueth they are not, abusinge the
true and honeste ancient name and trade of Broker or Brokerage :
And forasmuch as many Citizens Freemen of the Citie, beinge Men
of Manuall Occupation, and Handicraftesmen and others inhabiting
and remayninge neere the Citie and Suburbes of the same, have
lefte and given over, and daylie doe leave and give over, their
handie and manuell Occupations, and have and daylie doe set up a
Trade of buyinge and selling, and taking to pawne of all kinde of
worne Apparell, whether it be olde or little the worse for wearinge,
Houshold Stuffe and Goods of what kind soever the same be of,
findinge therebie that the same is a more idle and easier kinde of
Trade of livinge, and that there riseth and groweth [p. 1039] to them
a more readie, more greate, more profitable and speedier Advantage
and Gaine then by theire former manuall Labours and Trades did
or coulde bringe them : And Forasmuch as the said kinde of counter-
feit Brokers, and Pawnetakers upon Usurie, or otherwise for readie
Money, are growne of late to many Hundreds within the Citie of
London, and other places next adjoyninge to the Citie and Liberties
of the same, and are like to increase to farre greater Multitudes,
being Friperers, and no Brokers, nor exercisinge of any honest and

lawfull Trade, and within the memorie of many yet livinge, such kinde of persons Tradesmen were verie fewe and of small number: And forasmuch as there are not any Garment*es*, Apparell, Housholde Stuffe or other Goods of any kinde, whatsoever the same be of, either beinge stollen or robbed from any, or badlie or unlawfullie purloyned or come by, but these kinde of upstarte Brokers, under colour and p*re*tence they be Freemen of the saide Citie of London, or inhabitinge in Westminster, where they pretende to have the like overt Market, as the Citie of London, and therebie p*re*suminge to be lawfull for them to use and set up the same idle and needlesse Trades, being the verie meanes to uphold, maintaine, and embolden all kind of lewde and bad p*er*sons to robbe and steale, and unlawfullie to get and come by true Mens Goods, knowinge and findinge that no sooner the same Goods can be stollen or unlawfullie come by, but that they shall and may p*re*sentlie utter, vent, sell and pawne the same to su'ch kinde of new upstart Brokers for readie Money: For Remedie whereof, and for the avoidinge of the saide Mischiefes and Inconveniences, and for repressinge and abolishinge of the sayd idle and needlesse Trades, and upstart Brokers, and for the avoidinge of Theftes, Robberies and Felonies, and bad People, and for the repressinge of such kinde of Nourishers and Ayders of Theeves and bad People, and for the defence of honest and true Mens p*ro*perties and Interest*es* in theire Goods: Be it enacted . . . That no Sale, Exchange, Pawne or Morgage of any Jewell, Plate, Apparell, Houshold Stuffe, or other Goods . . . that shall be wrongfullie or unjustlie purloyned, taken, robbed or stollen from any p*er*son or p*er*sons or Bodies Politicke, and which at any tyme hereafter shall be sold, uttered, delivered, exchanged, pawned, or done awaye within the Citie of London or Liberties thereof, or within the Citie of Westminster in the Countie of Middlesex, or within Southwarke in the Countie of Surrey, or within two miles of the saide Citie of London, to any Broker or Brokers, or Pawne takers, by any way or meanes whatsoever, directlie or indirectlie, shall worke or make any change or alteration of the p*ro*pertie or interest, of and from any p*er*son or p*er*sons or Bodie Politicke from whome the same Jewels, Plate, Apparell, Houshold Stuffe or Goods were or shalbe wrongfullie purloined, taken, robbed or stollen: Any Lawe, Usage of Custome to the contrarie notwithstandinge."

§ 2 enacts that Brokers and Pawntakers who refuse to produce Goods to the owner from whom they've been stolen, shall forfeit Double the Value of them.

§ 3, that the Act shall not affect those folk ' using and exercising the ancient Trade of Brokers betweene Merchant and Merchant.'

(V.) The evil of, and continued struggle of folk and lawmakers against Regrating or Ingrating,—that is, buying-up all the get-at-able Corn or other produce, and then selling it out at a large profit—are so well known that confirmation of Stubbes's complaints is hardly needed; but as the Dearth of 1594-6 has appeard before in our *Stafford*, p. xiv, and elsewhere with regard to the suppozed date of *Midsummer Night's Dream* and otherwise, I give here short extracts from Elizabeth's Proclamation of 1596 relating to Regraters, and the duty of continuing Hospitality:—

"BY THE QUEENE.

The Queenes Maiesties Proclamation, 1. For obseruation of former Orders against Ingrossers, & Regraters of Corne, 2. And to see the Markets furnished with Corne. 3. And also against the carying of Corne out of the Realme. 4. And a prohibition to men of hospitalitie from remoouing from their habitation in the time of dearth. 5. And finally a strait commandement to all Officers hauing charge of Forts to reside thereon personally, and no inhabitant to depart from the Sea coast.

THE Queenes Maiestie hauing had of late time consideration of great dearth growen in sundry parts of her Realme,[1] iudging that the Rich owners of Corne would keepe their store from common Markets, thereby to increase the prices thereof, and so the multitude of her poore people hauing no graine growing of their owne, to susteine great lacke, caused speciall orders to be made and published to all parts of her Realme, in what sort the Iustices of peace peace in euery quarter should stay all Ingrossers, Forestallers, and Regraters of Corne, and to direct all Owners and Farmers hauing Corne to furnish the Markets ratably and weekly with such quantities as vsually they had done before time, or reasonably might and ought to doe: By which orders, many other things were prescribed to be obserued for the staying of the dearth, and reliefe of the people: Yet neuerthelesse, her Maiestie is informed, that in some parts of her Realme the dearth doth not diminish, but rather increase for lacke of due execution of the sayd orders, and specially by the couetousnes of the Owners, forbearing to furnish the Markets, as reasonably they might do, and by secretly selling

---

[1] On July 31, 1596, in consequence of the scarcity of Corn, the Queen issued her Proclamation from Greenwich, forbidding Starch to be made of home-grown Corn, or even from Bran by the holders of the Patent for the manufacture of it from Bran.

In 1598 (May Ao. 40) she granted the sole right to import Starch to John Packington for 8 years.

out of their houses to a kinde of people that commonly are called Badgers, at prices vnreasonable, who like wise do sell and regrate the same out of the Markets at very high and excessiue prices. For remedy whereof, her Maiestie chargeth all officers to whom the obseruation of the sayd orders hath bene directed, presently as they haue any naturall care of their Christian brethren & Countreymen, being in need, to cause all and euery part of the sayd orders from point to point to be executed, and the offenders against the same to be seuerely punished, to the terrour of others. . .

Finally her Maiestie is particularly informed of some intentions of sundry persons, of abilitie to keepe hospitalitie in their Countreys, to leaue their said hospitalities, and to come to the Citie of London, and other Cities and townes corporate, thereby leauing the reliefe of theire poore neighbours, as well for foode, as for good rule, and with couetous minds to liue in London, and about the Citie priuately, and so also in other Townes corporate, without charge of company ; for withstanding whereof, her Maiestie chargeth all maner of persons, that shall haue any such intention during this time of dearth, not to breake up their housholds, nor to come to the said Citie, or other towns corporate : and all others that haue of late time broken vp their housholds, to returne to their houses againe without delay. And whilest her Maiestie had thus determined, for reliefe of her people, to stay all good householders in their Countreys, there is charitable sort to helpe hospitalitie, her Maiestie hath had an instant occasion giuen her to extend her commandement euen for the necessary defence of her Realme . . .

The obseruation of all which, her Maiesties commandement, is to be performed vpon paine of her Maiesties heauie indignation.

Giuen at her Maiesties Mannour of Richmond the second day of Nouember 1596, in the eight and thirtieth yeere of her Maiesties reigne.

God saue the Queene."

§ 3. On the subject of the Relief of the Poor, and Stubbes's reazonable demands on it, I refer the reader to Sir George Nicholls's *History of the English Poor Law* (1854), i. 161—239. Among these reazonable demands I shoud not now include hanging a man who *can* work and won't; but before Stubbes's time, in 1547, the 1st of Edward VI, chapter 3, enacted that every idle person who ran away from work set him shoud be branded with the letter V, and be adjudgd a slave for 2 years to any person who should demand him ; then, if he ran away again, he should be branded in the cheek with the letter S, and adjudgd a slave for life; and lastly, if he ran away a third time, he was to suffer death as a felon. This act was repeald in 1549-50, by the 3 and 4 Edw. VI, ch. 16; but in 1572-3, measures almost as harsh were re-enacted: beggars and vagabonds were to be grievously whipt, and burnt thro the gristle of the right ear with a hot iron of the compass of an inch about, unless any honest person would take them into service for a year. If he would, and the beggar ran away, then he was to be whipt, and burnt thro the ear; for a second offence to be treated as a felon, unless some honest person would take him into his service for 2 years, and he continued in it; while for a third offence he was adjudgd to suffer death, and loss of land and goods as a felon, without allowance of benefit of clergy or sanctuary. Stubbes was then, in 1583, only asking that the actual law shoud be allowd to take its course, when he wisht that sturdy Beggars who woudn't work, shoud be hangd.

The same Act of 1572-3 orderd 'abiding places' to be provided for the aged and infirm poor, appointed Overseers to raise and apply taxes for their benefit, and sanctioned a rate on richer neighbours in aid of poor parishes who couldn't support their own poor. This legislation was developt by 18 Eliz. ch. 3, A.D. 1575-6, which enacted that a competent stock of wool, hemp, flax, iron, or other stuff should be got, by taxation, to set the poor on work, and if they wouldn't work, they were to be sent to 'houses of correction' and made to work.

After Stubbes wrote in 1583, came the 39 Eliz. chaps. 3 and 4, in 1597-8; 3 for the Relief of the Poor, and 4 for the Punishment of Rogues, Vagabonds and Sturdy Beggars. Chap. 3 makes the appointment of Overseers in every parish compulsory, empowers them to tax inhabitants—and to levy a rate in aid on richer parishes —in order to get material to support the idle poor at work, and provide for the sick and aged, and the care and apprenticing of children. This Act establishes the mutual responsibility of parents and children to maintain one another.

It also, by § 5 (vol. iv, Pt. 2, Record Com. Statutes, p. 897), empowers the Churchwardens and Overseers 'to erect, buylde, and sett upp in fit and convenyent Places of Habitacion . . . at the gen*er*all Chardges of the Parishe . . . convenyent Howses of Dwellinge for the sayde ympotent Poore ; and allso to place Inmates or more Famylies than one in one Cottage or Howse.'

Chap. 4 provides for the whipping of sturdy Beggars who won't work, and their committal to gaol, their banishment beyond seas, or their death, in case they won't give up their roguish kind of life.

'We are now arrived,' says Sir Geo. Nichols, i. 192, 'at the important period when by *The* 43*rd Elizabeth, cap.* 2 (A.D. 1601), the principle of a compulsory assessment for relief of the poor was fully and finally established as an essential portion of our domestic policy.' This Act, 'the great turning-point of our Poor-Law Legislation, is still the foundation and text-book of English Poor Law' (i. 194). It carries out more effectually, and extends, the provisions of the prior Acts, and again sanctions the Rate in Aid. In 1610 the 7th of James I, chapter 4, provides for the building of Houses of Correction in every county ; but not till 1624 does the 21 James I—'An Act for the erecting of Hospitals and Workinghouses for the Poor '—carry out what I take to be Stubbes's demand for an Almshouse in every parish ; while not till 1834 does the Poor Law Amendment Act provide for the Poor the proper Medical Relief which Stubbes cald for in 1583.

As to Education, Harrison (see my Part I. p. 77), Latimer before him (*Sermons*, Parker Soc. edn. i. 186, 290, 291, 349), and many others, but utterd the same complaints about the jobbing of Scholarships, Fellowships, &c. that Stubbes makes, page 19 ; and not yet has the jobbing of the nominations of Bluecoat Boys to Christ's Hospital been done away with.

The hardship to the poor of wholesale enclosure of Commons— another complaint of Stubbes's—has been long admitted, and is now partially stopt by the Law. That Stubbes was right in calling for proper examination and licensing of Doctors, the keeping out of tag, rag, and quacks (p. 53), no one will deny. And that he took a reasonable and moderate view of the religious topics disputed in his day, I think every one will admit. His Part II, then, supports the character that I drew of him from his Part I.

§ 4.   Of Phillip Stubbes himself I have some fresh tidings ; of his family, none.

1.   He may have married again in 1593, when he wrote his *Motiue to good Workes*.   I have a melancholy interest in printing the late Col. Chester's letter to me on the point :—

124, *Southwark Park Road, London, S.E.*
18 *Nov.* '79.

"MY DEAR MR. FURNIVALL,

Did I ever send you the following Marriage from the Registers of St. Olave, Southwark ?

1593, April 3, Philip Stubbes and Elenor Powell—by License.

It has this moment met my eye in one of my volumes that has recently been indexed.

It would have been only 3 years after the death of your Author's wife Katharine Emmes.[1]

Or, were there 'two Richmonds in the field' ?

A search for the License would, I fear, be hopeless, as those for that date issued from the Faculty and Vicar General's Offices are not in existence, and one from the Bp. of London would not have availed in Southwark.

Sincerely yours

JOS. L. CHESTER.

"The Powell Wills of the period might reveal the Connection.

The marrying *by license*, at that period, indicates that they were certainly not of the lower orders."

2.   Our Phillip Stubbes may be the man of that name at Benefield in Northampton, who in July 1586 executed a Bond of which Mr. Henry Stubbes of Danby, Ballyshannon, got hold in 1879.   He writes on 13 Nov. 1879 :—

[1] Katharine Stubbes is alluded to in George Powell's ' *Very Good Wife*, a Comedy.   London.   S. Briscoe, 1693,' p. 21, Act III. sc. i.

" *Well*.   Death, fight now, or you'll die infamous, was your Mother a Whore ?

Squeez.   Comparatively she might be in respect of some Holy Women, as the late Lady *Ramsey*, Mrs. *Katherine Stubbs*, and such, ha, ha, is that a Cause ! "

'I have now very little doubt that I have in my possession the Autograph of the Author of the "Anatomie," and it may besides furnish a clue to his family, and perhaps bring to light some particulars of his life hitherto unknown. The following is the reason of my forming this opinion : The Bond relates to a "messuage or tenement" in Congleton, Cheshire, which Phil. S. is granting to Will. S. to hold for ever, and the former binds himself to leave the latter in undisturbed possession. The Bond itself is in Latin, the Conditions in English—Now, coupling this with what the Author of the "*Anatomie*" says of knowing a man "for a dozen or sixteene yeares togither" in Congleton (Part I. p. 136), whose death he relates as a warning to swearers, makes, I think, a very good case to show that they were one and the same person ; and the house referred to in the Bond was in all probability where the Puritan spent a good many yeares of his life. He is described in the Bond as "Philippus Stubbes de Benefeild al[ias] Beningfeilde in Com. Northt. generosus," and the other as "Will*el*mus Stubbes de Ratcliffe in Com. Midd. generosus"—

'I conjecture Phil. in the course of his rambles had settled for a time at Benefeild, as he did afterwards at Burton-on-Trent. It is not stated whether Willm. was any relative, but it seems probable he was ; perhaps brother. I enclose two extracts from the Chancery Proceedings relating to Willm., but I am not certain that the second extract refers to the same person. These I got the other day. I have made no searches at Congleton, Chester, or Benefeild.'

'CHANCERY PROCEEDINGS.

1 Nov. 1584. Bill filed by Robt. Wright, Citizen and Goldsmith of Lond. against William Stubbs of Ratcliff, Co. Middx., Gent.

23 Nov. 1598. Bill filed by William Stubbes of Radcliff, Co. Middx., Ropemaker (who about 4 yeares now last past inhabited and dwelt at Boston, Co. Linc., being unmarried and having a great family household by reason of his trade) against Thomas Strangrushe of the same town, Fuller.'

As to Phillip Stubbes's family, Prof. Stubbs felt sure that Phillip came from Congleton, and that a gentle family of the name was still in that neighbourhood. So I wrote there, and found that no Stubbes was known but a sweep. Still, Mr. J. P. Earwaker says in his *East Cheshire*, ii. 362: "In 1654 I find it stated in a MS. at Capesthorne that "Nell, Nan, and Bess Stubbs, being mother and two daughters, were hanged [at Chester] for bewitching to death Mrs. Furnivall, wyfe to Mr. Anth. [a mistake for Ralph] Furnivall, daughter to Mr. J. Fellowes." Prof. Stubbs sent me this bit, and he finds that in 1595, William Stubbes of Congleton, gentleman, presented to the living of Gauseworth. The Congleton Records are, he says, full of Stubbeses; he has traced three generations of Congleton Jurors in the Town book—Ralph· or Reynold, from 1540 onwards; John from 1565 or so; and then another Ralph at the beginning of James I's reign. He also found a Randall Stubbes in the first year of Elizabeth, who would do for our Phillip's father. He thinks the Astbury registers will most likely settle the matter. There is an account of some Stubbeses, he says, among the Rawlinson MSS. I paid for a search of the Chester Indexes, with the following result:

Chester Registry. List of Wills proved and Admons granted in the names of Stubbs and Stubbes from the earliest date of the Indexes, 1540 to 1630 both inclusive

1586 Will of Geffrey Stubbs of Ludlow
1591 Will of Willam Stubbs of Gawsworth, County of Chester
1595 Admoñ of Lawrence Stubbs of North Rode, Co. of Chester
1597 Will of Hugh Stubbs of North Rode, County of Chester
1603 Admoñ of Thomas Stubbs of Allostock in the County of Chester
1617 Will of George Stubbs of Lower Tabley, County of Chester
1617 Admoñ of John Stubbs of Heaton, County of Chester
1621 Will of Nicholas Stubbs of North Rode, County of Chester
1622 Will of Thomas Stubbs of Hulse
1622 Will of Thomas Stubbs of North Rode, County of Chester
1623 Will of George Stubbs of Knutsford, County of Chester
1624 Will of John Stubbs of Merton
1630 Will of Ann Stubbs of North Rode, County of Chester

None of these look likely.

Mr. Walter Rye felt sure that he'd find some traces of Phillip Stubbes at Donnington in Lincolnshire (where there's a town of that name as well as in Leicestershire): see Forewords to Part I. p. 59*),—but diligent search showd none, tho' the Will of a Richard Stubbes of Donnington in 1622 is in the Lincoln Consistory Court.

It is clear that our Phillip was not the son of Ralph Stubbes of St. Mary le Wigford in the City of Lincoln, whose will is dated 4 April 1558, prov'd 29 July 1559, and of whose estate a *de bonis non* grant was issued on Jan. 29, 1562-3. Ralph's will was registered twice over, being in 36 Chaynay and 5 Chare (Somerset House). It mentions his children John, Henry, Justinian, and Elizabeth Stubbes, &c. &c., of whom Justinian may well be the M.A. of Gloucester Hall, Oxford, mentiond by Wood, *Ath. Ox.*, in the note on p. 53* of my Forewords to Part I. In the Chancery Proceedings temp. Eliz., S. s. 25, no. 31, Ralph Stubbes's executors claim £11 6s. 8d. of one Edmund, and in S. s. 23, £4 17s. 11½d. of Thos. Burton's executor.

The Essex Stubbeses yield no result either. There was a Philip Stubbes of Little Clacton, Essex, Will dated 19 June 1551, to whose estate the first Letters of Administration were granted on Sept. 25, 1555, and the second Letters on Oct. 31, 1561. He had an only son John, and a daughter Margaret. This John Stubbs of Cocks, Little Clacton, Essex, and Cotton Hall, Suffolk, made his will dated in 1587, but his son Phillip was not then of age. The Will was prov'd in the Commissary Court of Essex and Hertfordshire on Sept. 10, 1596. The right of Administration to this Philip Stubbs, then late of Clacton Parva deceasd, was renounced by Elizabeth, his Relict, in March 1626; and in May 1627, Administration was granted to Edward Luckin of Tiltey, one of Philip Stubbes's Creditors.

In the Chancery Proceedings of the time of Elizabeth are notes of other Stubbeses:

Richard Stubbe, and Anne his wife, Norfolk. G. g. 4, no. 59.
John Stubbs of Norfolk. C. c. 14, no. 57.
Richard Stubbs of Norfolk and Shropshire in vol. 3.

John Stubbs of Rutland, with sons William and Thomas, and a grandson Henry, 21 Eliz. 1579.

Wm. Stubbs of Radcliffe, Ropemaker, 23 Nov. 1598.—S. s. 5.
Alexander Stubbes of Codsall, Staffordshire yeoman.   S. s. 6.
Richard Stubbs of Southwark, yeoman.   S. s. 13.
Christopher Stubbs of Berkshire and Hampshire.
Edward Stubbs of Norfolk.
William Stubbs of Devonshire.

The name Stubbes occurs in a book dated 1626.   John Gee. *New Shreds of the Old Snare:*—p. 121, " Factors employed for the conueying ouer of the said Women to the Nunneries. . . .

Master Peeters
Stubbes."

Then Mr. Ellacombe hoped that he'd hit on traces, in his parish, Bitton, Glo'stershire, of our Stubbes, and he sent me up his Register ; but the only Stubbes entries in it show that the Rev. Henry Stubbs or Stubbe, when doing duty at Bitton—not being Vicar of it, had a daughter and a son baptized there :

" Mary daught*er* of Henry Stubbs, C*lericus*, was baptised February xith 1643."

" John the sonne of Mr. Henrie Stubbs, was babt. October xxvii." 1647.

There is no entry of the burial of any Stubbes from 1594 to 1643 (and a few years later).

Whether our Phillip Stubbes had anything to do with any of the folk above-named, I must leave to some future searcher to decide.

I have not tried to get up many Notes for this 2nd Part.   Those to Part I. cost so much, that a second set, even were one possible, must not be indulged in.   The text is reprinted from the copy of *The Display of Corruptions* in the Grenville Library, British Museum.

What have Books like the present one to do with Shakspere ? They help us to realize the England of his day, and the social evils that he must have seen.

3, *St. George's Square, N.W.*
July 18, 1882.

NOTES FOR PART II.

———

p. xxvii† Wills of John and Phillip Stubbes of Essex, and Ralph Stubbes of Lincoln :—

Jn. Stubbes, 1587.

(In Room 32) Will of John *Stubbes* of Cocks, Little Clacton, Essex (and Cotton Hall, Suffolk), dated 1587, gives Cocks and appurtenances, and lease of Cotton Hall to his son Phillip (under age) when he attains 21. If he dies under 21, then to testator's wife Agnes for life, and then over. Provision for boy Phillip's maintenance, &c. Prov'd in Com. *Court* of Essex and Herts, 10 Septr. 1596. (Phillip livd. Admōn to him ab. 1622.—Grigson.)

19 *June,* 1551.

(P. C. C. Bucke, quire 25) *Will of Phillip Stubbes* of Little Clacton, Essex— most lands to wife Johane for life, part to son John on attg. 21—if he doesn't, then to daughter Margret. If she dies under 18, then her share of personalty to son John. Evidently, only son John, and daughter Margret. No son Phillip.

25 Septr. 1555, authority to administer Ph. Stubbes's goods, granted to Rd. Blaxton, Ed. Assheman, and Edwd. Shorte, the exōr Jn. Hockett having died.

31 Octr. 1561, Commission to Rd. Godfrey and Alice his wife to administer the goods not administerd.

Ralph Stubbes, Alderman of *Lincoln, April* 4, 1558 (of the parish of St. Mary's, Wygford, in the suburbs of the City of Lincoln). Will proved, *July* 29, 1559 :—

Gives all his property, less legacies and special bequests, to his 4 children, *John, Henry, Justynyan,* and *Elizabeth.* If any die without issue—they're evidently under age—his share is to go to the survivors.

Gives Christabell *Bartram* his sister, to her marriage, 20£; and if she die or she be maryed, then 16£ to go to his 4 children, and 4£ 'to my thre bretherne, *Henry* Stubbes, *Iohn* Stubbes and *Thomas* Stubbes'.

Gives to his 'father *Bartrame* xij li. to bye the rest of the said house whiche he shulde purchase. And I wille . . that John *Bartrame* shalhaue the said house' in fee . . (As to children's bringing-up) . 'I will that my mother in lawe [Margarete Smythe] shall haue the kepinge and bringyng vppe of my children durynge her lif, and after her death I will that John Stubbes and

Justynyan Stubbes, with theire part*es* and portions shalbe in the Rule, ordre, and kepinge of Mr. John Hutchynson, and Henrye Stubbes . . of Thomas *Dawson* my brother-in-lawe' (Eliz*th*. not given to any one). Residue to 4 ch*ild*ren Exōrs. 4 ch*ild*ren, and "Margarete Smythe my mother in lawe."

    p. xxviii† *Henry Stubbes.* See Ant. Wood's *Ath. Oxon.* ed. Bliss, 1817; 1255 :—

    HENRY STUBBE, son of a father of both his names of Bitton in Glocester-shire,[1] was born in that county, became a student in Magdalen hall in the latter end of 1623, aged eighteen years; admitted bachelor of arts the 26th of January 1627, & master of arts the 8th of July 1630, took holy orders, and became a curate or vicar, sided with the puritans in the beinning of the rebellion, took the covenant, preached seditiously—took the engagement, and as a minister of the city of Wells was constituted one of the commissioners for the ejecting of such whom they then (1654) called scandalous, ignorant, and insufficient ministers and schoolmasters. After his majesty's restoration, he lost what he had for want of conformity, retired to London, and lived there. He hath, among several things pertaining to divinity, written

    Great Treaty of Peace, Exhortation of making Peace with God. Lond. 1676-77, oct.

    Dissuasive from Conformity to the World. Lond. 1675, in oct.

    God's Severity against Man's Iniquity. Printed with the *Dissuasive.*

    God's Gracious Presence, the Saint's great Privilege—a farewel Sermon to a Congregation in London, on 2 Thes. 3, 16. Printed also with the *Dissuasive.*

    Conscience the best Friend upon Earth: or the happy Effects of keeping a good Conscience, very useful for this Age. London 1678, 8vo.; 1685 in twelves, and other things which I have not yet seen; among which is his *Answer to the Friendly Debate,* an. 1669 in octavo. When he died, I know not; sure I am that after his death, which was in London, his books were exposed to sale by way of auction the 29th of Nov. 1680.

    [See a very amiable character of this writer in Calamy, who adds

    1. *A Funeral Sermon for a Lady in Gloucestershire.*

    2. *A Voice from Heaven; with his last Prayer.*

    Granger, who mentions a small head of Stubbe, gives us the title of a third book omitted by Wood :

    3. *Two Epistles to the professing Parents of baptized Children,* written a little before his death.

    Calamy says that Stubbe was of Wadham college, which I cannot believe. He was certainly matriculated of Magdalen hall, April 16 [18, Col. Chester], 1624. See *Reg. Matric. Univ. Oxon.* PP. fol. 299, b.] He died on July 7, 1678, aged 73, and was buried in Bunhill Fields.—(Col. Chester.)

    Of this Henry Stubbes, Richard Baxter says in his *Reliquiæ Baxterianæ,* Part III. (written in 1670) p. 189 [After his *Answer to Mr. Dodwell and Dr. Sherlock,* &c.], § 66. In a short time I was called on, with a grieved heart,

---

    [1] He was born, says Calamy [wrongly], at Upton in this county, upon an estate that was given to his grandfather by king James I, with whom he came from Scotland. *Ejected Ministers,* ii. 319.

to Preach and Publish many Funeral Sermons, on the Death of many Excellent Saints.

Mr. *Stubbes* went first, that Humble, Holy, Serious Preacher, long a blessing to Gloucestershire and Somersetshire, and other parts, and lastly to London. I had great reason to lament my particular Loss, of so holy a friend, who oft told me, That for very many years he never went to God in solemn Prayer, without a particular remembrance of me : but of him before.—*Reliquiæ Baxterianæ*, 1696.

Part III. p. 95, § 205 (written 1670). But because there are some few who by Preaching more openly than the rest, and to greater Numbers, are under more Men's displeasure and censure, I shall say of them truly but what I know . . .

11. Old Mr. *Stubbs*, who joineth with him [Mr. *Turner*], is one of a Thousand, sometimes Minister at Wells, and last at *Dursley* in *Gloucestershire*, an ancient grave Divine, wholly given up to the Service of God, who hath gone about from place to place Preaching with unwearied Labour since he was silenced, and with great Success, being a plain, moving, fervent Preacher, for the work of converting impenitent sinners to God : And yet being settled in peaceable Principles by aged Experience, he every where expresseth [═ presses out, excludes] the Spirit of Censoriousness, and unjust Separations, and Preacheth up the ancient zeal and sincerity with a Spirit suitable thereunto. *Reliq. Baxt.* 1696.

Ant. Wood gives an account of another Henry Stubbes, whose father was a clergyman at Parterey in Lincolnshire, where he was born on Feb. 28, 163½. He was at Oxford, and ultimately turnd Doctor. He was drownd on July 12, 1676, and buried in the Abbey Church at Bath. Him, Baxter mentions in the following passage of his *Reliq. Baxterianæ*, 1696 : *Life*, Part I. (written 1664), p. 75-6, "being writing against the Papists, coming to vindicate our Religion against them, when they imparte to us the Blood of the King, I fully proved that the Protestants, and particularly the Presbyterians, abhorred it, and suffered greatly for opposing it ; and that it was the Act of *Cromwell's* Army and the Sectaries, among which I named the *Vanists* as one sort. . . . Hereupon, Sir Henry *Vane* being exceedingly provoked, threatened me to many, and spake against me in the House, and one *Stubbs* (that had been whipt in the Convocation House at *Oxford*) wrote for him a bitter Book against me, who from a *Vanist* afterwards turned a Conformist ; since that, he turned Physician, and was drowned in a small Puddle or Brook as he was riding near the Bath."

Chaucer and Stubbes. In a short poem 'The | Laurel, | and the | Olive' : | Inscrib'd to | George Bubb, Esq ; | By Geo. Stubbes, M.A. | Fellow of Exeter-College in Oxon. | London, | Printed for Egbert Sanger at the Post-Office at the | Middle Temple-Gate in Fleetstreet .M.DCC.X. are some lines 'To the Author' ending thus :

> So when revolving Years have run their Race,
> Bright the same Fires in different Bosoms blaze ;
> Known by his glorious Scars, and deathless Lines,
> Again the *Hero*, and the *Poet* shines.
> In gentler *Harrison*, soft *Waller* sighs,
> And *Mira* wounds with *Sacharissa's* Eyes.

Achilles lives, and *Homer* still delights,
Whilst *Addison* records, and *Churchill* fights.
This happy Age, each Worthy shall renew, ⎫
And all dissolv'd in pleasing Wonder, view ⎬
In ANN—*Philippa, Chaucer* shine in you. ⎭

p. 6. *Papal Plots, Jesuits,* &c. Stubbes may allude specially to Campion's conspiracy two years before, of which Stowe—or Antony Munday—gives the following account in his *Annales* (ed. 1605, p. 1169), and a longer one in his additions to Holinshed's (or Reginald Wolfe's) Chronicle :—

[1581].   "On the 20. of Nouember, Edmond Campion, *Jesuit*, Ralfe Sher-
Ant. Monday.   wine, Lucas Kerbie, Edward Rishton, Thomas Coteham, Henrie
Campion   Orton, Robert Iohnson & Iames Bosgraue, were brought to the
and others
arraigned.   high bar at Westminester, where they were seuerally, & al
together indicted vpon high treason, for that, contrary both to loue & duty, they forsooke their natiue country, to liue beyond the seas under the Popes obedience, as at Rome, Rheimes, and diuers other places, where (*the Pope hauing with* other princes *practised the death and depriuation of our most gracious princesse, and vtter subuersion of her state and kingdome,* to aduance his most abhominable religion), these men, hauing vowed their allegiance to the Pope, to obey him in all causes whatsoeuer, being there, gaue their consent, to aide him in this most traiterous determination. And for this intent & purpose, they were sent ouer to seduce the harts of her maiesties louing subiects, & to conspire and practise her graces death, as much as in them lay, against a great day set & appointed, when the generall hauocke should be made, those onely reserued that ioyned with them. This laid to their charge, they boldly denied ; but by a iurie they were approoued guilty, and had iudgement to be hanged, bowelled & quartered.

The first of December, Edmond Campion, *Jesuit*, Ralfe Sherwine and
Campion   Alexander Brian, seminarie priests, were drawne from the Tower of
and others   London to Tiborne, and there hanged, bowelled & quartered.
executed.   Looke more in my continuation of Reine Woolfes Chronicle."

p. 9, *as that blessed martyr of God, Maister* Latimer *hath said in a sermon made before King* Edward *the sixt.* This is 'The seconde Sermon of Master Hughe Latemer, whych he preached before the Kynges maiestie, wythin hys graces Palayce at Westminster yᵉ .xv. day of Marche M.CC[C]CC. xlix.' *Sign.* E. 1. "I must desyre my Lorde protectours grace to heare me in thys matter, that your grace would heare poor mens sutes your selfe. Putte it to none other to heare, let them not be delayed. The saying is nowe, that mony is harde euery wher : if he be ryche, he shall soone haue an ende of his matter. Other ar fayn to go home with weping teares, for ani help they can obtain at ani Iudges hand. Heere mens suets your selfe, I requyre you in godes behalfe, & put it not to the hering of these veluet cotes, these vp skippes. Nowe a man can skarse knowe them from an auncyent Knyght of the countrye.

"I can not go to my boke, for pore folkes come vnto me, desirynge me that I wyll speake that theyr matters maye be heard. . . . I am no soner in the garden and haue red a whyle, but . . some one or other . . . desireth me that I wyll speake that hys matter myght be heard, & that [*Sign.* E. ii.] he hathe layne thys longe at great costes and charges, and can not once haue hys matter come to the hearing . . . [E. ii. back]. I beseche your grace that ye wyll loke to these matters.

"Heare them your selfe ! Vieue your Iudges ! And heare pore mens causes. And you proude Iudges, herke*n* what God sayeth in hys holy boke. *Audite illos, ita parum ut magnum.* Heare theym, sayeth he, the small as well as the greate, the pore as well as the ryche. Regarde no person, feare no man—Why ? *Quia domini iudicium est.* The iudgment is Goddes.

"Marcke thys sayinge, thou proude Iudge ! The deuyl will [E. iii.] brynge thys sentence at the daye of Dombe. Hel wyl be ful of these Iudges, if they repente not and amende.

"They are worsse then the wicked Iudge that Christe speaketh of, that neyther feared God nor the worlde. There was a certain wyddowe that was a suter to a Iudge, & she met hym in euery corner of the streete, cryinge : 'I praye you heare me, I besech you heare me, I aske nothyng but ryght.' When the Iudge saw hyr so importunate, 'though I fear neyther God, sayth he, nor the worlde, yet bycause of hyr importunatenes I wyll graunte hyr requeste.' ·

"But our Iudges are worsse then thys Iudge was. For [*sign.* E. iii. back] they wyll neyther heare men for Gods sake, nor feare of the worlde, nor importunatenes, nor any thynge else. Yea, some of them wyll commaund them to ward, if thei be importunat."

p. 12, *an angell,* (*for that is called a counsellers fee*). The well-known lawyer's 'six and eightpence.' Miss Rochfort Smith sends me the following Epigram, 594, from *Wits Recreations :*—

"Upon Anne's marriage with a Lawyer.

Anne is an angel : what if so she be ?
What is an angel but a lawyer's fee ?"

p. 19. *Colleges, &c, abused and peruerted.* See my Harrison's *Description of England,* 1577-87, p. 77. On Education in Early England, see my Forewords to the *Babees Book,* or *Meals and Manners :* Early English Text Society.

p. 24, *stretching and thicking Cloth.* "I here saye, there is a certayne
Cloth makers connyng come vp in myxyng of wares.
are become
Poticaryes, yea "Howe saye you, were it not wonder to here that clothe makers
and amonge the should become poticaries.
Gospellers.
"Yea, and as I heare saye, in such a place, where as they haue professed the Gospell, and the word of God most earnestly of a long tyme. Se how busie the Deuell is to sclaunder the word of god. Thus the pore gospel goeth to wracke. Yf his clothe be xviii. yerdes lo*n*ge, he wyl set hym on a racke,
A pretti kind of and streach hym tyll the senewes shrinke agayne, whyles he hath
multiplyinge. brought hym to xxvii. yardes. Whe*n* they haue brought hym to
. that perfection, they haue a pretty feate [*sign.* E. iiii.] to thycke him againe. He
Flocke powder. makes me a pouder for it, an playes the poticary : thei cal it floke

pouder : they do so incorporate it to the cloth, that it is wonderfull to consider : truely a goodly inuention."

p. 24, *Dark Shops.* p. 49, *False Weights.* p. 22, *Merchants.* p. 47, *Farmers.* p. 29, *Griping Landlords.* These Shop-keepers that can blind mens eyes, with dym and obscure lights, and deceiue their eares with false & flattering words, be they not Vsurers?

These Tradesmen that can buy by one weight, and selle by another, be they not Vsurers?

These Marchants that doe robbe the Realme, by carrying away of Corne, Lead, Tinne, Hydes, Leather, and such other like, to the impouerishing of the common wealth, bee they not Vsurers?

These *Farmers* that doe hurde vppe their Corne, Butter, & Cheese, but of purpose to make a dearth, or that if they thinke it to rayne but one houre to much, or that a drought doe last but two dayes longer then they thinke good, will therfore the next market day hoyse vp the prises of all manner [p. 46] of victuall, be not these Vsurers?

The *Land-Lordes* that doe sette out their liuings at those high rates, that their *Tenants* that were wont to keepe good Hospitalitie, are not nowe able to giue a peece of Bread to the *Poore,* be they not Vsurers? 1614. Barnabee Rych. *The Honestie of this Age.* p. 45-6.

p. 27, *the commons . . . are inclosed, made seuerall.* Compare Shakspere's phrase, in *Loues Labor's Lost,* II. i. 223, Qo. 1 :—

> *Bo.* So you graunt pasture for me.
> *Lady.*   Not so, gentle Beast,
> My lippes are no Common, though seuerall they be.

Thomas Greene's Diary says, on 1615, Sept. 1. "Mr. Shakspeare told Mr. J. Greene that he was not able to beare the enclosing of Welcombe" Common. Leop. Shaksp. Introd., p. cix. See p. 45* and 116 in Stubbes, Part I.

p. 28. *Enclosures of Commons,* &c. See Harrison, Part I., p. 306-7, and Latimer's 7th Sermon before Edw. VI, Serm. 14, Parker Soc., p. 248.

p. 28, *rich men's game eating up poor men's corn, grass,* &c. This goes on still, as every one in a game-preserving county knows. I heard Joseph Arch once say how his garden was cleard by Lord Warwick's rabbits, and how in return took his own compensation in game.

p. 33, *Tailors.* "now it were a hard matter for me to distinguish betweene men, who were good and who were bad, but if I might giue my verdict to say who were the wisest men nowe in this age, I would say they were *Taylers:* would you heare my reason? because I doe see the wisedome of women to be still ouer-reached by *Taylers,* that can euery day induce them to as many new-fangled fashions, as they please to inuent : and the wisedome of men againe, are as much ouer-reached by women, that canne intice their husbandes to surrender and giue way to all their newe-fangled follies : they are *Taylers* then that canne ouer-rule the wisest women, and they be women that can besot the wisest men : so that if Ma. Maiors conclusion be good, that because *Iacke,* his youngest sonne, ouer-ruled his mother, and *Iackes* mother agayne ouerruled M. Maior himselfe,

and M. Maior by office ouerruled the Towne, *Ergo*, the whole Towne was ouer-
ruled by *Iacke*, Ma. Maiors sonne : by the same consequence, I may likewise
conclude, that *Taylers* are the wisest men : the reason is alreadie rendered, they
doe make vs all *Fooles*, both men and women, and doe mocke the whole worlde
with their newe inuentions : but are they women alone that are thus seduced by
Taylers? doe but looke amongst our gallants in this age, and tell me, if you
shall not finde men amongst them to be as vaine, as nice, and as gaudie in their
attyres, as shee that amongst women is accounted the most foolish . . . . .

"The holy scriptures haue denounced a curse no lesse grieuous to the *Idole-
maker*, then to the *Idole* it selfe ; now (vnder the correction of *Diuinitie*) I would
but demaund, what are these *Puppet*-making *Taylers*, that are euery day inuent-
ing of newe fashions, and what are these, that they doe call *Attyre-makers*, the
first inuenters of these monstrous Periwygs, and the finders out of many other
like immodest Attyres : what are these, and all the rest of these *Fashion
Mongers*, the inuenters of vanities, that are euery day whetting their wits to
finde out those *Gaudes*, that are not onely offensiue vnto God, but many wayes
preiudiciall to the whole Common wealth : if you will not acknowledge these to
be *Idolemakers*, yet you cannot deny them to be the *Deuils enginers*, vngodly
instruments, to decke and ornifie such men and women, as may well be reputed
to be but *Idolles*, for they haue eyes, but they see not into the wayes of their
own saluation, & they haue eares, but they cannot heare the Iudgements of God,
denounced against them for their pride and vanitie." 1614. Barnabee Rych.
The Honestie of this Age, p. 23.

    p. 35. *Ruffes.* See Part I, p. 52, 240-2.

    p. 41, 42. *The Poor, and Beggars.* See my Harrison, Part I, p. 213, &c.

    p. 51, *long hair.* In 1614, Barnabee Rych asks : "And from whence
commeth this wearing, & this imbrodering of long lockes, this curiositie that is
vsed amongst men, in freziling and curling of their hayre, this gentlewoman-
like starcht bands, so be-edged, and be-laced, fitter for *Mayd Marion* in a *Moris
dance*, then for him that hath either that spirit or courage, that should be in a
gentleman ? "— *The Honestie of this Age*, p. 35. "There are certaine new inuented
professions that within these fourtie or fiftie years, were not so much as heard
of," says Rich, p. 24, "& yet have become flourishing, namely, 'Attyre-
makers,' Coach-makers & Coachmen, Body-makers, and Tobacco-dealers. The
3 most gainful trades are," he says, p. 28, "the first is to keepe an *Ale house*, the
2. a *Tobacco House*, and the third to keepe a *Brothell House*."

    p. 57. *A marvellous strange coniunction.* This alludes to R. Harvey's
notorious tract addrest to his brother the author Gabriel Harvey, "An
Astrological Discourse upon the great and notable Conjunction of the two
superiour Planets, Saturne and Jupiter, which shall happen the 28 day of April,
1583," 18 mo. *black letter. H. Bynneman*, 1583. The years 1588 and 1593
were to be "dangerous years" too. See my note in *N. Sh. Soc. Trans.*,
1875-6, p. 151-4.

    p. 82. *Such a dish of apples as Master Latimer talketh of, with thirty angels
in every apple.* This is in "The fifte Sermon of Mayster Hughe Latimer, whyche

he prached before the kynges Maiestye wythin hys Graces Palaice at Westminster the fyft daye of Aprill " [1549]. *Sign.* R. iii. " Ther was a patron in England (when it was) that had a benefyce fallen into hys hande, and a good brother of mine came vnto hym, and brought hym xxx. Apples in a dysh, and gaue them hys man to carrye them to hys mayster. It is like he gaue one to his man for· his laboure to make vp the game, and so ther was .xxxi.

The merye tale of the patrone that sold a benefyce for a deyntye dyshe of Apples.

" This man commeth to his mayster, and presented hym wyth the dyshe of Apples, sayinge : ' Syr, suche a man hathe sente you a [*R. iii. back*] dyshe of frute, and desyreth you to be good vnto hym for suche a benefyce.' ' Tushe, tushe,' quod he, ' thys is no apple matter. I wyll none of hys apples. I haue as good as these (or as he hath any) in myne owne orcharde.' The man came to the preest agayne, and toulde hym what hys mayster sayed. ' Then,' quod the priest, ' desyre hym yet to proue one of them for my sake, he shal find them much better then they loke for.' He cut one of them, and founde ten peces of golde in it [£10 = 30 Angels]. ' Mary,' quod he, ' thys is a good apple. The pryest standyng not farre of, herynge what the Gentle man sayed, cryed out and answered, ' they are all one apples, I warrante you, Syr, they grewe all on one tree and haue all one taste.' ' Well, he is a good fellowe [*sign.* R. iiii.], let hym haue it,' quod the patrone, &c. Get you a grafte of thys tre, and I warrante you it shall stand you in better steade then all Sayncte Paules learnynge. Well, let patrons take hede, for they shall annswere for all the soules that peryshe throughe theyr defaute." See too the Third Sermon, p. 145-6, Parker Soc., on the bribe-taking Judge flayd alive by Cambyses ; the pudding-story, p. 140.

A graft of gold to get a benefyce wythal is worth a great deale of learnynge.

NOTES FOR PART I.

p. 60*, note 2. The woodcut is at the back of the Dedication, p. 2*.

p. 86*. See too the *Homily* against Idleness.

p. 89*. Dice, wine, and women, wonne, drunke, & spent all,

And now he liues a vassall at each call.

1600. *Quips vpon Questions*, sign. E. 2, back, ' On a ruind Gallant.'

p. 95*. The cut of Irish Costumes is from the Additional MS. 28,330 in the British Museum : a Dutch ' Short Description of England, Scotland & Ireland,' 1574.

p. 97*. There is no ornamental border round the original 1584 Title-page.

p. 231. *Velure*, &c. See note p. 363-4, Dekker's Works, 1874, vol. iii.

p. 232. Nash's *Anatomie of Abuses* was enterd in the Stationers' Registers in advance, on Sept. 19, 1588.

p. 236. *Farrefetched and deare bought*. " we vse to say by manner of

Prouerbe, 'things farrefet and deare bought are good for Ladies.'" 1589.
Puttenham, p. 193, ed. Arber.

p. 248. Andrew Boorde's cut is also alluded to in the Homily against
Excess of Apparel ; and by Dekker, p. 77* above.

p. 271, 273. *Women's face-painting.*

> "Whers the Deuill? . . .
>   He's got into a boxe of Women's paint. . . .
>   Where pride is, thers the Diuell too."
>   1600. *Quips vpon Questions*, sign. F. 2.

p. 280. See the Homily against Whoredom and Adultery.

p. 284. See the Homily against Gluttony and Drunkenness.

p. 293. *Prisons.* See too in 1618, Geffrey Mynshul's *Essayes and Characters
of a Prison and Prisoners.*

p. 296. *Sunday Sports*, &c. See Humphrey Roberts's, 'An earnest Complaint of diuers vain, wicked and abused Exercises practised on the Sabath day,'
1572. Hazlitt's *Collections and Notes*, p. 360-1.

p. 307, at foot : *beaten with a Brewers washing bittle*, drunk.

> "these people
> Are all brainde with a Brewers washing beetle."
>   1600. *Quips vpon Questions*, sign. F. 2, back.

p. 318. *Deaths at Football.* Coroner's inquest on one Gibbs kild in a game.
"The Coroner, in summing up, advocated a return to the rules practised in
football twenty years ago, for, *as now played, it was only worthy of a set of
costermongers.*" See also the notice of the Mayor of Southampton prohibiting
football under Association or Rugby rules, on the town's public lands.—*Echo,*
Dec. 11, 1880. On Saturday . . . Mr. Joseph Hunter at Sheffield had his arm
and three ribs broken ; at Mexborough a young man named William Howitt had
his arm and leg dislocated.—*Daily News*, Dec. 13, 1880.

p. 349. Insert *Abandon*, v. t. banish, 125. *Ames ace & the dice*, 37*.
Deuse ace, 272 ; a man's genitals.

p. 352, col. 2. Insert *Breasts :* see Bare, and Naked.

p. 356, col. 2. *Disgesture*, digestion. "Glut with gazing, surfet with seeing
and rellish with reading [my book] :—It may be there are some preseruatiues,
not poyson, though harsh in *disgesture.* 1600. *Quips vpon Questions*, sign.
A. iij.

p. 362, col. 1. Insert *Honeymoon*, p. 376, ii. 1.

p. 371, col. 2, to 'Spanish &c.' add 'boots, 242.'

p. 375, col. 1. Insert *Venetians* 250. '*Grecques ;* f. Gregs, Gallogaskins,
wide venitians.' 1611. Cotgrave ; and *Venetian hose*, 56.

THE

Second part

of the Anatomie of

Abuses, containing The display
of Corruptions, with a perfect description of such imperfections, blemishes, and abuses, as now reigning in euerie degree, require reformation for feare
of Gods vengeance to be powred vpon
the people and countrie, without
speedie repentance and con-
uersion vnto God : made
dialogwise by Phil-
lip Stubbes.

Except your righteousnes exceed the righteousnes of the Scribes and Phari-
ses, you cannot enter into the
kingdome of heauen.

LONDON.

Printed by R. W. for William Wright,
and are to be sold at his shop ioining
to S. Mildreds Church in the
Poultrie, being the mid-
dle shop in the rowe.

THE DISPLAY OF

corruptions, requiring refor-

mation for feare of Gods iudge-

ments to be powred vpon the people

and country without spee-

die amendement.

The speakers, THEODORVS and AMPHILOGVS.[1]

OD bleſſe you my friend, and well ouertaken.

Amphilogus. You are hartilie welcome, good ſir, with all my hart.

Theod. How farre purpoſe you to trauell this way by the grace of God ?

Amphil. As far as *Nodnol* if God permit.

Theod. What place is that, I pray you, and where is it ſcituate? Stubbes is going to London.

Amphil. It is a famous citie and the chiefeſt place in *Dnalgne :* haue you not heard of it?

Theod. No truely. For I am a ſtranger, and newly come into theſe countries, onely to ſee faſhions, and to learne the ſtate and condi[2]tion of thoſe things whereof I am ignorant.

Amphil. What country man are you, I pray you, if I may be ſo bold as to aſke?

Theod. I am of the country and nation of the *Idumeans,* a cruell, fierce, and ſeruile kind of people.

Amphil. I haue beene in thoſe countries my ſelfe ere now, and He says he's been in Idumea therefore it is maruell that you knowe me not.

Theod. Me thinke I ſhould knowe you, but yet I cannot call your name to remembrance.

Amphil. My name is *Amphilogus,* ſomtime of your acquaintance, though now you haue (through tract of time, which is *Omnium*

---

[1] *Amphilogus* is Stubbes. The side notes are all mine. Stubbes put notes to his First Part only.

[2] B 1, back. The headline all thro, is ' The Display of Corruptions.'

rerum edax, A deuourer of al things) forgot the fame. But notwithftanding that you haue forgot me, yet I remember you very well : is
not your name Maifler *Theodorus ?*

Theod. Yes truly, my name is *Theodorus ;* I neither can, nor yet
will, euer denie the fame.

Amphil. What make you in thefe countries, if I may afke you
without offence ?

Theod. Truly I came hither to fee the country, people, and
nation, to learne the toong, and to fee (as I told you) the ftate
generally of all things.

Stubbes will de-
scribe the state
of England.
[¹ Sig. B 2]
¹ *Amphil.* You are moft hartily welcome, and I, hauing beene a
traueler, borne in thefe countries, and knowing the ftate thereof in
euerie refpect, to congratulate your comming, will impart vnto you
the fubftance and effect therof in as few words as I can.

Theod. I praie you then giue me leaue (vnder correction) to afke
you fuch neceffary queftions, as are incident to my purpofe, and
which may ferue for my better inftruction in all the forefaide
premiffes ?

Amphil. Go to then, afke on in the name of God, and I will
addreffe myfelf to fatiffie your reafonable requefts in anything I can.

Theod. What be the inhabiters of this countrie ? Be they a
vertuous, godlie, and religious kinde of people, or otherwife cleane
contrarie ?

Amphil. Surely they are, as all other countries and nations be for
the moft part, inclined to finne, and wickednes, drinking vp iniquitie
as it were water ; but yet I am perfuaded that, albeit all flefh hath

No nation is so
proud, drunken,
and so full of
mischief, as Eng-
land is.

[² Sig. B 2, back]
corrupted his way before the face of GOD, yet is there not any nation
or countrey vnder the funne, that for pride, whoredome, droonkennes,
gluttonie, and all kinde of oppreffion, iniurie and mifchiefe, may
compare with this one country ² of *Dnalgne,* God be mercifull vnto
it, and haften his kingdome, that all wickednes may be done away.

Theod. Then, as in all other countries where euer I haue trauelled,
fo in this alfo is verified the old adage, namely, that the firft age of
the world was called *Aurea œtas,* the golden age, for that men liued

1. The Golden
Age.
2. The Silver.
godlie and in the feare of God ; the fecond age was called *Argentea
œtas,* the filuer age, for that men began fomewhat to decline, and fall
from their former holineffe, and integritie of life, to finne and wicked-

nes: the thirde and laft age, which is this that we are fallen into, is 3. The Iron or Leaden Age, our finful one. and may juftlie be called *Ferrea* or *Plumbea ætas*, the yron or leaden age, in as much as now men are fallen from all godlineffe whatfoeuer, and are as it were wedded to iniquitie, committing finne without any remorfe, and running into all kinde of abhomination and impietie, without reftraint. All which things dulie in the good hart of a faithful chriftian confidered & weied, may eafily perfuade a wife man to think their deftruction to be at hand, except they repent.

Amphil. You fay verie well. Therefore I would wifh them to take heed to themfelues, and to leaue their wickednes before the Lords wrath be gon out againft them; for let them be [1]fure, that [1 Sig. B 3] when the meafure of their wickedneffe is full, then will the Lord cut But God 'll cut the sinners off. them off from the face of the earth, if they repent not, and truely turne to the Lord. The wife man faith, that a little before deftruc- Destruction'll follow Pride, tion come, the hart of man fhall fwell into pride, and wickednes. Our fauiour Chrift faith, when men flatter themfelues, and 'faie "peace, peace, al things are well, we neede not to feare anything," then, euen then, fhall fudden deftruction fall vpon them, as forrow commeth vpon a woman trauelling with childe, and they shall not efcape, bicaufe they would not knowe the Lord, nor the day of his vifitation.' Which thing we fee to be true through all the hiftories of as it did with Sodom and Gomorrah, the facred Bible; for when the Sodomits and Gomorreans had filled vp the meafures of their iniquitie, and faciate themfelues in finne, then came there fire and brimftone raining from heauen vpon them and their citie, and confumed them all, from the vpper face of the earth. When all the worlde in the daies of Noah, was giuen ouer to in Noah's days, finne, and wickednes, immediatelie came the floud of Gods vengeance, and deftroied them all, eight perfons—to wit, Noah, his wife, his three fonnes and their wiues,—who ferued the Lord in true fimplicity of hart, onelie excepted. The Hierofoltinitanes [2]when their finne was [2 Sig. B 3, back] ripe, were they not confounded, and put to the edge of the fworde? When Pharao the king of Egypt his finne was ripe, did not the Lord with Pharaoh, harden his hart to purfue the Ifraelits, and fo drowned him and all his retinue in the read fea? Herod and Nabuchadnezer fwelling in Herod and Nebuchadnezzar. finne, and rifing vp againft the maieftie of God in the malice of their harts, was not the one ftroken dead in a moment, and eaten vp with worms, the other depofed from his kingdome, and conftrained to eate graffe with the beafts of the earth; with the like examples, which, for the auoiding of prolixitie, I omit.   By all which it appeareth, that

When Deftruc-
tion is nearest,
folk are securest.

when deftruction is neereft, then are the people the fecureft, and the moft indurate and frozen in the dregs of their finne; and being fo, the fequele is either confufion in this life, or perdition in the world to come, or both.   And therefore I befeech the Lord, that both this country, and all others, may repent, & amende euerie one their wicked waies, to the glorie of God and their owne faluation.

Theod.   Is this country fruitfull, and plenty of all things, or barren, and emptie ?

England is a
plentiful land,

Amphil.   There is no nation or country in the world, that for ftore, and abundance of all things, may compare with the fame; for

¹ Sig. B 4]

[1] of all things there is fuch plentie (God haue the praife thereof) as they may feeme to haue neede of no other nation, but all others of them.   In fo much as if they were wife people (as they be wife inough, if they would vfe their wifedome well) to keepe their owne fubftance within themfelues, and not to tranfport it ouer to other

but covetous
wretches export
its goods.

countries (as many couetous wretches for their owne priuate gaine doe) they might liue richly and in abundance of all things, whileft other countries fhould languifh and want.   But hereof more fhall be fpoken hereafter.

Theod.   I pray you how is this country adiacent vpon other countries ?

Amphil.   It lieth inuironed with the occean fea rounde about; vpon the one fide eaftwarde, it bordereth vpon the confines of France : vpon the other fide weftward, vpon Irelande; towards the feptentrionall or north part, vpon Scotland; and vpon the fouth fide it

It has Englifh-
men, Welfhmen,
Cornifhmen,
whofe fpeech
differs from one
another.

refpecteth Germanie.   And is inhabited with three fundrie fortes of people, Englifhmen, Cornifhmen, and welchmen, all which, if not in lawes and conftitutions, yet in language, doe differ one from another.   But as they doe differ in toong and fpeech, fo are they

[² Sig. B 4, back]

fubiect (and that *Patrio iure*, By iuftice and law) [2] to one Prince, and gouernour onely to whom they owe their allegeance.

Theod.   Is the country quiet, peaceable, and at vnitie within it felfe, or otherwife troubled with mutenies, wars, and ciuill diffentions?

Amphil.   The whole lande (God be praifed therefore, and preferue hir noble Grace by whom it is gouerned and maintained !) is, and hath beene, at peace and vnitie, not onely within it felfe, but alfo abroad, for this foure or fiue and twenty yeeres. During all which time there hath beene neither wars, inuafions, infurrections, nor any effufion of blood to fpeake of, except of a fort of arch-traitours, who haue receiued but the fame reward they deferued, and the fame that I pray God all traitours with their complices may receiue hereafter, if they practife the fame which they haue done. The like continuance of peace was neuer heard of, not this hundred yeeres before, as this country hath inioied fince hir maiefties reigne: the Lord preferue hir grace, and roiall Maieftie for euer!

England has been at peace for 25 years.

Theod. Are the other countries, lands, and nations about them (for as I gather by your former intimations, this country is fcituate as it were in the centrie, or midft of ¹others) their friends, and well-willers, or their enimies?

[¹ Sig. B 5]

Amphil. It is an old faieng and true: *Ex incertis, & ambiguis rebus optimum tenere fapientis eft:* Of things vncerteine, a chriftian man ought to iudge and hope the beft. They hope wel that all are their friends and welwillers: but it is thought (and I feare me too true) that they are fo far from being their friends (*Nifi verbo tenus*, From mouth outward onely) that they haue vowed and fworne their deftruction, if they could as eafily atchiue it, as they fecretly intend it. Which thing to be true, fome of their late practifes haue (yet to their owne confufion, Gods name be praifed) proued true. For how manie times hath that man of finne, that fonne of the diuell, that *Italian* Antichrift of *Rome*, interdicted, excommunicated, fufpended, and accurfed with booke, bell and candle, both the Prince, the No-bilitie, the Commons, and whole Realme? How often hath he fent foorth his roring buls againft hir Maieftie, excommunicating (as I have faid) hir Grace, and difcharging hir Highneffe liege people and naturall fubiects, from their allegeance to hir Grace? How often hath he with his adherents confpired and intended the death and ouerthrowe of hir Maieftie and Nobilitie, by con²iuration, necromancy, exorcifmes, art magike, witchcraft, and all kind of diuelrie befides, wherein the moft part of them are fkilfuller than in diuinity? And when thefe deuifes would not take place, nor effect as they wifhed, then attempted they by other waies and meanes to ouerthrowe the eftate, the Prince, nobles, people and country: fometime by fecret irruption, fometime

But it has lip-friends who hate it.

That son of the Devil, the Pope,

has conspired the Queen's death,

[² Sig. B 5, back]

and tried to over-throw the land.

by open inuafion, infurrection, and rebellion, fometime by open treafon, fometime by fecret confpiracie, and fometimes by one meanes, fometimes by another.   And now of late attempted they the ouerthrowe and fubuerfion of hir Maieftie, people, country, and all

The Pope has sent here blood-thirsty Papists

by fending into the realme a fort of cutthrotes, falfe traitors, and bloudthirftie Papifts, who vnder the pretence of religious men (in whom for the moft part there is as much religion as is in a dog) fhould not onely lurke in corners like howlets that abhorre the light, creepe into noble mens bofoms, thereby to withdrawe hir Maiefties

to stir up re-bellions.

fubiects from their allegeance, but alfo moue them to rebellion, and to take fword in hand againft Prince, country, yea, and againft God himfelfe (if it were poffible) and to difpenfe with them that fhall thus mifchieuouflye behaue themfelues.   And forfooth thefe goodlie

[¹ Sig. B 6] These Devil's agents are calld Jesuits,

fellowes, the diuels agents, that muft worke thefe feates, are called (in the ¹diuels name) by the name of Iefuites, feminarie preefts, and catholikes, vfurping to themfelues a name neuer heard of till of late daies, being indeed a name verie blafphemoufly deriued from the name of Iefus, and improperly alluded and attributed to themfelues. But what will it preuaile them to be like vnto Iefus in name onely, or how can they, nay, how dare they, arrogate that name vnto them-felues, whereas their doctrine, religion, life and whole profeffion, togither with their corrupt liues and conuerfations are directly con-

but their every deed and word is directly contrary to Christ's.

trarie to the doctrine, religion, life, and profeffion of Chrift Iefus? There is nothing in the world more contradictorie one to another, than all their proceedings in generall are to Chrift Iefus and his lawes, and yet will they, vnder the pretence of a bare and naked name, promife to themfelues fuch excellencie, fuch integritie, and perfection, as GOD cannot require more, yea; fuch as doth merite *Ex opere operato,*

They delude the world with their trash.

Eternall felicitie in the heauens.   And thus they deceiue themfelues, and delude the world alfo with their trafh: but of them inough.

Theod.   Surely that country had neede to take heed to it felfe, to

[² Sig. B 6, back

feare, and ftand in awe, ²hauing fo manie enimies on euerie fide.   And aboue all things next vnto the feruing of God, to keepe themfelues aloofe, and in any cafe not to truft them, what faire weather foeuer the make them.   The fweeter the *Syren* fingeth, the dangeroufer is it to lend hir our eares: the Cocatrice neuer meaneth fo much crueltie, as when he fawneth vpon thee and weepeth: then take heed, for he meaneth to fucke thy bloud. The ftiller the water ftandeth, the more perilous it is. Let them remember it is an old and true faieng : *Sub melle iacet venenum,* Vnder honey lieth hid poifon. *Sub placidis herbis latitat coluber,* vnder the pleafanteft graffe, lurketh the venemouft adder. Take heed of thofe fellowes that haue *Mel in ore, verba lactis,* fweet words and plaufible fpeeches : for they haue *Fel in corde,* and *Fraudem factis,* Gall in their harts, & deceit in their deeds. So falleth it out with thefe ambidexters, thefe hollowe harted friends, where they intend deftruction, then will they couer it with the cloke or garment of amity & friendfhip ; therefore are they not to be trufted.

These Jesuits are ambidexters, hollow-hearted friends,

Amphil. You fay the truth. For I am thus perfuaded, that he who is falfe to God (as all [1]Papifts with their complices and adherents are) can neuer be true and faithfull, neither to prince nor country. Therefore God grant they may be taken heed of betimes.

[1 Sig. B 7]

never true to prince or country

Theod. Confidering that this country of *Dnalgne* is enuied abroad with fo many enimies, and infefted within by fo many feditious Papifts, and hollowe harted people, it is great maruell, that it can ftand without great wars, and troubles. Belike it hath a wife politike prince, and good gouernors, either elfe it were vnpoffible to preferue the fame in fuch peace and tranquillitie, and that fo long togither. I pray you therefore by what prince is the fame gouerned, and after what maner ?

Amphil. The whole realme or country of *Dnalgne* is ruled and gouerned by a noble Queene, a chafte Maide, and pure Virgin, who for all refpects may compare with any vnder the funne. In fo much as I doubt not to call hir facred breaft the promptuarie, the receptacle, or ftorehoufe of all true virtue and godlines. For if you fpeake of wifdome, knowledge and vnderftanding, hir Grace is fingular, yea, able at the firft blufh to difcearne truth from falfehood, and falfehood from truth; in any matter, how ambiguous or obfcure foeuer : fo as it may iuftly be called into queftion whether [2]*Salomon* himfelfe had greater light of wifedome inftilled into his facred breaft, than hir Maieftie hath into hir highnes roiall minde. If you fpeake of learning and knowledge in the toongs, whether it be in the Latine, Greeke, French, Dutch, Italian, Spanifh, or any other vfuall toong, it may be doubted whether Chriftendome hath hir peere, or not. If you fpeake

England is governd by a noble Queen,

virtuous and godly, wise and understanding,

[1 Sig. B 7, back]

learned in the tongues.

modest, gentle, affable,
of fobrietie, modeftie, manfuetude and gentleneffe, it is woonderfull in hir Highneffe; yea, fo affable, fo lowly and humble is hir Grace, as fhe will not difdaine to talke familiarlie to the meaneft or pooreft

merciful,
of hir Graces fubjects vpon fpeciall occafions. If you fpeake of mercie, and compaffion to euery one that hath offended, I ftande in fufpence

religious, just,
whether hir like were euer borne.   If you fpeake of religion, of zeale and feruencie to the truth, or if you fpeake of the vpright execution or adminiftration of iuftice, all the world can beare witnes, that herein (as in all godlineffe elfe) hir Highnes is inferior to none

more divine than earthly.
that liueth at this day.   So that hir Grace feemeth rather a d'uine creature, than an earthly creature, a veffel of grace, mercie and compaffion, whereinto the Lord hath powred euen the full meafures of his fuperabundant grace, and heauenlie influence.   The Lord increafe

The Lord preserve her I
[¹ Sig. B 8]
the fame in hir ¹Highnes roiall breaft, and preferue hir Grace, to the end of the world, to the glorie of God, the comfort of hir Maiefties fubiects, and confufion of all hir enimies whatfoeuer.

Theod. What is hir Maiefties Councell?   It fhould feeme that they muft needes be excellent men, hauing fuch a vertuous Ladie and Phenix Queene to rule ouer them?

The Queen's Council are wise and experienst men,
Amphil. The Councell are Honorable and noble perfonages indeed, of great grauitie, wifedome, and pollicie, of fingular experience, modeftie and difcretion, for zeale to religion famous, for dexteritie in giuing counfell renoumed, for the adminiftration of iuftice incomparable, finally, for all honorable and noble exploits inferior to none, or rather excelling all.   So as their worthie deedes, through the golden trumpe of fame are blowne ouer all the worlde.   The whole regiment

who make the laws, which are carried out by Magistrates.
of the Realme confifteth in the execution of good lawes, fanctions, ftatutes, and conftitutions enacted and fet foorth by hir royall Maieftie and hir moft honorable Councel, and committed by the fame to inferior officers, and maieftrates to be put in practife, by whofe diligent execution thereof, iuftice is maintained, vertue erected, iniurie repreffed, and finne feuerely punifhed, to the great glorie of God, and

[² Sig. B 8, back]
²common tranquilitie of the Realme in euery condition.

Theod. Is the lande diuided into fhires, counties, precincts, and feuerall exempt liberties, to the ende iuftice may the better be maintained?   And hath euery county, fhire, and precinct, good lawes in the fame for the deciding and appeafing of controuerfies that happen in the fame, fo that they neede not to feeke further for redreffe than in their owne fhire?

Amphil. The whole land indeede is diuided (as you fay,), into fhires, counties, and feuerall precincts, (which are in number, as I take it, 40). In euerie which fhire or countie, be courts, lawe daies, and leets, as they call them, euery moneth, or every quarter of a yeere, wherin any controuerfie (lightlie) may be heard and determined, fo that uone needs (except vpon fome fpeciall occafions) to feeke to other courts for deciding of any controuerfie. But as there be good lawes, if they were executed dulie, fo are there corruptions and abufes not a few crept into them. For fometimes you fhall haue a matter hang in fute after it is commenced a quarter of a yeere, halfe a yeare, yea, a twelue month, two or three yeeres togither, yea, feauen or eight yeeres now and then, if either friends or money can [1] be made. This deferring of iuftice is as damnable before God, as the fentence of falfe iudgement is, as that bleffed martyr of God, Maifter *Latimer*, hath faid in a fermon made before King *Edward* the fixt. Befides this deferring and delaieng of poore mens caufes, I will not fay how iudgement is perverted in the end. I reed them take heed to it that be the authors thereof. Therefore the reformed churches beyond the feas are worthie of commendations; for there the Iudges fit in the open gates, ftreets, and high waies, that euery man that will, may fpeake vnto them, and complaine if he haue occafion. And fo farre from delaieng, or putting of [2] poore mens caufes be they, as they will not fuffer any matter, how weighty foeuer, to hang in fute aboue one day, or two, or at the moft three daies, which happeneth verie feldome. But if the lawes within euery particular countie or fhire were dulie adminiftred without parcialite, and truly executed with all expedition, as they ought, and not fo lingred as they be, then needed not the poore people to run 100, 200, yea 300, or 400 miles (as commonly they doe) to feeke iuftice, when they might haue it neerer home: through the want whereof, befides that their futes are like to hang in ballance peraduenture feuen yeeres, [3] they, hauing fpent al, in the end fall to extreme beggerie; which inconuenience might eafilie be remoued, if all matters and caufes whatfoeuer were heard at home in their owne fhire or countie with expedition. And to fay the truth, what fooles

England is divided into shires and precincts, in each of which Law-Courts are held monthly or quarterly.

But abuses have crept in : causes are delayd, and that's as bad as false judgment, as Latimer said.

[1 Sig. C 1]

Also poor folk have to go 100 miles off to get justice,

[3 Sig. C 1, back]
and perhaps wait for 7 years.

² off.

are they (yea, woorthie to be inaugured fooles with the laurell crowne of triple follie) that, whilft they might haue iuftice at home in their owne country, and all matters of controuerfie decided amongft their neighbors and friends at home, will yet go to lawe two or three hundred miles diftant from them, and fpend all that they haue to inrich a fort of greedie lawiers, when at the laft a fort of ignorant men of their neighbors muft make an end of it, whether they will or not. This, me thinke, if euerie good man would perpend in himfelfe, he would neither go to lawe himfelf, nor yet giue occafion to others to doe the like.

They spend their all, too, on greedy lawyers.

Theod. I gather by your fpeeches that thefe people are very contentious and quarellous, either elfe they would neuer be fo defirous of revenge, nor yet profecute the lawe fo feuerely for euery trifle.

Englishmen are very contentious, and fond of going to law.
[¹ Sig. C 2]

Amphil. They are very contentious indeed. Infomuch as, if one giue neuer fo fmall occafion to another, fute muft ftraight be commenced; and to lawe go they, as round as a ball, till ¹either both, or at leaft the one, become a begger all daies of his life after.

Theod. But on the other fide, if they fhuld not go to lawe, then fhould they fuftaine great wrong, and be iniuried on euery fide.

TheLaw was made to do right and to still strife, but it's now perverted to contrary ends.

Amphil. Indeed the lawe was made for the adminiftration of equitie and iuftice, for the appeafing of controuerfies & debates, and for to giue to every man (*Quod fuum eft*) That which is his owne, but being now peruerted and abufed to cleane contrarie ends (for now commonly the law is ended as a man is fr[e]inded) is it not better to fuffer a little wrong with patience, referring the reuenge to him who faith : *Mihi vindiĉtam, & ego retribuam.* ' Vengeance is mine, and I wil reward,' than for a trifle to go to lawe, and fpende all that euer he hath, and yet come by no remedie neither? Our fauiour Chrift biddeth vs, if any man will go to law with vs for our cote, to giue him our cloke alfo, and if any man will giue thee a blowe on the one cheeke, turne to him the other, whereby is ment, that if any man will iniúrie vs, and doe vs wrong, we fhould not refift nor trouble our felues, but fuffer awhile, and with patience refer the due reuenge thereof to the Lord.

Christ teaches us to suffer wrong patiently, and let God revenge it.

[² Sig. C 2, back]

Amphil. Why? Is it not lawful then for one Chriftian ²man, to go to lawe with another?

Amphil. The Apoftle faith ' many things are lawfull which are not expedient,' and therefore, though it be after a fort lawfull, yet for euery trifle it is not lawfull, but for matters of importance it is. And yet not neither, if the matter might otherwife, by neighbors at home, be determined.

Theod. Yet fome doubt whether it be lawfull or no for one Chriftian man to go to lawe with another for any worldly matter, bringing in the apoftle Paule rebuking the Corinthians for going to lawe one with another.

St. Paul rebukes the Corinthians, who were Christians, for going to law before Heathens.

Amphil. The apoftle in that place reprehendeth them not for going to law for reafonable caufes, but for that they, being chriftians, went to lawe vnder heathen iudges, which tended to the great difcredite and infamie of the Gofpell. But certeine it is, though fome anabaptifts *Quibus veritas odio eft,* and certeine other heritikes have taught the contrarie, yet it is certeine, that one chriftian man may go to lawe with an other for caufes reafonable. For it being true, as it cannot be denied, that there is a certeine fingularitie, intereft, and proprietie in euery thing, and the lawe being not onely the meane to conferue the fame propriety, but alfo to reftore it againe, [1]being violate, is therefore lawfull, and may lawfully be attempted out, yet with this prouifo, that it is better, if the matter may otherwife be apeafed at home, not to attempt lawe, than to attempt it. But if any fchifmatikes (as alas the worlde is too full of them) fhould altogether deny the vfe of the lawe, as not chriftian, befides that the manifeft word of God in euery place would eafilie conuince them, the examples and practifes of all ages, times, countries, and nations, from the firft beginning of the world, togither with the example of our fauiour Chrift himfelfe, who fubmitted himfelfe to the lawes then eftablifhed, would quicklie ouerthrow their vaine imaginations. The lawe in it felfe, is the fquare, the leuell, and rule of equitie and iuftice, and therefore who abfolutely contendeth the fame not to be chriftian, may well be accufed of extreeme folly. But if the lawes be wicked and antichriftian, then ought not good chriftians to fue vnto them, but rather to fuftaine all kind of wrong whatfoeuer.

But as it's Law's business to keep things straight, Christians may go to law.

[1 Sig. C 3]

Law is the square and level of Equity.

Theod. Then it feemeth by your reafon, that if the lawe be fo neceffarie, as without the which Chriftian kingdomes could not ftand, then are lawiers neceffarie alfo for the execution thereof.

[2]*Amphil.* They are moft neceffarie. And in my iudgement a man

[2 Sig. C 3, back]

Lawyers are
necessary, and
can serve God :
but English ones
don't, they've
such cheveril
consciences.

Lawyers take
bribes, and beg-
gar the poor, and

turn Law topsy-
turvy.

Their fee is an
Angel, 10s.

[¹ Sig. C 4]

The abuses of
our procedure
and Prisons are
frightful.

A man is clapt in
irons, thrown
into a dungeon,
with only a little
straw fit for a

dog : and there
he lies, lice-bit,
ill-fed, till he
looks like a
ghost, or dies.

He stops there
for 3 months, 3
years, perhaps
his whole life.

can ferue God in no calling better than in it, if he be a man of a good confcience, but in *Dnalgne* the lawiers have fuch chauerell confciences, that they can ferue the deuill better in no kind of calling than in that : for they handle poore mens matters coldly, they execute iuftice parcially, & they receiue bribes greedily, fo that iuftice is peruerted, the poore beggared, and many a good man iniuried therby. They refpect the perfons, and not the caufes ; mony, not the poore ; rewards, and not confcience. So that law is turned almoft topfie turuie, and therefore happy is he that hath leaft to doe with them.

Theod. The lawiers muft needes be verie rich if they haue fuch large confciences.

Amphil. Rich, quoth you ? They are rich indeede toward the deuill and the world, but towards God and heauen, they are poore inough. It is no meruaile if they be rich and get much, when they will not fpeak two words vnder an angell (for that is called a counfellers fee.) But how they handle the poore mens caufes for it, God and their owne confciences can tell ; and one day, I feare me, they fhall feele to their perpetuall paine, except they repent and amend.

¹ *Theod.* How be iudgments executed there vpon offenders, tranf-greffours, and malefactors ? with equitie, & expedition, or otherwife ?

Amphil. It greeueth me to relate thereof vnto you, the abufes therein are fo inormous. For if a felone, homicide, a murtherer, or elfe what greeuous offender foeuer, that hath deferued a thoufand deaths, if it were poffible, happen to be taken and apprehended, he is ftraightway committed to prifon, and clapt vp in as many cold yrons as he can beare, yea, throwne into dungeons and darke places vnder the ground, without either bed, clothes, or anything elfe to helpe himfelfe withall, faue a little ftraw or litter bad inough for a dog to lie in. And in this miferie fhall he lie, amongft frogs, toades, and other filthie vermine, till lice eate the flefh of² his bones. In the meane fpace hauing nothing to eate, but either bread and water or elfe fome other modicum fcarce able to fuffice nature ; and many times it hapneth, that for want of the fame pittance they are macerate and fhronke fo low, as they either looke like ghofts, or elfe are famifhed out of hand. And this extreme mifery they lie in fome time (perhaps) a quarter of a yeere, fometimes halfe a yeere, a

² off.

tweluemonth, yea, fometimes two or three yeeres, and perchance [1]all their life, though they haue deferued death, by their flagitious facts committed. Who feeth not that it were much better for them to die at once, than to fuffer this extreme miferie? Yea, the fufferance of this extremitie is better vnto them, than the taft of prefent death it felfe. And therefore in the cities reformed beyond feas, there is notable order for this: for as foone [as] any fellon or malefactor what-foeuer that hath deferued death is taken, he is brought before the magiftrate, witneffe comes in, and giues euidence againft him, and being found gilty, and conuict by iuftice, is prefently, without any further imprifonment, repriuation or delay, condemned, and being condemned, is led prefently to the place of execution, and fo com-mitted to the fword.

[1 Sig. C 4, back]

The oversea Re-formd Cities try culprits at once, and execute em.

Theod. What is the caufe why they are kept fo long before they go to execution in *Dnalgne.*

Amphil. Sometimes it commeth to paffe by reafon of (will doe all) otherwife called mony, and fometimes by freends, or both, for certeine it is, the one will not worke without the other. Hereby it commeth to paffe, that great abufes are committed. For if any man that hath freends and mony (as mony alwaies bringeth freendes with him) chance to haue [2]committed neuer fo heinous, or flagicious a deed, whether robbed, ftollen, flaine, killed or muithered, or what-foeuer it be, then letters walke, freends beftir them, and mony carrieth all away: yea, and though the lawe condemne him, iuftice conuicteth him, and good confcience executeth him, yet muft he needes be repriued, and in the meane time his pardon, by falfe fuggeftion forfooth, muft be purchafed, either for friendfhip or mony.

Will-do-all or money. In England the delay's due to Will-Do-All, money.

[2 Sig. C 5]

If a felon or murderer has friends and money, he's safe to get reprievd or pardond.

Theod. That is a great abufe, that he whom the lawe of God and of man doth condemne, fhould be pardoned. Can man pardon or remit him whom God doth condemne? Or fhall man be more mercifull in euill, then the author of mercie himfelfe? it is God that condemneth, who is he that can faue? Therefore thofe that ought to die by the lawe of God, are not to be faued by the lawe of man. The lawe of God commandeth that the murtherer, the adulterer, the exorcift, magician and witch, and the like, fhould die the death. Is it now in the power or ftrength of man to pardon him his life?

Amphil. Although it be wilfull and purpofed murther, yet is the

The crime is set down to chance medley, accident.
[¹ Sig. C 5, back]

prince borne in hande that it was plaine chance medley (as they call it) meere cafuall, and fortunate, and therefore ¹may eafily be difpenfed withall.   Indeede, the wifedome of God ordeined, that if any man chanced to kill an other againft his will, he fhould flie to certeine cities of refuge, and fo be faued, but if it were proued that he killed him wittingly, willingly, & prepenfedly, then he fhould without al exception be put to death.   And herein is great abufe, that two hauing committed one and the fame fault, the one fhall be pardoned and the other executed.   If it be fo that both haue committed offence worthy of death, let both die for it; if not, why fhould either die?   Experience prooueth this true, for if a Gentleman commit a greeuous offence, and a poore man commit the like, the poore shal

If a Gentleman and a Poor Man commit the same offence, the Gentleman gets pardond, and the Poor Man hung.

be fure of his *Sursum collum*?   But the other fhall be pardoned.   So Diogenes, feeing a fort of poore men going to hanging, fell into a great laughter.   And being demanded wherefore he laughed, he anfwered at the vanitie and follie of this blind word.   For, faith he, I

Yet isn't a grasping landlord or lawyer, a bigger thief than the poor man who steals from hunger?

fee great theeues lead little theeues to hanging.   And to fay the truth, before God, is not he a greater theefe that robbeth a man of his good name for euer, that taketh a mans houfe ouer his head, before his yeeres be expired, that wrefteth *from* a man his goods, his lands and liuings whervpon he, his wife, children and familie fhould

[² Sig. C 6]

²liue, than he that ftealeth a fheepe, a cow, or an oxe, for neceffities fake onely, hauing not otherwife to releeue his neede?   And is not he a great theefe that taketh great fummes of mony of the poore (vnder the names of fees), and doth little or nothing for them?   Though this be not theft before the world, nor punifhable by penall lawes, yet before God it is plaine theft, and punifhable with eternall torments in hel.   Let them take heede to it.

Theod. Cannot the prince then pardon any malefactor?

Amphil. Some are of opinion that the prince, by his power imperiall and prorogatiue, may pardon and remit the penaltie of any law, either diuine or humane, but I am of opinion that if Gods lawe

No prince should pardon him whom God's law condemns.

condemne him, no prince ought to faue him, but to execute iudgement and iuftice without refpect of perfons to all indifferently.   But in caufes wherein Gods lawe doth not condemne him, the prince may pardon the offender, if there appeere likelyhoode of amendment in him.   And yet let the prince be fure of this, to anfwere at the day of

iudgement before the tribunall feate of GOD, for all the offences that
the partie pardoned fhall commit any time of his life after. For if
the prince had cutte him off when the ¹lawe had paffed on him, that [¹ Sig. C 6, back]
euill had not been committed. To this purpofe I remember I haue
heard a certeine pretie apothegue vttered by a iefter to a king. The
king had pardoned one of his fubiectes that had committed murther,
who, being pardoned, committed the like offence againe, and by
meanes was pardoned the fecond time alfo, and yet filling up the
meafure of his iniquitie, killed the third, and being brought before
the king, the king being very forie, afked why he had killed three
men, to whom his iefter ftanding by replied, faieng : " No (O king)   How a king was
he killed but the firft, and thou haft killed the other two : for if thou   shown by his
  jester that, by
hadft hanged him vp at the firft, the other two had not beene killed,   pardoning a
  murderer, he had
therefore thou haft killed them, and fhalt anfwere for their bloud."   killd 2 men.
Which thing being heard, the king hanged him vp ftraightway, as he
very well deferued : yet notwithftanding, I grant that a prince by his
power regall and prerogatiue imperial may pardon offenders, but not
fuch as Gods lawes and good confcience doe condemne, as I faid
before. The power of a prince is comprehended *In Rebus licitis in
Deo*, but not *in Rebus illicitis contra Deum*: In things lawfull in God,
not in things vnlawfull contrarie to God. No power or principalitie
vpon the earth ¹whatfoeuer may difpenfe with the lawe of God, but [¹ Sig. C 7]
what it fetteth downe muft ftand inuiolable. Therefore if it be
afked me wherein a prince may pardon any malefactor, I anfwer, for   A prince can
  only pardon
the breach or violation of any humane lawe, ordinance, conftitution,   breaches of man's
ftatute, or fanction, but not againft Gods word and lawe in any   law, not God's.
condition.

    Theod. How is iuftice miniftered there, fincerely and truely, fo as
the poore haue no caufe iuftly to complaine, or otherwife ?

    Amphil. If any haue caufe to complaine (as alas too many
haue) it is for want of due execution of the lawes, not for lacke
of good lawes. For, God be praifed, there be many good lawes,
but indeed now and then through the negligence of the officers they
are coldly executed. But if the lawes there in force were without
parcialitie dulie executed, there fhuld be no iuft occafion for any to
complaine. And truly to fpeake my confcience there is great parcialitie   There's great
  partiality in Eng-
  lish magistrates
in the magiftrates and officers, nay, great corruption. For if a rich   and officers.

man and a poore man chance to haue to doe before them, the matter
I warrant you fhall quickly be ended, and, my life for yours, fhall go
vpon the rich mans fide, notwithftanding the poore mans right be

apparent to all the world.   But ¹if two poore men of equall eftate go
to lawe togither, then their fute fhall hang three or foure yeeres,
peraduenture feuen yeeres, a dozen, yea twentie yeeres, before it be

ended, till either the one or both be made beggers.   For reformation
whereof, I would wifh iudges and officers to refpect the caufe, not the
perfons, the matter, not the gaine ? and not to regard either letter or
any thing elfe, which might be fent them to peruert true iudgement.
And iuftice being miniftred, then to read ouer their commendatorie
letters in Gods name, remembring what the wife man faith : ' Gifts

blinde the eies of the wife, and peruert iudgement.'   The lawiers I
would wifh to take leffe fees of their clients.   For is not this a plaine
theft before God, to take ten, twentie, or fortie fhillings of one poore
man at one time, and fo much of a great fort at once, and yet to
fpeake neuer a word for the moft part of it ?   And notwithftanding that
they can be prefent but at one barre at once, yet will they take diuers

fees of fundry clients to fpeake for them at three or foure places in
one day.   The other officers who grant foorth the warrants, the

Subpœnas, the *Scire facias,* and diuers other writs, and thofe who
keepe the feales of the fame, I would wifh to take leffe fees alfo.   For

is not ²this too vnreafonable, to take a crowne, or ten fhillings for
writing fix or feuen lines, or little more.   And then the keeper of the

feale, for a little waxe, he muft haue as much as the other.   And
thus they fucke out (as it were) euen the very marrowe out of poore
mens bones.   The fhirifs, bailifs, and other officers alfo, I would wifh,
for fees, for bribes, for friendfhip and rewards, not to returne a *Tarde
venit,* or a *Non eft inuentus,* when they haue either fent the partie
word to auoid couertly, or elfe, looking through their fingers, fee him,
& will not fee him, forcing herby the poore plaintife to lofe not
only his great & importable charges in the lawe, but alfo peraduenture his whole right of that which he fueth for.   Thus let
euery officer by what kind of name or title foeuer he be called, or in

what kind of calling foeuer he be placed, doe all things with fingle
eie, and good confcience, that God may be glorified, the common
peace maintained, iuftice fupported, and their owne confciences dif-

·charged againft the great daye of the Lorde, when all flefh fhall be conuented before the tribunall feate of G O D all naked as euer they were borne, to render accounts of all their dooings, whether they bee good or badde, and to receiue a rewarde according to their deeds. [1]By all which it appeareth, that if any for want of iuftice haue caufe to complaine, it is thorow the corruption of iniquitie, auarice, and ambition of greedy and infaciable cormorants, who, for defire of gaine, make hauocke of all things, yea, make fhipwracke of bodies and foules to the deuill for euer, vnleffe they repent. [1 Sig. C. 8, back]

Theod. How farre are princes lawes to be obeied, in all things indifferently without exception? Princes are to be obeyd in all things not contrary to God's law.

Amphil. In all things not contrarie to the lawe of God and good confcience, which, if they be againft God and true godlineffe, then muft we fay with the apoftles, *Melius eft deo obedire, quam hominibus,* It is better to obey God than man.

Theod. If the prince than doe fet foorth a lawe contrarie to the lawe of God, and do conftraine vs to doe that, that Gods word commandeth vs we fhall not doe. In this or like cafe, may fubiects lawfully take armes, and rife againft their prince?

Amphil. No, at no hand, vnleft they will purchafe to themfelues eternall damnation, and the wrath of God for euer. For it is not lawfull tor the fubiects to rife up in armes againft their liege prince for any occafion what[2]foeuer. For proofe whereof we read that our fauiour Chrift was, not onely obedient to the maigiftrates, and fuperior powers in all things, but alfo taught his apoftles, difciples, and in them all people and nations of the world, the very fame doctrine. And therefore the apoftle faith, *Omnis anima poteftatibus fuperioribus fubdita fit :* Let euery foule fubmit himfelfe to the higher powers, for there is no power but of God. And he that refifteth this power, refifteth the ordinance of God, and purchafeth to himfelfe eternall damnation. Peter alfo giueth the like charge, that obedience in all godlines be giuen to the fuperior powers, and that praiers and interceffions be made for kings and rulers, and giueth the reafon why, namely, that we may lead *Vitam pacificam,* A peaceable life vnder them. But their subjects mustn't in any case take arms against them. [2 Sig. D. 1] If subjects do, they resist God's ordinance.

Theod. Why? How than? If we fhall not refift them, then we do obey them in any thing either good or bad.

Amphil. No, not fo neither. In all things not contrarie to Gods word we muſt obey the*m*, on paine of damnation. But in things contrarie to the word and truth of God, we are thus to doe. We muſt depoſe and lay foorth ourſelues, both bodie, and goods, life, and time, (our [1] conſcience onely excepted, in the true obedience whereof we are to ſerue our God) euen all that we haue of nature, and committing the ſame into the hands of the prince, ſubmit our ſelues, and lay downe our necks vpon the blocke, chooſing rather to die than to doe any thing contrarie to the lawe of God and good conſcience. And this is that, that the apoſtles ment when they ſaide : It is better to obey God than man. Not that obedience to man in all godlineſſe is forbid, but that obedience to God is to be preferred before the obedience to man.

Theod. What if the prince be a tyrant, a wicked prince, and an vngodly, is he notwithſtanding to be obeied ?

Amphil. Yea, truely in the ſame order as I haue ſhewed before. For whether the prince be wicked, or godlye, hee is ſent of GOD, bicauſe the Apoſtle ſaith : Thére is no power but of GOD. If the prince be a godlye prince, then is hee ſent as a great bleſſing from GOD, and if hee be a tyrant, then is he raiſed of GOD for a ſcourge to the people for their ſinnes. And therefore whether the prince be the one, or the other, he is to be obeied as before.

Theod. And bee kings and rulers to [2] bee beloued, and praied for of their ſubieƈts.

Amphil. That is without all doubt. For hee that hateth his prince in his hart, is a contemner of Gods ordinance, a traitour vnto GOD, and to his countreye : yea, hee is to loue his prince as well as himſelſe, and better, if better can bee, and to praye for him as for himſelfe. For that an infinite number doe reſt and depend vppon his Maieſtie, which doe not ſo vppon himſelfe. So that the miſcarrieng of him, were the deſtruction (peraduenture) of manye thouſands.

Theod. This being ſo, then hath *Dnalgne* great cauſe to praye for their prince, by whoſe woorthye indeuour, and wiſe gouernement, the ſtate of that realme is ſo peaceably maintained.

Amphil. They haue great cauſe indeede not onely to loue hir Maieſtie, but alſo to praye for hir Grace, and whoſoeuer will not doe ſo, I beſeech the LORDE in the bowels of his mercie, to ſtoppe their

If princes order things against God's law, subjects must lay down goods and life, and

[1 Sig. D. 1, back]

put their necks on the block, rather than disobey God.

Even if the prince is ungodly, he's sent by God,

and is to be obeyd.
[2 Sig. D. 2]

Every one is to love his prince as himself.

May every Englishman who won't love and pray for Queen Elizabeth, die straight off !

breath, and to take them awaye quicklye from the face of the earth.
For by hir Highneſſe wiſe gouernement, the realme is in peace, Gods
word flouriſheth, and aboundance ¹ of al things floweth in the ´fame, [¹ Sig. D. 2, back]
the Lord God be praiſed therefore, and preſerue hir noble Grace long
to reigne amongſt vs. Amen.

Theod. Let vs proceed a little further : I pray you how is the youth As to Education,
of that country brought vp, in learning or otherwiſe?

Amphil. The youth truely is well brought vp, both in good letters,
nurture, and maners for the moſt part. For the better performance
whereof, they haue excellent good ſchooles, both in cities, townes, we've good
schools, and
and countries, wherein abundance of children are learnedly brought plenty of children
at 'em,
vp. But yet notwithſtanding, ſome parents are much to be blamed in
the education of their children, for the moſt keepe their ſonnes to
ſchoole but for a time, till they can write and read, and well if all but the boys stay
only till they can
that too, and very ſeldome or neuer doe they keepe them ſo long at read and write ;
their bookes, as vntill they atteine to any perfect knowledge indeed.
So that by this means learning doth, and is like, greatly to decay. And
if one aſke them, why they keepe not their children to ſchoole till they
prooue learned, they will anſwer, " Bicauſe I ſee learning and learned then they're put
to business, be-
men are little eſteemed, and ne thinke the beſt of them can hardly cause they can't
live by Learning,
live by the ſame. And therefore I will ſet him to an occupation, which gets small
preferment now-
which will be alwaies ſure." As herein they ſay ²true, for I cannot adays.
but lament the ſmall preferment now adaies that learning gettéth in [² Sig. D. 3]
the world amongſt men, & the ſmal account that is made of the
ſame. This is the cauſe why learning doth, and will in time, greatly
decay. For who is he, that hauing ſpent all his ſubſtance vpon learning, yea, his bodie, ſtrength, and all, and yet can hardly line thereby,
and maintaine himſelfe withall, that will couet after learning, which is
both ſo chargeable, and painfull to be come by?

Theod. Be there not Vniuerſities, colledges, and free ſchooles, The free Colleges
and Schools
where youth may bee brought vp in learning *Gratis* without any are abused and
perverted
charges to their parents?

Amphil. There are ſuch places indeed. But alas they are abuſed
& peruerted to other ends than was intended by them at the firſt.
For whereas thoſe places had great liuings, rents, reuenues & poſ-
ſeſſions giuen to them, it was to this onely end and purpoſe, that
thoſe poore children whoſe parents were not able otherwiſe to main-

taine them at learning, fhould be brought vp vpon the charges of the houfe, and not thofe whofe parents are able to maintaine them of themfelues.   But now we fee the contrarie is true, and whereas they

from poor chil-
dren to rich ones.
[¹ Sig. D. 3, back]

were giuen to maintaine none but the poore only, now ¹ they main-taine none but the rich onely.   For except one be able to giue the

Unless a father
can bribe the
Master,

regent or prouoft of the houfe, a peece of mony, ten pound, twentie pound, fortie pound, yea, a hundred pound, a yoke of fatte oxen, or a couple of fine geldings, or the like, though he be neuer fo toward a

his son 'll not get
into College or
School.

youth, nor haue neuer fo much need of maintenance, yet he comes not there, I warant him.   If he cannot preuaile this way, Let him get him letters commendatory from fome of reputation, and per-chance he may fpeed, in hope of benefite to infue.   So that the places

The places are
jobd, not given
to the needy.

in the vniuerfities and free fchooles, feeme rather to be folde for mony and frienfhip, than giuen *gratis* to them that haue neede, as they ought to be.

   Theod. Are there not many inferior fcholes in the country befides, both for the inftruction and catechifing of youth?

   Amphil. There are fo, almoft in euery parifh.   But alas, fuch

In poor schools,
Schoolmasters
are so badly paid
that pupils snort
in palpable ignor-
ance all their
days.

fmall pittance is allowed the fchoolmaifters, as they can neither buy the libraries, nor which is leffe, hardly maintaine themfelues; which thing altogither difuadeth them from their bookes, and is occafion why many a one fnorteth in palpable ignorance all daies of their life.

   Theod. Would you haue any man without exception, to take

[² Sig. D. 4]

vppon him the office of a ²fchoolmaifter, and to teach the youth?

   Amphil. No, at no hand.   Firft I would wifh that euery one

Every School-
master should be
examind for
character and
knowledge,

that is a fchoolmafter, how learned or vnlearned foeuer, fhould be examined, as wel for his religion, and his fufficiencie in knowledge, as alfo for his integritie of life, & being found found in them all, to be alowed & admitted to teach.   For if euerie one that wold, fhould take vpon him to teach without further triall, then might there great inconuenience follow.   For papifts and other fchifmatikes, apoftataes, or elfe whatfoeuer, might thruft in themfelues, & fo corrupt the youth.   Ignorant & vnlearned would take vpon them high learning & fo delude their fchoolers.   And if his life fhould not be anfwer-able to his profeffion, then fhould he peruert his auditorie alfo.   Therefore in my iudgement is there great choife to be made of

and then pay no
fees to teach.

fchoolmaifters.   Thus they being tried, let them be admitted *gratis*,

by authoritie. But now there is great abufes herein, for being found
fufficient in all refpeⱨs, yet muft he be conftrained to take a license,
whether he will or not, and muft pay xxvi. or xx. fhillings for it, &

Now he must pay 26s. or 30s. for a license for every diocese he teaches in.

yet will this ferue him no longer than he tarieth in that dioces, &
comming into another he muft pay as much there for yᵉ like licenfe
alfo, whereas peraduenture he fhall fcarcely get ¹fo much cleere in

[¹ Sig. D. 4, back]

three or foure yeeres in that dioces, they haue fuch fat pafture. But
if they would needes haue them to haue licenfes, (which I grant to
be very good,) I would wifh they might haue them *gratis*, without
mony, for if it be lawfull for them to teach for mony, it is alfo lawfull

Licenses should be given to fit men gratis.

without. And if they be not woorthie it is pittie that mony fhould
make them woorthie; and againe, if they be woorthie, it is pittie that
without mony they cannot be fo accepted.

Theod. What way were beft to be taken for the good education of
youth?

Amphil. It were good (if it might be brought to paffe) that in

Every Parish ought to have its Schoolmaster with a good stipend.

euery parifh throughout the Realme, there were an indifferent able
man appointed for the inftruⱨion of youth in good letters, hauing a
reafonable ftipend alowed him of the fame parifh for his paines, But
now they teach and take paines for little or nothing, which vtterly
difcourageth them, and maketh manie a cold fchooler in *Dnalgne,* as
experience daily teacheth.

Theod. Be there men of all kinde of trades, occupations, and

As to Tradesmen,

artes, as there be in other countries.

Amphil. Yea, truely: there are men of all fciences, trades,

English Artisans are as clever as any under the sun.

myfteries, faculties, occupa²tions, and artes whatfoeuer, and that as
cunning as any be vnder the funne. Yea, fo expert they be, as if

[² Sig. D. 5]

they would let a thing alone when it is well, they were the braueft
workmen in the world. But as they feeke to excell and furpaffe
al other nations, in finenes of workmanfhip, fo now and than they
reape the fruits of their vaine curiofity, to their owne detriment,
hinderance, and decay.

Theod. How liue the marchant men amongft them? are they rich
and wealthy, or but poore?

Amphil. How fhould they be poore, gaining as they do, more then

The Merchants are rich, making from 100 to 400 per cent.

halfe in halfe in euerie thing they buy or fell? And which is more,
fometimes they gaine double and triple; if I faid quadruple, I lied not.

Theod. I pray you how can that be fo?

Amphil. I will tell you.   They haue mony to lay foorth vpon euerie thing, to buy them at the firft and beft hand, yea, to ingroffe, and to ftore themfelues with abundance of al things.   And then will they keepe thefe marchandize till they waxe verie fcarse, (and no maruaile, for they buy vp all things) and fo confequently deere.   And then will they fell them at their owne prices, or elfe (being able to beare the mony) they will keepe them ftill.   By this [1] meanes they get the deuill and all; befides thefe, they haue a hundred flights in their budgets to rake in gaine withall.

Theod. I pray you, what be thofe?

Amphil. They will go into the countries, and buy vp all the wooll, corne, leather, butter, cheefe, bacon, or elfe what marchandize foeuer they knowe will be vendible, and thefe they tranfport ouer feas, whereby they gaine infinit fummes of mony.

Theod. That is woonderful that they are fo permitted : are there no lawes, nor prohibitions to the contrarie, that no wooll, corne or leather, fhoulde be tranfported ouer feas?

Amphil. There are good lawes, and great reftraints to the contrary, in fo much as they be apparent traitors to God, their prince and country, that carrie any of the forefaid things ouer without fpeciall licence thereto.   Yet notwithftanding, either by hooke or crooke, by night or day, by direct or indirect meanes, either knowne or vnknowne, they wil conueigh them ouer, though their owne country want the fame.   But to auoide all dangers, they purchafe a licence & a difpenfation for mony, bearing the prince in hand that they do it for fome good caufe, when indeed the caufe is their owne [2] priuate gaine.   And for the fpeedier obtaining of their defires, they demand license for the cariage ouer but of fo much and fo much, when in truth they conuey ouer, vnder the colour of this their licenfe, ten times, twenty times, yea, a hundred times, fiue hundred times, yea, a thoufande times as much more.   And thus they delude their prince, impouerifh their country, and inrich themfelues, feeding, clothing and inriching our enimies with our owne treafure.   Hereby it commeth to paffe that all things are deerer, and fcarfer, than otherwife they would be if reftraynt were had, and I warrant them many a blacke curfe haue they of the poore commons for their doing.

They buy up the whole stock of an article, hold it till it gets dear, and then sell it at their own price.

[1 Sig. D. 5, back]

Merchants also buy up English goods and export them.

Traitors to God and their country they are, dodging the laws by buying the Queen's license,

[2 Sig. D. 6]

and then exporting 500 times as much as they've leave to.
They thus make things dear ; and

many a black curse do they get from the poor for it!

Theod. Would you not haue licenfes granted for the tranfporting ouer of fuch things for no caufe?

Amphil. Yes. But firft I would haue our owne people ferued, that they wante not in any cafe. For it is very vnmeete to feede forren nations, and our owne country famifh at home. But if it were fo, that *Dnalgne* flowed in abundance and plentie of all things, whatfoeuer are neceffarie for the vfe and fuftentation of man in this life, and other nations (prouided that they bee our freendes [1] and of chriftian religion) wanted the fame then would I wifhe that fome of our fuperfluitie might be erogate to them, to the fupplie of their neceffities, but not otherwife. And this ftandeth both with the lawes of God, charitie, and good confcience.

We ought to feed our own folk first.

Then we may export our surplus to friendly lands.

[1 Sig. D. 6, back]

Theod. Thefe are marueilous fleights to get mony withall. But I pray you, haue they no more?

Amphil. They want none, I warrant you; for rather than to faile, they haue their falfe weights, their counterfet ballances, their adulterate meafures, and what not, to deceiue the poore people withall, and to rake in mony. But the Wife man telleth them, that falfe ballances, counterfet weightes, and vntrue meafures, are abomination to the Lord. And the Apoftle telleth them, that God is the iuft reuenger of all thofe that deceiue their brethren in bargaining. And yet fhall you haue them, in the fale of their wares, to fweare, to teare, and proteft, that 'before God, before Iefus Chrift, as God fhall faue my foule, as God fhall iudge me, as the Lord liueth, as God receiue me, as God helpe me, by God and by the world, by my faith and troth, by Iefus Chrift,' and infinite the like othes, that fuch a thing coft them fo much, & fo much, and it is woorth [2] this much and that much, when in truth they fweare as falfe, as the liuing Lord is true, as their owne confciences can beare them witneffe, and I feare me will condemne them at the day of the Lord, if they repent not. For if a thinge coft them ten fhillings, they will not blufh to afke twentie fhillings for it. If it coft them twentie fhillings, they will not fhame to afke forty fhillings for it, and fo of all others, doubling, tripling, and quadrupling the price thereof, without either feare of God, or regard of good confcience.

Merchants use false weights and measures too.

And they swear by all that's holy that their wares cost so much, and are worth so much, lying loudly.

[2 Sig. D. 7]

They'll not blush to ask 20s. for what cost 'em 10s.! having no fear of God.

Theod. What fay you of the Drapers and cloth fellers? liue they in the fame order that the other doe?

Amphil. Of Drapers I haue little to fay, fauing that I thinke them cater cofins, or cofin germans to merchants. For after they haue bought their cloth, they caufe it to be tentered, racked, and fo drawne out, as it fhall be both broader and longer than it was when they bought it almoft by halfe in halfe, or at left by a good large fife Now the cloth being thus ftretched forth in euery vaine, how is it poffible either to endure or hold out; but when a fhower of raine taketh it, then it falleth and fhrinketh in, that it is fhame to fee it. Then haue they their fhops and places where they [1] fell their cloth commonly very darke and obfcure, of purpofe to deceiue the buiers. But *Caueat empto* (as the old faieng is) Let the buiers take heed. For *Technas machinant, & retia tendant pedibus,* as the faieng is : 'They meane deceit, and lay fnares to intrap the feet of the fimple.' And yet notwithftanding, they will be fure to make price of their racked cloth, double and triple more than it coft them. And will not fticke to fweare, and take on (as the other their confraters before) that it coft them fo much, and that they doe you no wrong. God giue them grace to haue an eie to their confciences, and to content themfelues with reafonable gaines.

Theod. I thinke there is great fault to bee found in the firft makers of the cloth, for the naughtineffe thereof, as well as in the Drapers, is there not ?

Amphil. No doubt of that. For fome put in naughty wool, and caufe it to be fpun & drawne into a very fmall thred, and then compounding with the Fuller to thicke it very much, and with the Clothier alfo to fheare it very lowe, and with fome liquide matter to lay downe the wooll fo clofe, as you can hardly fee any wale, and then felleth it as though it were a very fine cloth indeed. Other fome mixe good [2] wooll and naughty wooll togither, and vfing it as before, they will fell it for principall good cloth, when it is no thing leffe. And then for their further aduantage, euery vaine, euery ioint, and euery thred muft be fo tentered and racked, as I warrant it for euer being good after. Now, it being thus tentered at his hands, and after at the Drapers handes, I pray you how fhould this cloth be ought, or endure long ?

Theod. Be there Goldfmithes there any ftore alfo, as in fome other countries there be ?

Amphil. There are inow, and more than a good meanie. They are (for the moſt part) very rich and wealthye, or elſe they turne the faireſt ſide outwards, as many doe in *Dnalgne.* They haue their ſhops and ſtalles fraught and bedecked with chaines, rings, golde, ſiluer, and what not woonderfull richly. They will make you any mouſter or antike whatſoeuer, of golde, ſiluer, or what you will. They · haue ſtore of all kinde of plate whatſoeuer. But what? Is there no deceit in all theſe goodlye ſhewes? Yes, too many. If you will buy a chaine of golde, a ring, or any kinde of plate, beſides that you ſhall paye almoſt halfe iu halfe more than it is woorth (for they will per-ſuade[1] [2] you the workmanſhip of it comes to ſo much, the faſhiou to ſo much, and I cannot tell what:) you ſhall alſo perhaps haue that golde which is naught, or elſe at leaſt mixt with other droſſie rubbage, and refuſe mettall, which in compariſon is good for nothing. And ſome-times, or for the moſt part, you ſhal haue tinue, lead, and the like, mixt with ſiluer. And againe, in ſome things ſome will not ſticke to ſell you ſiluer gilt for gold, and well if no worſe too now and then. But this happeneth very ſeldome, by reaſon of good orders, and con-ſtitutions made for the puniſhment of them that offend in this kind of deceit, and therfore they ſeldome dare offend therein, though now and then they chance to ſtumble in the darke.

Theod. Haue you good wines in *Dnalgne?*

Amphil. Indeede there are excellent wines as any be in the world, yet not made within the Realme, but comming from beyond ſeas: which when the vintners have once got into their clouches, and placed in their ſellers, I warrant you they make of one hogſhead almoſt two, or at leſt, one and a halfe, by mixing & blenting one with another, & infuſing other liquor into them. So that it is almoſt vnpoſſible, to get a cup of pure wine of it ſelfe at the tauerne. But harſhe, rough, ſtipticke, and hard [3] wine, neither pleaſant to the mouth, nor wholſome to the bodie. And notwithſtanding that they gaine (welneare) one hogſhead in another, yet ſhall their meaſures, their gallons, pints, and quarts be ſo ſpare, and their prices ſo hie, that it is woonderful to ſee. And if a poore ſimple man go to drinke a pint of wine for the ſtrengthening of his bodie, and for neceſſities ſake onely, he ſhall be ſure to haue that wine brought him, that is too bad, though his monie (I am ſure) is as good as the rich mans. But

---

Side notes:

are very rich, and have shops and stalls loaded with gold and silver ornaments.

[1 usade *orig.*]
[2 Sig. D 8, back]
Goldsmiths mix gold with base alloy; and some sell silver-gilt for gold.

Vintners mix bad wine with good;

[3 Sig. E 1]

give short measure, and palm off bad wine on poor men.

if a man of countenance come to drinke for pleafure & niceneffe, he fhall haue of the beft wine in the feller, though his mony be no beter than the poore mans.   With infinite the like abufes, which I omit.

Theod. Haue you anything to fay of Butchers, and thofe that kill and fel meate to eate ?

Butchers are impudent enough to try and make 100 per cent profit !

Amphil. Nothing but this : that they are not behind in their abufes, fallacies, and deceits.   For whereas they pay a certeine price for a fat beefe, they are fo impudent that they thinke their market is naught, except they may gaine halfe in halfe, or the beft quarter at

Butchers let the blood soak into their meat.

the leaft.   And to the end their meate may be more faleable to the eie, the fairer, and the fatter, they will kill their beafts, and fuffer the

[¹ Sig. E 1, back]

bloud to remaine within them ftill, for this caufe that ¹ it may incorporate it felfe in the flefh, and fo thereby the flefh may not onely be the weightier (for in fome places they buy all by waight) but alfo may feeme both frefher, fairer, newer, tenderer, and yonger.   And,

They puff lean meat up with air, and pin fat on it.

which is more commonly, they vfe to blowe and puffe it vp with winde, to the end it may feeme bigger, fatter, and fairer to the eie. Or if the meate it felfe be leane, and naught, then will they take the fat of other meate, and pin vpon the fame very artificially, and all to delude the eies of the beholders.   And though it be neuer fo old meate, tough, and ftale, yet will they fweare, proteft, and take on woonderfully, that it is very new, frefh and tender.   So that no more

Some 'll also sell meat that has died in a ditch.

in them than in others, there is little confcience at all.   There be fome of them alfo now and then that will not fticke to fell meate which hath died (perchance) in a ditch, if it be worth the eating (which is moft lamentable), and yet wil beare the world in hand that it is excellent meate, that it died kindly, and fo foorth.   So that hereby infinite difeafes are caught, and manie times prefent death infueth to the eaters thereof.

[² for for, orig.]

Theod. Is meate deere or good cheape there for ² the moft part ?

[³ Sig. E 2]

Meat is dear. Greedy grasiers keep up the price of beasts.

Amphil. It is commonly deere, feldom good ³ cheape, and the reafon is, bicaufe a fort of infaciable cormorants, greedie grafiers I meane, who, hauing raked togither infinite pafture, feed all themfelues, and will not fell for anie reafonable gaine, and then muft the Butchers needes fell deere, when as they buie deere.

Theod. Why? would you haue no grafiers? then how coulde there bee anie meate fatted?

Amphil. Yes I would haue grafiers. But I would not haue a few rich cobs to get into their clowches almoſt whole countries, ſo as the poore can haue no releeſe by them. For by this meanes paſtures and groundes are not onely exceſſiuely deere, but alſo not to be got of any poore men for monie, whereby it commeth to paſſe, that the poore are impoueriſhed, and the rich onlie benefited. Yea, ſo greatly are the poore hereby inthralled, that they can hardly get a peece of ground to keepe ſo much as a poore cow or two vpon for the maintenance of themſelues, and their poore families. This is a great abuſe : for by this meanes rich men eate vp poore men, as beaſts eate vp graſſe.

Theod. Doe the gentlemen and others, take in commons & inclofures (as your words ſeeme to implie) for their better feeding?

[1] *Amphil.* Yea, almoſt all indifferently. For whereas before was any commons, heathes, moores, plaines, or free places of feeding for the poore and others, euen all in generall, now you ſhall haue all ſeuerall, incloſed, and appropriate to a few greedy gentlemen, who will neuer haue inough, till their mouths be full of clay, and their bodie full of grauell. Commons and moores which were woont to be the onely ſtaie of the poore, & whervpon eche might keepe cattle, both neate and ſheepe, according to his eſtate, are now taken from them, wherby manie are conſtrained either to famiſh, or elſe to beg their breade from doore to doore. So that in proces of time, if theſe incloſures be ſuffered to continue, the ſtate of the whole Realme will mightily decay, a few ſhall be inriched, & many a thouſand poore people, both men, women, and children, in citie and country, vtterlie beggered. Oh it was a goodlie matter, when the poore man might turne out a cow, or two, & certeine numbers of ſheepe to the commons, and haue them kept well vpon the ſame, both winter & ſommer, freely without coſting them ought; whereas now they are incloſed, made ſeneral, and imploied to the priuate commoditie of a few ambicious gentlemen, so as the poore man cannot keepe ſo much as a pig or a gooſe vpon [2] the ſame.

Theod. It is great pittie that ſuch oppreſſion of the poore ſhould be borne withall or ſuffered in any of what degree ſoeuer.

A few rich cobs get whole counties into their hands,

and stop poor folk keeping a cow.

Rich men eat up poor ones as beasts do grass.

[1 Sig. E 2, back]

The gentry enclose the poor folk's commons,

and make em starve.

A good time it was when a poor man could keep a cow on the common!

Now he can't keep a goose. [2 Sig. E 3]

Amphil. It is fo. But what than? You fhall haue fome that, not for the benefit of grafing and feeding onely, will take in commons, and inclofures, but alfo fome that for vaineglorie, worldly pompe, promotion & foolifh pleafure, will not fticke to pull downe whole townes, fubuert whole parifhes, and turning foorth all a begging, rather than to faile, make them parkes, chafes, warrants, and I cannot tell what of the fame. And when they haue thus done, their bucks, their does, their ftags, harts, hinds, conies and the like, not onely not fead *intra gyrum fuum*, Within their circuit, but eate vp and deuoure all the poore mens fields, corne, graffe and all. So that it is hard if any poore mans corne fcape their fangs within a dozen myles com- paffe, which is a pitifull and a lamentable cafe.

Theod. Would you not haue parkes, and chafes for game?

Amphil. I difalow them not. But I would not haue them to be made of the poore mens liuings, nor yet to ftand to the preiudice of the whole country adioining. Therefore if they [1] will haue parkes and chafes, Firft let them fee that they be of their owne proper lande, and then that they be no annoiance to the country about, and then let them haue them, in the name of God.

Theod. Be there any grafiers of fheep there alfo?

Amphil. Two [2] manie, if it pleafed God. For nowe euerie meane gentleman, if he can pretend (though neuer fo little) title to any common, heath, moore or pafture, he will haue it, *quo iure, quaue iniuria,* Either by hooke or crooke. And wheras before time there hath bin a whole parifh or towne maintained vpon the fame, now is there no bodie there dwelling, but a fheepeheard and a dogge lolling vnder a bufh. Thus are whole parifhes and townes made praies to rich grafiers. Yea, you fhall haue fome grafiers to keepe fiue hundred, a thoufand, fiue thoufand, ten thoufand, twentie thoufand fheepe of his owne at one time: now iudge you what infinite com- modities arifeth hereof. Befides that, when they fell their wooll (as though they gayned not inough otherwife), it is a worlde to fee what fubtilties, (I will not faie what falfities), they vfe in the fale thereof. As firft to intermixt and blente the good and naughtie wooll [3] togither, to winde it vppe cloofelie that it fhall not be feene within. And which is more, becaufe they fell all by waight, they will not fticke to vfe finifter meanes to make it peafe well in waight. Some lay it, after it

Then vain rich men pull down villages to make parks and warrens;

and their conies eat up poor men's corn.

Parks must not be made out of poor men's livelihoods.

[1 Sig. E 3, back]

[2 *read* Too]

Commons are inclosd: and in- stead of a village you've only a shepherd and a dog.

Some grasiers keep from 500 to 20,000 (?) sheep.

[3 Sig. E 4] They cheat in selling their wool, mixing bad with good;

is clipped from the fheepes backe, in a moyft feller, vnderneath the
grounde, to the ende that the moyfture, humiditie and wette of the
feller may inftill into it, and fo may peafe the more. Otherfome will
caft wette falt into it, which in time will liquifie, and caufe it to be
the waightier. With manie other the like wicked fleights and leger-
dimeanes, whereof, for that I would rather giue them a tafte in hope
of amendment, then a plaine defcription for feare of difpleafing
them, at this time I will omit to fpeake any more till further occafion
be offered.

wetting it,
putting salt into
it, &c.

Theod. Is the lande there poffeffed in common, or elfe is their
propertie in all things, and fo confequently landlords?

Amphil. There is not onelie a propertie in lands there, but alfo in
all things elfe, and fo landlords inow more than be good ones iwis.

Landlords

Theod. Doe they let out their lands, their farmes, and tenements,
fo as the poore tenants may liue well vpon them?

[1]*Amphil.* Oh no. Nothing leffe. But rather the contrarie is
moft true. For when a gentleman or other hath a farme or a leafe
to let: firft he caufeth a furueior to make ftrict inquirie what may be
made of it, and how much it is woorth by yeere; which being found
out, and fignified to the owner, he racketh it, ftraineth it, and as it
were fo fetteth it on the tenter hookes, ftretching euery vaine, and
ioint thereof, as no poore man can liue of it. And yet if he might
haue it freely for this racked rent too, it were fomewhat well. But
(out alas, and fie for fhame) that cannot be. For though he pay
neuer fo great an annuall rent, yet muft he pay at his entrance a fine,
or (as they call it) an income of ten pound, twenty pound, forty
pound, threefcore pound, an hundred pound, whereas in truth the
purchafe thereof is hardly woorth fo much. So that hereby the
poore man, if hee haue fcraped any little thing togither, is forced to
difburfe it at the firft dafh, before he enter the doores of his poore
farme, wherein, what through the exceffiue fine, and the vnreafonable
rent, he is fcarfe able to buy his dog alofe, liuing like a begger, or
little better, all his life after. The time hath beene, and not long
fince, when men feared God & loued their brethren, that one might
haue had a houfe, with pafture [2]lieng to it, yea good farmes, leafes and
liuings for little or nothing. Or (as fome hold) for a Gods penie, as
they called it. But howfoeuer it be, certeine it is, that that farme or

[1 Sig. E 4, back]

get their farms
valued, and not
only rack the
rent higher,

but make the
tenant pay a fine
as an Incoming,

so that he's
hardly enough
left to buy his
dog a loaf.

[2 Sig. E 5]

Rents have risen twentyfold of late years.

leaſe, which one might haue had then for ten ſhillings, is now woorth ten pound.   For twentie ſhillings, now is woorth twentie or three-ſcore pound.   For fortie ſhillings, is now woorth fortie pound, or a hundred pound and more.

Theod. Then I perceiue, they let not out their land after the old rent : doe they ?

Amphil. No. You may be ſure of that, they loue nothing worſe. They cannot at any hand brooke or digeſt them that would counſel them to that.

Theod. Why ?   Haue not landlords authoritie, and may they not make as much of their owne lands as they can ?   They count that good policie, and I haue heard them ſay : Is it not lawfull for me to liue vpon mine owne, and to get as much for it as I can ?

Landlords should think that they've only the use of the land ; and so they ought to give the poor a chance nf living by it.
[¹ Sig. E 5, back]

Amphil. They muſt firſt conſider that the earth is the Lords (as the Pſalmograph ſaith : *Domini eſt terra, & plenitudo eius,* The earth is the Lords, and the fulneſſe thereof) and all that dwelleth therein. And therefore being the Lords in propertie, it is theirs but in vſe onely.   And yet not ſo.   But that they [1] ought to lay it foorth to the ſupport of the poore, that all may liue iointly togither, & maintaine yᵉ ſtate of the common wealth to Gods glorie.   For other wiſe, if a few rich cobs ſhuld haue al, & the poore none, it ſhuld come to paſſe, that the ſtate of the common wealth would ſoone decay, & come to confuſion.   They ought alſo to conſider how they came by their lands, whether by right or wrong.   If by right, then are they bound by Gods lawe, and good conſcience, to let forth the ſame ſo as the poore may well liue vpon them.   But if they poſſes them wrongfully, then ought they to ſurrender their tytle, and giue it to the right heire :

No man ought to plunder his fellow-man,

but take them with that fault, & cut of their necks : No man ought to poole and pill his brother, nor yet to exact and extort of him more than right and reaſon requireth, being ſure that the ſame meaſure which he meaſureth to others, ſhal be meaſured to him againe.   Euery one muſt ſo deale with his owne, ſo let it out, & ſo liue, as others may liue by him, and not himſelf alone, for the earth is comon to al *Adams* children ; & though fortune haue giuen more abundance to ſome than to other ſome, yet dame nature hath brought foorth al alike, & will receiue them againe into hir wombe alike alſo.   And

but do to him as he'd be done by.

therefore ought euerie chriſtian to doe to others, as they would wiſh to

be done to : which ¹lawe, if it were obferued well, would cut of all [¹ Sig. E 6]
oppreffion whatfoeuer.

Theod. I pray you, how came noble men and gentlemen by their
lands at the firſt?

Amphil. Cicero faith that in the beginning, before the world was
impeopled, men comming into huge & waſt places inhabitable,
either toke to themfelues as much land as they would, or elfe wan it
by yᵉ fword, bought it by purchafe, had it by gift, or elfe receiued it
from their forefathers, by lineal difcent, or hereditary poffeſſion.
Which faieng of his muſt needes be true, both in the people of the
former world & in vs alfo. Then feeing this is fo, ought not euery   Christian land-
good chriftian to fet forth his lande, fo as poore men may liue upon   lords are bound
  to let their land
it as wel as himfelfe : whofoeuer doth not this, efchewing al kind of   at moderate
  rents.
exaction, polling, pilling & fhauing of his poore tenants, he is no
perfect member of Chriſt, nor doth not as he would be done by.

Theod. You talked before of fines, and incomes : what if a poore
man be not able to paye them, what then?

Amphil. Then may he go fue yᵉ goofe, for houfe gets he none,
yᵉ deuill fhal haue it before him, if he will giue him mony inough :
no, if yᵉ fine be not paid (thogh the rent be neuer fo gret) he fhall
haue a fig, affone as a houfe. If yᵗ a poore man haue got neuer fo   [² Sig. E 6, back]
litle a ſtock to liue vpon and to ²maintaine his occupation or trade   Poor men have
  to sell all their
withall, yet fhall he be conſtrained to fell the fame, yea, peraduenture   stock to pay
  Fines to Land-
all the goods and implements he hath, to pay this fine, fo that during   lords;
yᵉ whole terme of his life, he fhall hardly recouer the fame againe.
And then his leafe being expired, out of doores goes he, for that he is   and at the end
not able to pay as great a fine or greater than before. Thus are   of their lease,
  out they go.
many a one, with their wiues, children, and whole families, turned out
a beging, and die, not a fewe of them, in extreeme miferie.

Theod. I thought one might haue had a farme or a leafe for a
reafonable rent yeerely, without any fine or income paieng.

Amphil. One would thinke fo. For, paieng as much yeerely, as can
be made of the thing it felfe : I wonder what deuill put it into their
heads to receiue fuch fines and incomes, to vndoe the poore withall.
The deuill himfelfe, I thinke, will not be fo ſtraite laced, nor yet fo   The Devil himself is not so
nigard to his feruants, as they are to their poore tenants. For whereas   niggardly as
  some Landlords.
they will not let out a farme or a leafe for one and twentie yeeres

without a great fine, the deuill will giue them his whole territorie and kingdome of hell, to their inheritance for euer, and that freely, paieng nothing for the fame.   And yet notwith¹ftanding all this. There are fome landlords, (nay lewdlords) that hauing racked their rents to the vttermoft, exacted fines, & made all that euer they can of their farmes, will yet proceede further, and as men neuer content with inough, will haue their poore tenants to pay a yeere or two yeeres rent before hande, promifing them (before they haue it) that they fhall pay no more rent yeerelie, till the fame be runne vp.   But when they haue it, they pay their yeerely rent notwithftanding, and neuer receiue any reftitution for the other.   And at euerie change forfooth they muft take newe leafes, and pay new fines, being borne in hand that their leafes before are infufficient, and of no effect.   And fometimes foure or fiue yeres, yea ten, twentie, fortie, or fiftie yeeres before their former leafe be expired, fhall they be conftrained to renue their leafes, and difburfe great fomes, or elfe haue their houfes taken ouer their heads.   Befides, as though thefe pollages and pillages were not ill enough, if their leafes be not warely and circumfpectly made (all quirks and quiddities of the lawe obferued), they will finde fuch meanes (or elfe it fhal go verie hard) that the poore man fhall forfait his leafe, before his leafe be expired : which thing if it happen, out goes the poore man, ²come on it what will.

Theod. Are the inftruments, the writings, & conueiances in that land fo intricate, as they are hard to be kept, for fo I gather by your words ?

Amphil. Yea, truly.   For whereas in times paft when men dealt vprightly, and in the feare of God, fixe or feuen lines was fufficient for the affurance of any peece of land whatfoeuer, now 40. 60. 100. 200. 500. nay a whole fkin of parchment, and fometimes 2. or 3. fkins will hardly ferue.   Wherin fhalbe fo many prouifoes, particles, & claufes, & fo many obferuances, that it is hard for a poore ignorant man to keep halfe of them : and if he fail in one of the left, you knowe what followeth.   In former time a mans bare word was fufficient, now no inftrument, band, nor obligation can be fure inough.   Fy vpon vs ! what fhal become of vs ? we are they of whom the prophet fpeaketh, faieng : There is no faith, there is no truth nor righteoufnes left vpon the earth.   God be mercifull vnto vs !

[¹ Sig. E 7]

[² Sig. E 7, back]

Some cheat their tenants out of the first year or two's rent when paid in advance.

Landlords force tenants to renew their Leases at heavy fines,

and make 'em forfeit their Leases too.

Leases and Conveyances are also terribly long, and contain so many provisoes that a poor man can hardly keep em all.

Theod. Seing that farms and leafes are fo deere, I am perfuaded that euerie thing elfe is deere alfo : is it not fo ?

Amphil. Yea truly it cannot be chofen. And yet it is ftrange, that in abundance of althings there fhuld be dearth of all things, as there is.

Theod. Who is it long of, can you tell ?

[1]*Amphil.* Truly of the landlords onlie in my fimple iudgment : for whenas they inhance the rents, & fet their fines on tenter as they do, how fhould the poore man do ? Muft he not fel al his things a great deale the deerer ? Elfe how fhuld he either faue him-felfe, pay his rent, or maintaine his familie : fo that thefe greedy landlords are the very caufers of al the derth in *Dnalgne;* for truly they are worfe than the caterpillers & locufts of Egypt, for they yet left fome thing vndeuoured, thefe nothing ; they fpoiled but for a time, thefe for euer : thofe by commandement from God, thefe by com-miffion from the diuel.

[1 Sig. E 8]

Landlords are the only cause of high prices.

Landlords are worfe than the Locusts of Egypt.

Theod. How, I pray you, doe thefe iollie fellowes fpend thefe wicked gotten goods ?

Amphil. I fhame to thinke, & I blufh to tell you how. For, for the moft part, they fpend it in dicing, carding, bowling, tennife plaieng, in rioting, feafting & banketing, in hauking, hunting, & other the like prophane exercifes. And not onlie vpon thefe things do they fpend their goods (or rather the goods of the poore) but alfo in pride their *Summum gaudium,* & vpon their danfing minions, that minf it ful gingerlie, God wot, tripping like gotes, that an egge would not brek vnder their feet. But herof inough, & more than perchance wil plefe their deinty humors.

They spend their ill-gotten gains in rioting, prophanities, and women.

Theod. Do they exceed in pride of apparel, or are they very temperate, & fober minded people ?

As to Apparel,

[2]*Amphil.* They are not onely not inferior to any nation in the world in the exceffe of apparell, but are farre woorfer, if woorfer can be. For the taylers doe nothing elfe but inuent new fafhions, difguifed fhapes, and monftrous formes of apparell euery day. Yea furely I thinke they ftudie more in one day for the inuention of new toies, and ftrange deuifes in apparell, than they doe in feauen yeeres, yea, in all the daies of their life, for the knowledge of Gods word.

[2 Sig. E 8, back]

Tailors invent new fashions every day,

Theod. Me thinke then by your reafons it feemeth, that Tailors

and are the causers of all the monstrous English dress.

are the caufers of all that monftrous kind of attire worne in *Dnalgne,* and fo confequently are guiltie of all the euill committed by the fame.

Amphil. You fay very truly.   For *Mali alicuius author, ipfius mali, & malorum omnium, quae ex inde orientur, reus erit coram Deo,* The author of any euill, is not onely giltie before God of the euill committed, but alfo of all the euill which fpringeth of the fame. Therefore I would wifh them to beware, and not *Communicare alienis peccatis,* To be partakers of other mens finnes, for be fure they fhall finde inough of their owne to anfwer for.   But fo far are they from making confcience hereof, that they heape vp finne vpon finne.

[' Sig. F 1]

Tailors ask one fourth too much cloth, and more lace, for a coat.

For if a man [1]afke them how much cloth, veluet, or filke wil make a cote, a dublet, a cloke, a gowne, hofen, or the like, they muft needs haue fo much, as they may gaine the beft quarter thereof to themfelues.   So play they with the lace alfo : for if tenne yards would ferue, they muft haue twentie; if twentie would ferue, they muft haue fortie; if fortie woulde ferue, they muft haue fixtie; if fixtie would ferue, they muft an hundred, and fo forward.   Befides that, it muft be fo drawne out, ftretched, and pulled in in the fowing, as they

And they charge too high for making it.

get the beft quarter of it that way too.   Then muft there as much go for the making, as halfe the garment is woorth.   Befides this, they are in league, and in fee, with the Drapers and Clothfellers, that if a man come to them to defire them to helpe them to buy a peece of cloth,

They're in league with the *Draper*, to cheat their customers.

and to bring them where good is, they will ftraightway conduct them to their feer, and whatfoeuer price hee fetteth of the cloth, they perfuade the buier it is good, and that it is woorth the money, whereas indeed it is nothing fo, nor fo.   And thus they betwixt them diuide the fpoile, and he (the tailor) receiues his wages for his faithfull feruice done.   If a man buy a garment of them made, hee fhall haue

[2 Sig. F 1, back]

it very faire to the eie (therfor it is true : *Omne quod glifcit non* [2]*eft aurum,*   Euerie faire thing is not the beft) but either it fhall be lined with filthie baggage, and rotten geare, or elfe ftretched & drawne out vpon the tenter, fo as if they once come to wetting, they fhrinke almoft halfe in halfe, fo as it is a fhame to fee them.   Therefore I aduife euery one to fee to his garments himfelfe, and according to the old prouerbe : *Sit oculus ipfi coquus,* Let his eie be his beft cooke, for feare left he be ferued of the fame fauce, as manie haue beene to their great hinderance.

Theod. I haue heard it faide that they vfe great ruffes in *Dnalgne:* do they continue them ftill as they were woont to doe, or not?

Amphil. There is no amendement in any thing that I can fee, neither in one thing nor in other, but euery day woorfer and woorfer, for they not only continue their great ruffes ftill, but alfo vfe them bigger than euer they did. And whereas before they were too bad, now they are paft al fhame & honeftie, yea moft abhominable and deteftable, and fuch as the diuell himfelfe would be afhamed to weare the like. And if it be true, as I heare fay, they haue their ftarching houfes made of purpofe, to that vfe and end only, the better to trimme and dreffe their ruffes to pleafe the diuels eies withall.

Theod. Haue they ftarching houfes of purpofe made to ftarch in? Now truly that paffes [1] of all that euer I heard. And do they nothing in thofe brothell houfes (ftarching houfes I fhuld fay) but onelie ftarch bands and ruffes?

Amphil. No, nothing elfe, for to that end only were they erected, & therefore now are confecrate to Belzebub and Cerberus, archdiuels of great ruffes.

Theod. Haue they not alfo houfes to fet their ruffes in, to trim them, and to trick them, as well as to ftarch them in?

Amphil. Yea, marry haue they, for either the fame ftarching houfes (I had almoft faid farting houfes) do ferue the turn, or elfe they haue their other chambers and fecret clofets to the fame vfe, wherein they tricke vp thefe cartwheeles of the diuels charet of pride, leading the direct way to the dungeon of hell.

Amphil. What tooles and inftruments haue they to fet their ruffes withall. For I am perfuaded they cannot fet them artificially inough without fome kind of tooles?

Amphil. Very true: and doe you thinke that they want any thing that might fet forth their diuelrie to the world? In faith fir, no, then the diuell were to blame if he fhould ferue his clients fo, that maintaine his kingdome of pride with fuch diligence as they doe. And therefore I would you wift it, they haue their tooles and inftruments for the purpofe.

[2] *Theod.* Whereof be they made, I pray you, or howe?

Amphil. They be made of yron and fteele, and fome of braffe kept as bright as filuer, yea, and fome of filuer it felfe; and it is well,

if in proceſſe of time they grow not to be gold.   The faſhion where-
after they be made, I cannot reſemble to anything ſo well as to a

like a Squirt or
Squib,

ſquirt, or a ſquibbe, which little children vſed to ſquirt out water
withall; and when they come to ſtarching, and ſetting of their ruffes
then muſt this inſtrument be heated in the fire, the better to ſtiffen
the ruffe.   For you know heate will drie and ſtiffen any thing.   And
if you woulde know the name of this goodly toole, forſooth the deuill

calld *Putters*
or Putting-Sticks.
Setting-Sticks
they have too,
for their cursed
Ruffs.

hath giuen it to name a putter, or elſe a putting ſticke, as I heare
ſay.   They haue alſo another inſtrument called a ſetting ſticke, either
of wood or bone, and ſometimes of gold and ſiluer, made forked wiſe
at both ends, and with this (*Si diis placet*) they ſet their ruffes.   But
bicauſe this curſed fruit is not yet grown to his full perfection of
ripeneſſe, I will therefore at this time ſay no more of it, vntil I here
more.

Theod. What is the leather in that country ? excellent good, and
wel tanned, or but indifferently ?   I haue heard ſome complaine of it.

[¹ Sig. F 3]

[1]*Amphil.* There is of both ſorts, as of all things elſe; but as there
is ſome naught (I can not denie) ſo is there otherſome as good as any
is vnder the ſunne.   And yet I muſt needes confeſſe, there is great
abuſe in the tanners, makers, curriers, and dreſſers of the ſame : for

Some *Leather*
is only half
tand,

you ſhall haue ſome leather ſcarcely halfe tanned, ſo that within two
or three daies or a week wearing (eſpecially if it come in any weat)
wil ſtraight-way become browne as a hare backe, and which is more,
fleete and run abroad like a diſhclout, and which is moſt of all, will

and won't
keep out water.

holde out no water, or very little.   And the ſaieng is (*Erubeſco dicere,*
I ſhame to ſpeake it) that to the ende they may ſaue lyme and barke,
and make the ſpeedier returne of their mony, they will take vp their
hides before they bee halfe tanned, and make ſale of them.   And as
herein they are faultie and much to be blamed, ſo in the ſurpriſing of
their hides, they are worthie of reprehenſion.   For that which they
buy for ten ſhillings, they will hardly ſell for twentie ſhillings ; that
which they buy for twentie ſhillings they will not willingly ſell for
fortie ſhillings.   And thus by this meanes, they make ſhooes vnrea-
ſonable deere.

Theod. Then the fault is not in the ſhoomakers onely, that ſhooes
be ſo deere ?

[² Sig. F 3, back]

[2]*Amphil.* There is fault inough in them alſo.   For whereas the

others inhanſe the price of their hides excefſiuely, theſe felowes racke
it very vnconcionably. And yet if the ſhooes were good, though
deere, it were ſomwhat tollerable; but when they ſhall be both naught,
and yet deere too, it is too bad, and abhominable. Now if you aſke
the ſhoomakers in whom the fault doth confiſt, they will anſwere you
ſtrait, in the tanner. But this is certeine, that as there is a horrible fault
in the tanner, ſo there is more, or as much in the ſhoomaker. For firſt
of all the ſhoomaker liquoreth his leather, with wateriſh liquor, kit-
then ſtuffe, and all kinde of baggage mingled togither. And as
though that were not ill inough, they ſaie they vſe to put ſalt in the
liquor, wherewithall they greaſe the leather of purpoſe, to the ende
that the leather ſhal neuer hold out water. And truelie it is verie
likelie they doe ſo, or ſome ſuch like thing, for ſurelie almoſt none of
their leather will holde out water, nor ſcarſelie durt neither. Beſides
this, it is a worlde to ſee how lowſely they ſhall be ſowed, with hotte
alles, and burning threedes, euerie ſtitch an inch or two from another,
ſo as with-in two or three daies you ſhall haue them ſeamerent and all
too betorne. And yet as though this were not [1]ill inoughe, they adde
more. Sometimes they will ſell you calues leather for cow leather,
horſe hides for oxe hides, and truelie I thinke rotten ſheepe ſkins for
good ſubſtantial & dureable ſtuffe. And yet ſhall a man pay for
theſe as well as for better ſtuffe. And to the ende they may ſeeme
gaudie to the eie, they muſt be ſtitched finelie, pincked, cutte, karued,
raſed, nickt, and I cannot tell what. And good reaſon, for elſe
would they neuer be ſold. The inwarde ſoole of the ſhooe commonlie
ſhall be no better than a cattes ſkinne, the heeles of the ſhooes ſhall
be little better. And if the ſooles be naught (as they be indeede
yet muſt they be vnderlaied with other peeces of leather, to make
them ſeeme thicke and excellent ſtuffe, whereas indeede they are
nothing leſſe. And to make the ſooles ſtiffe, and harde, they muſt be
parched before the fire, and then they are moſt excellent ſooles, And
ſuch as will neuer be worne, no, I thinke not in halfe a coopple of
daies, which is a woonderfull thing. Oh, farewell former worlde,
for I haue hearde my Father ſaie, and I thinke it moſt certeinely
true, that a paire of ſhooes in thoſe daies woulde haue kept a man as
drie as a feather, though he had gone in water all the daye thorowe,
[2]yea, all the weeke thorow, to the very laſt day, and would haue

Shoemakers

liquor their leather,

and salt it, so that it won't keep out water.

They sow with hot awls and rotten thread

[1 Sig. F 4]

They sell you horse-hide for ox-hide,

and use cat-skin for inside soles.

They parch the soles too.

Why, in my Father's days, a pair of shoes 'ud keep the wet out, and last a year.

[2 Sig. F 4, back]

Now, they'll
hardly last a
month.

ferued a man almoſt a whole yeere togither, with a little repairing.
But now fiue or ſixe paire, halfe a ſcore, yea, twentie paire of ſhooes
will ſcarſely ſerue ſome a yeere, ſuch excellent ſtuffe are they made
of. But let all ſhooemakers, tanners, and the reſt, take heed, for at
the day of iudgement they ſhal render accounts for this their doing.
And here-of hitherto.

Theod. Be there any Brokers, or ſuch kind of fellowes in your
country ?

Amphil. If it be a thing that is good, it is a doubt whether it be
there, or no, but if it bee naught (as brokerie is) then paſt peraduenture it is there.

Brokers are

Theod. What maner of fellowes are thoſe Brokers, for truly their
profeſſion, and the vſe thereof, is vnknowne to me, ſaue only that I
haue heard of ſome of their dealings ?

Amphil. Seeing that you are ignorant of this goodly myſterie, and
high profeſſion of brokerie, and alſo ſo deſirous to knowe the truth of
them, I will in few words (as brieſly as I can) declare vnto you the

jolly fellows

ſubſtance thereof. Theſe Brokers are iolly fellowes forſooth, and
ſuch as in the beginning of their occupation, haue either iuſt nothing,

[¹ Sig. F 5]
who, not being
able to live by
anything else,

or elſe very little ¹at all, who, when they haue attempted, and aſſaied
by all kind of meanes and waies to liue, and cannot by any of them
al either any thing thriue, or which is leſſe, not ſo much as maintaine
their poore eſtate withall, though but meanly, then fall they into

make friends
with thieves,
and buy every-
thing these steal,

acquaintance with looſe, diſſolute, and licentious perſons, either men
or women, to whom all is fiſh that comes to net, and who haue
limed fingers, liuing vpon pilfering, and ſtealing, and of theſe they
buy for little or nothing, whatſoeuer they ſhal haue filched from any.
And thus by this meanes in proceſſe of time, they feather their neſts
well inough, and growe (many of them) to great ſubſtance and
wealth.

Theod. Will they buy any thing whatſoeuer commeth to hand?

Amphil. Yea, all things indifferently without any exception. All
is good fiſh with them that comes to net. They will refuſe nothing,
whatſoeuer it be, nor whom-ſoeuer bringeth it, though they be neuer
to ſuſpitious, no, although it be as cleere as the day, that it hath beene
purloined by ſiniſter meanes from ſome one or other. And can you

for half its value :

blame them   For why? They haue it for halfe it is woorth.

Amphil. What wares be they (for the moſt part) which theſe Brokers doe buy and ſell?

[1]*Amphil.* I told you they wil refuſe nothing. But eſpecially they buy remnants of ſilks, veluets, ſatins, damaſks, grograins, taffeties. laſe, either of ſilke, gold, ſiluer, or any thing elſe that is worth ought Otherſome buy cloakes, hoſen, dublets, hats, caps, coates, ſtockings, & the like. And theſe goodly marchandize, as they haue them good cheape, ſo they will ſel them againe to their no ſmall gaines.

drapers' and haberdashers' goods chiefly.

Theod. If this be true, that they will receiue all, and buy al that comes to hand, than it muſt needes be that this is a great prouocation to many wicked perſons, to filch & ſteale whatſoeuer they can lay their hands vpon, ſeing they may haue ſuch good vent for yͤ ſame. Is it not?

Amphil. You ſay very true. And therefore I am perſwaded that this dunghill trade of brokerie newly ſprong vp, & coined in the deuils minting houſe, the ſhoppe of all miſchiefe, hath made many a theefe more than euer would haue bin, & hath brought many a one to a ſhamefull end at Tiburne, & elſe where. Yea, I haue hard priſoners (and not any almoſt but they ſing the ſame ſong) when they haue gone to execution, declaime & crie out againſt brookers. For, ſaid they, 'if brokers had not bin, we had not come to this ſhamefull death; if they would not haue receiued our ſtollen goods, we woulde neuer [2]haue ſtollen them; and if we had not ſtollen them, we had not bin hanged.'

This dunghill Brokery's made many thieves, and brought many a man to the Gallows.

[2 Sig. F 6]

Theod. Then it ſeemeth by your reaſons, that brokers are in effect acceſſary to the goods feloniouſlie ſtolen, & are worthie of the ſame puniſhment *that* the others that ſtale them are worthy of?

Brokers ought to be hung with Thieves.

Amphil. They are ſo, if before they buy them they know preciſely that they are ſtolen, & yet notwithſtanding will not onely willingly buy them, but alſo rather animate, than diſanimate them to perſeuere in their wickednes, as this their greedy buieng of their wares doth argue *that* they doe. This maketh many a tailer to aſke more cloth, more ſilk, veluet, & lace, than he nedeth, & all to the ende the broker may haue his ſhare; for, be they neuer ſo litle ſcraps or ſhreds or ſhort ends of lace, or ſmal peces of veluet, ſatan, ſilk or yͤ like, the broker will giue mony for them, with a wet finger. This maketh many ſeruants to pilfer, filch, & purloin from their maſters,

Brokers' willingness to buy

makes Tailors cheat, and

servants pilfer.

fome a yard or two of veluet, fatin, taffety, lace, filk, & what not, fome hats, cots, cloks, & the like, & fome one thing, fome another: this hindereth the merchant man, is difcomodious to y⁻ tailer, & benefioial vnto none, but to themfelues: & therfore, as they be the feminaries of wickednes, fo I befech God, they may be fupplanted, except they amend, which I hardly looke for at their hands.

[¹ Sig. F 6, back]

¹ *Theod.* What woulde you haue them to do, that they may exercife their trade, with good confcience, both before God, and the world?

Amphil. I would wifh them to doe thus, which, if they would doe, they might vfe their trade in the feare of G O D, both with good confcience before the Lord, with honeftie before the world, and finallie to the leffe detriment of the common wealth. Firft, let them be fure, that the goods which they buy be truely and juftly come by of the fellers thereof. And to the end, that herein they may not be deceiued, Let them examine the matter ftrictly, where they had it, whofe it is, vpon what occafion they would fel it. And in conclufion not to buy it, vntill they haue gone themfelues to the right owners of the goodes, and if they find all things well, that they may with good confcience buy it, let them give reafon for it, elfe not. And if euerie brooker would deale thus, their would not fo many falfe knaues bring them fuch lauifh of ftollen goods, as they do, neither fhould their trade grow, as it doth, into hatred and contempt.

Theod. You faide before (except I be deceiued) that if they know before they buy any wares, that the fame is ftollen, if they than buy them, they are acceffary to the fame goods fo ²felonioufly ftollen, & fo are worthie of the fame punifhment, that the principals are woorthie of. I pray you, what punifhment is inflicted vpon acceffaries in *Dnalgne.*

Amphil. Acceffaries are punifhable by the lawes of *Dnalgne* with the fame punifhment that the principals are to be punifhed withall (for fo the lawe ftandeth); but in the execution thereof, we fee the cleane contrarie practifed. For when as a theefe, or a fellon ftealeth any thing, hee bringeth it to his receiuer, who, though he knowe it to be ftolen, yet with alacritie admitteth it into his cuftodie, and reteineth it, hereby making himfelfe acceflorie, and guiltie of the felonie committed. And yet notwithftanding when execution is to be done for the fame, the principall is (peraduenture) hanged vp, the other that

Brokers are seed-beds of villainy.

To deal honestly, Brokers should buy only goods honestly come by,

and should find out the owners themselves.

[² Sig. F 7]

Brokers get out of the claws of Justice.

is the accefforie is not once fpoken of, nor none can faie 'blacke is his eie.' But howfoeuer it be, I cannot be otherwife perfuaded, but that the receiuers and accefories are a great deale more woorthie of death (by the penall lawes) than he who ftealeth the thing it felfe, whatfoeuer it be. Bicaufe if they had [not] any to receiue their ftolen goods, they would not fteale at all. And therefore are the receiuers (in my fimple opinion) rather the authors, and the principals (efpecially if ¹they know before they receiue it, that it is ftolen) then they that commit the fact, and being the authors of the euill comitted, they are to be punifhed rather than the perpetrators of the fact it felfe. But for want of due punifhment to be executed as well vppon the one as vppon the other, we fee greeuous crimes, and flagicious facts without all remorfe, or feare of God, daily committed. Good lawes there are, both for the repreffing of thefe, and al other enormities whatfoeuer, but the want of the due execution thereof, is the caufe why all wickednes and mifchiefe dooth reigne and rage euerie where as it doth : God amend it, if it be his good pleafure ! And thus much briefly of the noble fcience of brokerie.

Theod. What hofpitalitie is there kept, or reliefe for the poore ?

Amphil. Very fmal. For as for the poore tenants and commons, they are not able to maintaine any hofpitalitie, or to giue any thing to the poore, their rents are fo raifed, & their fines fo inhanfed, and yet notwithftanding they minifter (I am perfuaded) more releefe to the poore than the rich & wealthie doe : more poore are fed at their dores than at the rich : more clothed at their hands than at the rich, & more lodged and harboured in their poore houfes, than in the ²rich. But yet can I not denie but that the gentlemen, & others, keepe fumptuous houfes, lufty ports, and great hofpitalitie, but fo as the pore hath the left part thereof, or rather iuft nothing at all. If the poore come to their houfes, their gates be fhut againft them, where they, ftanding³ froft and fnow, haile, wind or raine whatfoeuer, are forced to tary two houres, 3. 4. yea fometimes halfe a day, and then fhal they haue but the refufe, and the very fcraps neither. And well if they haue anything too ; in fteed whereof they are fometimes fent to prifon, clapt in irons, manicled, ftocked, and what not. This is the almes that moft men giue.

Marginal notes:
But Receivers deserve hanging more than the Thieves they tempt.

[¹ Sig. F 7, back]

Against these, and like evils, we have good Laws, but they're not put in force.

As to *Hofpitality*, the poor can't afford it,

tho in fact they help other poor more than the rich do.

[² Sig. F 8]

Gentlemen keep grand houses, but make poor folk stand for hours in the cold for a few scraps.

³ ?=fuffering, putting up with ; or is 'in' left out ?

Theod. Then it feemeth that the poore are fimplie prouided for ?

Amphil. They are fo indeed, God amend it.   And yet I am not
so full of foolifh pittie that I would haue all kind of beggers indifferently without any exception to be fed and nourifhed vpon the
sweat of other mens browes.

Theod. Doe you make a difference of beggers then ?   Are there
two forts of them ?

Amphil. Yea, there are two forts.   One fort is of ftout, ftrong,
luftie, couragious, and valiant beggers, which are able to worke, and
will not.   Thefe at no hand are not to be relieued (for *qui non
operatur non manducet,* [1]faith the apoftle, He that will not worke, let
him not eat) but are to be compelled to worke, and not to liue vpon
other mens labours.   For he that releeueth thefe, maintaineth them
in their idleneffe, and taketh awaie the childrens bred, and giueth it to
dogs.   Thefe are as drone bees, that liue vpon the fpoile of the poore
bees that labour and toile to get their liuing with the fweat of their
faces.   If fuch fellowes as thefe will not worke, but liue vpon begging, let them be punifhed and imprifoned till they be content to
worke.   The other fort of beggers are they that be old, aged, impotent, decrepite or lame, ficke, fore, or difeafed : thefe I would wifh
fhould be looked vnto : and thefe are they that euerie Chriftian man
is bound in confcience to releeue.

Theod. What order would you haue obferued in thefe refpects ?

Amphil. The former fort of fturdie valiant beggers, which are
able to worke and will not, I would wifh them to be compelled to
worke, or elfe not to haue any releefe giuen them.   And if they
would not work, to punifh them ; if that will not ferue, to hang
them vp.   But herein I would wifh a prouifo, that being content to
worke, they might haue maifters prouided the*m*, with reafonable
wages, for many would faine [2]worke, and can get none ; and than if
they will not worke, to Tiburne with them.   The other fort of
beggers, which are either halt, lame, impotent, decrepite, blind, ficke,
fore, infirme and difeafed, or aged and the like, I woulde wifh that
they fhould be maintained, euerie one in his owne parifh, at the cofts
and charges of the fame.   And if the parifh be not able to maintain
fo manie, then that there fhould be collections & contributions made
in other parifhes to fupplie their want, and fo the former poore people

Of *Beggers*

we have two
kinds, the Strong,
(who won't work ;

[1 Sig. F 8, back]

Drones, who
ought to be put
in prison till
they *do* work ;)

and the old,
sick, and
diseasd.

The Sturdy
Beggars who
can work, and
won't,

I'd just hang.

[2 Sig. G 1]

The aged and
sick ones I'd
have kept in
their own
parish, and
rate richer
parishes for em.

to be maintained therevpon. For wante of which godlie order and conftitution, there are infinite of the forefaid perfons that die, fome in ditches, fome in holes, fome in caues and dens, fome in fields, fome in one place, fome in another, rather like dogs than chriftian people. For notwithftanding that they be neuer fo impotent, blind, lame, fick, old, or aged, yet are they forced to walke the countries from place to place to feeke their releefe at euery mans doore, except they wil fterue or famifh at home, fuch unmercifulnes is in *Dnalgne.* Yea, in fuch troups doe they flocke, and in fuch fwarmes doe they flow, that you can lightlie go no way, but you fhall fee numbers of them at euerie doore, in euerie lane, and in euerie poore caue ; and as though this were not extremity inough [1]they driue them from citie to citie, from parifh to parifh, from towne to towne, from hundred to hundred, from fhire to fhire, and from country to country, like flocks of fheepe. Here they dare not tarrie for this Iuftice, nor there for that Iuftice, here for this man, nor there for that man, without a licence or a pafport, wheras a man woulde thinke their old age, their hoare haires, their blindneffe, lameneffe, and other infirmities, fhoulde bee pafports good inough for them to go abrod withal, if they cannot get releefe at home. But if the former order, that euery parifh fhould maintaine their poore, were taken, then fhould they neither need to go abroad, nor otherwife want their daily releefe.

Theod. Are there no hofpitals, fpittles, lazar houfes, almes houfes, nor the like, for the releefe of thefe poore people ?

Amphil. Yes there are fome fuch in cities, townes, and fome other places, wherein manie poore are releeued, but not the hundred part of thofe that want. For the fupplie wherof would God there might be in euerie parifh an almes houfe erected, that the poore (fuch as are poore indeede) might be maintained, helped and relieued. For vntill the true poore indeed be better prouided for, let them neuer thinke to pleafe God. Is it not great pity when a man can paffe [2]no waie almoft neither citie nor country, but fhall haue both halt, blind, lame, old, aged, ficke, fore, & difeafed, hanging vpon his fleue, and crauing of releefe ? Whereas, if the former order were eftablifhed, then fhould none at al need to go abroad, but al fhuld haue fufficient at home. The reformed churches beyond feas, and euen the French, Duch, & Italian churches in *Dnalgne* are worthie of great com-

---

Side notes:

Now, many die in the fields like dogs.

They get no relief except by wandering about and begging.

You see poor aged and sick Beggars at every door ; and they're driven from town to town like flocks of sheep.

[1 Sig. G 1, back]

Not a hundredth part can be relievd in our Hospitals.

We want an Almshouse in every Parish,

[2 Sig. G 2]

and then the poor 'ud get enough at home.

mendations herin, & fhal rife vp at the day of iudgment to our condemnation except we repent & amend our vnmercifulneffe

The Reformd Churches abroad and the forin ones here, set us a good example in this.

towards the poore. Thefe good churches, folowing the counfel of the almighty who biddeth that there be no begger amongft vs, fuffer neuer a one of their countrymen, nor yet any other dweling in their parifh, to beg or afke almes without his parifh, nor yet in his parifh neither; but by mutual contributions and collections maintaine them, & minifter to their neceffities in all things, Which thing G O D grant the churches of *Dnalgne* may once begin to practife amongft themfelues, that God may be glorified, and the poore members of Chrift Iefus releeued and maintained.

Our *Husbandmen,* or Farmers, are as skilld as any in the world.

Theod. Be there hufbandmen there & fuch others as manure and till the ground, for the further increafe of fruits, to the maintenance of the commonwealth?

[¹ Sig. G 2, back]

¹*Amphil.* There are of fuch indeed good ftore, and as excellent men in that kinde of exercife, as any be vpon the earth. They know exactly, I warrant you, the times and feafons of the yeere, when euerie kinde of graine is to be fowed, and what ground is beft for euerie kinde of corne. They are not ignorant alfo, howe to culture & dreffe the fame; and if it be barren, what kind of dung is beft to fatten the fame againe. They know the nature, the propertie, and qualitie of euerie foile, and what corne it will bring. They know alfo when the ground is to be tilled, when not, how long it will bring foorth good corne, how long not, when it ought to reft, when not, with all things elfe incident to the fame.

Theod. I thinke they haue good farmes and tenements, that are able to furnifh their ground in this fort, for otherwife they were not able to keepe their oxen, their horfes, their feruants, and other neceffaries, belonging thereto: haue they not fo?

But many have very poor farms,

Amphil. No truely haue they not. For fome haue fuch fatte farmes, and tenements, as either will bring forth no corne at all (in a manner) or if it doe, verie little, and that not without great coft

and others only houses with no land,
[² Sig. G 3]

beftowed vpon it. Otherfome haue houfes with no lande belonging to ²them at all, and yet notwithftanding fhall pay a good round fome for the fame alfo. And no marueile, for landlords and gentlemen take all the lands and lyuelode wherevpon there poore tenants fhoulde liue, into their owne hands, and fuffer not the poore hufbandmen to haue fo much ground as will fiude them corne for the maintenance of their poore families, nor which is more, fcarcely to keepe one cow, horfe, or fheepe vpon, for their continuall releefe. Or if they haue any, they fhall pay tenne times fo much as it is worth, to their vtter vndooing for euer. But if landlords would confider that the earth is the Lords, and all that is therein, and that it is theirs, but onely in title, intereft and propertie (hauing their fouereigntie, or chieftie thereof) and the poores in vfe and poffeffion, and if they would remember that the poore ought to liue vpon the earth as well as they, than would they not vfe fuch tirannie, fuch exactions, fuch pooling, and pilling, and the like, as they doe without all compaffion.

Theod. There being fuch ftore of hufbandmen, and the fame fo expert in their agriculture as your words import they be, it muft needes follow, that there is great plentie of corne, and all kinde of other graine, and the fame verie good cheape : is it not fo ?

[1]*Amphil.* There is great ftore of corne, and all kind of graine, no nation vnder the funne like vnto it ; but as I told you before, thorowe the infatiable greedines of a few couetous cormorants, who for their owne priuate commoditie, tranfport ouer feas whole mountaines of corne, it is made fometimes very fcarfe. Other-wife there would be gret ftore at al times. And whereas you fay it is good cheape, it is nothing leffe[2], as euerie daies fucceffe prooueth true.

Theod. How can that be, that there being fuch ftore of corne, yet fhould be deare alfo.

Amphil. I will tell you. It commeth to paffe three manner of waies. Firft, for that landlords racke their rents fo extreemely, and aduance their fines fo vnreafonably, that the poore man is forced to fell euerie thing deere, otherwife he fhould not be able to pay his landlord his due, whereas if he had his fearme good cheape, he might afforde to fell good cheape. The fecond caufe is (as I haue faid), for that the fame is carried and conueighed ouer Seas. The third caufe is, thorow a forte of ingrators, or foreftallers, who intercept euerie thing before it come at the market, or elfe being come to the market, and hauing mo[3]ney at will, buy vp either all, or the moft part, and carieng it into their celles, and garners at home, keepe it till time of the yeere that corne is fcarfe, and fo confequentlie deere.

[2] It's any thing but that. It's dear.

Margin notes:

or hardly enough to keep a cow on.

Landlords are so grasping.

We've lots of Corn,

[1 Sig. G 3, back]

but the export of it often makes it scarce.

Its dearness comes from

1. Rack-rents,

2. Export over seas,

3. Ingraters or Forestallers buying it up, [3 Sig. G 4] and keeping it till it gets scarce and dear.

And when there is want of it, then they fell it deere, and when there is plentye, then they make it deerer by buying it vppe in whole heapes as they doe.   Thus you fee, by this meanes, thefe hellifhe ingratours, and foreftallers make corne and all thinges elfe deere, all times of the yeere.   Nowe iudge you what a horrible abufe is this, for one man to buy vppe all things, and that not for anie neede or want in himfelfe, but to fell it againe, deerer then they bought it, thereby to inriche himfelfe with the impouerifhing of many a thoufande.

Theod. Is there not punifhment for this horrible abufe, for me thinke great inconueniences doe followe it ?

Amphil. There be great penalties, and forfaitures ordained, as well for the repreffinge of this, as of any other outragious abufe ; but they playe with this as with all other good lawes, they inuente quirckes and quiddities, fhiftes, and put offes ynough [1] to blinde the eies of the magiftrates, and to deliuer themfelues (trimly, trimly) from the danger and penaltie of the lawe.   For they will fay that they buy but for the neceffarie prouifion of their owne families, and not to fell againe.   And then when they doe fell it againe, they will beare you in hande it was of their owne tillage.   Or if this way will not ferue the turne, then procure they another man to buy it with their owne mony vnder his owne name, and fo to fell it againe when hee feeth tyme ; but who hath the commoditie, iudge you.   But if all thefe waies faile, then buie they it couertly, and fell it againe as couertly ; and thus they buy and fell their owne foules for corruptible monie, which in the laft day fhall beare witneffe againft them, and confume them : yea, as Saint Iames faith : The monie which they haue vniuftlie got with the polling and pilling of the poore, fhall rife vp in iudgement againft them, and the ruft thereof fhall eate and deuoure their flefh as it were a canker.   But let thefe iollie felowes (as fubtil and as politike as they would feeme to be) take heed vnto themfelues, and beware : for though they can blinde mens eies, and deceiue their iudgements, yet let them be fure that they can not deceiue the iudgement of the Lord, but he [2] that made the eies fhall furely fee, and he who knoweth the fecrets of all harts, fhall one day declare the fame to their perpetuall confufion, except they repent.

Theod.   What be thefe hufbandmen ? honeft, plaine dealing and

fimple perfons, and fuch as in whom there is no abufe ; or elfe fraudulent, deceitfull and craftie perfons?

Amphil. They are for the moft part verie fimple and plaine men
in outward appeerance, yea, fuch as if you fawe them, and heard them
talke, you would thinke they had no gall, or that there were nothing
in them in the world.   But if you looke into their dailie exercifes,
practifes, and deeds, you fhall find them as craftie and fubtill in their
kind, as the deuill is in his, if it be poffible.   For the fimpleft of
them all, if he make a bargaine with another, he wil be fure to make
it fo as he himfelfe may gaine by it.   And it is well, too, if the other
though neuer fo wife, circumfpect, or prouident, be not vtterly
deceiued (or to fpeake in plainer termes, cofoned at their hands), fuch
fubtiltie, fuch policie, and fuch craftie conueiance, they practife vnder
the garment of fimplicitie.   Yea truly, it is growne to be almoft their
profeffion to deceiue, defraud, and beguile their brethren, infomuch
as they count him a wife man, a worldly [1]felow, and fuch a one as
will liue in the world, that can not deceiue, and beguile men in bargaining.   This is their [2] *Columbina fimplicitas,* (Nay rather, *Vulpina, et
ferpentina aftutia*) which Chrift would haue al his children to practife
in all things, all daies of their life.   But fo farre from this chriftian
fimplicitie are many, that their whole life (almoft) is nothing elfe,
than a continuall practife of fraud, and deceit, as for example: You
fhall haue fome that, fending corne to the market to be fould, they
will put good corne in the top or mouth of the bag, to feeme faire to
the eie, and in the bottome of the facke, very good alfo (that when it
is powred forth of the fame, it may yet feeme exceeding good ftill,)
but in the middeft fhall be neuer a good corne, but fuch as is muftie,
fprouted, and naught.   Whereof can be made neither good bread
nor drinke, for mans bodie.   I haue knowne otherfome, that hauing
a barren cow, and being defirous to put hir away, haue taken a calfe
from another melch cowe, and fo folde the former barren cowe with
hir adulterate calfe, for a melche cowe, whereas fhee was nothing
leffe.[3]   With infinite the lyke fleights, which for breuities fake I
omit.

Theod. I perceiue then it is good for a man to be warie, that
deales with thefe fimple [4]fooles?

Marginal notes:
- tho they look so simple,
- are as crafty as the Devil himself.
- It's almost their business to cheat.
- [1 Sig. G 5, back]
- Nearly their whole life is a fraud.
- They'll put musty corn in the middle of a sack.
- They'll sell a barren cow with another cow's calf as if it were hers.
- [4 Sig. G 6]

[2] *Orig.* there.   [3] Anything but that.   See p. 45; p. 54, l. 2.

Amphil. It were good fo indeede, elfe he may chaunce to cough

The Fox may go to school to em.

himfelfe a dawe for his labour.   For I tell you, the foxe, for all his crafte, may go to fchoole to thefe felowes, to learne the rudiments of deceit and craft.   Such fkilfull Doctors are they herein.   If they fell you a cow, an oxe, a horfe, or a mare, they will fet the price on him,

They tell lies about the animals they want to sell.

I warrant you, and with-all will proteft and take on woonderfullie, that hee is but this olde, and that olde, this yoongue, and that yoongue. And which is woorft of all, though they knowe a hundred faultes by them, yet will they not reueale anye vnto him that buyeth the fame, which is a playne, and a mainfeft deceite before the LORDE, and one daye fhall be anfwered for, I dare be their warrante.

Theod. Would you haue euerie man to declare to the buyers the

Every seller ought to tell the buyer the faults of the things he sells.

faultes and imperfections, which they knowe to be in thofe thinges they fell? then fhould he fell but a little.

Amphil. Euery true chriftian ought to do fo, or elfe, befides that he doth not to others, as he would wifh to be done to (for this is the chaine wherwith euery chriftian is bound to another,) he alfo breketh

[¹ Sig. G 6, back]

the cords of charity, & commiteth ¹moft horrible cofonage, and wil-ful prefumptuous deceit before God, which is a fault punifhable in the iuftice of God, with eternall death, in the lake that burneth with

We should do to others as we wish they'd do to us.

fire and brymeftone for euer.   And feing we ought to doe to others as we would wifh to be done vnto vs, let *the* deceiuer afke of him-felfe when he goeth about to deceiue, thefe queftions: Would I be coofoned?   Would I be vndone and fpoiled?   Would I count him an honeft man, or a good chriftian, that would fupplant me in bargain-ing?   Oh no.   No more ought I to doe to others, that which I would not fhould be done to my felfe.   Befides this, confider that the apoftle faith, The Lord is the reuenger of all fuch as deceiue their brethren in bargaining.   If they would fall into this or the like confideration, I doubt not, but fraude, deceit, lieng, diffimulation, coofonage, and guile, would be abandoned and put to flight in fhorte time; which God grant.

But we can't live without husband-men;

Theod. Well, notwithftanding, I cannot fee how we could liue without hufbandmen anie maner of waie, could we?

Amphil. No truly.   Neither king, prince, earle, duke, lord, knight, efquire, high nor low, rich nor poore, nor yet any potentate,

[² Sig. G 7]

power or principalitie vpon the earth (how great a mo²narch foeuer)

could liue or continue without the vſe of huſbandrie and huſband-
men.   And therefore they are not only to be beloued of vs, but alſo
to be preferred and to be made much of amongſt vs, without whoſe
induſtrie and labour no man could liue long vpon the face of the   their labour is
needful for our
life.
earth.   For this cauſe we read the uſe of huſbandry to be commended
vnto vs in ſundry places of holy ſcripture ; and which is more, the
kingdome of heauen many times to be compared and aſſimiled to the
huſbandman for diuers purpoſes and reſpeᵭs.   And when Adam our   Adam was bidden by God to
till the ground.
firſt parent was expulſed paradiſe, he was by God himſelfe inioined to
manure, to dreſſe and till the ground ; whereby we may ſee both the
antiquitie, auncientie, and excellencie of huſbandrie, euen from the
verie beginning of all things.   And therefore doubtles is it to be had
in reuerence and eſtimation of all men.   But hereof inough.

   Theod. Be there any Chandlers there as in other places ?   *Chandlers*

   Amphil. Yea, that there are inow, I warrant you, and more than
deale iuſtly in euerie reſpe᭬.

   Theod. What do they ſell for the moſt part ?

   Amphil. Almoſt all things, as namelie butter, cheeſe, fagots, pots,   sell cheese, pots,
pans, and other
trinkets.
pannes, candles, and a ¹thouſand other trinkets beſides.   [¹ Sig. G 7, back·

   Theod. What be the abuſes which they commit, I pray you ?

   Amphil. Abuſes, quoth you ?   They dare not commit anie, I
trowe.   But ſeeing you would ſo faine knowe, I will giue you an
inkling of them.   Firſt they buy that butter, cheeſe, and other things,   They buy bad
goods cheap, and
sell em dear.
which is naught, bicauſe they may haue it for a little monie, and then
ſell it for verie good : this, manie a poore prentiſe and other can tell to
be true.   Or if they buy that which is good, then they either ſell it
wonderfull deere, or elſe keepe it till it be paſt the beſt, and yet vtter
it for as much and more than it coſt them.   Beſides this, that they
keepe their butter & cheeſe till it be muſtie and mould, yea, till it
ſmell that no man can eate it, they haue alſo their falſe waights &   They have
false weights and
measures.
counterfet meaſures to deceiue the poore people withall.   And notwithſtanding that they buy ſometimes 2. or 3. fagots for a penie, yet
wil they not ſel one, be it neuer ſo litle, vnder a penie, gaining aboue
the one halfe in the other.   And as for the ſtuffe whereof they make
their candles, I am aſhamed to ſpeake of it.   For whereas they ſhould   They make their
candles of stink-
ing baggage,
make them of good liquor and ſweet, they make them of all kind of
kitchen ſtuffe, & other ſtinking baggage, ſo that they ſhal waſte &

[¹ Sig. G 8]

and their wicks
of rope-ends.

confume ¹away like vnto ware againft the fire, and yet fhall neuer burne cleere, nor giue good light, but run ouer, and about the candlefticke too fhamefully. And as for the wikes within the*m*, they are of hurds, rope ends, & fuch other good ftuffe. Befides all this, they haue fleights to make the liquor of the candles alwaies to remaine foft, to the end it may wafte & confume the fafter, with legions of the like diuifes, God be mercifull vnto vs!

Barbers:

Theod. What fay you of the barbers and trimmers of men? are they fo neate, and fo fine fellowes as they are faid to be?

There are no
finer fellows
under the sun!

Amphil. There are no finer fellowes vnder the funne, nor experter in their noble fcience of barbing than they be. And therefore in the fulnes of their ouerflowing knowledge (oh ingenious heads, and worthie to be dignified with the diademe of follie and vain curiofitie) they haue inuented fuch ftrange fafhions and monftrous maners of cuttings, trimmings, fhauings and wafhings, that you would

Our Barbers
have all kinds of
cuts of beards.

wonder to fee. They haue one maner of cut called the French cut, another the Spanifh cut, one the Dutch cut, another the Italian, one the newe cut, another the old, one of the brauado fafhion, another of the meane fafhion. One a gentlemans cut, another the common

[² Sig. G 8, back]

cut, one ²cut of the court, an other of the country, with infinite the like vanities, which I ouerpaffe. They haue alfo other kinds of cuts innumerable; and therefore when you come to be trimed, they will

They ask you
whether you'll
be trimd to look
fierce or pleasant.

afke you whether you will be cut to looke terrible to your enimie, or amiable to your freend, grime & fterne in countenance, or pleafant & demure (for they haue diuers kinds of cuts for all thefe purpofes, or elfe they lie.) Then, when they haue done al their feats, it is a

Your Mous-
tachios are
twisted up like
horns; the scis-
sors go snip snap,

world to confider, how their mowchatowes muft be preferued and laid out, from one cheke to another, yea, almoft from one eare to another, and turned vp like two hornes towards the forehead. Befides that, when they come to the cutting of the haire, what fnipping & fnapping of the cycers is there, what tricking & toying, and al to tawe out mony, you may be fure. And when they come to wafhing, oh how gingerly they behaue themfelues therein. For then fhall your

your face is
washt with sweet
balls;

mouth be boffed with the lather, or fome that rifeth of the balles (for they haue their fweete balles wherewith-all they vfe to wafhe); your

snap go the
fingers;
[³ Sig. H 1]

eyes clofed muft be anointed therewith alfo. Then fnap go the fingers, ful brauely, god wot. Thus this tragedy ended, ³ comes me warme clothes, to wipe and dry him withall; next, the eares muſt be picked, and cloſed togither againe artificially forſooth. The haire of the noſtrils cut away, and euery thing done in order comely to behold. The laſt action in this tragedie is the paiment of monie. And leaſt theſe cunning barbers might ſeeme vnconſcionable in aſking much for their paines, they are of ſuch a ſhamefaſt modeſtie, as they will aſke nothing at all, but ſtanding to the curteſie and liberalitie of the giuer, they will receiue all that comes, how much ſoeuer it be, not giuing anie againe, I warrant you: for take a barber with that fault, and ſtrike off his head. No, no, ſuch fellowes are *Raræ aues in terris, nigriſque ſimilimi cygnis,* Rare birds vpon the earth, and as geaſon as blacke ſwans. You ſhall haue alſo your orient perfumes for your noſe, your fragrant waters for your face, wherewith you ſhall bee all to beſprinkled: your muſicke againe, and pleaſant harmonie, ſhall ſound in your eares, and all to tickle the ſame with vaine delight. And in the end your cloke ſhall be bruſhed, and 'God be with you Gentleman!'

Theod. All theſe curious conceits, in my iudgement are rather done for to allure and prouoke the minds of men to be bountifull and [1] liberall towards them, than for any good elſe, which they bring either to the bodie or health of man?

Amphil. True it is that you ſay, and therefore you muſt needes think they are maiſters of their ſcience that can inuent al theſe knacks to get money withall. But yet I muſt needs ſay (theſe niſities ſet apart), barbers are verie neceſſarie, for otherwiſe men ſhould grow verie ouggliſom and deformed, and their haire would in proceſſe of time ouergrowe their faces, rather like monſters, than comlie ſober chriſtians. And if it be ſaid that any man may cut off the haire one of another, I anſwer, they may ſo, but yet not in ſuch comelie and decent maner as theſe barbers exerciſed therein can doe, and beſides, they knowe that a decorum in euerie thing is to be obſerued. And therefore I cannot but maruell at the beaſtlineſſe of ſome ruffians (for they are no ſober chriſtians) that will haue their haire to growe ouer their faces like monſters, and ſauage people, nay rather like mad men than otherwiſe, hanging downe ouer their ſhoulders, as womens haire doth: which indeed is an ornament to them, being giuen them as a ſigne of ſubiection, but in man it is a ſhame and reproch, as

Side notes:
warm cloths are brought,
your noſtril-hairs cut,
and then you're to pay 'What you pleaſe, Sir.'
You have fragrant waters, and music;
your cloak bruſht, and good-bye!
[1 Sig. H 1, back]
Barbers are neceſſary.
Without em men ud look like monſters.
I wonder at the beaſtlineſs of ſome ruffians letting their hair grow ſo long.

[¹ Sig. H 2]

the Apoftle prooueth. And thus much of barbers and their
¹fcience.

Theod. Haue you furgeans, and phyficians there, as in other
places, and are they fkilfull and expert in their myfterie; and not
onelie fkilfull, but alfo confcionable in their dealings, as well toward
the poore as toward the rich?

Surgeons and
Physicians

Amphil. There are both furgeans and phyficians, good ftore.
And as they be manie, fo are they verie vnconfcionable in their
dooinges, for, as for both the one and the other, fo farre from godlineffe
and good confcience in all things are they, as if a poore man that hath

'll only work for
money.

not monie to giue them at their pleafure, ftande in need of their
helpe, they will either not come at him, or if they doe, they will fo
handle him, as it were better for him to be hanged, than to fuftaine

Doctors 'll do

the paines that they will put him to.   But for the moft part, neither
of them both will come at him, but rather contemne him, and reiect

nothing for a
poor man with-
out money.

him as a thing of naught, yea, as much will they doe for the diuell
himfelfe, as for a poore man, if hee haue not money. And againe, as
long as moneye runneth, they will applye gentle and eafie potions,
medicines, and falues, bearing their patient in hand, that he fhall

[² Sig. H 2, back]

recouer without ²all doubt, with what difeafe, maladie, or fore foeuer
he be infected, wheras in truth they can do nothing leffe.   But

As soon as that
fails, they give
you the nastiest
stuff they can.

Deficiente pecunia, Monie wanting, they applie bitter potions, nipping
medicines, gnawing corrofiues, and pinching plaiftures to greeue their
patient withal, therby to ftraine out what liquor of life (that is, what
monie or goods) they are able to giue.   And thus they abufe their
gifts, to the difhonor of God, the hurt of their felow brethren, and
their owne damnation, except they repent.

Theod. Are furgeans and phifitians then neceffarie in a common
wealth, as you feeme to inferre?

Amphil. Salomon faith the Phifition (by the which worde he
vnderftandeth both the phifition and the furgean, bicaufe the one
is coofin germaine to the other) is to be honored for neceffitie.   And
if for neceffitie, then muft it needes follow, that the fame is moft
neceffarie in a common wealth.   But as the good, learned, and

We've many ill-
taught doctors.

difcreet phifitions and furgeans, are neceffarie, and may doe much
good, fo the vnlearned, and naughtie (as the world is to full of
them) may and doe much hurt dailie, as experience teacheth.

Theod. You fay truth. But are all indifferently fuffered to practife the fame noble miſfteries of phificke and furgerie, without any
choyfe or exception at all?

[¹ Sig. H 3]

Amphil. There is to great libertie permitted herein. For now
a daies euerie man, tagge, and ragge, of what infufficiencie foeuer, is
fuffered to exercife the mifterie of phifick, and furgerie, and to
miniſter both the one, and the other, to the difeafed, and infirmed
perfons; but to their woe, you may be fure. Yea, you fhall haue
fome that know not a letter of the booke (fo farre are they from
being learned, or fkilful in the toongs, as they ought to be, that
fhoulde practife thefe mifteries) both men and women, yoong and
old, that, prefuming vpon experience forfooth (for that is their greateft
fkill) will arrogate great knowledge to themfelues, and more than
the learnedſt doctor vpon the earth will doe. And yet notwithſtanding, can doe in manner nothing at all. But if they chance at any time
to doe any good (as *forte lufcus capiat leporem* fomtime by chance a
blind man may catch a hare) it is by meere chance, and not by any
knowledge of theirs. And yet fhall this exploit of theirs be founded
foorth with a trumpet, which indeede may hardly be blowne vp
with an oten pipe, for any praife it deferueth. This bringeth the
laudable fciences of phifick and furgerie, into hatred, obloquy, &
contempt, ²maketh it of no eftimation in the world, and vtterly dif-
crediteth it amon[g]ſt men. For when as any fick, infirmed, or difeafed,
either mifcarieth vnder the hands of his phifition or furgean, or elfe
when the medicine or falue worketh not his effect, then fall they to
accufe the fcience it felfe, and to reproch it altogither, whereas in
truth the whole blame confifteth in the ignorance of the practicioner
himfelfe. Great pitie it is therefore, that there is fuch libertie in
permitting euery one that luft, to prophane and to abufe thefe venerable fciences of phificke and furgerie as they doe. For euery man,
though he know not the firſt principles, grounds or rudiments of his
fcience, yᵉ lineaments, dimenfions, or compofitions of mans body, the
poores, arteries, temperament, or conftitution, no, nor yet fo much as
the naturall complexion, qualitie, or difpofition of the fame, will yet
notwithſtanding take vpon him the habite, the title, yᵉ name, and
profeffion, of a phifition or furgean. This we fee verified in a fort of
vagarants, who run ftragling (1 wil not faie roging) ouer the countries,

Any man, tag
and rag, can
practise both
physic and sur-
gery.

If any person
makes a cure, he
puffs it every-
where.

[² Sig. H 3, back]

If any doctor
loses a patient,
then the Science
is abus'd.

Any Ignorant

can set up as a
Surgeon or
Physician.
Vagrant Quacks
make a lot of
money.

and beare men in hand of gret knowledg, when as there is nothing leſſe in them.   By which kind of theft, (for this cooſoning ſhift is no better) they rake in great ſomes of mony, which when they haue got, they leaue their [1] cures in the duſt, I warrant you, and betake them to their heeles as to their beſt refuge.   And thus be the noble ſciences of phiſicke and ſurgerie vtterly reproched, the world deluded, and manie a good man and woman brought to their endes, before their time.

[1 Sig. H 4]

Theod. If phiſicke be good, would you not haue euery man to practiſe it that will, without reſtraint ?

Amphil. Phiſicke is good, and yet would I not haue euerie ignorant doult that knoweth not the vſe nor benefit thereof, to practiſe the ſame.   For that maketh it to take ſo little effect, and ſo ſmally to be eſteemed of, as it is now a daies ; (for reformation wherof) I would wiſh that euery ignorant doult, & eſpecially women, that haue as much knowledg in phiſick or ſurgery as hath Iackeanapes, being but ſmatterers in the ſame noble ſciences (nor yet al that), ſhould be reſtrained from the publike vſe therof, yet not from priuate exercife thereof either for their owne ſinguler benefit, or any other of their freends (prouided that they do it *gratis*) not making an occupation of it, but rather for deſire to helpe, then for lucre of gaine.   Than woulde I wyſhe that the others who ſhoulde exerciſe the vſe of Phiſicke and Surgerie ſhoulde firſt bee Graduates in [2] either of the vniuerſities ; and being graduates, yet not to be admitted therefore, but firſt to be tried and examined, as well for their knowledge, diſcretion, and ſufficiencie in their art, profeſſion and calling, as alſo for their god- lines, chriſtian zeale, pure religion, compaſſion, and loue to their brethren ; and being found ſufficient for the foreſaid reſpects, to be admitted and licenſed, vnder hand and ſeale authentike, by thoſe that be of authoritie.   And if he abuſe himſelfe or his facultie, then out with him, let him be *Officiperda*, Iacke out of office, make him a *Quondam*, and let him go to plow and cart, rather than to robbe the poore (as manie of them doe) yea, to murther and kil them without reprehenſion.   And as I would wiſh none but godlie, learned, and ſuch as feare God, to be admitted to the exerciſe and practiſe hereof, ſo I would wiſh, that either they might be allowed annal ſtipends, for their better ſuccouring of the poore diſeaſed, or elſe

I'd let no stupid Dolt or Woman practise medicine or surgery except *gratis*.

I'd have all doctors Graduates,

[2 Sig. H 4, back]

examind for character as well as learning,

and then licenst to practise ; and if they did wrong, out with em !

I'd pay em

might be conftrained to take leffe of their poor patients than they doe. For now they ruffle it out in filckes and veluets, with their men attending vpon them, whereas many a poore man (GOD wot) fmarteth for it. Yea, fo vnreafonable, and fo vnconfcionable are they, as fome of them will not fet one foot out of his owne doores, without [1]twentie fhillings, fortie fhillings, three pound, twentie nobles, ten pound, twentie pound, and fome more, fome leffe. And hauing this importable fee, If they minifter anything to the partie difeafed, than befides, muft they haue twenty fhillings, for that that ftands them not in twentie pins; fortie fhillings, twentie nobles, for that that coft them not twentie pence, & fo foreward. This is a great wickednes, God be mercifull vnto vs, and fuch as the Lord will one day reuenge, if they preuent not his iudgements by fpeedy repentance. Befids thefe abufes, there are otherfome, that if they owe euill will to any, man or woman being ficke, or if they hope for any preferment by their deaths, wil not make any confcience of it, to giue them fuch medicines, fuch potions, and drinkes, as will foone make a hand of them; and this fhall be done inuifible in a clowde, Vnder the pretence of phificke, forfooth; and if he die, why it was not the medicine that killed him (no it were *Blafphemia in fanctos ruminare,* blafphemie to thinke it of thefe holie fathers) but it was death, that cruell tyger, that fpareth none. And to fuch corruption are they grown, that for mony I am perfuaded they can make away with any whom they haue acceffe vnto. Therefore I aduife euery man to be careful to whom [2]he committeth the cure of his bodie. They are likewife in league with the apothecaries, in whome there are great abufes alfo, as well in compounding and mixing of their elements & fimples togither, as alfo in felling chalke for cheefe, one thing for another, & the like, fo as it is hard to get anything of them that is right pure and good of it felfe, but druggie baggage, and fuch counterfait ftuffe as is ftarke naught. But of them inough.

Let vs fpeake a worde or two of a certeine kinde of curious people, and vaineglorious, called aftronomers, and aftrologers, the cor- ruptions and abufes of whom are inexplicable. This done, we will make a final ende at this time of fpeaking any further conferning the abufes, corruptions, and imperfections, of the temporaltie, till occafion of more matter hereafter fhall be offered.

Theod. Thefe names of aftronomers, aftrologers, prognofticators, and the like, are fo vnquoth and ftrange to my eares, that I knowe not what to make of them. Wherefore I pray you fhewe me as neere as you can, the meaning of them, and what kinde of marchants the profeffors thereof be ?

Amphil. The' aftronomers, aftrologers, prognofticators (and all others of the fame focietie, and brotherhoode, by what name or title foe¹uer they be called) are a certeine kinde of curious phantafticall and vaineglorious fellowes, who *fecreta dei temere remantes,* Searching the fecrets of God rafhlie, which he would haue kept clofe from vs, and onely knowne to himfelfe, take vpon them, & that vpon thefe grounds (forfooth), namely, the obferuation of times & feafons,

the afpects & coniunctions of the fignes and planets, with their occurrents, to prefage, to diuine, and prognofticate, what fhall come or happen afterwards, as though they fate in Gods lap, knew his fecrets, & had the world and the difpofement thereof in their own hands. It is an olde faieng, and verie true, *Quæ fupra nos, nihil ad nos,* Thofe things that are aboue our reach, conferne vs not, and therefore we ought not to enter into the bowels & fecrets of the Lord—(for as the wife man faith, *Qui fcrutatur abfcondita dei, obruetur gloria eius,* hee that feacheth out the hidden things of

G O D, fhall bee ouerwhelmed with the glorye of the fame,—but to content our felues with fo much as hee hath reuealed vnto us in his facred worde, committing the euent, the' fucceffe, and difpofement of all things elfe to his facrede Maieftie, the G O D of all glorie. For to them that goe about, and labour fo bufelye by fpeculations, by

aftronomie, ²aftrologie, and the like curious arts to iudge of things to come, and thinke they can tell all things by the fame (but *Dum par-turiunt montes nafcetur ridiculus mus,* whilft the mountains doe trauell,

a feely moufe will be brought forth) Chrift our fauiour faith, *non eft veftrum noffe tempora, & momenta temporum, quæ ipfe pater in fua ipfius conftituit poteftate,* It is not for you to knowe the times and feafons, which the Lord God hath referued to himfelfe. And how much our fauiour Chrift difliketh this vaine curiofitie, of aftronomicall & aftrologicall fpeculations, we may gather by that vehement reprehen-fion or commination in the 16. of Matthew, thundred out againft the people of the Iewes, who were, as it feemeth, too much addicted to the fame. Where he fharply rebuketh them, and calleth them diffembling hypocrites, in that they obferued and marked with fuch ferious attention and diligence, the elemental fignes & tokens in the firmament, being in the meane time, ignorant of greater things, namely of the fignes and tokens of the fonne of G O D Chrift Jefus, the true Meffias, and fauiour of the world.

Theod. Vppon what grounds, certeinties, rules, and principles doth this curious fcience confift ?

[1]*Amphil.* It ftandeth vpon nothing elfe, but meere conie&ures, fuppofals, likelihoods, gheffes, probabilities, obferuations of times and feafons, coniun&ions of fignes, ftarres, and planets, with their afpe&s, and occurrents, and the like, & not vpon anie certeine ground, knowledge, or truth, either of the word of God, or of natural reafon. But to argue the vntruth and the vncerteintie of this foolifh curious fcience, we need not to go farre for examples and arguments. For the contrariety that euer hath beene in all ages amongft the verie do&ors and maifters themfelues, but moft fpecially of late, doth approoue the fame to be moft fantafticall, curious, vaine, vncerten and meere prophane. For there being a maruellous ftrange coniunction (as they faid) of two fuperiour planets, So manie as writ of the fame, neither iumped togither in one truth, nor yet agreed togither, either of the day, houre, or moneth, when it fhould be : but in al things fhewed themfelues like themfelues, that is, plaine contradi&orie one to another. Infomu'ch as they writ in defence of their errors, and confutation of the contrarie, one againft another, fhamefully to behold. By which more than prefumptuous audacitie, and rafh boldneffe of thefe, they brought the world into a woonderfull perplexi[2]tie and ceafe, expe&ing either a woonderfull alteration of ftates and king-domes (as thefe foolifh ftarre tooters promifed) or elfe a finall confummation and ouerthrowe of all things. Or if not fo, yet the ftrangeft things fhould happen, that euer were heard or feene fince the beginning of the world. Wheras, God be thanked, at the verie houre and moment when (as fome of them fet downe) thefe woonders and portents fhould haue happened, there was no alteration nor change of any thing feene or heard of, the element being as faire, as bright, as calme, and as pleafant, and euerie thing as filent, and in as perfe& order and forme, as euer they were fince the beginning of the world.

Marginal notes:

rebukes em, and calls em hypocrites.

[1 Sig. H 7]

Their science is founded only on guesses and star-gazing.

On April 28, 1583 (see *Holinshed*, 1587, iii. 1356), or some other day that they couldn't agree on,

[2 Sig. H 7, back]

the foolish star-tooters foretold fearful events,

and yet everything passed off quietly as usual.

By all which appeereth the vanitie and vncerteintie of their curious
fcience. I woonder where thefe fellowes fate, whether vppon the
earth, or in the firmament of heauen, when they faw thefe coniunctions.
Or with what eies they could fee that, that no man elfe could fee.
But peraduenture they haue *Argus* eies, and can fee all things, euen
thofe things that be not. I maruell whether they haue dwelt in the
region of the aire, and who told them the names, the fcituation, the
houfes, afpects, and locall places of the fignes and planets, of the funne,

[¹ Sig. H 8]

moone, and ftarres, with the number ¹thereof alfo, which indeed are
innumerable. I woonder what fpirite tolde them which planets were
higher than other, and which lower than other, which be good and
which be euill, which be moift and which be drie, which bee colde,
and which be hote, which be gentle and affable, and which bee
cruell and terrible, which giue good fortune, and which giue euill,
which be good to take iourneies in hand, or to attempt any great
thing, and which bee naught, which bee good for a man to take a

Where did these
astrologing
fellows learn all
their fooleries?
Not in the book
of God, I know.

wife in, that fhe may be amiable and gentle, and which be contrarie,
which be dangerous to take difeafes in, or to fall ficke, and which
bee not, with infinite the like fooleries, which I ouerpaffe. Now
from whence they haue learned thefe things I cannot tell, but certeine I am, that out of the booke of G O D, they neuer fetched them,
the fame being in euerie point contrarie vnto them, and reproouing,
yea, condemning to hell, their vaine curious fearching of Gods fecrets,
and the fucceffe of things by fuch fallible and vncerteine accidents.

Theod. Me thinke this is the next way to withdrawe men from
G O D the Creator, to depende and hang vpon creatures, is it not?

[² Sig. H 8, back]

For if the Planets
give good and
evil,
and rule men,

²*Amphil.* It is the onely waie: For who, hearing that the creatures,
as the fun, the moone, the ftarres, the fignes & planets doe giue
both good things and euill, bleffing and curfing, good fucceffe, and
euill fucceffe, yea, life and death, at their pleafure (as thefe brainefick
fooles hold they doe) and that they rule, gouerne, and difpofe al
things whatfoeuer, yea, both the bodies and foules of man (for fo
fome fhame not to fay) who, hearing this, I fay, would not fall from

men 'll turn from
God, and worship
the stars.

God, and worfhip the creatures that giue fuch bleffings vnto man?
What can be a neerer way to withdrawe the people, not onelie from
God, but alfo to hale them to idolatrie, and wholy to depend vpon
creatures as the heathen do to their eternall damnation for euer.

But, fay they, though we giue authoritie, great power, great rule and gouernement to the creatures, yet we giue vnto God the cheefeft ftroke and the cheefeft rule in all things, all other creatures being but the inftrumentall, or fecundarie caufes, or (that I may fpeake plainlie) as it were his deputies, fubftitutes, or inftrumentes whereby he ruleth and worketh all things. Is this any thing elfe, than to faie with certeine heretikes, that though God made all things, yet he ruleth them not, nor hath no care ouer them, but hath committed the rule ¹and gouernement of them to his creatures. Then which, what blafphemie can be greater? is not this a flatte deniall of the prouidence of God, which fcripture fo much fetteth forth and commendeth vnto vs? Shall we thinke that God made all things, and now as one wearie of his worke, committeth the gouernemente of them to other creatures? Saith not our Sauiour Chrift, *Pater et ego operamur*, my father worketh, and I worke? Meaning thereby, that as he wrought in creating all things, fo he worketh ftill in ruling them by his power, gouerneing them by his wifdome, and preferuing them by hys prouidence, and will do to the end of the world. But when they haue proued that he hath committed the rule and gouernement of his creatures, to his creatures, then I will faye as they fay. In the meane time I fay & holde, that it derogateth greatly from the glorie and maieftie of God, to faye or affirme that creatures haue the gouernement of all things committed vnto them. For if there fhould be many kings, princes and rulers in any one realme or country, muft not the dominion and rule of the chief prince or regent be leffer, than if he ruled and gouerned alone? Woe were vs, if wee were at the rule and gouernement of creatures; but bleffed be our God, who, as he knoweth our ²frailtie (hauing therefore compaffion of our infirmities) fo he ruleth and gouerneth all things, whether in heauen, earth, hell, or elfe wherfoeuer, according to the good pleafure of his will. In the 1. and 2. chapters of Genefis, befides infinit the like places in holie fcriptures, we read that the fun, the moone, the ftars, with all creatures elfe, were created & made for the vfe and commoditie of man, being made fubiect to him, and he conftitute lord ouer them; & yet notwithftanding, are they becom now his lords, and he their fubiect, vaffal bondflaue? This is prepofterous geare, when Gods ordinance is turned topfie turuie, vpfide downe. It is time thefe phantafticall

To pretend that Planets are God's deputies, is blasphemous nonsense too.

[¹ Sig. I. 1.]

God works and rules still, as he did at the Creation.

[² Sig. I. 1. back]

God made the stars for the use of man. Who made them his lords?

These fantastical
fellows turn God
into a Jack out
of office.
fellowes were looked to in time, that wil go about to difthronize the
mightie God Jehoua of his regall throne of maieftie and glorie,
makin gan *Officiperda* of him, a iacke out of office, & to pul him
(as it were) *E cælis*, Out of the heauens, downe to the earth, giuing
him no power nor authoritie at all.

Theod. Haue the fignes and planets then no power nor authoritie
at all vpon things on the earth?

Amphil. Yes, they haue their power, their operation, force, ftrength
and effect in thofe things whereto G O D hath created them, as namely
in the growing, increafing, cherifhing, foftering, renewing, comforting
[¹ Sig. I. 2.]
& reuiuing of ¹all natural things, And alfo they haue their influence &
operation in mans bodie, for letting of bloud, receiuing of purgations &
the like. But to fay they worke thefe effects of their own proper force
& ftrength, or that they rule or difpofe the fpirits & foules of man,
is vtterly falfe, & at no hand true. And yet notwithftanding, fo
The busy-headed
astronomers as-
sign every kind
of man to a par-
ticular Sign,
far infatuat are thefe bufie heded aftronomers, & curious ferching
aftrologers, that they attribute euery part of mans body to one particular figne & planet, affirming that part of the bodie to be ruled
by that figne, or planet. And therefore to Aries they haue affigned
the gouernement of the head & face. To Tau[rus] the necke and
throte. To Gem[ini] the fhoulders, the armes & the hands. To Leo
the hart and back. To Can[cer] the breft, ftomake and lungs. To
Lib[ra] the raines and loines. To Vir[go] the guts & bellie. To
Scor[pio] the priuie parts & bladder. To Sag[ittarius] the thighes.
To Capr[icornus] the knees. To Aqu[arius] the legs. To Pifc[es]
the feet. And thus haue they, & doe, beare the world in hand that
the whole bodie of man both *Interne & externe*, within & without,
and every month
too.
is ruled and gouerned by the xii. fignes, by ftarres, and planets, &
not by God only. For the confirmation of which fained vntruth,
they pretend the xii. moneths in the yere to be ruled & gouerned
by the xii. fignes in the element, and the feuen daies in the weeke
The 7 Days they
put to the 7
Planets.
[² Sig. I. 2. back]
to be ruled by the feuen planets ²alfo. Befides this, they haue their
particular houres, times and feafons, wherein they chiefly worke their
effects, and haue greateft ftrength. So that by their reafons, no
moneth in the yere, nor day in the weeke, no, nor houre in the day
nor night, but it is ruled and gouerned by the influence and conftel-

lation of the ftarres and planets, and nothing is effected or brought to paffe, but what they will, and intend.

Theod. Are the fignes and planets, liuing creatures and reafonable, or infenfible creatures, and things without life ?

Amphil. They are no liuing or reafonable creatures, it is without all controuerfie, but meerely infenfible, and without life. And being without life and reafon, how is it poffible that they fhould bring life or death (as thefe fellowes hold) fickneffe or health, profperitie or aduerfitie, heate or cold, faire weather or foule, beautie or deformitie, long life or fhort, or any thing elfe ? And if they be not able to giue thefe things, how much leffe able are they then, to gouerne, rule, and difpofe all thinge[s] in heauen, earth, the aire, or elfe wherfoeuer, to ouerthrowe monarchies, kingdoms, nations, countries, and people, and finally to work althings after their owne defire and will ? Will they ¹haue dumbe and vnreafonable creatures to rule the reafonable ? If that were true, why fhould God be praifed either for his mercie, or feared for his iuftice and iudgement, and not rather the planets, fignes, and ftarres, which worke all in all in all creatures ? If bleffing come by the influence of ftarres and planets, then let men praife them, and not God, for the fame. And if curfes proceed from the ftarres, let them be feared for them. Briefly, if life and death, and all things elfe, come by the force of the elementall creatures, and celeftiall bodies, then let them be honoured with diuine worfhip. If thefe effects iffued from creatures, then why fhould the homicide, the murtherer, adulterer, or wicked perfon be punifhed, wheras he might fay, it was not I, it was *Planetarum iniuria*, The force of the planets that compelled me to finne* ? Or why fhould the godlie man be praifed for dooing well, whereas he is inforced thereto, by the ftarres and planets ? *In Summa*, why fhould not planets and ftarres be adored and worfhipped as gods, if they coulde worke thefe effects ? They that attribute thus much to the ftarres, not onelie rob the maieftie of God of his honour, but alfo ftrenhthen the hands of the heathen, pagans, infidels, and idolatrous people, to perfeuere in their curfed ido²latrie ftill. Nay, do they not rather fhake hands with them, that as they worfhip the

* Cp. Edmund in *Lear*, I. ii. 134-5 : "Drunkards, liars, and adulterers, by an enforced obedience of planetary influence."

funne, the moone, the ftarres, fire, water, and other creatures, for their God, fo doe thefe worfhip the fame, though not for their chiefe Gods, yet for their fecond gods, whereby they commit moft filthie idolatrie, and are giltie of moft hainous tranfgreffion.

I confess that Stars have effect; but yet they're not Efficient Causes. Indeede, I confeffe they haue effects and operations, but yet are they not the efficient caufes of any thing either good or bad. Otherwife than thus, that it pleafeth the maieftie of God to worke by them, as by his inftruments, whatfoeuer is his good wyll and pleafure, and not after any other fort.

Theod. I haue heard of fome of thefe aftronomers that would take vpon them to tell a mans fortune, onely by their conftellation : forfooth, is it poffible, fuppofe you ?

Amphil. No, at no hand. For if it were fo, that all things were, and man himfelfe, gouerned and ruled by the ftars alone (as who is fo forfaken of God to beleeue it?) And that they knew the minds, the purpofes, the intents, the inclination, the difpofition & qualities of euery ftarre, then might it be (peraduenture) true, that they might

Let these star-gazers show me, if they can,

tell the fortune, and defteny of any man. But otherwife they can tel as much as a horfe. I would faine learne of thefe ftarre ¹gaifers,

[¹ Sig. I. 4.]

who teach that man is drawne to good or euill by the conftellations, and influence of ftars, whether all the people that were euer borne fince the beginning of the world, or fhal be borne to the ende of the fame, were al borne vnder one planet or ftar? For they had all one fortune, all finned in *Adam,* & all were in the iuftice of God condemned to euerlafting fire. I would know alfo whether all the

that all the sinners in Sodom and Gomorrah, who had one fate, were born under one star;

Sodomits and Gomorreans being confumed with fire & brimftone from heauen were borne all vnder one ftarre & planet? For they had all one deftinie, and all one end. Whether all the whole world in the daies of *Noah,* was borne vnder one and the fame ftar, or planet, for they had all one deftenie, being ouerwhelmed with an vniuerfall deluge. Whether the whole hoft of *Core, Dathan,* and *Abiram,* were borne all vnder one ftar or planet, who had al one iudgment, one deftinie, and one kind of death. Whether all the hoft of *Pharao* were borne vnder one and the fame ftarre and planet,

why Esau and Jacob, who were born under one star, had different ends;

who all fuftained one kinde of death, and had all one deftinie. Whether *Efau,* and *Iacob* were not borne both in a moment, and both at one birth, and yet had they contrarie natures, qualities, dif-

pofitions and ends. Finally I would learne of them, whither none
that euer liued fince the [1]firft beginning of the worlde, nor any that
fhall be borne to the end of the fame, hath not, or may not be borne
in the fame houre, and vnder the fame planet & conftellation, that
Chrift Iefus was borne in. If they fay there haue not beene any
borne in the fame houre that Chrift Iefus was borne in, common
reafon, and daily experience would difprooue them, for there is not one
minute of an houre wherein there are not infinite children borne into
the world. And if they fay that there are that haue beene borne in
the fame houre, and vnder the fame ftarre and planet, than muft it
needes follow (if man fhould neceffarily be ruled, gouerned, difpofed
& affected according to the naturall difpofition, and inclination of
the planets & ftars) that he that hath bin, is, or fhall be, borne in the
fame howre, and vnder the fame planet or ftar that Iefus Chrift was
borne vnder, fhould bee as good & as perfect in euery refpeƐt, as
Chrift Iefus himfelfe; and fo fhould we haue had manie chrifts before
this time. But God bleffe all his children from once thinking of any
fuch impietie, and blafphemie. By all which reafons and arguments
it apeareth manifeftly that man is nothing leffe, than ruled, gouerned
or deftined, after the inclination, or influence of ftars or planets, but
onely by the liuing God, who doeth [2]whatfoeuer pleafeth him in
heauen & in earth. This being fo, twife vnhappy be thofe parents
that thinke any moneth, day or houre, infortunate for their children
to be borne in, or that fome be more fortunate and happie than otherfome. And thrife curfed be thofe wicked deuils, that taught them
thofe leffons. What? Doe they thinke that the Lorde is a fleepe
thofe houres; or being wake, hath no power to rule? Hath he not
made all things pure and good? Then cannot the good creatures of
God make vs euil, or incline vs to finne. But it is the malice of the
deuill, the corruption of our nature, and the wickednes of our owne
harts, that draweth vs to euill, and fo to fhamefull deftinies, and
imfamous ends, and not the ftarres, or planets. Whereof if we were
truely perfwaded, we wold leaue of, when we come to any fhamefull
end, to faie: " Oh, I was borne to it, it was my deftonie," and I cannot tell what: whereas in truth we were borne to no fuch ends. But
rather to glorifie our heauenly father by integritie of life & godlines
of conuerfation, whilft we liue vpon the face of the earth. Certein

[1 Sig. I. 4. back]

why the children
born when Christ
was, were not
like him.

Man is not
swayd by Stars,
but by the living
God.

[2 Sig. I 5]

It's the Devil
and our own
wickedness, and
not planets, that
make us sin.
(Cf. Edmund in
Lear I. ii.)

Tho God sees that some men will come to a bad end, he doesn't fore-ordain them to it.
[¹ Sig. I 5, back]

it is, that God by his prouidence, & prefcience, doth forefee that fuch a man through his wickednes fhall come to fuch an ende, yet did not the Lord foreordeine, or foreappoint him to the fame, [1]but rather dehorteth him from comitting that wickednes, which may purchafe fuch an end. Wherefore to conclude. Seing it is finne that bringeth man and woman to fhamefull ends, and neither fate, deftonie, birthftar, figne or planet, conftellation, nor anything elfe whatfoeuer, let euerie one endeuour himfelfe to ferue his G O D truelie, in finglenefle

Serve God, and

and purenefle of heart, and himfelfe to liue well and vprightlie; Walking in the lawes, and commandements of the Lord; and I warrant him for euer comming to anie euill end or deftinie. That

Hell preserve you.

God whom he hath ferued, will keepe him as he kept *Sidrach*, *Mifaac*, and *Abednago*, from the rage of the fire, *Sufanna* from the ftake, *Daniel* from yᵉ chawes of the greedie lions, & manie others that ferued him in feare.

Theod. I haue hea[r]d fome that woulde take vpon them to tell a man whither he fhoulde be poore or rich, a feruant or a lord, a theefe or a true man, cruell or gentle, and what kinde of trades he fhould haue profperous fuccefle in: how fhoulde they doe this?

Amphil. I will tell you how they pretende to doe it. There are

Some say that the 12 Signs of the Zodiac and the 7 Planets and their Aspects fix men's natures and fates.
[² Sig. I 6]

(as they faye) certeine fignes in the element (but yet I maruell what Apollo tolde them fo, when they were there, and fawe them, or how they knew the fhape [2]and proportion of them) as Aries, Taurus, Gemini, Cancer, Leo, Virgo, Libra, Scorpio, Sagittarius, Capricornus, and Pifces, with their planets, and afpects, as Sol, Luna, Mars, Mercurie, Iupiter, Venus, and Saturne. Now fay they, he that is borne vnder Aries, (which is a figne in the *Nufquam region*, Like to a ramme, or fheepe vpon earth) fhall be a riche man and too too wealthie. And whie fo? Marke their droonken reafon. Forfooth

But what a drunken reason they give for it!

becaufe the rame is a fruitfull beaft vpon earth, and yeldeth to his mafter two or three fleeces a yeere. Againe, he that is borne vnder Taurus (which is a figne (fay thefe liers) in the element like vnto a bull, vpon earth); now fir, he that is borne vnder him, fhall be pore,

Because a Bull is a yoke-beast here, *therefore* a man borne under him shall be a bond-slave!

& a bondflaue all his daies. And why fo? Mary, fay they, bicaufe the bull on earth is a beaft vfed to the yoke, and to much flauerie & drudgery. He that is borne vnder Leo (which is a figne quoth thefe iuglers like to a lion) fhal be ftrong, couragious, & feared of al men, & fhal be lord & ruler ouer many, And why fo? Bicaufe the lion is a ftrong & mightie beaft, & is lord & king ouer all other beafts. He that is borne vnder Scorpio, fhal be a murtherer, a robber, a theefe, and a wicked perfon. Why fo? Forfooth bicaufe the Scorpion is a ferpent full of poyfon & malice vpon earth. [1]He [1 Sig. I 6, back] that is borne vnder Gemini fhall be rich, and haue manie children, bicaufe Gemini is a figne of two twinnes. He that is borne vnder Virgo fhall be beloued of women, fhall be amiable, faire, gentle, and I cannot tell what, bicaufe maids are fo affected. He that is borne vnder Cancer, fhall be crabbed and angrie, bicaufe the crab fifh is fo inclined. He that is borne vnder Libra, fhall be fortunate in merchandize, in waights and meafures, bicaufe Libra is a figne of a paire of ballance. He that is borne vnder Sagittarius, fhal be a good fhooter, bicaufe Sagittarius is a figne like to a fhooter. He that is borne vnder Capricornus fhall be a flouenly, ill fauoured, and vncleane fellowe, bicaufe the gote is a beaft filthie, ftinking and vncleane. He that is borne vnder Aquarius and Pifces fhall be fortunate by water, bicaufe watermen haunt the waters, and fifhes fwim in the fame. Thefe be cupftantiall reafons and well feafoned arguments, and as ftrong to prooue their purpofe, as a caftell of paper to refift the enimie. Thus you may fee they haue no other reafons, than to heape one lie vpon another. As firft that thefe fignes and planets in the heauens are like to earthly creatures, then that their natures, and qualities are knowne by the natures and qualities of [2]earthly creatures. Iefu God, what cunning felowes are thefe, that can knowe the nature of heauenly bodies, and celeftiall creatures, by thefe terreftriall bodies and earthly creatures? Thefe are profound fellowes indeed, and by all likelihood, haue dwelt long in the clouds, that are fo perfect in euery thing there, and can iudge of future accidents with fuch fingular dexteritie. By this time I thinke they are afhamed of their profeffion, therefore I need to fay no more of them; till further occafion be offered, befeeching the Lorde God to giue them grace to fearch for the truth of the worde of God, letting all fuch curious fearchings of Gods fecrets alone to God, who onely knoweth all fecrets whatfoeuer.

Theod. If you condemne aftronomie, and aftrologie altogither, as you feeme to doe, then it followeth that you condemne prognofticators, and fuch as make almanacks for euerie yeere: doe you fo?

Margin notes:
He that's borne under Capricorn shall be uncleanly, *because* the goat's a stinking beast!

[2 Sig. I 7]

These Astrologer fellows must have livd long in the clouds to know so much about heavenly bodies.

Prognosticators and *Almanac-makers* I condemn too,

Amphil. I neither condemne aftronomie nor aftrologie, nor yet the makers of prognofticatious, or almanacks for the yeere.   But I condemne the abufe in them both, and wifh they were reduced to the fame perfection that they ought, and to be vfed to the fame endes and purpofes which they were ordeined for.   [1] The funne, the moone, the ftarres, and the celeftiall bodies whatfoeuer, created by the Lord not onelie to fructifie and increafe the earth by their influence, but alfo to fhine and giue light to man in this life, and to diuide the light from darknefe, the day from the night, winter from fommer, and to diftinguifh one feafon and time from another.   Now how much may make or conduce to the knowledge hereof, fo much I doubt not is verie tollerable, and may be vfed.   But when we go about to enter into Gods fecrets, and to diuine of things to come, by coniectures, and geffes, then make we the fame wicked and vnlawfull. Therefore prognofticators are herein much to be blamed, for that they take vpon them to forefhew what things fhall be plentie, and what fcarfe, what deere, what good cheape.   When fhal be faire weather, when foule, and the like, whereas indeede the knowledge of thefe things are hid in the fecrets of G O D, and are beyond their reach, therefore ought they not to meddle with them.   But if they would keepe them within their compaffe, as namely to fhew the times and feafons of the yere, feftiuals, vigils, to diftinguifh winter from fommer, fpring from harueft, the change of the moone, the fall of euerie day, the ecclipfes, epacts, dominical letter, golden num[2]ber, circle of the funne, leape yeere, and other the like neceffarie points, then were their profeffion laudable, and greatly for the commoditie of the commonwealth.   And thus much with their patience be it fpoken briefly hereof.

Here ende the abufes of the
Temporalitie.

[1 Sig. I 7, back]

when they pretend to pry into God's secrets,

and foretell what 'll be plentiful and what scarce.

Let Almanac-makers keep to their proper business,

[2 Sig. I 8]

and then they'll be useful folk.

THE CORRVPTIONS

AND ABUSES OF THE

SPIRITVALITIE.

Theodorus.

Auing now fpoken fufficiently of the corruptions and abufes of the temporalitie, if I might be fo bold, I would requeſt you fomewhat to fay concerning the corruptions and abufes of the fpiritualitie, or (as fome call it) of the ecclefiafticall hierarchie. For I am fully perfuaded, that the one being fo corrupt, the other can hardly bee without blemifh.

As to the corruptions of the Ecclesiastical Hierarchy,

[1]*Amphil.* I am verie loth to enter into that fielde, the view where-of offereth fuch ftore of matter to intreat of, as if I fhoulde enter the fame, I fhoulde rather not knowe where to end, then where to begin. Befides, you knowe the olde prouerbe, *Non bonum eſt ludere cum fanƐtis,* It is not good to meddle with thefe holie ones, for feare of thunderbolts, to infue. But for that, he is not onely a falfe prophet, and a traitor to the truth, that teacheth falfe doctrine, but as well he that knoweth the truth, and either for feare of death, or defire of life, wil not expreſſe the fame to the worlde. And for that, not onely the author of any euill or mifchiefe is giltie of offence before God, But alfo he that might by [2] difcouerie thereof preuent the fame, and yet either will not, or for feare of death dares not. And for that as the olde prouerbe faith, *Qui tacet, confentire videtur,* he that concealeth the truth, feemeth to confent to errors, for thefe and the like caufes, I will laye downe vnto you fome fuch corruptions and abufes, as feeme to be inormous, and ftande in neede of reformation, omitting in the meane time to fpeake perticularly of all (for that they be innumerable) vntill I fee how thefe fewe will be brouked of them.

[1 Sig. I 8, back]

let the meddler with them look out for thunder-bolts.

But I'll tell you some of our worst Abuses in the Church.

[2] *Orig.* vy   F 2

For it is a point of good phyficke, you knowe, to fee how the former [1]meate receiued into the ftomacke, will be digefted, and concoĉted, before we receiue anye more into the fame.

[1 Sig. K. 1.]

Theod. You fay very well.   Giue me leaue then (by your patience) to afke you fuch queftions as I thinke conuenient for my further inftruĉtion, that by your good meanes, I knowing the truth, may praife God in you, and alfo haue iuft occafion to giue you thanks for the fame.

Amphil. Afke what you thinke good, in Gods name, and I will doe the beft I can, to refolue you in anything that you fhall demand.

All our churches and congrega-tions

Theod. Then this fhall be my firft demand.   Be the churches, congregations, & affemblies there, diftinĉted into particulars, as into parifhes and precinĉts, one exempt from another, or are they difperfed here and there abroad, without any order, exemption, or limitation of place at all ?

are divided into parishes,

Amphil. Euerie particular church, congregation, affemblie, or con-uenticle, is diuided one from another, and diftinĉted into parifhes and precinĉts, which feuerall precinĉts and parifhes are fo circumgired and limited about with bounds and marks, as euerie one is knowne of what parifh he is, and vnder whofe charge he liueth.   So that euerie fhepheard knoweth [2]his flocke, euerie paftor his fheepe.   And

[2 Sig. K. 1. back]
so that every flock knows its pastor.

again, euerie flocke knoweth his fhepheard, and euerie fheepe his paftor, verie orderlie and well, in my fimple iudgement.

Theod. Doe you allow then of this partition of churches, and of one particular congregation from another ?

In early days,,

Amphil. Yea trulie.   It is not amiffe, but a verie good order, for thereby euerie paftor doth knowe his owne flock, euery fhepheard his owne fheepe, which without this diuifion could not be.   Befides that, we read that euen in the apoftles daies (who writ to particular churches themfelues, as to the Rom. Corint. Thes. Phil, &c.) in the daies of Chrift, & in the times of the prophets before Chrift, churches,

assemblies were always separate.

affemblies, and congregations were euer diftinĉted one from another, & diuided into feueral flocks, companies, and charges.   So that although they had not the name of this word ' parifh' amongft them, yet had the thing ment thereby, in effeĉt.

Theod. Then it followeth by your reafon, that there are infinite churches in *Dnalgne ;* and I haue learned out of the book of God that there is but one true church, and faithful fpouse of Chrift vpon the earth. How reconcile you thefe two places?

Amphil. Verie well. For although there be [1]infinite particular churches, congregations, and affemblies in the world, yet doe they all make but one true church of God, which being diuided in time and place, is notwithftanding one church before God, being members of the myftical body of Chrift Iefus, & felow members one of another, fo as they can neuer be diuided, neither from themfelues, nor from their head, Chrift.

Theod. Who doe you conftitute the head of the vniuerfall church of Chrift vppon earth? Chrift Iefus, the pope, or the prince?

Amphil. Chrift Iefus, whofe the bodie is, muft needs be, & is the onely true head of the vniuerfall church. Then next vnder him euerie chriftian prince in his kingdom. And as for the pope, he is head ouer the malignant church, the church of the deuil, and not of Chrift Iefus. No, he is fo far from being head ouer the vniuerfal church of Chrift, that he is no true member of the fame, but rather the childe of perdition, the firft borne of fatan, a diuell incarnate, and that man of fin (euen Antichrift himfelfe) that muft be deftroied with the breath of Gods mouth.

Theod. By whom be thefe particular churches and congregations gouerned & ruled?

Amphil. By bifhops, paftors, and other inferiour officers.

Theod. Do you fhut out the prince then from gouerning the church?

[2]*Amphil.* No, God forbid. For take awaye *Brachium feculare,* The lawfull power, and gouernement of the temporal magiftrate from the regiment of the church, and ouerthrow the church alto-gither. And yet notwithftanding the neceffitie hereof, the dooting anabaptifts and braineficke papifts haue moft deuilifhly denied the fame. The anabaptifts denie (moft abfurdly) the authoritie of the magiftrate altogither. The papifts feing themfelues conuinced by the manifeft worde of G O D, denye not their authority abfolutely; but that their authority extendeth to the gouernement of the church, forfooth they vtterly denie, hereby exempting themfelues, and plucking away their neckes from vnder the yooke of chriftian obedience due vnto

[1 Sig. K. 2.]

But thefe separate churches all make up One true Church,

whofe Head is Christ; under Him each King in his kingdom;

(The Pope's the head of the Devil's Church)

and under them Bishops, Pastors, &c.,

[2 Sig. K. 2. back]

and temporal Magiftrates.

The Anabaptists deny the temporal power altogether;

the Papists deny its extending to Church Government.

magiſtrates[1], contrarie to the expreſſe word of our ſauiour Chriſt, and his apoſtles, who ſaith *Omnis anima ſubdita ſit poteſtatibus ſupereminentibus !*   Let euery ſoule be ſubieĉt to the higher powers, for there is no power but of God.   And therefore they are to be obeyed as the miniſters of God of all whatſoeuer.

Theod. Well than I gather thus much, that euery king, prince, or potentate, is ſupreame head next vnder God, ouer the church of G O D diſperſed through his kingdomes, and domini[2]ons : is not this true ?

But every King is supreme head over the Church in his realm.
[² Sig. K. 3.]

Amphil. Verie true.   And therefore that antichriſt of Rome, hath plaide the traitor a long while, both to Chriſt Ieſus and all chriſtian kings, in arrogating and vſurping to be ſupreame head ouer all the world.   Whereas indeed he, being a greaſie prieſt, & ſmered prelate, hath no more authority than other oiled ſhauelings haue, nor ſo much neither, and yet that authoritie is but ouer the malignant church of antichriſt, and not of Chriſt Ieſus.   I beſeech the Lord therefore to breake of that power, to grind in peces that ſtumbling blocke of offence, and to wipe off the heads of that monſtrous hidra, ſo as neuer any mo may growe thereof againe.

The Pope is a mere greasy priest, like other oild shavelings are.

Theod. Seeing you ſay that euerie prince is ſupreame head ouer the church of God within his dominions, what authoritie therfore aſſign you to the prince to execute in the church.

Amphil. It is the office and dutie of a prince, not onely to ſee eleĉted, ſent forth, & called, good, able, & ſufficient paſtours, for the inſtruĉtion of the church, but alſo to ſee that good orders, conſtitutions & rites be eſtabliſhed, and duely performed, that the worde be preached, the ſacraments truely miniſtred, excommunication, diſcipline and eccleſiaſticall cenſures orderly [3]executed to the honor of God, and benefit of his church.   But if it be ſaid that theſe thinges are to bee executed of the eccleſiaſticall perſons onely, I anſwere, true it is ; but if the eccleſiaſticall magiſtrate be negligent, ſecure, ſlouthfull, and careleſſe about the execution hereof (as who ſeeth not ſome be) than ought the prince to ſhew his authoritie in commanding and inioining them to doe their office.   Beſides this, it is the office of the prince to ſee all kind of ſinne, as well in the church men themſelues, as in all others of the church, ſeuerely puniſhed.

A King has to see good Pastors elected, proper rites establisht, and Church censures executed.

[³ Sig. K. 3. back]

The King should see sin punisht

¹ *Orig.* migiſtrates.

And though I grant the prince to haue the foueraigntie and primacie ouer the church of G O D, within his dominions, yet my meaning is not, that it is lawfull for the prince to preach the word, to minifter the facramentes, or to execute the fentence of excommunication, and other ecclefiafticall difcipline and cenfures of the church, but (as before) to fee them done, of them to whom it apperteineth. For faith the apoftle, *nemo fumat fibi honorem, nifi qui legittime vocatus fuerit, vt fuit Aaron.* And againe, *vnufquifque in ea vocatione, qua vocatus eft, maneat apud deum?* But in times paft the papifts bare the worlde in hande, that no temporall power whatfoeuer coulde, nor ought not, to ¹meddle wyth the clergie, and therefore made they vaffals of moft chriftian Princes. Yea, that pernicious antichrift of Rome, in thofe daies of ignorance hath not beene afhamed to make Kings, Queenes, Emperours, Dukes, Lords, and all other, how honorable or noble foeuer, his lackeis, his pages, his horfekeepers, and compelled them to hold his ftirups, to leade his horfe, and to proftrate themfelues before him, whileft he trod vpon their neckes. But God be praifed, this great antichrift is difcouered to all the world, and his fhame fo laid open, as euery childe iuftlie laugheth him to fcorne.

Theod. You faid before, that the churches there were gouerned by bifhops, and paftors : how by them?

Amphil. The bifhops are graue, ancient, and fatherlie men, of great grauitie, learning, and iudgement (for the moft part) conftituted by the Prince ouer a whole country or prouince, which they call their dioces. Thefe graue fathers hauing authoritie aboue all other of the minifterie, in their dioces, do fubftitute vnder them in euerie particular church a minifter, or minifters according to the neceffitie of the fame. And thus doeth euery bifhoppe in hys owne dioces thorow out the ²whole realme. So that no church, how fmall foeuer, but it hath the truth of Gods word, and of his facraments, truly deliuered vnto it.

Theod. Are thofe preaching prelates, that the bifhops do place in euerie congregation, or elfe reading minifters?

Amphil. It were to be wifhed that all were preaching prelates, and not reading minifters only, if it could be brought to paffe, but though all be not preachers, yet the moft part be, God be praifed therefore.

Theod. Be any, readers onlie, and not preachers : that is a great

and the Church's orders carried out.

[¹ Sig. K. 4.]

The Antichrist of Rome formerly had kings as lackeys,

but his shame is laid open now.

The Bishops are graue and learned men, set over Dioceses.

[² Sig. K. 4, back]

All our ministers don't preach, some read only.

abufe. For I am perfuaded that he that cannot preach, ought not to fupplie a place in the church of God to read onlie : how fay you ?

Amphil. It is no good reafon to fay, bicaufe all ought to be preachers, that therefore readers are not neceffarie. But indeed I am of this iudgement with you, that whofo can but read onelie, and neither is able to interpret, preach, expound, nor explane the fcriptures, nor yet to refell and conuince the aduerfarie, nor to deliuer the true fenfe and meaning of the fcriptures, ought not to occupie a place in the church of God, as the paftor thereof. For God commandeth that the paftors be learned, faieng : *Labia facerdotum cuftodiant verita*[1]*tem, and edifcant populi verbum dei ex ore eorum,* Let the lips of the priefts preferue knowledge, and let the people learne the truth out of their mouthes. And therefore thofe that haue not this dexteritie in handling the worde of God, they are not fent of God, neither are they Chrifts vicegerents or paftors to inftruct his flocke. To fuch, the Lord faith : They rule, but not by me ; they run, but I fent them not ; they crie, thus faith the Lord, whereas hee neuer fpake it. Thefe are thofe idoll fhepheards, and dumbe dogs, of whom fpeaketh the prophet, that are not able to barke againft finne. And therefore I befeech the Lord to remooue them, and place able and fufficient paftors ouer his church, that G O D may be glorified, and the church edified in the truth.

Theod. Bare reading, I muft needs fay, is bare feeding : but what then ? Better it is to haue bare feeding than none at all.

Amphil. Verie true. And therefore are not they more fcrupulous than they ought, more curious than needes, and more precife than wife, that bicaufe they cannot haue preaching in euerie church, doe therefore contemne reading as not neceffarie ? This is as though a man fhould defpife meane fare, bicaufe he cannot come by better, whereas I thinke it is [2]better to haue meane fare than none at all, or as though a man, bicaufe he cannot come by the carnell at the firft, will therefore caft awaie both the nut and the carnell. It were good (as faith the apoftle) that all could prophefie, that is, that all could preach and expound the truth, but bicaufe that al haue not the gift, is therefore reading naught ? And therefore a fort of nouatians lately fprong vp, haue greatly faulted herein, in that they hold that no reading minifters only ought to be permitted in the church of God, as though

Sidenotes:

But Readers

ought not to be Pastors.

[1 Sig. K 5]

They are not Christ's Vicegerents,

only dumb dogs.

But bare Reading is better than nothing.

[2 Sig. K 5, back]

If you can't get at a kernel at first, don't throw away the whole nut.

(as I fay) becaufe a man can not haue daintie fare, therefore it is good to haue none at all. But to be plaine, as I will not defende a dumbe reading minifterie only, fo I will not condemne it for neceffities fake, when otherwife euery place cannot be fufficiently furnifhed at the firft with good and fufficient men as it ought.

Keep your Reading Ministers till you can get Preaching ones.

Theod. But it is thought that there are inow able men in the vniuerfities and elfewhere to furnifh euery particular church with a preaching minifter?

Amphil. Truely I thinke there are fo, if they were fought for & preferred: but alas thofe that are learned indeed, they are not fought for nor promoted, but the vnlearned for the moft part, fomtimes by frendfhip, fomtime by mony [1](for they pay wel for their orders, I heare fay) and fomtimes by gifts, (I dare not fay bribes) are intruded. This maketh many a good fchoolar to languifh, and difcourageth not a fewe from goyng to their bookes. Whereby learning greatlie decaieth, and barbarifme, I feare me, will ouerflow the realme, if fpeedie remedie be not had herein.

We've enough learned men, but, alas they don't get Preferment.

[1] Sig. K 6]

Theod. As farre as I can gather by your fpeeches, there is both a reading and a preaching minifterie: whether doe you prefer before the other?

Amphil. I preferre the preaching minifterie before a reading minifterie only: and yet the reading minifterie, if the other can not be had, is not therefore euill, or not neceffarie.

Theod. But tell me this. If there might a preaching minifterie be gotten, ought not the reading minifterie to giue place to the fame?

Amphil. Yea, doubtleffe. And therefore the bifhops ought to feeke for the learned fort, and as it were to fue and make inftance to them, and finding them worthy, as well for their life as doctrine, to call them lawfully according to the prefcript of Gods word, & fo to fende them forth into the Lords harueft. And where the forefaide dumbe minifterie is, to difplace the fame, and place the other. By this meanes [2] the word of God fhould flourifh, ignorance (mauger the head of fatan) be abandoned, the church edified, and manie a one incouraged to go to their bookes, whereas now they practife nothing leffe, and all by reafon that by their learning they haue no promotion nor preferment at all.

Bishops ought to seek out learned Ministers.

[2] Sig. K 6, back]

Preaching
Ministers
preach mainly
in their own
parishes,

Theod. Do thefe preaching minifters preach onely in their owne cures, flockes and charges, or elfe indifferently abroad elfe where?

Amphil. They preach for the moft part in their owne charges and cures whereouer the holie Ghoft hath made them ouerfeers, and for which they fhall render a dreadfull account at the day of iudgement, if they doe not their dutie diligently, as God hath commanded. But though they preach moft commonly in their owne cures, yet doe

but sometimes
out of them,
and rightly so,

they fometimes helpe their felowe brethren to breake the bread of life to their charges alfo. Wherein me thinke they do not amiffe. For if a watch man appointed by a whole citie, or towne to giue warning when the enimie commeth, feeing an other citye or towne to be in danger, giueth fufficient warning to his owne citie, and goeth and warneth the other citie alfo, and fo by this meanes deliuereth them both, I fay, that in fo doing, hee doth well, and according to

[¹ Sig. K 7]
notwithstanding
the Brownists,

charitie.   And yet [1] notwithftanding, diuers new phangled felows fprong vp of late, as the Brownifts, and there adherents, haue fpoken verie blafphemouflie hereof, teaching in their railing pamphletes, that thofe who are lecturers or preach els wher than in their owne cures are accurfed before god. Than the which, what can be more abfurdlie, or vntruely fpoken? For if they grant (as they cannot deny) that the word of God is good, then cannot the declaration of that which is good in one place, be hurtfull in another. And read we not that the

for the Apostles
went from place
to place
preaching.

apoftles themfelues went from place to place, preaching the word to euerie congregation? Chrift Iefus did the fame, & alfo taught vs, that he came not to preach to one citie onely, but to many?

Theod. Doe the reading minifters onely continue and read altogither in their owne charges, or not?

Amphil. The reading minifters, after they be hired of the parifhes (for they are mercenaries) they read commonly in their owne charges, and cures, and except (which is a horrible abufe) that they haue two

Evils of
Pluralities.

or three cures to ferue, all vpon one day, and peraduenture two or three myles diftant, one from another. Which maketh them to gallop it ouer as faft as they can, and to chop it vp with all poffible

[² Sig. K 7, back]

expediti[2]on, though none vnderftand them, and as fewe be edified by them.

Theod. Be thefe reading minifters well prouided for, fo as they want nothing, or not?

Amphil. No truly. For if the other preaching minifters be not well prouided for (as in truth they be not) then how can the other be well maintained? And therfore they haue, fom of them ten pound a yeere (which is the moft), fome eight pound, fome fixe pound, fome fiue pound, fome foure pound, fome fortie fhillings; yea, and table themfelues alfo of the fame. And fometimes failing of this too, they runne roging like vagarents vp & downe the countries like maifterleffe men, to feeke their maintenance. Whereby fome fall to one mifchiefe, fome to another, to the great flander of the Gofpell of Iefus Chrift, and fcandall of the godlie. And yet part of thefe reading mifters be too well prouided for, for fome of them haue two or three, yea foure or fiue benefices apeece, being refident but at one of them at once, and peraduenture at neuer a one, but roift it out elfewhere, purchafing a difpenfation for their difcontinuance, and then may no man fay: *Domine, cur ita facis?* Sir, why doe you fo? For hee hath [1]plenarie power and authoritie granted him fo to doe.

Reading Ministers' pay runs from £10 to £2 a year, and keep themselves.

Some have 3 or 4 benefices apiece,

[1 Sig. K 8]

Theod. That is an horrible abufe, that one man fhould haue two or three, or halfe a dozen benefices apeece as fome haue: may anie man haue fo manie liuings at one time, by the lawe of God, and good confcience?

Amphil. As it is not lawfull for anie man to haue or enioie two wiues at once, fo is it not lawfull for any man, how excellent foeuer, to haue mo benefices, mo flockes, cures or charges in his handes, than one at once. Nay, I am fullie perfuaded that it is more tollerable (and yet it is a damnable thing) for a man to haue two wiues or mo, than for a man to have two benefices at once, or mo. For by poffibilitie a man might difcharge the dutie of a good hufband to two or three wiues (yet to haue mo than one is the breach of Gods commandements), but no man, though he were as learned as Saint Paule, or the apoftles themfelues to whome were given fupernaturall and extraordinarie giftes and graces, is able fufficientlie to difcharge his dutie in the inftruction of one church, or congregation, much leffe of three or foure, or halfe a dozen, as fome haue. And as one father cannot bee manie fathers, one paftor [2]manie paftours, nor one man diuerfe men, fo one fheepeheard or paftour cannot, nor ought not, to haue diuers charges, and flocks at once. Is it poffible for any fhepheard though he were neuer fo cunning a man, to keepe two or

which is worse than having 2 or 3 wives.

[2 Sig. K 8, back]

One Pastor cannot take charge of

three flocks or mo at once, and to feed them wel and in due feafon, dooing the dutie of a good fhepheard in euerie refpeact, they being diftant from him, ten, twentie, fortie, fixtie, an hundred, two hundred, or three hundred miles? Much leffe is there any man able to dif-

charge the dutie of a good paftor ouer fo manie flocks, churches, and congregations fo farre diftant in place, wheras the fimpleft flocke that is, requireth a whole, and perfeact man, & not a peece of a man. Therfore I aduife al benefice mongers, *that* haue mo charges then one, to take heede to themfelues, and to leaue them in time, for the blood of al thofe within their cures, or charges, that die ghoftlie for want of the truth of Gods word preached vnto them, fhall be powred vpon their[1] heads, at the day of iudgement, and be required at their hands.

Theod. If they haue fo many benefices a peece, and fome fo farre diftant from another, then it is not poffible that they can be refident vpon them all at once. But the matter is in difpute, whether they

may not as well be ab²fent, or prefent: what is your iudgment of that?

Amphil. To doubt whether the paftor ought to be refident with his flocke, is to doubt whether the foule fhould be in the bodie, the eie in the head, or the watchman in his tower. For this I am fully perfuaded of, that as the foule is the life of the bodie, and the eie the

light of the fame, fo the word of God preached is the life, and light, as well to the bodie as to the foule of man. And as neceffarie as the one is to the bodie, fo (and much more) neceffarie is the other both to foule and bodie. Now certein it is, thefe things cannot be applied without the prefence of the preacher or paftor; and therefore is his abfence from his flocke a dangerous and a perilous thing, and as it were a taking away of their life and light from them, which commeth by the preaching of Gods word vnto them.

Theod. But they fay, though they be not prefent by themfelues, yet be they prefent by their fubftitutes and deputies: is not that a fufficient difcharge for them before God?

Amphil. I grant they are prefent by their deputies and fubftitutes, but if a man fhoulde looke into a great fort of them, he fhould finde them fuch as are fitter to feed hogs, than chriftian foules. For as for

[1] *Orig.* their their.

fome of them, are they [1]not fuch as can fcarcely read true englifh ? ['Sig. L. 1. back]
And for their zeale to Gods worde and true religion, are they not
fuch as can fcarce tell what it meaneth ? The truth of Gods word
they cannot eafily preach nor expound. The aduerfarie they cannot
refell : barke againft finne they dare not, bicaufe their liues are
licentious. They will read you their feruice faire and cleanly (as the *Tho they can read the Service,*
doting papifts did their blafphemous maffes out of their porteffes), and *yet after it,*
when they haue done, they will to all kinde of wanton paftimes and
delights, with come that come will, and that vpon fabboth day,
feftiuall day, or other ; no day is amiffe to them. And all the weeke *and on week-days, they'll*
after, yea all the yeere (if I faid all the yeeres of their life, I lied not) *swill all day at the Alehouse.*
they will not fticke to keepe companie at the alehoufe from morning
till night, tipling and fwilling till the figne be in Capricornus. Infomuch as if you would know where the beft cup of drinke is, go to
thefe malt woormes, and I warrant you you fhall not miffe of your
purpofe. By thefe mercenaries their deputies, and the like, I grant
they are prefent in all their flocks, but fo as it were better or as good
they were abfent, for any good they doe, but rather hurt by their euill
example of life. The refidence of thefe their deputies is no difcharge for them [2]before the tribunall feate of God : for notwithftand- [² Sig. L. 2.]
ing the fame, let them be fure to anfwere for the blond of euerie
one of their fheepe, that mifcarrieth through their default, or their
deputies. Their deputies fhall not excufe them at the day of iudgement, I dare be their warrant. Therefore I wifh them to take heed
to it betime, leaft afterward it be too late.

Theod. But I heare fay, that what is wanting either in their depu- *Pluralists may preach once a*
ties, or in themfelues for not being daily refident, they fupply either *quarter, but that's no more*
by preaching their quarter fermons themfelues, or elfe (if they be not *good*
able) by procuring of others to do it for them. Is not that well ?

Amphil. It is as though a man euery quarter of a yeere once, *than if a man plowd one furrow*
fhuld take his plow, & go draw a furrow in a field, & yet notwith- *every quarter.*
ftanding fhould looke for increafe of the fame : were not he a foolifh
hufbandman that wold do thus ? And euen fo he is no leffe vnwife,
that plowing but one furow, that is, preaching but one poore fermon
in a quarter of a yeere (& perchance but one in a whole yeere, nay
in 7. yeeres) will notwithftanding loke for gret increfe of the fame.
Now the caufe why this ground bringeth not forth fruit is, for that it

is not plowed, furowed, & tilled al togither as it ought to be. So the caufe wherefore the pore churches doe not bring forth fruit [1] is, for that they are not furrowed, manured, and tilled, as they ought, and bicaufe the word of God is not preached vnto them, and as it were braied, punned, interpreted, and expounded, *that* it, finking down into the good ground of their harts, might bring forth fruit to eternal life. If the ftrongeft mans body that liueth vpon the earth fhould be nourifhed with nothing for a whole quarter of a yeeres fpace, but onely with two or three drops of aqua vite, aqua angelica, or the like, euery day, and at euery quarters end fhould be fed with all manner of dainties, I am perfwaded that his bodie notwithftanding would foone be weake inough. Nay, do you thinke it were poffible to liue one quarter of a yeere? Euen fo falleth out in this cafe. For although our foules (which liue by the word of God, as our bodies doe by meate) be daily fedde with hearring the word read as it were with aqua vite, or fweet necter, and at euerie quarters ende, haue a moft excellent & fumptuous banquet to pray vpo*n*, yet may they macerate and pyne away notwithftanding, for lacke of the continuance of the fame. And therfore the worde of God is to be preached night and day, in time, and out of time, in feafon and out of feafon, and that without ceafing, or intermiffion. And if that faieng of the prophet be [2] true (as without all controuerfie it is moft true) that he is accurfed, *Qui fecerit opus domini negligenter*, That doth the worke of the Lord negligently, or fraudulently, then muft it needs be, that thofe who hauing cure of foules, and doe feldome, or neuer preach, are within the compaffe of this curfe. Let them take heede to it. The apoftle Paule faid of himfelfe, *Væ mihi nifi euangelixauero*, Woe be to me if I preach not the gofpel; and doe they thinke that the fame wo is not proper to them if they prech not? Haue they a greater priuiledge than the bleffed apoftle faint Paule had? No, no, thefe vaine excufes will not ferue them; therfore, as they tender the faluation of their owne foules, and many others, I wifh them to take heede, and to fhew themfelues painefull laborers in the Lords harueft.

Theod. As far as I remember, by the lawes of *Dnalgne* there is a reftraint, that none fhall haue no more benefices at once than one: how is it then, that they can holde fo manie a peece, without danger of the law?

[1 Sig. L. 2. back]

Our churches don't bring forth fruit because they're not tilld with preaching.

God's Word should be preacht night and day without ceasing.

[2 Sig. L. 3.]

Woe to Ministers who won't preach it!

Tho there's a law against Pluralism,

Amphil. They make the lawes (as it were) ſhipmens hooſen, or as a noſe of waxe, turning and wreſting them at their pleaſure, to anie thing they luſt. But bicauſe they will auoide the lawes, they purchaſe a diſpenſation, a li¹cence, a commiſſion, a pluralitie, a qualification, and I cannot tell what elſe, by vertue whereof they may hold totquots ſo manie, how manie ſoeuer, and that with as good a conſcience as *Iudas* receiued the mony for the which he ſold Chriſt Ieſus the Sauiour of the world. Or if this way will not ſerue, then get they to be chaplines to honorable & noble perſonages, by prerogatiue whereof they may holde I cannot tell how manie benefices, yea, as manie as they can get. But I maruell whether they thinke that theſe licenſes ſhall go for good paiment at the daie of iudgement. I thinke not. For ſure I am that no licenſe of man can diſpenſe with vs, to doe that thing which is againſt Gods worde (as theſe totquots is) and therfore vnlawful. They may blind the fooliſh world with pretended diſpenſations, and qualifications, but the Lorde will bring them to account for it in his good time: G O D grant they may looke to it !

it's avoided by buying a dispensation,
[¹ Sig. L. 3. back

getting a chaplaincy to a Noblemao, &c.

But God 'll be down on these folk.

Theod. In whome doth the patronage, right, and gifture of theſe eccleſiaſtical promotions and benefices conſiſt ? in the churches them-ſelues, or in whom elſe ?

Amphil. Indeede you ſaie well. For who ſhoulde haue the patronage, the right, the intereſt, and gifture of the benefices, but the ² churches themſelues, whoſe the benefices are by right, and to whome, *Proprio iure,* They doe apperteine ? For doe not the benefices con-ſiſt either in tithes, or contributions, or both ? Nowe, who giueth both the one and the other ? Doe not the Churches ? Then by good reaſon ought they to haue the gifture and beſtowing of them, and the right and intereſt thereof ought to remaine in the power of the church, and not in anie other priuate man whatſoeuer.

The Patronage of Benefices ought to be in the Churches' hands.
[² Sig. L. 4.]

Theod. Why ? Then I perceiue you would not haue anie priuate or ſinguler man of what degree ſoeuer, to haue the patronage, the right, or gifture of anie eccleſiaſtical liuing, but the churches them-ſelues : is not that your meaning ?

Every parish Church ought to have the patronage of its own Living.

Amphil. Yes truely, that is my meaning, and ſo I am of opinion it ought to be.

Theod. Why ſo, I beſeech you ?

It wouldn't abuse it as private Patrons do.

Amphil. Bicaufe one man may eafily be corrupted, and drawne to beftowe hys benefice eyther for fauour, affection, or monie, vppon fuch as bee vnworthie; the whole Church will not fo. Againe, the whole liuing is nothing elfe but pure almes, or deuocion, or both, the [¹ Sig. L. 4. back] Gentelman or other that pretendeth the gifture thereof, ¹giueth not the whole liuing himfelfe, *ergo* hee ought not to haue in his owne power, the only gifture of the fame. Thirdly, the whole church will not giue the fame for fimonie; one priuate man may be induced to doe it. Fourthlie, the church will keepe no part of the liuing backe from the paftor, if he doe his dutie, nor imploie it to ther owne vfe; the fingularitie of one man may eafilie be abufed: nay, the moft patrones keepe the fatteft morfels to themfelues, and giue fcarcely the crums to their paftors. But if the benefice be woorth two hundred pound, they will fcarcely giue their paftor foure fcore. If it be woorth an hundred pound, they will hardly giue fortie pound. If woorth forty pound, it is well if they giue ten pound, imploieng the better halfe to their owne priuate gaine. Now if this be not facrilege, and a robbing of the poore churches of their fubftance, as alfo defrauding of the Lords minifter of his dutie and right, then I knowe not what facrilege, and fraude meaneth. Yea there are fome, that hauing ground in another parifh than where they dwell, againft the time that their fheepe, kine, and other cattell fhould bring foorth increafe, will driue them thither, fo that the fruit falling in the other parifh, he fhall not need to pay tithes for the fame to his owne paftor [² Sig. L 5] ²where he dwelleth. And againft the time that the other paftor of that parifh where his cattell fell, fhall demand his tithes thereof, they will haue fetched home their cattell, so that by thefe finifter kinde of meanes, they will neither pay in the one parifh, nor in the other. But if the one commence fute againft him, he anfwereth, they fell not in his parifh: if the other doe the fame, he pleadeth that he is not of his parifh, nor oweth him ought. But indeed they wil pay for their ground in the other parifh a little herbage (as they call it), a thing of nothing, to ftop his mouth withall. So that hereby the poore paftors are deteined from their right, and almoft beggered in moft places that I haue come in.

Private Patrons often cheat their Pastors of half their income.

And they move their cattle and sheep so as to avoid paying tithes on em.

Theod. How came temporall men by the right of their patronages, and how fell they into their clowches, can you tell?

Amphil. I will·tell you, as farre as euer I could coniecture, how they fel into their hands.   In the beginning, when Antichrift the pope exercifed his vfurped authoritie, and challenged the title of fupreme head ouer the vniuerfall church of Chrift vpon the face of the earth, to whomfoeuer would either erect churches, temples, and oratories (as the then world was giuen to blinde fuperftition, as to inftaurate ab[1]beies, prieries, nunries, with other fumptuous edefices, and houfes of religion, thinking the fame a worke meritorious, and to gilte, croffes, images, and the like fooleries) or elfe giue ground for the fame to be built vpon, his vnholie holines did giue the patronage and pretenfed right of the fame church, and benefice belonging to the fame.   Otherfome thinke (to whome I willinglie fubfcribe) that the Churches (confifting of fimple and ignorant men for the moft part) abufing the fame benefices, and beftowing them vpon vnmeete perfons, the princes haue taken them out of their handes, and giuen the right patronage and poffeffion of the fame to the temporalitie, to the ende they might beftowe them better.   But as they were taken from the churches for fome caufes, fo ought they to be remooued and giuen againe to the Churches for greater caufes.   For nowe are they bought and foulde for fimonie, euen as an oxe or a cow is bought and fold for mony.

Theod. Are there no lawes for the reftrainte of fimonie, being for horrible and deteftable vice in the church of God?

Amphil. Yes, that there are.   As he that is patrone taking monie for his benefice, to loofe the patronage of the fame, and the [2]ecclefiafticall perfon, that giueth it, to loofe the fame benefice, the monie giuen or promifed to be giuen, and to remaine incapable of anie other ecclefiafticall promotion afterwarde for euer.   But doe you thinke they are fooles?   Haue they no fhift to defeate the lawe?   Yes, I warrant you.   For though they giue two hundred, or three hundred pound for a benefice, yet it fhall be done fo cloofely, as no dogges fhall barke at it.   But bicaufe at the time of their initiation, inftitution, induction and admiffion, they are fworne whether they came by it by fimonie or no, whether they gaue anie monie for it or no, therefore, to auoide the guilte of periurie, they, the paftors themfelues, will not giue anie monie, but their friendes fhall doe it for them; and than may they fweare (with as good a confcience as euer Iudas betraied Chrift) that they gaue not a penny, but came

Marginal notes:

Laymen get their Church Patronage by the *Pope* having given it to all men who'd build churches or give ground for em;

[1 Sig. L 5, back]

and by the King having taken the patronage from congregations, and given it to individuals.

We have laws against *Simony*,

[2 Sig. L 6]

but they're easily evaded.

Simony is avoided by pastors getting friends to pay money for them.

Or they buy a
worthless thing
for £100.

by it freely, as of gifte.   Or if this waie fayle them, than muſt they
giue the patrones a hundred pounde, or two hundred pounds vpon
ſome bargayne, that is not woorth a hundred pence, and then maye
they ſweare, if neede be, that they came by the benefice frankelye,
and freelye, and that they gaue the money vppon ſuch and ſuch a

[¹ Sig. I. 6, back]

bargaine, ¹without ſome of theſe practiſes, or without ſuch a diſh of
apples as Maſter Latimer talketh of, with thirty angels in euery apple,
thogh he be neuer ſo learned a man, I warrant him he gets nothing.
But if he can get a graffe of this tree loden with ſuch golden apples,
it will ſerue him better then all Saint Paules learning.   For theſe

Private
Patronages
should be
abolisht.

and the like abuſes infinite, if the patronages were taken away from
them that now enioy them, nay, that make hauocke of them, and
either to reſt in the right of the Prince (as they ought) or elſe in the
right of the churches, who will not be corrupted, it were a great

Poor Pastors
haven't money
to buy books.

deale better than nowe they bee.   For now the poore paſtours are
ſo handled at the hands of their patrones, that they neyther haue
mony to buy them bookes withall, nor, which is leſſe, not to maintaine themſelues vppon, though but meanelye, but are manye times
conſtrained either to wander abroad to ſeeke their liuings, or els to
take vp their Inne in an alehouſe, or in ſome od corner or other, to
the great diſcredite of the goſpell of Chriſt, and offence of the godlie.
This argueth flatly that we loue not Chriſt Ieſus, who make ſo little
of his meſſengers, and ambaſſadors.   He that deſpiſeth you, deſpiſeth

[² Sig. L 7]

me, and he that receaueth and maketh much of you, he receiueth ²me,
and maketh much of me, ſaith Chriſt.   The heathen gentils, and

Pagans take
better care of
their Priests.

pagans, prouide better for their idolatrous prieſts, then we doe for the
true preachers of the goſpell, and diſcloſers of the ſecrets of God.
For when the Egyptians were ſore pooled of Pharao, the prieſts, by
his commandement, were excepted, and permitted to haue all neceſ-
farie maintenance whatſoeuer.   But we are of another mind, for
we thinke whatſoeuer we get of them is won, it is our own good,
whereas in truth, what we withdrawe from them (prouided that they
be diligent preachers of the goſpell) we withdraw it from God, and
ferrie it to the deuil.   But hereof more ſhal be ſpoken (Chriſt willing)
hereafter, when we come to this queſtion, whether it be lawful for
preachers and miniſters of the Goſpell, to receiue wages and ſtipends
for preaching of the worde.

Theod. By what law may a minifter of the Gofpell-make claime to tithes, and other profits, emoluments, duties, and commodities, belonging to him, by ye law of God, or of man? Ministers can claim Tithes

Amphil. God, in the law of Mofes, gaue fpeciall commandement that tithes, and other oblations, commodities and profits fhould be giuen to the priefts, to the end that they might attend vpon the diuine feruice of God and not [1] bufie themfelues in worldly affaires, which ordinance or fanction being meere ceremonial, is now fully abrogate by Chrift (for in him the truth, al ceremonies, fhadowes, types & figures ceafed, & toke their end) And therfore cannot a preacher of the Gofpel claime his tithes by the lawe of Mofes, but by the pofitiue lawes of Chriftian princes which are to be obeied in all things (not directly againft true godlineffe) vpon paine of damnation. [1 Sig. L 7, back]

by the positive law of Christian kings,

Theod. Are tithes then due to be paid by the pofitiue lawe of man, and not by the law of God?

Amphil. Yea truly, by the pofitiue lawe of man: which godlie conftitution is now no leffe to be obeied vnder the Gofpel (being commanded by a chriftian prince) than the diuine inftitution was to be obeied vnder the law. And although tithes bee due by the pofitiue lawes of man, yet are the fame grounded vpon the word of God, as commanded as well by God as by man. And therefore he that breaketh this ordinance (being an excellent policie) violateth the commandements of God, and breketh the conftitution of his liege prince to his damnation, except he repent. grounded on the word of God.

Theod. Muft euerie one pay his tithes truely to euery paftor, whether he be ought or [2] naught, learned or vnlearned, without any exception; or may he deteine it with good confcience from him that is an vnfit and vnable minifter? [2 Sig. L 8]

Amphil. If he be a good paftor, and diligent in his calling, and withal able to difcharge the dutie of a faithful fhepheard ouer his flock, then ought he to haue al tithes paid him whatfoeuer with the better; and if any fhould withhold the left mite from him, he finneth againft the maieftie of God moft greeuoufly. And although he be a wicked man and not able to difcharge his dutie, though but in fmall meafure, yet ought euerie man to pay him his due faithfully and truly. For in denieng him his dutie, they might feeme to withftande authoritie, which they ought not to doe. In the meane time giuing Even tho a Minister's a wicked man, his tithes should be paid him, themfelues to praier, and fuing to them that haue the authoritie for his difplacing, and placing of another that is more able in fome meafure to difcharge the dutie of a faithfull paſtor. Notwithſtanding I know fome are of opinion that if any man giue either tithes, or anie dutie elfe, to their paſtor being an vnfit and an vnable perfon, he is partaker with him of his finne, he communicateth with other mens offences,

[¹ Sig. L 8, back]

and he maintaineth him in his idleneffe, floth, ignorance, ¹ and fecuritie, and therefore offendeth greeuoufly. ˎBut I am of opinion that euerye man ought to pay their dutie (for elfe he might feeme, as I faid, to

but his parishioners should try to get him removed.

refiſt the power) & if he be not able to difcharge his dutie, to pray for his remoouing, and to make inſtance to them that are in authoritie appointed for the redreffe of fuch inormities, for his difplacing, and fo not to attempt anything without good and lawfull authoritie grounded vpon the word for the fame.

Theod. May a paſtor that hath a charge and a flocke affigned him to watch ouer (hauing a maintainable liuing allowed him of his flock) preach in other places for monie?

An endowd Minister may not

Amphil. Hee may fometimes, obteining licence for fome reafonable caufe of his owne flocke, preach the word of God abroad in other places, but then he ought to doe it *gratis*, contenting himfelfe with the liuing allowed him at home of his owne parifh. Notwithſtanding, if the other churches where he fhall have preached, ꞏwill voluntarily impart any thing to the fupplie of his neceffities, in refpeꞓt of his

force men to pay him for preaching in other places.

painſtaking, he may thankfully receiue the fame, but he may not compell, nor conſtraine them to giue it him whether they will or not, againſt their wils, as manie impudently doe.

[² Sig. M. ɪ.]

Theod. Then I perceiue if it be not law²full for a paſtor that hath a flocke, and a ſtipend appointed him, to receiue monie vppon conſtraint of ſtrangers for preaching the worde abroad in other places, then is it not lawfull for him to take monie in his cure for preaching funerall fermons, marriage fermons, chriſtening fermons, and the like, as many do. What fay you to this?

Ministers may not take fees for sermons

Amphil. There are manie woorthie of great blame in this refpeꞓt. For though they receiue fortie pound, a hundred pound, or two hundred pound a yeere, of fome one parifh, yet will they hardly preach once a moneth, nay happily not once in a quarter of a yeere, and fometimes not once a twelue moneth, for the fame. And if a man requeft them to preach at a burial, a wedding, or a chriftening, they will not doe it vnder an angell, or a noble at the left. And therefore the papifts and aduerfaries to the Gofpel call our Gofpel, 'a polling Gofpel,' our fermons 'roiall fermons, angell fermons, and noble fermons.' You call, fay they, our bleffed maffe 'a polling maffe;' but, fay they, your preachings are more polling. For we fay they would haue fold a maffe for a grote; you will not fell a fermon vnder a roiall, or a noble. And thus thefe fellowes are a flander to the Gofpel, and robbers of their fellowe brethren. If I fhould hire a [1]man for fortie pound, an hundred pound, or more, or leffe, to teach my children nurture or knowledge, if he for the execution therof fhould afke me more for the fame than we agreed for, were not this man a naughtie, exacting, and fraudulent felowe? Nay, if I compound with him to teach them in the beft maner he is able for fo much, and he doth it not, and yet receiue my monie, haue not I good lawe againft him? If he fhould fay vnto me, I will not doe it except you giue me more, were not this a very vnreafonable man? For, hauing his monie that was couenant, is hee not bound both by lawe and confcience to teach them to the vttermoft of his power? Or if he fhall not doe it, and yet take my monie, is not he a theefe and robber? Is this true in a priuate man, & not in an ecclefiafticall perfon? Is he not hired to that end & purpofe to preach the word of God to his flocke? And hath hee not wages for the fame? Shall he now denie to preach the fame word except he haue more monie? Or is he not bound in confcience to preach the fame night and day without ceafing? And if he doe not, is he not a deceiuer, a theefe, & a robber? The paftor therefore, hauing taken vpon him the cure & charge of his flocke, and hauing his ftipend appointed for the fame, is bound to preach the worde of [2]God to all his flocke indifferently whether it be at buriall, wedding, chriftening (yea then efpecially) or at any other time whenfoeue, without taking or requiring of any more monie, than the ftipend he was hired for. For if he take any more, it is plaine theft before God, and one day fhall be anfwered for: let them be fure of it.

Theod. You condemne not funerall fermons then, fo that they be good, doe you?

Amphil. No, God forbid. Why fhould not godlie fermons be as

at Burials, Weddings, &c.

Those that do are a slander to the Gospel.

[1 Sig. M. 1. back]

They get their salary, and yet won't preach without more pay.

[2 Sig. M. 2.]

I think godly
Sermons at
Funerals are
very needful,
and do great
good.

wholfome (and as neceffarie) at the burials of chriftians, when wee haue fuch liuely fpectacles before our eies, of our mortality, miferie, and end, as they be at all other times? Yea truely at that prefent I thinke godlie fermons verie neceffarie to put the people in remembrance of their mortalitie, of their great miferie, and frailtie, of their fatall end, of the immortalitie of the foule, of the generall refurrection at the laft day, and of the ioie, felicitie, and beatitude of the life to come, with the like godlie inftructions, that they may the better prepare themfelues to the fame when God fhall call them hence to himfelfe. And although of late fome phantafticall fpirites haue

[¹Sig. M. 2. back] taught that the vfe of them is naught, in that they ¹ftand in place of popifh diriges, and I cannot tell what, yet cannot I be eafilie drawne to affent vnto them, for that I fee them in that refpect a great deale more curious than godlie wife.

Ministers
ought to have
Stipends, so as

Theod. Is it lawfull, thinke you, for minifters, and preachers of the Gofpell, to receiue ftipends, and wages for their preaching?

to be free from
worldly business,
and keep their
families.

Amphil. Why not? Otherwife how fhould they bee able to keepe themfelues free from worldly occupations, and trauels of this life (as they ought) to applie their ftudies for the difcharge of their duties, to maintaine themfelues, their family, and houfhold; or how fhuld they keepe hofpitalitie for the releefe of the poore? all which they are bound to doe both by Gods lawe, and good confcience. Therefore take away liuings and wages from the preachers, and ouerthrowe preaching altogither, the ordinarie meane to faluation in Chrift. This caufed the apoftle to enter difputation of this point, where he prooueth by inuincible arguments, that a preacher or minifter of the Gofpell of Chrift Iefus, may (*Salua confcientia,* With a good confcience) receiue wages and ftipends for his peines fufteined in the affaires of the Gofpell, and that for the caufes abouefaid. Therefore faith this apoftle:

[² Sig. M. 3.] *Boui* ²*trituranti non ligabis os,* Thou fhalt not muffle the mouth of the oxe that treadeth foorth the corne. Whereby is ment, that he that laboreth and taketh paines in any good exercife, ought not to be denied of his meed for his paines. Againe he faith: *Dignus eft operarius mercede fua,* The workman is woorthie of his reward. And

St. Paul says
that Ministers
who preach the
Gospel should
live by it.

ftill infifting in the fame argument, hee faith: *Qui euangelium prædicant, ex euangelio viuant,* They that preach the Gofpell, let them liue vpon the Gofpell. And yet further profecuting the fame more at

large, he faith : *Quis militat*, etc. ' Who goeth on warfare at any time
of his owne charges ? Who planteth a vineyard, and eateth not of
the fruit ? Who feedeth a flocke, and eateth not of the milke of the
flock ? ' By al which reafons and arguments it appeareth, that he who
preacheth the Gofpel ought to liue of the Gofpell.   But as euerie
paftor that hath a peculiar flocke affigned him, may, with the teftimonie
of a good confcience, receiue wages and maintenance of his flocke,
for his paines taken amongft them : fo may he not, nor ought not, to
take wages or falarie of any other flocke adioining, if fo be it, that
either vpon requeft, or his owne voluntarie good will, he preach the
word of God amongft them.   To them that are thus prouided for,
Chrift our ¹ fauiour faith : *Gratis accepiftis, gratis date,* Freely you haue
receiued, freely giue againe.   But if any haue not a fpeciall flocke or
charge affigned him, then may he with good confcience receiue the
beneuolencie, the friendly contributions and rewards, of the churches
to whom he hath preached.   And this is probable, both by the word
of God, and the examples of the apoftles themfelues.

Theod. What fay you of preachers, and lecturers, that haue no
peculiar flockes, nor charges appointed them ; are they neceffarie, and
may they receiue wages, with a good confcience, of the flockes and
charges where they preach the word of God ?

Amphil. Firft you afke me whether preachers and lecturers that
haue no peculiar flocks nor charges of their owne to-attend vpon,
be neceffarie.   Whereto I anfwere.   That confidering the ftate &
condition of the church at this day, they are moft neceffarie.   But if
it were fo, that euerie church and congregation had his preacher (as
euery one ought to preach, elfe is he not fent by the Lord) then were
they not fo neceffarie ; but confidering that moft churches are planted
and fraught with fingle reading minifters, they are verie behouefull to
helpe to fupplie the defect of the others, that ²through the good induf-
trie as well of the one, as of the other, the churches of G O D may
bee inftructed and nourifhed with the worde of G O D to eternall life.
Then you afke mee whether thefe lecturers and preachers may receiue
wages of the churches to whom they preach, with a good confcience,
whereto I anfwere, that they may.   But yet I am perfuaded, that it
were much better for them to haue particular flocks of their owne,
to the end that they, receiuing fufficient maintenance of them, might

[Marginal notes:]

But benefist
Ministers may
not take extra
pay.

[¹ Sig. M. 3. back]

Unbenefist
preachers are
now necessary,

as most
Churches have
only Readers.

[² Sig. M. 4.]

Unbenefist
clergy may
take pay for
Preaching.

(if they were at anie time difpofed to beftowe any fpirituall graces abroad) doe it *Gratis*, frankly and freely, without any charges to the poore churches of Iefus Chrift.

Theod. But what if the paftors liuing be not maintaineable nor fufficient for him to liue vpon, may hee not take wages of other flocks abroad ?

Amphil. I am perfuaded no. For if his liuing be too little, then ought the church to mend it ; but if the church, either for want of zeale will not, or through extreame pouertie cannot, increafe his liuing, then ought the paftor to content himfelfe with that little which God hath fent him, following the example of the apoftle, who biddeth the children of G O D [1] to be content with their wages, bee it little or be it much : for if they haue meate, drinke, and cloth, it is inough, and as much as nature requireth. We brought nothing (faith he) into this world, neither fhall we carrie any thing out. Againe, thofe that will be rich, fall into diuers temptations, and fnares of the diuell, which drowne men in perdition and deftruction. Therefore if it be fufficient to yeelde him meate, drinke, cloth, and other neceffaries, he is bound to content himfelfe with the fame. Which if he doe (for the zeale he beareth to his flocke), I doubt not but the L o r d will open the harts of his flock towards him, and both make them able and willing to fupport his neceffities. For if hee deliuer vnto them fpirituall things, doubtleffe the Lord will moue them to giue vnto him temporall things. And therfore ought he to perfeuere ; and in his good time, without all peraduenture, the Lord will looke vpon him, as he hath promifed.

Theod. Doe you allow of that vagarant minifterie, which is in manie countries, but moft fpecially in *Dnalgne* fprong up of late, to the difcredite of the Gofpell of Iefus Chrift, and offence of the brethren ?

Amphil. Allow of it, quoth you ? No, God forbid ! But I rather deplore it with all my hart, [2] knowing that it is moft directly againft the word of God, the example of the primitiue age and all good reformed churches thorough the world. Is it not a pitifull cafe that two hundred, three hundred, fiue hundred, a thoufand, fiue thoufand, yea poffible ten thoufand, fhall be called into the minifterie, in one countrie, not a quarter of them knowing where to haue any liuing or

Margin notes:

But benefift ones may not, even if their Livings are very poor.

[1 Sig. M. 4. back]

They must be content with em,

and wait till the Lord opens men's hearts to give them more.

[2 leaf M 5]
The present *Vagrant Ministers,*

charge? And what do they then? Runne ftragling and rouing ouer countries, from towne to towne, from citie to citie, from fhire to fhire, and from one place to another, till they haue fpent al that euer they haue, and then the moft of them either become beggers, or elfe attempt wicked and vnlawfull meanes to liue by, to the great dif-honour of God, and flander of the word.

Theod. Me thinke this is a great abufe, that fo manie, or any at all, fhould be called into the minifterie, not hauing flocks and charges prouided for them before.

Amphil. It is a great abufe indeed. For if paftor come of *Pafco,* to feed, if he be not a fhepheard that hath no flock, and if he be not a feeder, that giueth no fuftinance, nor a father that hath no childe, then are they no fhepheards, nor no watchmen fent from the Lord, that haue neither flocks, nor charges to watch ouer. For [1] he that is made a fhepheard (or a minifter) that hath no particular flocke readie to receiue him, is fo far from being a lawfull fhepheard, by reafon of his former admiffion, that he is rather made a paftor by the church that hireth him to be their watchman and guide, than of him that firft called him into that function. And therefore woulde I wifh that bifhops and others to whome it doth (*Ex officio*) apperteine to call, and admit paftors, and teachers in the church of G O D, to bee verie carefull heerein, and not rafhly to lay their handes vpon any, before they haue had fufficient triall, as well of their life and doctrine, as alfo of the flock and charge where they fhal be refident, that they go not like maifterleffe hounds, vp and downe the countries, to the flander of the Gofpell.

Theod. Why? Then I perceiue you would haue none called into the minifterie, before there be a place void for him: is not that your meaning?

Amphil. That is my meaning indeed.

Theod. But are you able to prooue your affumption out of the word of God, or elfe I will giue but fmal credit to you in fuch matters of controuerfie as this is?

Amphil. I haue not, neither doe I meane to fpeake anie thing vnto you touching thefe matters, but what I am able (I truft) to [2] prooue by the worde of G O D. And yet I grant *Errare poffum* (for *Hominis eft labi, & decipi,* Man may bee deceiued and fall) but

Margin notes:
roaming all over the country, I condemn.

[1 leaf M 5, back]

Bishops should stop these men running about like masterless dogs.

No one should be ordaind till a place is ready for him.

Bible examples prove this.
[2 leaf M 6]

Hereticus effe nolo, Erre I may, but heretike I will not be. No, fo foone as I fhall be conuinced by the manifeft worde of God, of any of my former pofitions or affertions, I will willingly fubfcribe to the truth. But being perfuaded as I am, giue me leaue, I befeech you (vnder correction) to fpeake what I thinke. But now to the purpofe. In the firft chapter of the Actes of the apoftles recorded by the Evangelift Saint *Luke,* wee read that *Matthias* fucceeding *Iudas* the traitour in the adminiftration of the apoftlefhip, was not chofen nor elected (notwithftanding that the apoftles by the reuelation of the Spirite of G O D, knew that he fhould fall from the fame in the end) vntill the place was voide, and emptie. In the fixt chapter of the Actes of the apoftles wee reade alfo of feuen deacons, which were chofen for the dailie miniftring to the poore; but when, I pray you? Not before the church (deftitute of their feruice) had need of them, nor before there [1] were places readie to receiue them, wherein they might exercife their function, and calling. Then if the apoftles would not choofe not fo much as deacons, which is an office in the church of God farre inferiour to the office of the paftor, or preacher, before places were void and readie to receiue them, much leffe would they, or did they choofe or call any paftor into the church of God, before the church ftood in need of him, and before there be a place readie to receiue him. Befides that, we read not thorough the whole euangelicall hiftorie, that euer the apoftles called any to be paftors and preachers of the word, before fuch time as there were places void for them. Common reafon, me thinke, and daily experience, fhould teach us this truth fufficiently, if we were not wilfully blinded, that when any church or congregation is deftitute of a paftor, it were better to place there one able perfon, than to make two or three hundred or mo vnable fellowes, and they, for want of liuing, to runne ftragling the countries ouer, without any liuing or maintenance at. all, being glad of any thing. For as the old faieng is : Hungrie dogs eate fluttifh puddings.

Theod. What order would you have obferued in this?

[2] *Amphil.* Me thinke this were a verie good order: That euerie church or congregation being deftitute of a paftor, fhould prefent to the bifhops, and others to whom it dooth apperteine, one or two, three or foure able perfons, or mo, or leffe, as they conueniently can,

Matthias wasn't elected

till Judas's place was empty.

The Apostles wouldn't choose Deacons until [1 leaf M 6, back] places were ready for em.

Common sense says, better wait and get one able man than have 200 unfit ones struggling about after places.

[2 leaf M 7] Any congregation wanting a Pastor, should propose 2 or 3 tried men to the Bishop,

whofe liues and conuerfations they haue had fufficient triall of, whofe
foundneffe in religion, integritie of life, and godly zeale to the truth
they are not ignorant of. Then the bifhops and others to whom it
doth apperteine, to examine and trie them thoroughly for their
fufficiencie in learning, foundneffe in doctrine, and dexteritie in teaching, and finding them furnifhed with fufficient gifts for fuch an
honorable calling, to admit them, to lay their hands vppon them, and
to fend them foorth (the chiefeft of them) to that congregation or
church fo deftitute. Which order, if it were ftrictly obferued and
kept (as it ought to be) then fhould not fo manie run abroad in the
countries to feeke liuings, then fhould not churches bee peftered with
infufficient minifters. Then fhould not the bifhops be fo deceiued in
manie as they be. And no maruell. For how fhould the bifhop
choofe but be deceiued in him, whom he neuer fawe before, whofe
conuerfation he knoweth not, whofe difpofition hee is ignorant of,
and [1] whofe qualities and properties in generall, he fufpecteth not ?
Whereas if this order were eftablifhed, that euerie church deftitute of
a paftor fhould prefent certeine able men, whofe conuerfation and
integritie of life in euerie refpect they perfectly knowe (for the whole
church is not likely to erre in iudging of their conuerfations, who
haue been either altogither, or for the moft part conuerfant among
them) then (as I fay,) fhould not the bifhop be deceiued in any, nor
yet any church fcandalized with the wicked liues of their paftors (or
rather depaftors) as they be. For now it is though fufficient for the
certeintie of his conuerfation, if he either haue letters dimifforie from
one bifhop to another (whereas they little or nothing knowe the
conuerfation of the man) or elfe letters commendatorie from any
gentleman, or other, efpecially if they be of any reputation. If he
can get thefe things, he is likely to fpeede, I warrant him. Which
thing is fcarce well, in my iudgement. For you knowe one priuate
man or two, or three, or foure may, peraduenture either write vpon
affection, or elfe bee corrupted with bribes or gifts, whereas the
whole church cannot, nor would not. Therefore is the other the
furer way.

 [2] *Theod.* How prooue you that the churches that are deftitute of a
paftor, ought to prefent him whom they would haue admitted, to the
bifhop, and not the bifhop to intrude vpon the church whom he will ?

Marginal notes:

and he should ordain the best for that Church.

[1 leaf M 7, back]

Now, a Bishop gets but small proof of a candidate's fitness.

[2 leaf M 8]

Bishops ought not to intrude their nominees on churches,

Amphil. In the firft chapter of the Actes of the apoftles before cited, we read, that after the defection of Iudas the traitour, the apoftle *Peter* knowing it neceffarie that one fhoulde be chofen in his place, to giue teftimonie and witneffe of the refurrection and afcenfion of Chrift Iefus, commanded the church to prefent one or two, or mo, as they thought good, that hee with his fellowe brethren might confirme and allow them.   And therevppon, faith the text, they chofe two, to wit, *Matthias,* and *Iofeph,* furnamed *Berfabas.*   And the church hauing prefented them, they were elected, confirmed and allowed of the apoftles and elders.   Alfo in the forefaide fixt chapter of the Acts of the apoftles, when the deacons (whofe office was to make collections for the poore, and to fee the fame beftowed vpon them without fraud or deceit) were to be chofen, the text faith, that the apoftles defired the church to choofe foorth feuen men from amongft them, of honeft report, & ful of the holie Ghoft, which they might appoint to that bufineffe. [1] By all which reafons appereth, that the church ought to prefent him, or them, whom they would haue to be admitted, and not that the bifhop ought to prefent, to allow, or to intrude him vpon the church at his pleafure, againft the will thereof.

Theod. Why would you not haue paftors to be thruft vpon the churches, whether the churches will or not ?

Amphil. Bicaufe it is manifeft that no church will fo willingly receiue, nor yet fo louingly imbrace, him that is intruded vpon them againft their wils, as they will doe him that they like of, choofe, and allow of themfelues.   And if the churches beare not a fingular loue, fauour, good will, and affection to their paftor, it is vnpoffible that they fhould heare him, or learne of him with profit to their foules. And if they heare him not *Auide & fitienter* (as we fay) Greedily and thirftily thereby to profit, then fhal they perifh euerlaftingly, in that the word of God is the ordinarie meane appointed by the diuine maieftie.   And therefore in conclufion, if there be not a mutual amitie, loue, and affection betwixt the paftor and his flocke, and if that the one loue not the other, as themfelues, it is not to be looked for that either the one fhall teach, or the other receiue, any thing to their foules [2] health, but rather the cleane contrarie.

Theod. I pray you what is your iudgement in this ?   What if a

Margin notes:

for the Apostles

bade the Church present successors to Judas Iscariot.

They also bade the Church choose Deacons.

[1 leaf M 8, back]

So now each Church should choose its Pastor.

If it doesn't, it won't like him.

[2 Sig. N. 1.]

man be once lawfully called into the minifterie, may he euer vpon anie occafion whatfoeuer, leaue off the fame function, and applie himfelfe to fecular affaires?

Amphil. There is a twofold calling. The one a diuine calling immediately from God, the other a humane calling immediately from and by man. Now he that hath the firft diuine calling (his confcience fuggefting the fame vnto him, and the fpirit of God certifieng his fpirit of the certeintie thereof) being furnifhed with gifts and graces neceffarie for fuch a high function and office (as God calleth none, but he indueth them firft with gifts, and graces neceffarie for their calling) and afterwards is lawfully called of man according to the prefcript of Gods word, hauing a flocke appointed him wherevpon to attend, this man may not, nor ought not at any hand to giue ouer his calling, but to perfeuere in the fame to the end, for that he hath both the diuine and humane callings, being furnifhed with all gifts and graces neceffarie (in fome meafure) for the difcharge of his high function and calling. Yet notwithftanding, in time of extreame perfecution, when Gods truth is perfecuted, and his glorie defa[1]ced, if he haue not wherewithall to maintaine his eftate otherwife, he may for the time giue himfelfe to manuall occupations, and corporall exercifes in the affaires of the worlde, as we fee the apoftles themfelues did, who, after Chrift Iefus was crucified, gaue themfelues to their old occupations of fifhing, making of nets, tents, pauilions, and the like. But vpon the other fide, if a man haue not this diuine calling, his confcience bearing him witneffe thereof, nor yet the graces, gifts, and ornaments of the minde, fit for his calling (which, whofoeuer hath not, it is a manifeft argument that the Lorde hath not fent him, for thofe that hee fendeth, hee furnifheth with all kinde of graces and giftes neceffarie for their callings) this man, though he be called by humane calling neuer fo precifely, yet he may, nay, hee ought, to leaue his function, as vnwoorthie to occupie a roome in the church of God, reprefenting (as an idoll doth) that thing which hee is not. Befides, hee that is compelled and inforced either by friendes (as manie are), or by pouertie (as not a few bee), or for anie other refpect elfe, to take that high function vpon him, without the teftimonie of a good confcience, being not furnifhed with gifts, and graces fit for fuch a calling (which argueth di[2]rectly that God hath not called him)

As to a Minister giving up his office,

if he's calld by God's Spirit,

and then by man, and is given a flock, he must continue a Minister to the end.

[1 Sig. N. 1. back]

But if he's not calld by God, and hasn't fit gifts for his work, he

should at once give up his office.

Men forst by friends or poverty into the Ministry, and being unfit,

[2 Sig. N. 2.]

ought to leave
their callings.

hee, I fay, is fo farre from being bounde neuer to leaue his function
and calling, that hee ought not one minute of an houre to continue in
the fame, though he bee called by man a thoufande times.   Therefore
he that is a minifter, and hath charge of foules committed vnto him,
let him if hee bee not furnifhed with fuch gifts as his high calling
requireth, in the name of G O D make no doubt of it to giue ouer his
function vnto others that are able for their giftes to difcharge the
fame, in the meane time giuing himfelfe to godlie exercifes of life, as
God may be glorified, his confcience difburthened, and the commonwealth profited.

 Theod.   But I haue heard of fome that, confidering the naughtineffe
of their calling, and their owne infufficiencie to difcharge the fame,
haue therefore left off their function, giuing themfelues to fecular
exercifes, and in the ende haué beene inforced to refume their former
function vpon them againe, and that whether they would or not.
How thinke you of this?

 Amphil.   I thinke truely that they who compelled them to take

[¹ Sig. N. 2. back]
Those who
would drive
them back into
Orders, offend
grievously.

againe that function which they were not able to difcharge, and ¹ therefore left it, haue greeuoufly offended therein.   This is as if I, knowing
a fimple ignorant foole prefumptuoufly to haue taken vpon him a
great and waightie charge, yea, fuch a charge as all the wifedome in
the world is not able thoroughly to performe, and when he, in taking a
view of his owne infufficiencie, fhuld be mooued to leaue his charge
to others better able to execute the fame than hee, I fhould notwithftanding not onely counfell, but alfo compell him to refigne againe
his former great charge, which I knowe he is neither woorthie, nor
yet able, euer to accomplifh.   Thinke you not that he that compelleth
him to take againe that office or calling which before he had leaft for
his inabilitie, fhall not anfwere for the fame?   yes truely, you may be
fure of it.   In conclufion, he that is fufficiently furnifhed with fuch
gifts as are neceffarie for his calling, & withal is found able to difcharge in fome fort his duty, ought not to leaue his function (for to
fuch a on that fo doth, Chrift faith ' hee that laieth hande vppon the

No unfit Pastors
should be
re-appointed.

plough, and looketh backe, is not fit for the kingdome of God ').   But
againe, he that hath not thefe gifts, and graces fufficient for his
calling, to the difcharge of his dutie, ought not to occupie a place in

[² Sig. N. 3.]

the church of God, as the paftor thereof, much leffe ought he, ² when he hath (for his inabilitie) leaft the fame, to be conftrai[n]ed to refume againe his former function and calling, which he is not able to difcharge. But hereof inough.

Theod. Then I perceiue that any minifter or ecclefiafticall perfon that hath not gifts fufficient to difcharge his duty, may with good confcience leaue their functions, and giue themfelues to liue by their labors, as other temporall men doe : may they not?

They'd better work for their bread.

Amphil. Yes, with a better confcience than to retaine them, being not able to difcharge them in any fmall meafure. For with what confcience can he receiue temporall things of his flocke, and is not able to giue them fpirituall? With what face can a fhepeheard receiue of his fheepe, the milke, the wooll, and fleece, and yet will not, or cannot giue to the fame either meate or drinke fufficiently? With what confcience can he receiue fortie pound, a hundred pound, or two hundred pound, a yeere, of his poore flocke, and is not able to breake to them the breade of life, in fuch forme and maner as he ought? Nay, how can he euer haue quiet confcience that knowing that the blood of all thofe that die ghoftlie for want of inftruction fhal be powred vpon his head at the day of iudgment, and be demanded at his handes, will yet not[1]withftanding reteane the fame charge and function to himfelfe ftill, not being able to difcharge the leaft iote of the fame? Therefore would I wifh euery man of what office, function, or calling foeuer he be, if he be not able to difcharge his dutie in the fame, to giue it ouer, and not for greedineffe of a little mucke or dung of the earth, (For monie is no better) to caft away their foules, which Iefus Chrift hath bought with his moft precious blood.

How can a Pastor fairly take pay for what he can't give?

[1 Sig. N. 3. back]

Let unfit men resign at once.

Theod. Is it lawfull for a paftor or minifter that hath a flocke to departe from the fame, In the time of plague, peftilence, or the like, for feare of infection?

Amphil. Is he a good fheepeheard that, when he feeth the wolues comming, will take him to his heeles and runne away? Or is he a fure freend that, when a man hath moft neede of his helpe, will then get him packing, not fhewing any freendfhip towardes him at all? I thinke not? And truly no more is he a good paftor, or minifter, (but rather a depaftor, and minifter) that in time of any plague, peftilence or ficknes whatfoeuer, will conuey himfelfe away

A minister is no Pastor, but a Depastor, who 'll run away for fear of infection.

from his flocke, for feare of infection, at the houre of death, when the poore people haue moſt need of comfort aboue all other times, then is he their paſtor that ſhoulde feede [1]them, the furtheſt from them. When they ſtande vppon the edge, as it were, of ſaluation or damnation, then permits he the wolfe to haue the rule ouer them. Our Sauiour Chriſt ſaith *Bonus paſtor animulam dat pro ouibus,* A good ſhepheard giueth his life for his ſheepe, but theſe felowes are ſo far from giuing their liues for their ſheepe, that they ſeeke to ſaue their owne liues with the deſtruction of their whole flocke. This is the loue that they beare vnto their flocke, this is the care they haue ouer their ſoules health, which Chriſt Ieſus bought ſo deere with the price of his blood. Out vpon thoſe ſhepheards that for feare of incurring of corporall death (which is to the Godly an entraunce into parpetuall glorie) will hazard manie a thouſande to die a corporall and a ſpirituall death both, yea, a death of damnation both of body & ſoule for euer. Do they thinke that their blod ſhall not be aſked at their handes at yᵉ gret day of the Lord. Do they thinke *that* their flieng away from their flock, is a mean to preſerue their liues yᵉ longer vpon earth? Is not God able to ſtrike them as well in the fields, as in the city, as well in the country as in the towne, in one place, as well as in another? Is not his power eueriewhere? Is not his meſſenger death in al places? Saith he not in the booke of Deuteron. that if we doe [2]not thoſe things which he hath commanded vs in his ſacred word, curſed ſhall wee bee at home, and curſed in the fields. And ſaith he not further, that the plague and peſtilence, the botch, bile, blaine, or elſe what deadly infection ſoeuer, ſhall followe vs, and lay hold vpon vs, in what place ſoeuer we be, and ſhall neuer depart from vs, till it haue quite conſumed vs from the face of the earth? And doe theſe fugitiues that ouerrun their flocks in time of infection, thinke that they ſhall eſcape the heauie wrath and vengeance of God for their tergiuerſation and backſliding from their duties? Doe they thinke that God cannot ſaue them from corporal death but with the breach of their duties towards God? Is not the Lord as well able to defend them from any deadly infection, if it be his good pleaſure, as he was to defend *Sidrach, Miſaach,* and *Abednego* from the flaming fire? *Daniell* from the mouth of the lions, *Ionas* from the iawes of the mightie whale, with manie others that truſted

[¹ Sig. N. 4.]

Such runaways, to save their bodies, will hazard a thousand souls.

[² Sig. N. 4. back]

But God will follow and strike them.

Cannot God protect his servants now from death?

in him? D>e they thinke that his arme is fhortened, or his power weakened? Is he not able to deliuer his children, that in dooing of their duties depend vpon his prouidence? And to bee plaine with them, me think that in flieng away from their flockes, they fhew themfelues to thinke [1]that either God is not almightie, or elfe not mercifull, or neither. For if they beleeued that he were almightie, and that hee were able to faue them, then they would neuer run awaie from their flocke, but depending vpon his prouidence, beleeue that he is as well able to deliuer them in one place as in another, if it bee his good pleafure. And if they beleeued that he were mercifull, then would they reft vpon the fame, not doubting, but as he is almightie, and omnipotent, and therefore can doe al things, fo he is moft mercifull, and therfore wil preferue al thofe that put their truft in him. If a temporall magiftrate that exercifeth but a ciuil office in the commonwealth, fhuld go away from his charge for feare of infection or plague, wheras his prefent abode might do more good than his abfence, he greatly offendeth; how much more then offendeth he, that being a paftor or feeder of foules, flieth away from his charge, wheras his prefence might doe a thoufand times more good than his abfence? And if it pleafe the Lord to take them away to himfelfe, are they not moft happie? Enter they not into eternall glorie? And haue they not an end of all miferies and paines in this life, and the perfect fruition of perpetuall ioie in the heauens? Are they not bleffed, if when the Lord fhal call them, he find [2]them fo well occupied as in feeding, & breaking the bread of life to, the pore members of Chrift Iefus for whofe fakes he fhed his hart blood?

Theod. But they fay, we ought not to tempt God, which thing they muft needs doe if they fhoulde tarrie when they fee death before their face. And they fay further, that it is written that we muft keepe the whole from the ficke, and the ficke from the whole. Befids, faie they, *Natura dedit, poteftatem tuendi vitam omni animanti,* Nature hath giuen power of defending of life to euerie liuing creture. Againe, euery thing fleeth from his contrarie, but death is contrarie to nature, for it came through the corruption of nature, therfore we flie from the fame by the inftinct of nature. Thefe and the like fond reafons they alledge for their excufe in flieng from their flocks and charges: what fay you to them?

Marginal notes:

[leaf N 5]

He will preserve all those who trust in him.

And if he takes them to himself, happy are they.

[2 leaf N 5, back]

Cowardly Pastors' excuses for fleeing from infection.

These refuted :

Amphil. I can faie little to them. But onelie this, that none of all thefe reafons doe priuiledge them to difcontinue from their flockes and charges. And whereas they faie, that their ftaieng were a tempting of God, it is verie vntrue, it is rather a reuerent obedience to this

God has bidden his Pastors to feed his Sheep.

tripled commandement, *Pafce oues meas, pafce oues meas, pafce oues meas,* Feede my fheepe, feede my fheepe, feede my fheepe. But

[¹ leaf N 6]

indeede if it were fo that a priuate man who hath no ¹kind of function nor office, neither ecclefiafticall nor temporall, feeing himfelfe if he

Men with no duty to stay in danger may go from it.

ftaie ftil in great danger of death, & might auoid the danger by flieng, & fo by the grace of God prolong his life, and yet will not, this man, if he tarrieth, tempteth the Lord, and is a murtherer of himfelfe before God. And to fuch it is faid, 'thou fhalt keepe the whole from the ficke, & the fick from the whole.' This is the meaning & fence of thefe words, and not that they do priuiledge any man for not doing of his dutie. But notwithftanding all that can be faid in confutacion of this great & extreeme contempt of

But Ministers

their duties, I haue knowne and doe know fome minifters (nay, wolues in fheepes clothing) in *Dnalgne* that in time of any plague, peftilence or infection, thogh there hath bin no gret danger at all, that haue bin fo far from continuing amongft their flock, *that* if any one of them were ficke, although of neuer fo common or vfuall difeafe, yet fearing to be infected with the contagion thereof, they haue abfented themfelues altogither, from vifiting *the* fick according as they ought, & as dutie doth bind them. Yea, fome of them (fuppofe you of mercenaries, & hirelings, but not of good paftors) are fo nice, fo fine & fo feareful of death forfoth, *that* in no cafe they cannot abide

[² leaf N 6, back]

to vifit the ficke, neither by day nor ²by night. But in my iudgement it is as incident to their office and dutie, to vifite, to comfort, to

are specially bound to be at the deathbeds of their flocks.

inftruct, and relieue the ficke, at the houre of death, as it is for them to preach the word of God to their flocke al the daies of their life. And peraduenture they may doe more good in one howre at the laft gafpe, then they haue done all the daies of their life before. For he that in his life time hath had in fmall eftimation the bleffed worde of

Many who've led a wicked life

God, but following his owne humors in hope to liue long, hath lead a very wicked and impenitent life, nowe through the confideration and fight of death, which he feeth before his eies, togither with godly exhortations, admonitions, and confolations, out of the word of

God, may eafilie be withdrawne from his former wicked life, and
dieng in the faith of Iefus Chrift, with true repentance for his finnes
to-fore committed, liue for euer in ioye both of body & foule,
whereas, if exhortations had not bin, he might (happily) haue died
irrepentant or vtterly defperate to his euerlafting deftru&tion for euer.
Yea, it is commonly feene, that thofe who could neuer be wonne to
Chrift Iefus, all the daies of their life before, yet at the laft howre
they are foone recouered. Therefore ought not the paftors to
negle&te their duties therein, but [1]warely and carefully to watche
ouer their flocks night and day without ceafing, that when the great
fhephard of the fheepe commeth, he may rewarde them with the
immerceffible crowne of eternall glory. And thus much be it fpoken
hereof.

may easily be drawn to repent on their dying beds.

[1 leaf N 7]

Theod. In whome doth the ele&tion of the minifter or paftor confift? in the church ouely, or in the bifhops?

The Election of Pastors.

Amphil. I tolde' you before (as I remember) that the church
might examine the life, the conuerfation, and difpofition of him, or
them, whome they would haue to be their paftor, and finding the
fame good, to prefent him, or them, to the bifhops or elders to
whome it apperteineth, to examine for his fufficiencie in knowledge,
and dexteritie in teaching and handling the word of God; and finding
him a man furnifhed with gifts and graces neceffary for fuch a high
vocation, to call him lawfullie according to the word of God, and fo
to fende him foorth into the Lords harueft, as a faithfull laborer
therein.

Their lives should be lookt into by the Church; then the men should be presented to the Bishop.

Theod. But fome are of opinion that the churches themfelues of
their owne abfolute and plenarie power ought to choofe their paftor,
and not bifhops.

Amphil. The churches haue no further [2]power in the ele&tion of
their paftor, than as I haue told you, that is, to iudge of his conuerfation & integritie of life, referring the whole a&tion befides to the
bifhops and elders. For if the churches fhould ele&t their minifter
or paftor of themfelues abfolutely, befides that it would breed confufion (for fome would choofe one, fome another, fome this, and fome
that, neuer contenting themfelues with any) the church fhould doe
that alfo, which were dire&tly contrarie to the word of God. For
certeine it is, the church hath no abfolute power by the word of God

[2 leaf N 7, back]

Churches should not elect their Ministers with-out the Bishop's approval.

to elect their paſtor, to chooſe him, to cal him orderly in ſuch forme as is appointed in the word, obſeruing all kinde of rites, ceremonies, & orders belonging thereto. Neither was it euer ſeene that any church did euer practiſe the ſame. For in the dais of the apoſtles, did the churches any more than chooſe foorth certeine perſons of a tried conuerſation, & preſented them to the apoſtles? And did not the apoſtles then, (whom our biſhops now in this action do repreſent) lay their hands vpon them, approue them (after triall had of their ſufficiencie in knowledge) and ſent them foorth into the Lords vineyard? The churches laid not their hands vpon them, or as ſome call it, conſecrated them not, nor vſed not any other ceremoniall rite in the ¹election of them, as the apoſtles did. But as I grant that the church for ſom cauſe, and in ſom reſpects, is not to be excluded from a conſultatiue voyce (as before) or from being made priuie at al to the election of their paſtor, ſo I denie that the church may abſolutely of his owne plenarie power cal their paſtor, all ceremonies and rites thereto belonging obſerued, for that is to be done and executed of the biſhops & elders, and not of the churches conſiſting of lay men, and for the moſt part rude, and vnlearned.

Theod. What ſay you to a ſeigniorie or elderſhip? were it not good for the ſtate of the church at this day that yᵉ ſame were eſtabliſhed in euery congregation, as it was in the apoſtles daies.

Amphil. The ſeueral eſtates and conditions of the apoſtolicall churches, and of ours (al circumſtances duly conſidered) are diuers and much different one from another, and therefore, though a ſeigniorie or elderſhip then in euerie particular church were neceſſarie, yet now vnder chriſtian princes it is not ſo needfull. The churches then wanted chriſtian princes and magiſtrates to gouerne the ſame, and therefore had need of ſome others to rule in the church. But God be thanked, we haue moſt chriſtian kings, princes, and gouernors, to rule and gouerne the church, & therfore ²we ſtand in leſſe need of the other. And yet notwithſtanding, I grant that a ſeigniorie in euery congregation were to be wiſhed, if it could be brought to paſſe, yet cannot I perceiue, but that it would rather bring confuſion, than reformation, conſidering the ſtate of the church at this day. For in the apoſtles times when ſeigniories were ordeined, we read not of any ſhires, dioces, or precincts, where biſhops and eccleſiaſticall magiſtrates

Bishops repreſent the Apostles.

[¹ leaf N 8]

But a Church should have a voice in its Pastor's call.

Seignory or Eldership in every Church is not needful now.

[² leaf N 8, back]

A Seignory in every Congregation, as in the Apostles' time,

might exercife their authoritie and gouernement, as now they doe, and therefore, there being neither bifhops, ecclefiafticall nor ciuill magiftrates (as we haue now), it was neceffarie that the feigniories fhuld be ordeined. But now we, hauing al thefe things, ftand not in is not needed now. fuch neceffitie of them, as the churches in the apoftles daies did. Befides, the inftitution of elders was but meere ceremoniall, and temporall, and therefore not to continue alwaies, neither ought the neceffitie thereof to binde all churches. Neither doe I thinke that all churches are bound for euer to one forme of externall gouerne- Every Church may alter its form of external government from time to time. ment, but that euery church may alter, and change the fame, accord- ing to the time and prefent ftate therof, as they fhal fee the fame to make for the glorie of God, and the comon peace of the church.

[1]*Theod.* What fay you to deacons? Is their office neceffarie or [¹ Sig. O. 1.] not in the church of God at this day?

Amphil. Their office (which was to make collections for the The office of *Deacon* is still very necessary. poore, to gather the beneuolences, and contributions of euerie one that were difpofed to giue, and to fee the fame beftowed vpon the poore and needie members of the church) is very neceffarie, and without doubt ought to be continued for euer. But yet is not the church tied to their names onely, but to their office. Which office is Now it is filld by Church- wardens, who daily gather alms and give em to the poor. executed by honeft fubftantiall men (called Churchwardens or the like) chofen by the confent of the whole congregation to the fame end and purpofe, who daily gathering the friendlye beneuolencies of the churches, beftow, or fee the fame beftowed vpon the poore and indigent of the fame church, which was the greateft part of the deacons duties in the apoftles daies. So that albeit wee haue not the name, we yet hold their office in fubftance and effect.

Theod. What is your iudgement, ought there to be any bifhops in the churches of chriftians?

Amphil. To doubt whether there ought to be bifhops in the churches of chriftians, is to doubt of the truth it felfe. For is there not [2]mention made of their names, dignities, functions, and callings, [² Sig. O. 1. back] almoft in euery chapter of the new teftament, in all the epiftles of *Paule,* of *Peter,* of *Iohn,* of *Iude,* and of all the reft? Befides that, The Apostles ordaind Bishops. did not the apoftles themfelues conftitute and ordeine bifhops and elders; and doe they not woonderfully commende the excellencie of their calling, inferring that thofe that rule well, are worthye of double honour? Whereby appeereth that bifhops are not onlye needefull in the churches of chriftians, but alfo moft needfull, as without whome I can fcarcely fee how the ftate of the church could well bee main-

The state of the Church couldn't be kept up without em.

tained. And therefore thofe that contend that they are not neceffarie in a Chriftian Common wealth, fhewe them felues either wilfull, waiwarde, or malicioufly blinde, and ftriuing to catch their owne fhadowes, they labour all in vaine, giuing manifeft demonftration of their more than extreame follie to all the world.

Theod. Well. Let it bee granted (as it cannot bee denied) that they are mofte neceffarie, yet in this I would verie gladlye bee abfolued, whether they maye lawfully vendicate or challenge to themfelues

[1 Sig. O. 2.]

fuperioritie, and primacie aboue their fellowe [1]brethren of the minif-terie or no? for fome holde that there ought to be equalitie in the minifterie, and no fuperioritie at all: how fay you?

They don't claim superiority to other Pastors as to their calling, but only as to the dignity that the prince has given em.

Amphil. They doe not vendicate or challenge anie fuperioritie or primacie to themfelues ouer their brethren in refpect of their common callings and functions (for therein the pooreft paftor or fhepheard that is, is coequall with them, they themfelues will not denie) but in refpect of dignitie, authoritie, and honour, which the prince and church doth beftowe vpon them. So that the fuperioritie that they haue ouer their brethren, refteth in dignitie, authoritie, and honour, which it hath pleafed the prince to dignifie them withall aboue their felowe brethren, and not in calling, function, or office, for therein they are all coequall togither. But if any curious heads fhould demand why the prince fhould aduance any of the cleargie to fuch high dignitie, authoritie, and primacie aboue his brethren, I anfwer as it is in the Gofpell: 'Is thine eie euill, bicaufe the prince is good?' May not the prince giue his gifts, his dignities, and promotions to whom he will? And if the prince of his roiall clemencie be minded to beftowe vpon his fubiect any dignity or promotion, is it chriftian

[3 Sig. O. 2. back]

obedience[2] [3]to refufe the fame? Nay, is it not extreeme ingratitude towards his prince? Befides, who feeth not, that if there fhould

There must be superiority in dignity.

be no fuperioritie (I meane in dignitie, & authoritie only) the fame honorable office or calling would growe into contempt? For is it not an old faieng, and a true, *Familiaritas, fiue æqualitas parit con-*

Familiarity breeds contempt.

temptum, Familiaritie, or coequallitie doth euer bring contempt. And

[2] *Orig.* abedience.

therefore take awaye authoritie and honor from the magiftrates either temporall or fpirituall, and ouerthrowe the fame altogither.   If authoritie fhould not be dignified, as well with glorie and eternall pompe the better to grace the fame, & to fhew forth the maieftie thereof, would it not foone grow to be difpifed, vilipended, and naught fet by ?   And therefore the more to innoble and fet foorth the excellencie of this honorable calling of a bifhop, hath the prince & the churches thought it good to beftow fuch authoritie, dignitie, and honor vpon them, and not for anie other caufe whatfoeuer.   And therefore, feeing it is the pleafure of the prince to beftowe fuch dignitie, authoritie, and honor vpon them, me thinke, any fober chriftians fhould eafely tolerate the fame.

Sober Christians should tolerate Bishops.

Theod. Yea, but they faie, that there ought to be no fuperioritie in the minifterie, [1]bringing in the example of the apoftles themfelues, amongft whom was no fuperiority, inequalitie, or principallitie at all ?

[1 Sig. O. 3.]

Amphil. Indeede amongft the apoftles there was no fuperioritie, I grant, neither in office, calling, authoritie, nor otherwife, but al were equall in ech refpecte, one to another. But what than ? The apoftles were fent to preach to the churches, and not to gouerne (and therefore they choofe elders to rule the fame) but our bifhops are as well to gouerne and to rule the churches in fome refpects, as to preach the worde.   And therfore, though there were no fuperioritie amongft the apoftles, yet maye there be amongft our bifhops in refpect of gouer[n]ment, dignitie and authoritie.   And wheras they faie there ought to be no fuperioritie in the minifterie at all, I anfweare, no more there is in refpect of euerie ones function, forme of calling, and office to preach the word and minifter the facraments. But in refpect of gouernement, authoritie, dignitie, and honor, there is fuperioritie, and I am perfwaded fo ought to be. In which opinion, vntill they haue difprooued it, I meane, Chrift willing, to perfifte.

Bishops have to rule as well as preach.

Theod. But they adde further, and fay that it ftrengtheneth the hands of the aduerfaries, [2]the papifts. For, faie they, the papifts may as well affirme that chriftian emperours, kings and potentates, and euen the churches of God themfelues, haue giuen to the pope that authoritie, that dignitie, and honor which he hath or claimeth aboue his fellowe brethren, as well as the bifhop may fay fo. Befides, it confirmeth the opinion of foueraigntie ouer all the churches in the

[2 Sig. O. 3. back]

The Papist argument that the

Pope has his
power from
Kings, &c., as
Bishops do.

world. For, fay they, may not the pope faie that he receiued plenarie power to be head ouer all the world, from chriftian kings, emperours, and potentates, as well as the bifhops may fay, we receiued this power to be fuperior to our brethren from chriftian kings and princes. Now whether thefe reafons be a like, I would gladly know.

Amphil. They be verie vnlike, and fo vnlike as there is no

equallitie, comparifon, or femblance betwixt them. For, firft of all, let them note, that the pope nor any of his complices and adherents doe not holde, nor pretende to holde, (no, they dare as well eate off their fingers as to fay fo, for then were there ftate in a wofull cafe)

the Pope gets
his power from
God.
Not true.

that their archdiuell, their god, the pope, I fhould fay, doth receiue his power either of authoritie, fuperioritie, primacie, foueraigntie, or head ouer all the world, from any earthly creature, but immediately from

[1 Sig. O. 4.]
The Pope didn't
get his superi-
ority from God,

God [1]himfelfe. But whereas hee fayth that hee receiued his power of fuperioritie ouer all the worlde from no earthie creature, but from God himfelfe, it is manifeft that he receyued it neyther from God (for his vfurped power is contrarie to God, and to his worde in euerie

but from the
Devil, whose
Lieutenant-
General he is.

refpecte) nor from anie chriftian man, but from the Deuill himfelfe, whofe vicegerent or Liefetenant generall in his kingedome of impietie he fhewes himfelfe to be. Than let them note, that although hee pretended to holde his vfurped authoritie from man (as hee doth not,) yet is there no man howe mightie an Emperour, King, Prince, or Potentate foeuer, that is able *proprio iure* to giue him authoritie ouer all the worlde, without great and manifefte iniurye done to all other Princes, as to giue the foueraigntie, or chieftie of their Landes from

them, to a ftraunger. But a Prince may lawfullye beftowe and geue to his fubiectes anie prerogatiue, title, authoritie, office, function, gouernment, or fuperioritie of anie thing within his owne dominions and kingdomes, but no further he maye not. And therefore this reafon of theirs holdeth not, that the Pope maye as well arrogate the one to himfelfe, as the Byfhops may the other to themfelues.

[2]*Theod.* Seeing now it cannot be denied, but that bifhops are moft neceffarie, and that they may alfo lawfully hold fuperioritie ouer their brethren (in refpect of gouernement, regiment or authoritie) being giuen them of the prince, what fay you then to this? Whether

may a bifhop be called by the name of an archbifhop, metropolitane, primate, or by the name of ' my Lord bifhop, my Lords grace, the

right honourable,' and the like, or not? For, me thinke, thefe titles
and names are rather peculiar to the temporalitie than to them, &
do fauour of vainglorie, and worldly pompe, rather than of any thing
elfe. And which is more, me thinke they are againft the expreffe
word of God. Wherefore I couet greatly to heare your iudgement
thereof?

Amphil. Thefe names and titles may feeme to fauour of vaineglorie indeed, if they fhould arrogate to themfelues *Iure diuino,* as
they doe not. But if you wil confider by whom they were giuen
them, and how they doe require them, you will not thinke it much
amiffe, nor farre difcrepant from the finceritie of the Gofpell. Firft
therefore note that they were giuen them by chriftian princes to
dignifie, to innoble, to decore, and to fet foorth the dignitie, the
excellencie, and worthines of their cal¹lings. Secondly let them note
that they require them as due vnto them by the donation and gifture
of men, and not *Iure diuino,* and therefore being giuen them for the
caufes aforefaid by chriftian kings and prinees, they may in that
refpeƈt hold them ftill without any offence to the diuine goodneffe, or
his faithfull fpoufe vpon the earth. But if they fhuld claime them as
due vnto them by the lawe of God, as they doe not, then fhould they
offend. For our fauiour Chrift, feeing his difciples and apoftles
ambicioufly to affeƈt the fame vaineglorious titles and names, fet
before them the example of the heathen kings, thereby the rather to
withdrawe them from their vaine humour, faieng: *Reges gentium
dōminantur eis,* &c. The kings of the gentils beare rule ouer them,
and thofe that exercife authoritie ouer them, be called gratious Lords,
but *Vos autem non fic,* You fhall not be fo. In the which words he
vtterly denieth them (and in them, all others to the worlds end, that
in the fame office and funƈtion of life fhould fucceed them) the titles
of Lords, graces, or the like. The apoftle alfo biddeth them to
beware that they challenge not thofe vaine titles to themfelues by the
lawe of God, when he faith (fpeaking to bifhops and paftors) Be not
Lords ouer your flocks, &c. By ²thefe and manie other the like places
of holie writt, it is cleare that they cannot arrogate thefe names or
titles to themfelues by yᵉ word of God; neyther doe they, but (as I
haue faid) by the donation, the beneuolence, and gifture of chriftian
Princes, for the reuerent eftimation they bare and ought to beare to

Side notes:

Yes, tho' these titles look vainglorious. God doesn't give 'em, but the Prince does.

[¹ leaf O 8]

If Bishops claim these titles by God's law, they do wrong.

Christ 'ud have none of this.

[² Sig. O 5, back]

These titles of 'Bishop,' &c., are not given by God's Word, but only by Christian Princes,

their high function and calling, in that they are his Liefetenants, his vicegerents in his Church, his meffengers, his Ambaffadors, the dif-clofers and proclaimers of his fecretes, and his Aungels (for fo are they called in the fcriptures) & therfore, in refpecte of the excel-lencie hereof, thefe names were giuen and attributed vnto them. And truely to fpeake my fimple iudgement, I fee not but that thefe names doe dignifie their callinges, fhewe forth the maieftie thereof, and doe moue the Churches to haue the fame high calling in more reuerence, & honor, than otherwife they would, if they were called by bare & naked names onelie. But notwithftanding either this that hath beene faide, or anie thinge els that can be faid herein, there are fome waiward fpirits lately reuiued, who hold the fame names to be meere Antichriftian, blafphemous and wicked, and fuche as at anie hande a Minifter of the Gofpell ought not to bee called by. But whereas they holde them to bee Antichri[1]ftian, I holde them to be Chriftian names, and geuen by Chriftian Princes to the innobling and garnifhing of their offices, functions, and callinges, which doubtleffe is a glorie to God, denie it who will, or who can. And therefore in conclufion I fay, that Byfhops, though not by the lawe of God, yet by the pofitiue law, donation, and gifture of Chriftian Princes, maye lawfully affume the faide titles and names to them, for the caufes before cited. And therefore thefe names and titles beeing meere indifferent, and not derogating from the glorie of God, but rather making for the fame, they are not, of anye wife, fober, or faythfull Chriftian, neyther to bee inueighed againft, nor yet to bee in anye refpecte diflyked beeing vfed as before. And thus much of the names and titles of Byfhops.

Theod. Maye Byfhops exercife temporall authoritie together with Ecclefiaficall; and maye they bee Iuftices of peace, Iuftices of Quorum, Iuftices of Affifes, Ewer, Determiner, and the lyke; or maye they, as Capytall Iudges, geue definytiue fentence of lyfe and death vpon malefactors and others, that by the iudiciall lawe of man haue deferued to dye?

2Amphil. There is neither of the callings temporall, nor ecclefi-aficall, but it requireth a whole and perfect man, to execute the fame. And if there were neuer founde any one man yet fo perfect, as could throughly and abfolutelie performe his office in either of

Margin notes

and they dignify their holders callings.

They are not Anti-christian but Christian,

[1 Sig. O 6]

and Bishops may lawfully assume them.

[2 Sig. O 6, back]

A man can only fulfill one calling.

the callings temporall or ecclefiafticall, much leffe can there euer one man be found, that is able to difcharg them both. It is hard therefore that thefe two callings fhould concurre in one man. This is as though a man hauing an importable burthen alreadie vpon his backe, fhould yet haue an other almoft as burthenous vrged vppon him. And therefore as it were abfurde to fee a temporall magiftrate mount into the pulpit, preach the worde, and minifter the facraments, fo abfurde it is to fee an ecclefiafticall magiftrate exercife the authoritie temporall, and to giue fentence condemnatorie of life, & death, vpon any criminous perfon, which properlie belongeth to the temporall power. Befids, it is a great difcredite to the temporall magiftrate, becaufe it may be thought that they are not wife nor politique inough to execute their office, nor difcharge their duties without the aide and affiftance of the other. And which is more, it hindereth them from the difcharge of their duties in their owne calling, for [1]it is written, no man can ferue two mafters but either he muft betraie the one or the other. When the woman taken in adultery was apprehended, and brought vnto Chrift, he refufed to giue iudgement of hir; and yet it was a matter in effect ecclefiafticall, & appertained to an ecclefiafticall iudge. Then what ought they to do in matters meere ciuil? Againe, our fauior[2] Chrift, when the yong man requefted him to deuide the inheritance betwixt his brother, & him, refufed the fame, faieng, *Quis me conftituit iudicem inter vos?* Who made me a iudge or a deuider betwixt you? Whereby appeareth how farre ecclefiafticall perfons ought to bee from hauing to doe with temporal matters. But whereas they fay the bifhops of *Dnalgne* do exercife temporall authoritie, and doe it as iudges capitall, giuing fentence condemnatorie of life and death, it is verie vntrue otherwife than thus, to be prefent at the fame, & to haue a confultatiue exhortatiue, or confentatiue voice onely. Which vfe me thinkes is verie good and laudable in my iudgement. For whereas the temporal magiftrates not vnderftanding in euerie point the deapth of Gods lawe, if they fhoulde doe anie thing either againft the fame, or the lawe of a good confcience, they might informe them thereof, that [3]all things might bee done to the glorie of God, the comforte of the poore members of Chrifte Iefus, and the benefit of the common welth.

[2 fauior do *Orig.*]

Marginal notes:

No ecclesiastical officer

should exercise temporal authority, like condemning men to death.

[1 Sig. O 7]
No man can serve 2 Masters.

Christ refuzd to be a Judge.

And English Bishops have only a consultative voice in giving temporal Judgments.

[3 Sig. O 7, back]

Theod. What fafhion of apparell doe the paftors and Minifters weare vfually in their common affaires?

Amphil. The fame fafhion that others doe, for the moft parte, but yet decente, and comlie, obferuing in euerie point a *decorum.* But as others weare their attire, fome of this colour, fome of that, fome of this thinge, fome of that, fo they commonly weare all their ap-

parell, at leaft the exteriour part, of blacke colour, which, as you know, is a good, graue, fad, and auncient colour. And yet notwithftanding herein fome of them (I fpeake not of all) are muche to bee blamed, in that they cannot content themfelues with common, and vfuall fafhions, but they muft chop and chaunge euerie day with the worlde.

Yea, fome of them are as fonde in excogitating, deuifing, and in-uenting of new fafhions euerie day, & in wearing the fame, as the verieft Royfter of them all. And as they are faultie in this refpeĉt, fo are they herein to be blamed, in that they cannot contente them-felues with cloth, though neuer fo excellent, but they· muft weare

filkes, veluets, fatans, damafkes, grograms, taffeties, and the like. I fpeake not agaynft ¹thofe that are in authoritie, for wearing of thefe thinges (for they both maie, and in fome refpeĉtes ought to weare them for the dignifying of their offices and callings, which otherwife mighte growe into contempte), but againft thofe that bee meane paf-tours and Minifters, that flaunt it out in their faten doblets, taffetie

doblets, filke hofen, garded gownes, cloakes, and the like. Alas, how fhoulde they rebuke pryde, and exceffe in others, who are as faultye therein as the refte? Therefore fayde Cato verye well, *Quae culpare foles, ea tu ne feceris ipfe :* for, fayeth he, *Turpe eft doĉtori, cum culpa redarguit ipfum.* Which is, thofe thinges which thou blameft in others,

fee that thou thy felfe bee not guiltye in the fame, for it is a foule blemifh and a great fhame and difcredit, what that euyll which thou reproueft in an other, is apparent in thy felfe. For in fo doing, a man repre-hendeth as well himfelfe as others, is a hinderance to the courfe of the Gofpell, and what he buildeth with one hand, he pulleth down with the other. Chrift Iefus, the great paftor of the fheepe, was him-

felf contented to go daily in one poore coat, beeing knit, or wouen all ouer without feeme, as the maner of yᵉ Paliftinians is to this day.

This me think was but a fimple cote ²in the eie of the world, and yet Chrift Iefus thought it pretious inough. Samuel was accuftomed to walke in an old gowne girded to him with a thong. *Elias* and *Elizeus* in a mantell, Iohn the baptiſt in camels haire, with a girdle of a ſkin about his loines. The apoſtle Paùle with a poore cloke, and and Paul a poor cloak. the like ; wherby appeareth, how farre a miniſter of the Goſpell ought to be from pride, and worldly vanitie, obſeruing the rules of chriſtian ſobrietie, as well in apparell, as in al things elſe, knowing that he is as Let the Minis-ters be sober in dress. a citie ſet vppon an hill, and as a candle ſet vppon a candleſticke to giue light, and ſhine to al the whole church of God. Therfore ſaith Chriſt : *Sic luceat lux veſtra coram hominibus,* &c. Let your light ſo ſhine before men, that they, ſeeing your good works, may glorifie your father which is in heauen : which God grant we may all doe.

Theod. Haue they no other kind of apparell different from the common ſort of men ?

Amphil. Yes, marie, haue they. They haue other attire more But, when officiating, they proper, and peculiar vnto them (in reſpeƈt of their funƈtions and wear Cap, Tip-pet, Surplice, &c offices) as cap, tippet, ſurpleſſe, and the like. Theſe they weare, not commonly, or altogither, but in eſpecial when they are occupied in, or about, the execution of their offices and callings, to [1]this end and [2] [¹ Sig. P. 1.] purpoſe, that there may be a difference betwixte them and the com-mon forte of people, and that the one maie be diſtinƈte from the other by this outward note or marke.

Theodo. Is it of neceſſitie than required, that the Paſtors and Miniſters of the worde, ſhoulde be diſtinƈted from other people, by anie ſeuerall kind of attire ?

Amphil. It is not required as of neceſſitie, but thought meete and conuenient to be vſed for a decencie, and comlines, in the Church of God. But notwithſtanding the chiefeſt thyng wherby a paſtor or But their chief distinction miniſter oght to be known from the common & vulgare forte of should be in Preaching and people is, the preaching of the word of God, the adminiſtration of Holy Life, the ſacraments, the execution of eccleſiaſtical diſcipline, and other cenſures of the Church, and withall his integritie of lyfe, and ſound-neſſe of conuerſation in euerie reſpeƈte. Theſe are the true notes and markes wherby a Miniſter of the Goſpell ought to bee knowen and diſtinƈted from the other common forte of people. And yet though theſe bee the chiefeſt notes whereby they are diſtinƈt from others of the temporalitie and laitie, yet are they not the onelie notes,

[² end end *Orig.*]

or markes, for they are known and difcerned from others alfo, by exteriour habite, and attire, as namely by cappe, tippet, fur[1]pleffe, and fuch like: That as the firft doth diftinguifh them from others, whileft they are exercifed about the fame, (for who is fo doltifhe, that feeing a man preache, minifter the facraments, & execute other ecclefiafticall cenfures of the church, that will not iudge him to bee a Minifter of the Gofpell) fo the other notes of apparell (the furpleffe except) may make a difference, and diftinguifhe them from others of the laitie abroad. To this end, that the reuerence which is due to a good paftor, or minifter of the Gofpell may be giuen vnto them. For as the Apoftle faith, thofe elders that rule well, are worthie of double honour.

Theod. But I haue heard great difputation and reafoning *pro &* *contra*, to and fro, that the paftors and minifters of the Gofpell, ought not to be difleuered from the common forte of people, by anie diftinéte kinde of apparell, but rather by founding the Lordes voice on high, by miniftring the facramentes, and the like: what fay you to the fame?

Amphil. Indeede there are fome, I confeffe, that are of that opinion, and they bring in the example of Saule, enquiring of Samuell for the feers houfe, inferring that the Prophet was not diftinét from other common people in his attire, for than Saule fhould eafelie [2]haue knowen him by the fame. And the example of the damofell that fpake to Peter, inferring that whereas the mayde fayde, *Thy fpeech bewrayeth thee*, if he had bene diftinéte from others in attire, or outwarde apparell, fhee would than haue fayd, *Thy apparel fheweth thee to bee fuch a fellowe.* Thefe, with the like examples, they pretende to prooue that paftors and Minifters are not to bee difcerned and knowen from the lay people, by anye kinde of apparell. But as I will not faie that they are to bee knowen and difcerned from others by apparell or habite onelye, (but rather by the lifting vp of their voices like Trumpets, as faith the Prophet,) fo I wyll not denye the fame to bee no note or marke at all to knowe a Paftour or Minifter of the Gofpell by, from others of the temporaltie, and laitie. And truelye for my parte, I fee no great inconuenience, if they bee by a certaine kinde of decente habite (commaunded by a Chriftian Prince) known and difcerned from others. Yet fome more curious than wife,

[1 Sig. P. 1., back]
tho their outward mark is Cap, Surplice, &c.

As to those who object to a different dress for Pastors,

and try to justify their opinion by the Bible,

[2 Sig. P. 2.]

I can't agree with em.

I think a different dress justifiable.

before they would weare anie diftinct kind of apparell from others, they haue rather chofen to render vp both liuinges, goods, families, and all, leauing their flockes to the mouth of the wolues.

[1]*Theod.* Is it lawfull for a minifter of the Gofpell to weare a furpleffe, a tippet or forked cappe, and the like kind of attire?

Amphil. As they are commaunded by the Pope, the great Antichrift of the worlde, they ought not to weare them; but as they be commaunded, and inioyned by a Chriftian Prince, they maie weare them without fcruple of confcience. But if they fhould repofe any religion, holineffe or fanctimonie in them, as the doting Papifts doe, than doe they greeuoufie offende; but wearing them as things meere indifferent (although it be controuerfiall whether they bee things indifferente or not), I fee no caufe why they maie not vfe them.

Theod. From whence came thefe garments, can you tell? from Rome, or from whence els?

Amphil. The moft hold that they came firft from Rome, the poifon of all the world; & moft likelie they did fo; but fome other fearching the fame more narrowlie, do hold *that* they came, not from Rome, but rather from Grecia, which from the beginning, for the moft part, hath euer been contrarie to the Church of Rome. But from whence foeuer they came it fkilleth not much, for beeing mere indifferent, they maie be worn or not worne without offence, according to the pleafure of the Prince, as things which of them[2]felues bee not euill, nor cannot hurte, excepte they be abufed.

Theod. Notwithftanding they holde this for a *maxime*, that in as much as they came firft from the Papiftes, and haue of them bene idolatroufie abufed, that therefore they are not, nor ought not to bee, vfed of anie true paftors, or Minifters of the Gofpell. Is this their *affumption* true, or not?

Amphil. It is no good reafon to fay fuch a thing came from the Papiftes, *ergo* it is naught. For we read that the Deuils confeffed Iefus Chrift to be the fonne of God: doth it follow therefore that the fame profeffion is naughte, becaufe a wicked creature vttered the fame? All thinges are therefore to bee examined, whether the abufe confift in the thinges themfelues, or in others that abufe them. Which being found out, let the abufes be remoued, and the thinges remaine ftill. A wicked man maye fpeake good wordes, doe good

[1] Sig. P. 2. back

If Tippets, forke Caps, &c.,

are orderd by a Christian Prince,

I think Ministers may wear them,

even tho they first came from Rome.

[2] Sig. P. 3.]

Use of a good thing by Papists, doesn't make the good thing bad.

If a good thing is abuzd,

works before the world, (but becaufe they want the oile of faith to fouple them withall, they are not good workes before the Lord) and maie ordaine a good thing which maie ferue to good ends, and pur-pofes. And becaufe the fame hath afterward beene abufed, fhall the thing it felfe therefore be quite taken away? No, take away the abufe, let the thinge [1]remaine ftill, as it maye very well without anie offence, except to them, *quibus omnia dantur fcandalo,* to whom all thinges are offence. And further, if thefe preficians would haue all things remoued out of the Church which haue beene abufed to Idola-trie, than muft they pull downe Churches (for what hath bene abufed more to Idolatrie and fuperftition?) pulpits, belles, and what not. Than muft they take away the vfe of bread and wine, not onely from the church, but alfo from the vfe of man in this life, becaufe y[e] fame was abufed to moft fhamefull idolatrie in beeing dedicate to *Ceres,* and *Bacchus,* twoo ftinking Idols of the Gentiles. Than muft they take away not onely the Epiftles, and Gofpels, but alfo the whole volume of the holy fcriptures, becaufe the Papiftes abufed them to idolatrie. By all which reafons, with infinite the like, it manifeftly appeareth, that manie things which haue beene inftituted by Idolaters. or by them abufed to Idolatrie, may be applied to good vfes, and may ferue to good ends, y[e] abufes being taken away. Yet wold I not that any thing that hath been idolatroufly abufed by the papifts, fhould be reteined in the churches of Chriftians, if by any meanes they might be remoued, and better put in place.

Theod. Is the wearing of thefe garments [2]a thing meere indifferent, or not? for fome hold it is, fome hold it is not?

Amphil. It is a thing without all controuerfy mere indifferent; for, whatfoeuer gods word neither exprefly commandeth, neither directly forbiddeth, nor which bindeth not y[e] confcience of a chriftian man, is a thing mere indifferent to be vfed, or not to be vfed, as the prefent ftate of y[e] church, & time requireth. But it is certen that the wearing of this kind of attire is not exprefly commanded in the word of God, nor directly forbid by the fame, & therfore is mere indifferent, and may be vfed, or not vfed, without burthen of confcience, as y[e] prefent ftate of time fhall require. And therfore feeing they be things indifferent, I wold wifh euery wife chriftian to tollerate y[e] fame, being certen that he is neither better nor worfe, for wearing or not wearing of them.

take away the Abuse, and let the Good Thing stay.
[1 Sig. P. 3. back]

If everything that idolatrous Papists have uzd is to be done away with,

the Bible and most other good things 'll have to go.

[2 Sig. P. 4.]

These Garments are a mere matter of Indifference : do as you like about em.

Put up with Garments : a man's no better or worse for em.

Theod. Being things, as you fay, mere indifferent, may any man lawfully refufe ye wearing of them againft the commandement of his prince, whom, next vnder God, he ought to obey?

Amphil. Euery man is bound in confcience before God to obey his prince in all things, yea in things directly contrary to true god-lines hee is bound to fhew his obedience (but not to commit ye euil) namely to fubmit himfelfe life, lands, liuings or els whatfoeuer he hath, to ye wil of his ¹Princes, rather than to difobeie. If this obedi- ence than be due to Princes in matters contrarie to true godlineffe, what obedience than is due to them in matters of fmall waight, of fmall importaunce, and meere triffles as thefe garments be, iudge you? He that difobeieth the commaundement of his Prince, difobeieth the commaundement of God; and therfore, would God all Ecclefi-afticall perfons that ftande fo muche vpon thefe fmall pointes, that they breake the common vnitie, & band of charitie in the church of God, would nowe at the laft quallifie themfelues, fhewe obedience to Princes lawes, and fall to preaching of Chrift Iefus truelie, that his kingdome might dailie bee increafed, their confciences difcharged, and the Church edefied, which Chrifte Iefus hath bought with the fhedding of his precious hart bloud.

[¹ Sig. P. 4. back]

And if your Prince orders them, of course obey him in such a Trifle.

Theod. Maie a paftor, or a Minifter of the Gofpell, forfake his flocke, and refufe his charge, for the wearing of a furpleffe, a cappe, tippet, or the like, as manie haue done of late daies, who being in-forced to weare thefe garmentes, haue giuen up their liuings, and forfaken all?

Amphil. Thofe that for the wearing of thefe garments, being but the inuentions, the traditions, the rites, the ceremonies, the ordinances & conftitutions of man, will leaue their flocks, ²and giue ouer their charges, not caring what become of the fame, doe fhew themfelues to be no true fhepheards, but fuch as Chrift fpeaketh of, that when they fee the Wolfe comming, will flie away, leauing their flocke to the flaughter of the greedie wolfe. They giue euident demonftration alfo, that they are not fuch as the holie Ghoft hath made ouerfeers ouer their flocke, but rather fuch, as being poffeffed with the fpirite of pride and ambition, haue intruded themfelues, to the deftruction of their flocke. If they were fuch good fhepheards as they ought to be, and fo louing to their flocke, they would rather giue their life for

Any Pastor who leaves his Flock because he won't wear a Surplice, &c.,

[² Sig. P 5]

shows that he's no good Shepherd.

their ſheepe, if neede required, than to runne from them, leauing them to the bloodie teeth of the mercileſſe wolues. Is hee a good ſhepheard that watcheth dailie vppon his flocke, or hee that runnes from them for euerie light trifle? I thinke we would count him a verie

How can he be a good Shepherd who should give his Life for his Sheep, when he'll leave em for trifles like Garments?

negligent ſhepheard. And ſhall wee thinke him a diligent, or a good paſtor, and one that would giue his life for his ſheepe, as a good paſtor ſhould doe, that for ſuch trifles wil eſtrang himſelfe from his flocke for euer? Therefore I beſeech God to giue them grace to looke to their charges, and to let other trifles alone, being no part of our ſaluation or damnation.

[¹ Sig. P 5, back]

Theod. But they ſaie they refuſe the wea¹ring of theſe garments, becauſe they are offenſiue to the godlie, a ſcandall to the weake brethren, a hinderaunce to manie in comming to the Goſpel, & an induration to the papiſts hardning their hearts, in hope that their trumperie will once come in again, to their ſingular comfort.

Amphil. It is an old ſaying, Better a bad excuſe, than none at all. And truly it ſeemeth they are driuen to the wall, and ſore graueled, that will flie to theſe ſimple ſhifts. But whatſoeuer they ſay or affirme, certain it is, that offenſiue to the godly they cannot be, who haue already learned to diſtinguiſh betwixt the things abuſed, and the abuſes themſelues. And who know alſo how to vſe things mere indifferent, to good ends and purpoſes. And therfore this queſtion

If these Garments are orderd by a Christian Prince, no good Christian should be offended by em.

thus I ſhut vp in few words, that the wearing of theſe garmentes beeing commaunded by a Chriſtian Prince, is not offenſiue, or ſcandalous to anie good Chriſtians; and to the other, it mattereth not what it be. For they are ſuch as the Lorde hath caſt off into a reprobate ſence, and preiudicate opinion, abuſing all things, euen the truth it ſelfe, to their owne deſtruction for euer, excepte they repent, which I praye God they maye doe, if it bee his bleſſed will.

² Sig. P 6]

²*Theod.* I pray you why doe they weare white in their ſurpleſſes, rather than any other colour? and why a forked cappe rather than a rounde one? for the Papiſtes (if they were the authors of theſe garmentes) haue their miſteries, their figures, & their repreſentations in all things. Wherfore I deſire to know your iudgment herein.

The Papists say that White signifies Holiness;

Amphil. You ſay the truth, for the Papiſtes haue their miſteries in all thinges after their maner. Therfore thus they ſay, that white doth ſignify holines, innocency, & al kind of integrity, putting them in mind what they ought to be in this life, and reprefenteth vnto them the beatitude, the felicitie, and happines of the life to come. And thys they prooue *ab exemplis apparitionum*, from the example of apparitions and vifions, in that aungels, and celeftial creatures haue euer appeared in the fame colour of white. Therefore forfooth they muft weare white apparell. The cornered cappe, fay thefe mifterious fellows, doth fignifie, and reprefent the whole monarchy of the world, Eaft, Weft, North, & South, the gouernment whereof ftandeth vpon them, as the cappe doth vppon their heades. The gowne, faye they, doth fignifie the plenary power which they haue to doe all things. And therefore none but the Pope, or hee [1] with whome hee difpenceth, maie weare the fame euerie where, bicaufe none haue *plenariam poteftatem*, plenarie power, in euerie place, but (Beelzebub) the Pope. Yet the Minifters, faith he, maie weare them in their Churches, & in their owne iurifdictions, becaufe therein they haue full power from him. Thus foolifhlie do they deceiue themfelues with vaine fhewes, fhadows, and imaginations, forged in the mint of their owne braines, to the deftruction of manie. But who is he, that becaufe thefe fottifhe Papiftes haue and doe greeuouflie abufe thefe thinges, wili therefore haue them cleane remoued? If all thinges that haue beene abufed, fhould be remooued becaufe of the abufe, than fhould we haue nothing left to the fupply of our neceffities, neither meat, drinke, nor cloth for our bodies, neyther yet (which is more) y[e] word of God, the fpirituall food of our foules, nor any thing els almoft. For what thing is there in y[e] whole vniverfall world, that eyther by one Hereticke or other hath not beene abufed? Let vs therfore take the abufes away, and the things maie well remaine ftill. For may not we chriftians vfe thefe thinges which the wicked Papjfts haue abufed, to good ends, vfes, and purpofes? I fee no reafon to the contrarie. And therefore in conclufion I befeech the Lorde that wee [2] may all agree together in one truth, and not to deuide our felues one from another for trifles, making fchifmes, ruptures, breaches, and factions in the church of God, where we ought to nourifh peace, vnitie, concord, brotherly loue, amitie, and frendfhip, one amongft another. And feeing we do all agree togither, and iump in one truth, hauing al one God our father, one Lord Iefus Chrift our fauiour, one holy fpirit of adoption, one price of redemption, one faith, one

the Cornerd Cap the Monarchy of the World,

and the Gown the Pope's plenary power:

[Sig. P 6, back]

all this is gammon.

But because Papists have abuzd these things,

as well as the Word of God,

aren't we to uze em? Surely we are.

[2 Sig. P 7]
Do let us Reformers all agree, and not make rows.

We've all one God and Saviour,

let us then
agree about
outward
rites, &c.

hope, one baptifme, and one and the fame inheritance in the kingdome of heauen, Let vs therefore agree togither in thefe externall
fhadowes, ceremonies and rites.　For is it not a fhame to agree
about the marrow, and to ftriue about the bone? to contend about

We've got the
Kernel.　Don't
let's wrangle
over the Shell.

the karnell, & to vary about the fhell? to agree in the truth, and
to brabble for the fhadow?　Let vs confider that this contention
of ours among our felues, doth hinder the courfe of the Gofpell
from taking fuch deepe roote in the heartes of the hearers, as otherwife it would doe.　And thus for this time, brother *Theodorus*, we
will breake off our talke concerning this matter, vntill yt pleafe God
that we may meete againe.　Which if it pleafe God we doe, I promife
you in another woorke to difcourfe of the fame more at large.　In

[¹ Sig. P 7, back]
Let us fast and
pray, and be-
seech God to
keep our Queen
Elizabeth as the
apple of His
eye ; and grant
us Eternal Life
in Heaven, thro
Christ's Death.

the mean time let vs giue our felues, ¹to fafting, and prayer, moft
humbly befeeching his excellent maiefty to bleffe our noble Queen,
and to keepe hir grace as the apple of his eie from all hir foes, to maintaine his word and gofpell amongft vs, to plant vnity and concord
within our walles, to increafe our faith, to graunt vs true and vnfained
repentaunce for our fins, and in the end eternall life in the kingdome
of heauen, thorow yᵉ precious death, paffion, bloodfhedding, and
obedience of Chrifte Iefus our Lord, and onely fauiour, to whom,
with the father and the holy ghoft, one true, and immortal God, be
al honor, praife, power, empire, and dominion throughout all congregations for euermore.　And thus, brother *Theodorus,* I bid you farewell
in the Lord, till I do fee you againe.

Theodo.　And I you alfo good brother Amphilogus,
befeeching the Lord that if we meete not
vpon earth, we maye meete yet in the
kingdome of heauen, there to reft
in perfect felicitie
for euer.

May you and I
meet again, if
not on Earth,
yet to rest for
ever in Heaven !

Amphil. The Lord grant it
for his mercies fake.
Amen.

FINIS.

LONDON
Printed by Roger
Ward for William Wright,
and are to be solde at his shop ioy-
ning to Saint Mildreds Church in
the Poultry, being the mid=
dle shop in the row.

1 5 8 3.

INDEX.

BUNGAY: CLAY AND TAYLOR, PRINTERS, THE CHAUCER PRESS.